VOICE OVER!
SEIYU ACADEMY
VOL. 9
Shojo Beat Edition

STORY AND ART BY
MAKI MINAMI

TECHNICAL ADVISORS
Yoichi Kato, Kaori Kagami, Ayumi Hashidate,
Ayako Harino and Touko Fujitani

Special Thanks
81produce
Tokyo Animator College
Tokyo Animation College

English Translation & Adaptation/John Werry
Touch-up Art & Lettering/Sabrina Heep
Design/Yukiko Whitley
Editor/Pancha Diaz

SEIYU KA! by Maki Minami
© Maki Minami 2012
All rights reserved.
First published in Japan in 2012 by HAKUSENSHA, Inc., Tokyo.
English language translation rights arranged with
HAKUSENSHA, Inc., Tokyo.

Printed in the U.S.A.

Published by VIZ Media, LLC
P.O. Box 77010
San Francisco, CA 94107

10 9 8 7 6 5 4 3 2 1
First printing, February 2015

www.viz.com   www.shojobeat.com

Maki Minami is from Saitama Prefecture in Japan. She debuted in 2001 with *Kanata no Ao* (Faraway Blue). Her other works include *Kimi wa Girlfriend* (You're My Girlfriend), *Mainichi ga Takaramono* (Every Day Is a Treasure), *Yuki Atataka* (Warm Winter) and *S•A*, which was published in English by VIZ Media.

Voice Over!
Seiyu Academy

9

Vol. 9
Story & Art by
Maki Minami

TECHNICAL ADVISORS
Yoichi Kato, Kaori Kagami, Ayumi Hashidate,
Ayako Harino and Touko Fujitani

Voice Over! Seiyu Academy

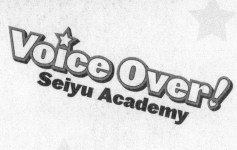

Vol. 9

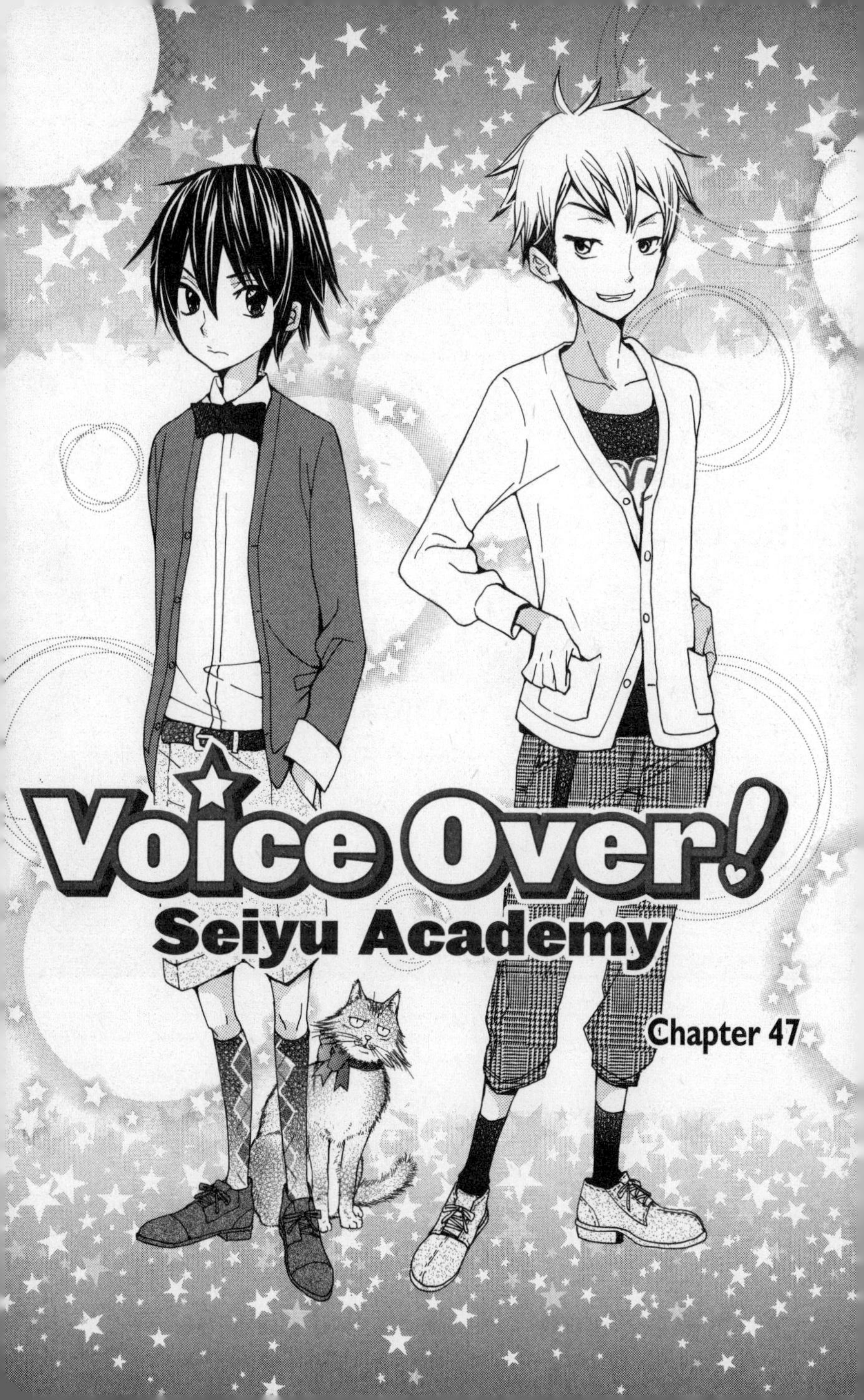
Voice Over!
Seiyu Academy
Chapter 47

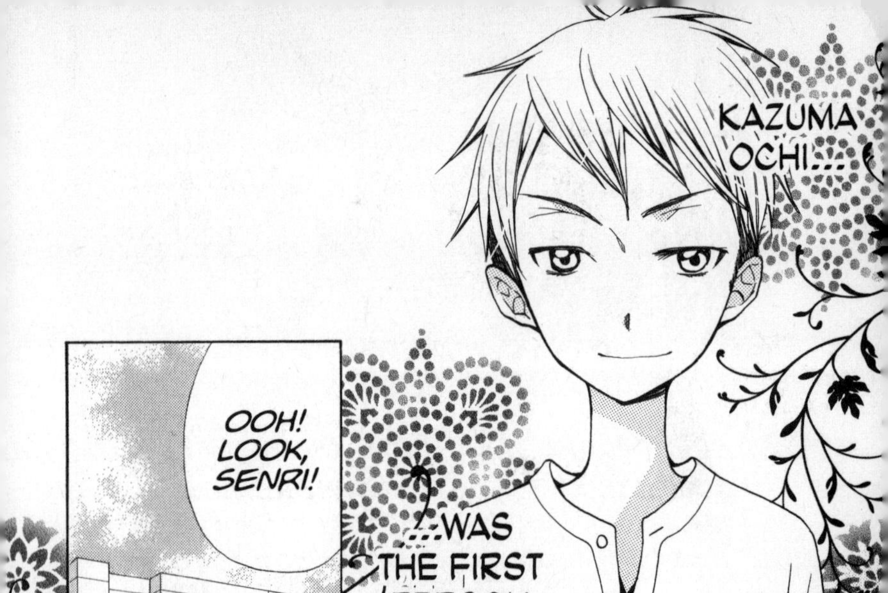
KAZUMA OCHI...
...WAS THE FIRST PERSON I EVER MET WHO WAS LIKE ME.
OOH! LOOK, SENRI!
Libros Theater Group
OOH!! WHAT IS THAT?!

•Cover & Various Things•

• The cover this time is Mizuki & Shiro. Both with glasses! Those two get along so well!!

This time, I was enthusiastic about using a different coloring technique than usual, but the next thing I knew, it was just like usual. *Urrgh...*

1

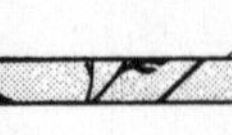

•And now join me for Volume 9!!

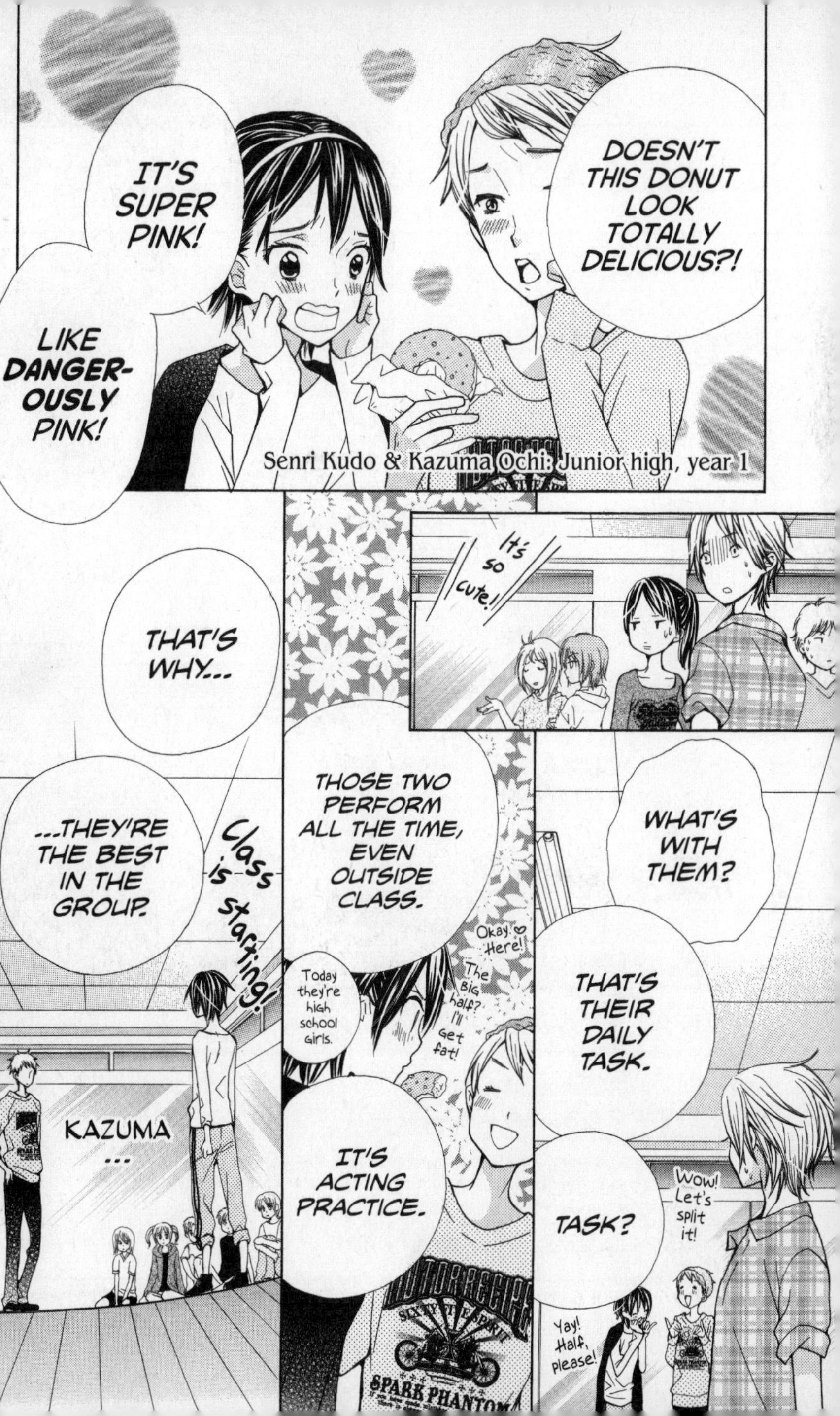
DOESN'T THIS DONUT LOOK TOTALLY DELICIOUS?!
IT'S SUPER PINK!
LIKE DANGEROUSLY PINK!
Senri Kudo & Kazuma Ochi: Junior high, year 1
It's so cute!
WHAT'S WITH THEM?
THAT'S THEIR DAILY TASK.
TASK?
Wow! Let's split it!
Yay! Half, please!
THOSE TWO PERFORM ALL THE TIME, EVEN OUTSIDE CLASS.
Okay. ♡ Here!
The big half? I'll get fat!
Today they're high school girls.
IT'S ACTING PRACTICE.
THAT'S WHY...
...THEY'RE THE BEST IN THE GROUP.
Class is starting!
KAZUMA...

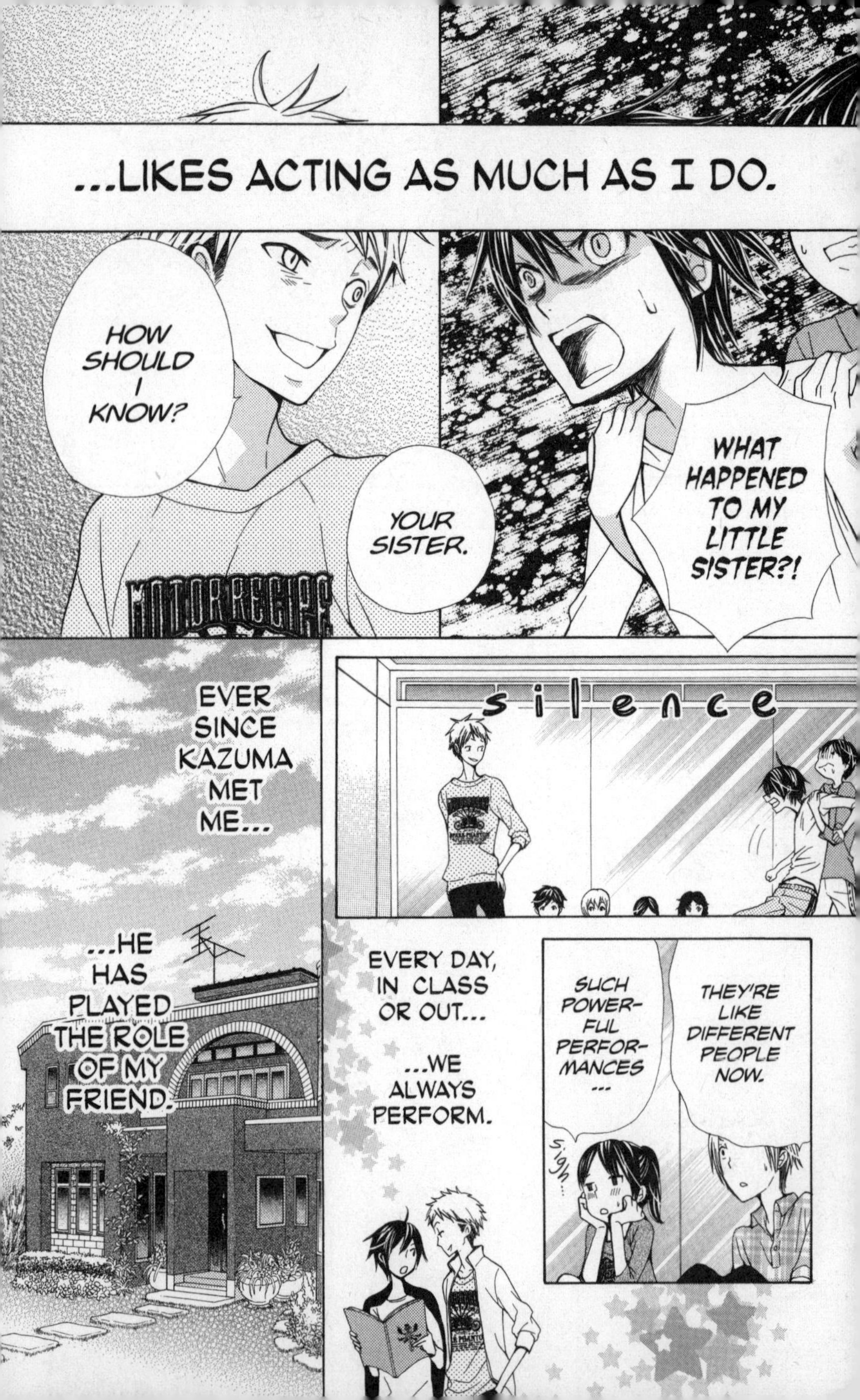
...LIKES ACTING AS MUCH AS I DO.
WHAT HAPPENED TO MY LITTLE SISTER?!
HOW SHOULD I KNOW?
YOUR SISTER.
silence
THEY'RE LIKE DIFFERENT PEOPLE NOW.
SUCH POWER-FUL PERFOR-MANCES...
sigh...
EVERY DAY, IN CLASS OR OUT...
...WE ALWAYS PERFORM.
EVER SINCE KAZUMA MET ME...
...HE HAS PLAYED THE ROLE OF MY FRIEND.

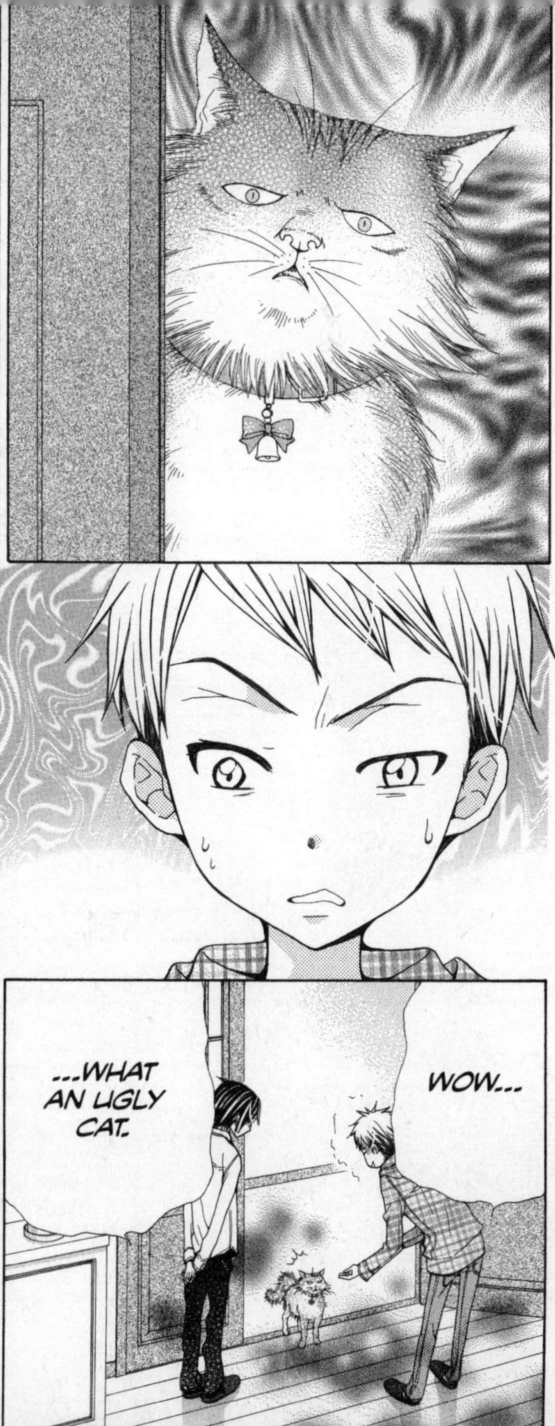
WOW...
...WHAT AN UGLY CAT.

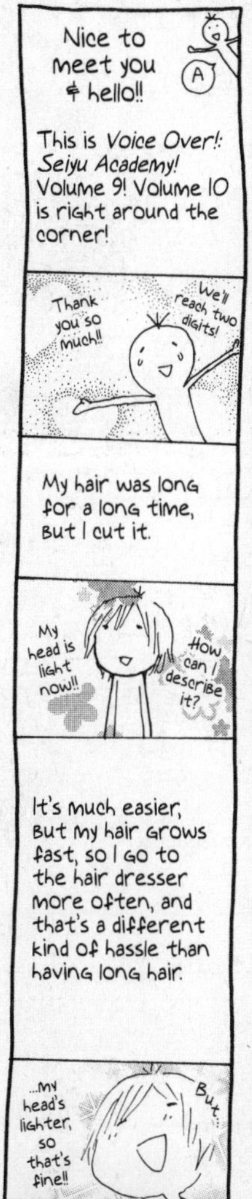
Nice to meet you & hello!!
A
This is *Voice Over!: Seiyu Academy!* Volume 9! Volume 10 is right around the corner!
Thank you so much!!
We'll reach two digits!
My hair was long for a long time, but I cut it.
My head is light now!!
How can I describe it?
It's much easier, but my hair grows fast, so I go to the hair dresser more often, and that's a different kind of hassle than having long hair.
But...
...my head's lighter, so that's fine!!
Senri

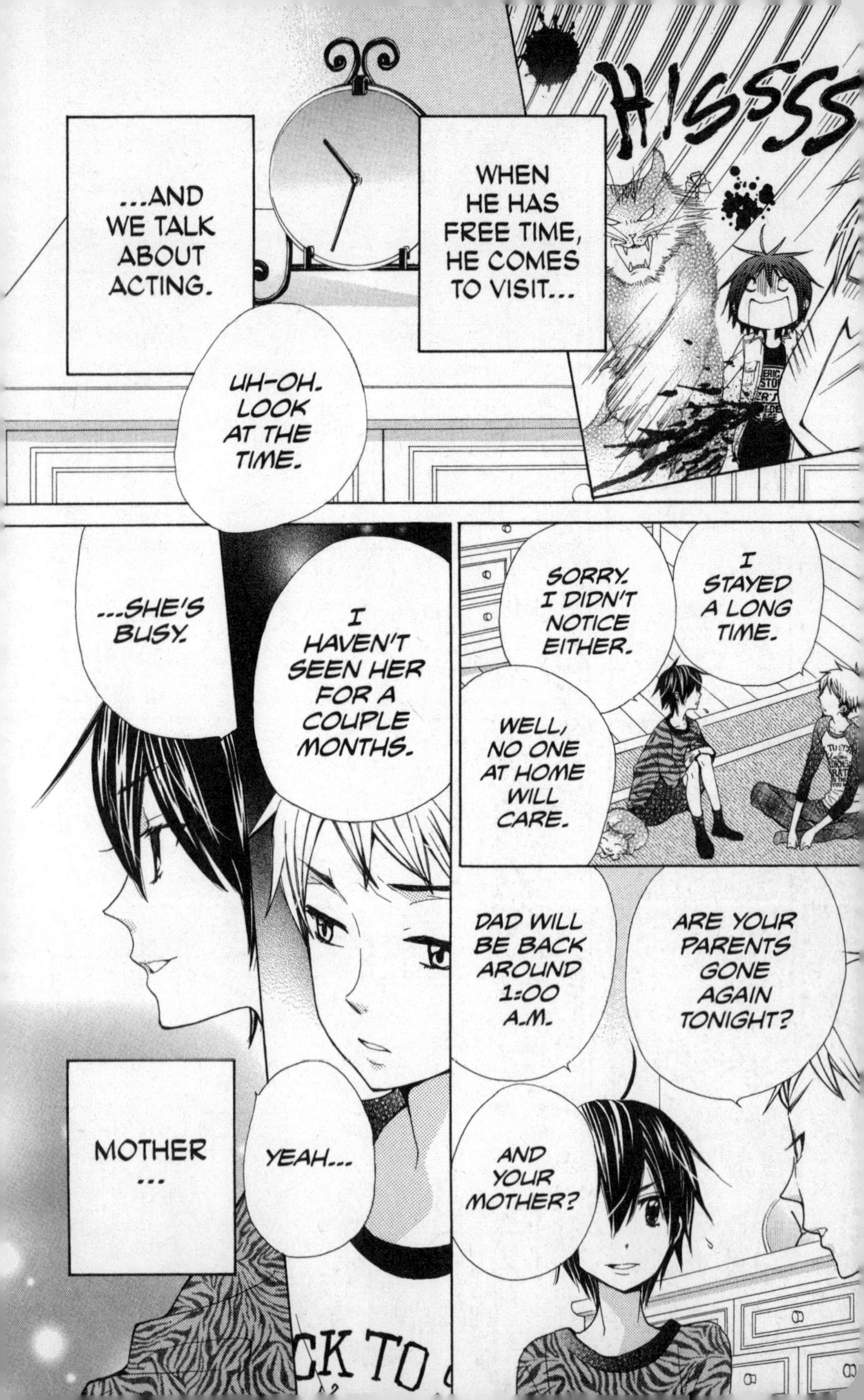
HISSSS
WHEN HE HAS FREE TIME, HE COMES TO VISIT...
...AND WE TALK ABOUT ACTING.
UH-OH. LOOK AT THE TIME.
I STAYED A LONG TIME.
SORRY. I DIDN'T NOTICE EITHER.
WELL, NO ONE AT HOME WILL CARE.
ARE YOUR PARENTS GONE AGAIN TONIGHT?
DAD WILL BE BACK AROUND 1:00 A.M.
AND YOUR MOTHER?
I HAVEN'T SEEN HER FOR A COUPLE MONTHS.
...SHE'S BUSY.
YEAH...
MOTHER...

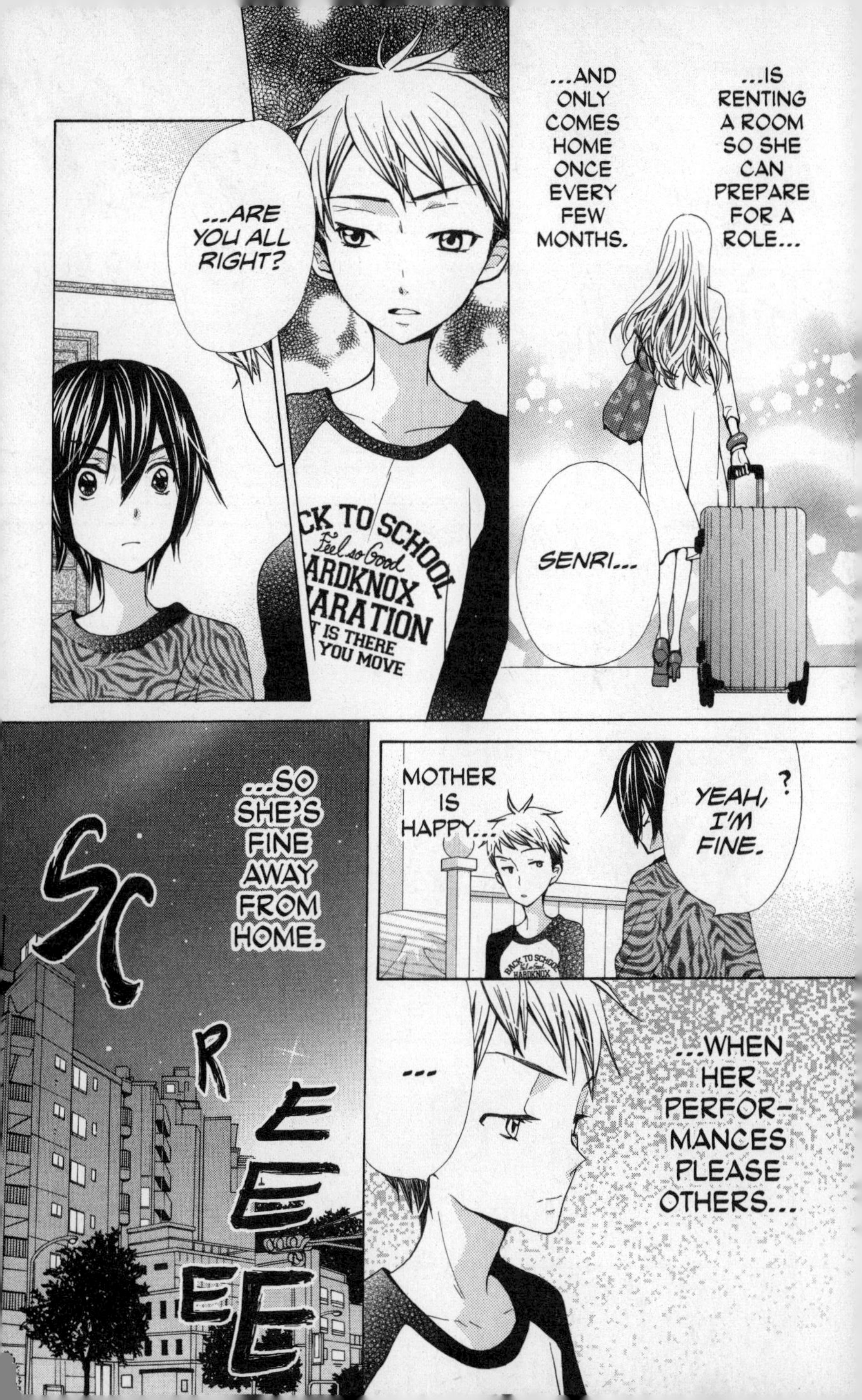
...IS RENTING A ROOM SO SHE CAN PREPARE FOR A ROLE...
...AND ONLY COMES HOME ONCE EVERY FEW MONTHS.
SENRI...
...ARE YOU ALL RIGHT?
YEAH, I'M FINE.
?
MOTHER IS HAPPY...
...WHEN HER PERFORMANCES PLEASE OTHERS...
...
...SO SHE'S FINE AWAY FROM HOME.
SCREEEE

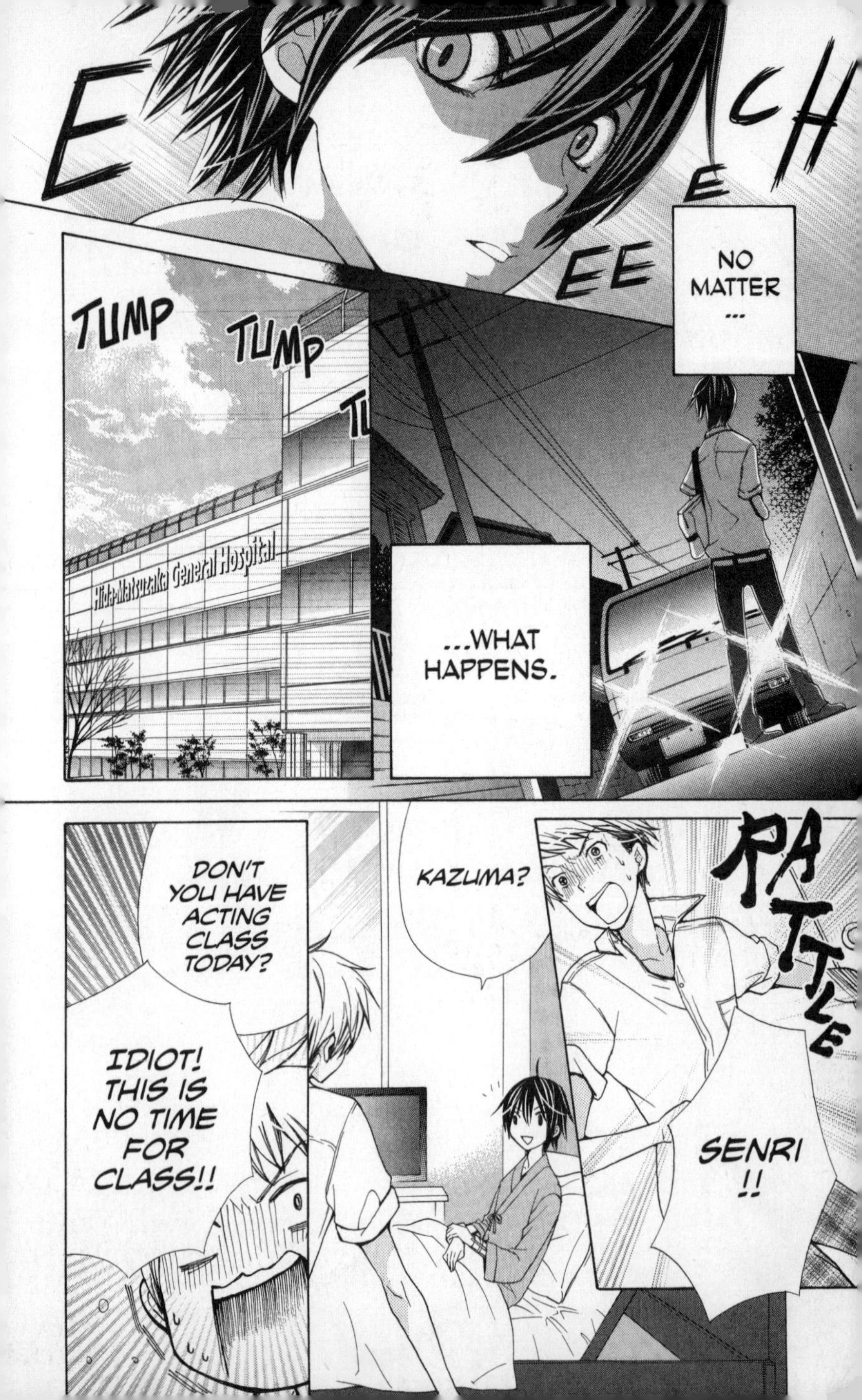
EEEEECH
NO MATTER ...
...WHAT HAPPENS.
TUMP
TUMP
TU
Hida-Matsuzaka General Hospital
RATTLE
SENRI!!
KAZUMA?
DON'T YOU HAVE ACTING CLASS TODAY?
IDIOT! THIS IS NO TIME FOR CLASS!!

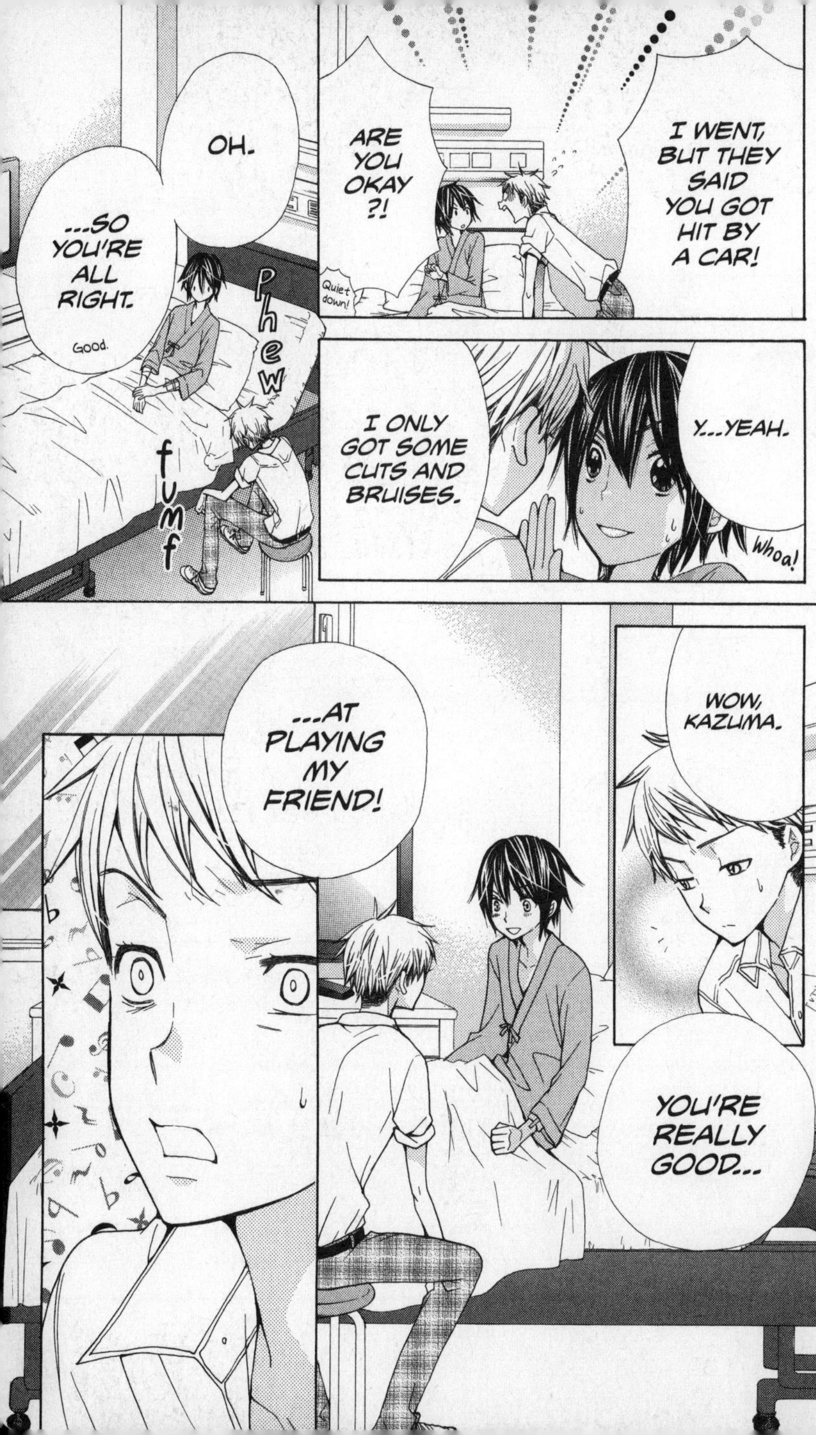
I WENT, BUT THEY SAID YOU GOT HIT BY A CAR!
ARE YOU OKAY?!
Quiet down!
Y...YEAH.
Whoa!
I ONLY GOT SOME CUTS AND BRUISES.
OH.
...SO YOU'RE ALL RIGHT.
Good.
phew
fumf
WOW, KAZUMA.
YOU'RE REALLY GOOD...
...AT PLAYING MY FRIEND!

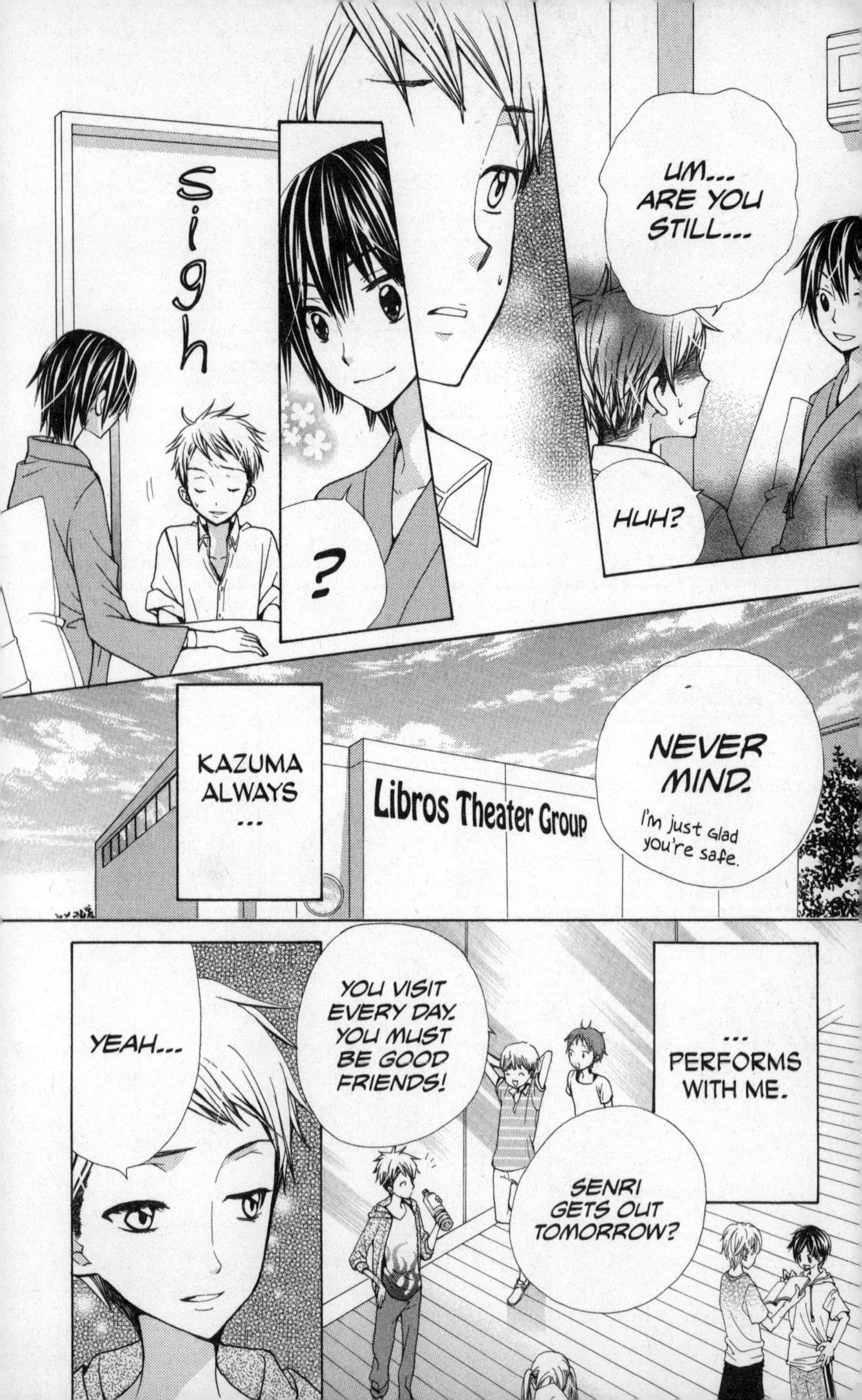
UM... ARE YOU STILL...
HUH?
?
Sigh
NEVER MIND.
I'm just glad you're safe.
Libros Theater Group
KAZUMA ALWAYS ...
... PERFORMS WITH ME.
YOU VISIT EVERY DAY. YOU MUST BE GOOD FRIENDS!
SENRI GETS OUT TOMORROW?
YEAH...

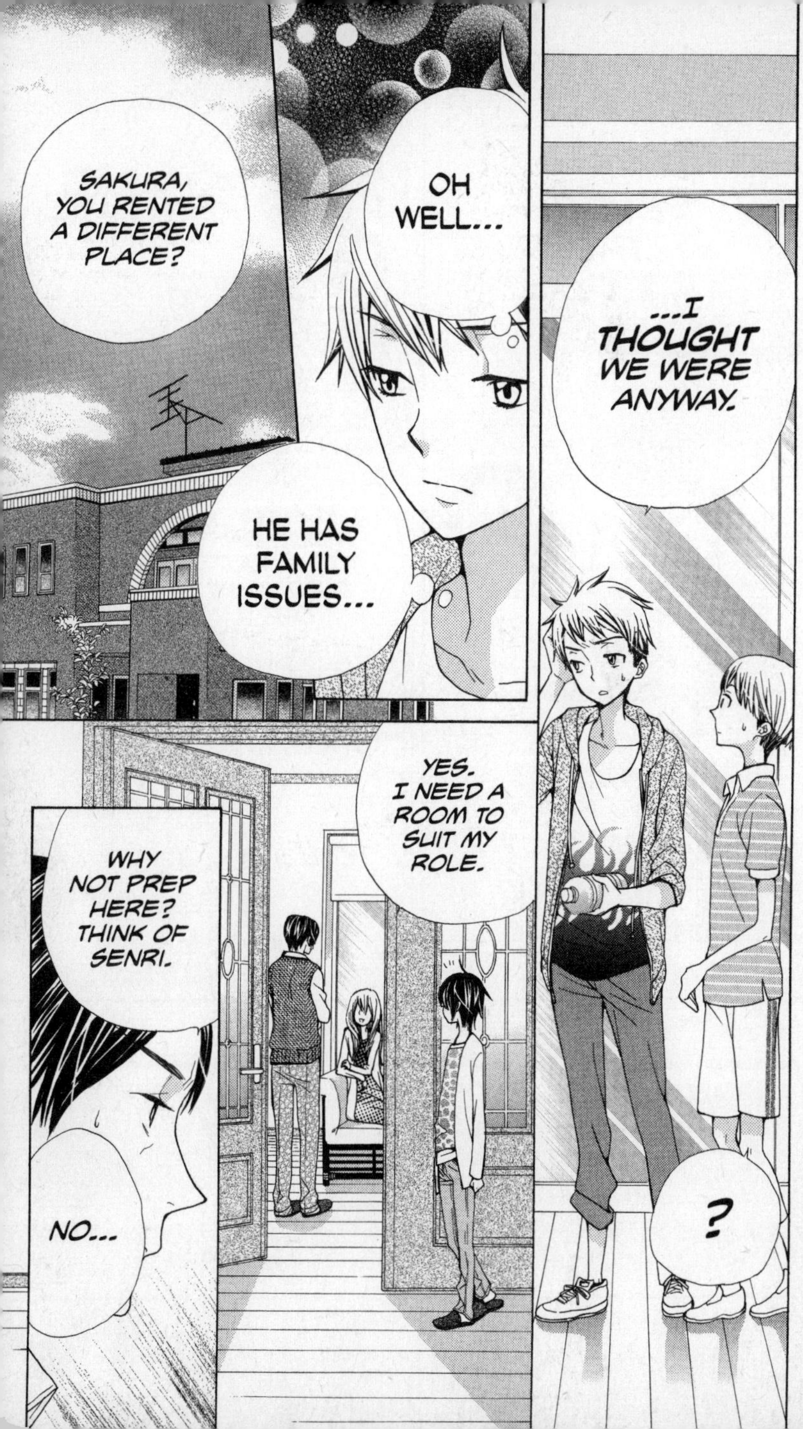
...I THOUGHT WE WERE ANYWAY.
?
OH WELL...
HE HAS FAMILY ISSUES...
SAKURA, YOU RENTED A DIFFERENT PLACE?
YES. I NEED A ROOM TO SUIT MY ROLE.
WHY NOT PREP HERE? THINK OF SENRI.
NO...

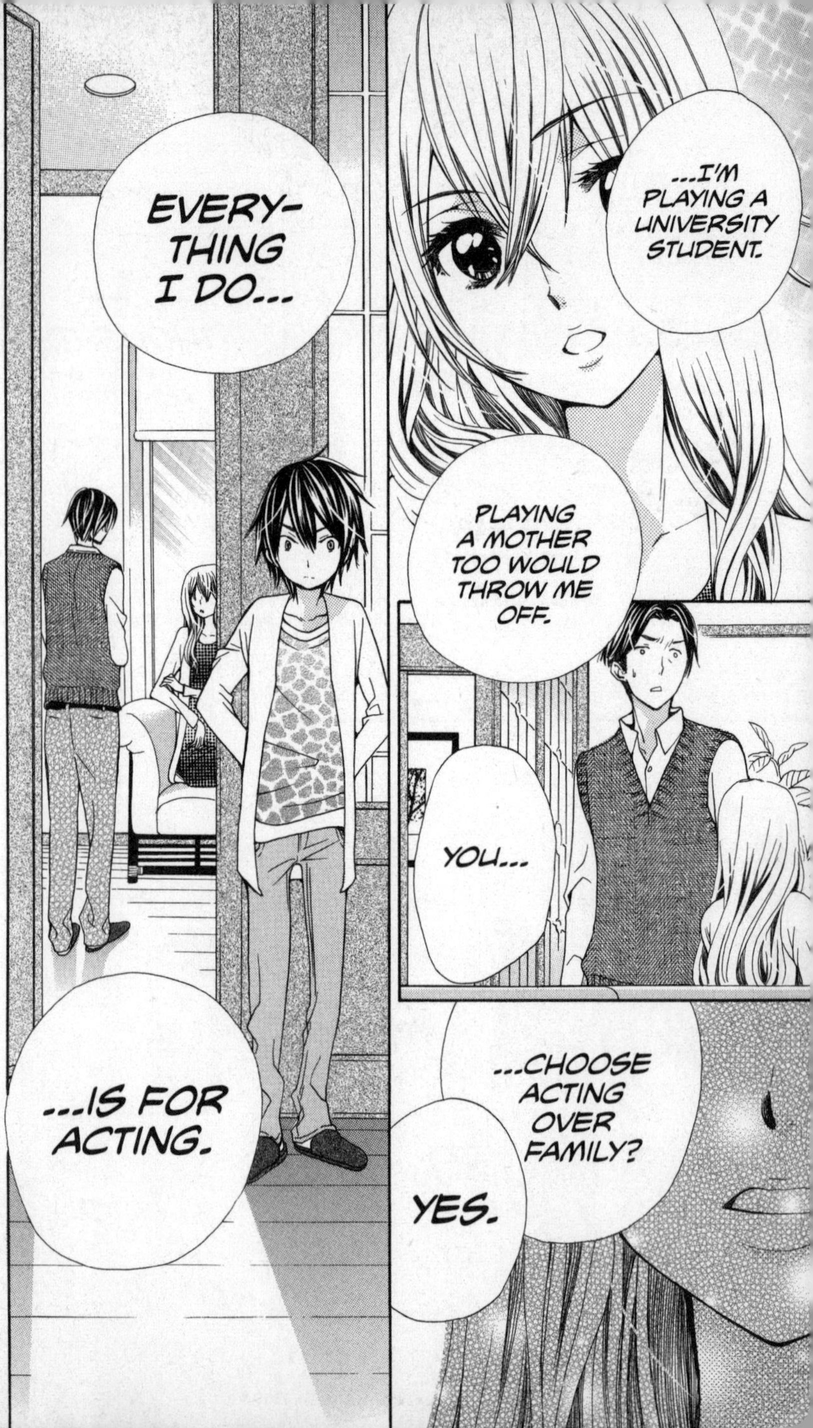
...I'M PLAYING A UNIVERSITY STUDENT.
PLAYING A MOTHER TOO WOULD THROW ME OFF.
YOU...
...CHOOSE ACTING OVER FAMILY?
YES.
EVERY-THING I DO...
...IS FOR ACTING.

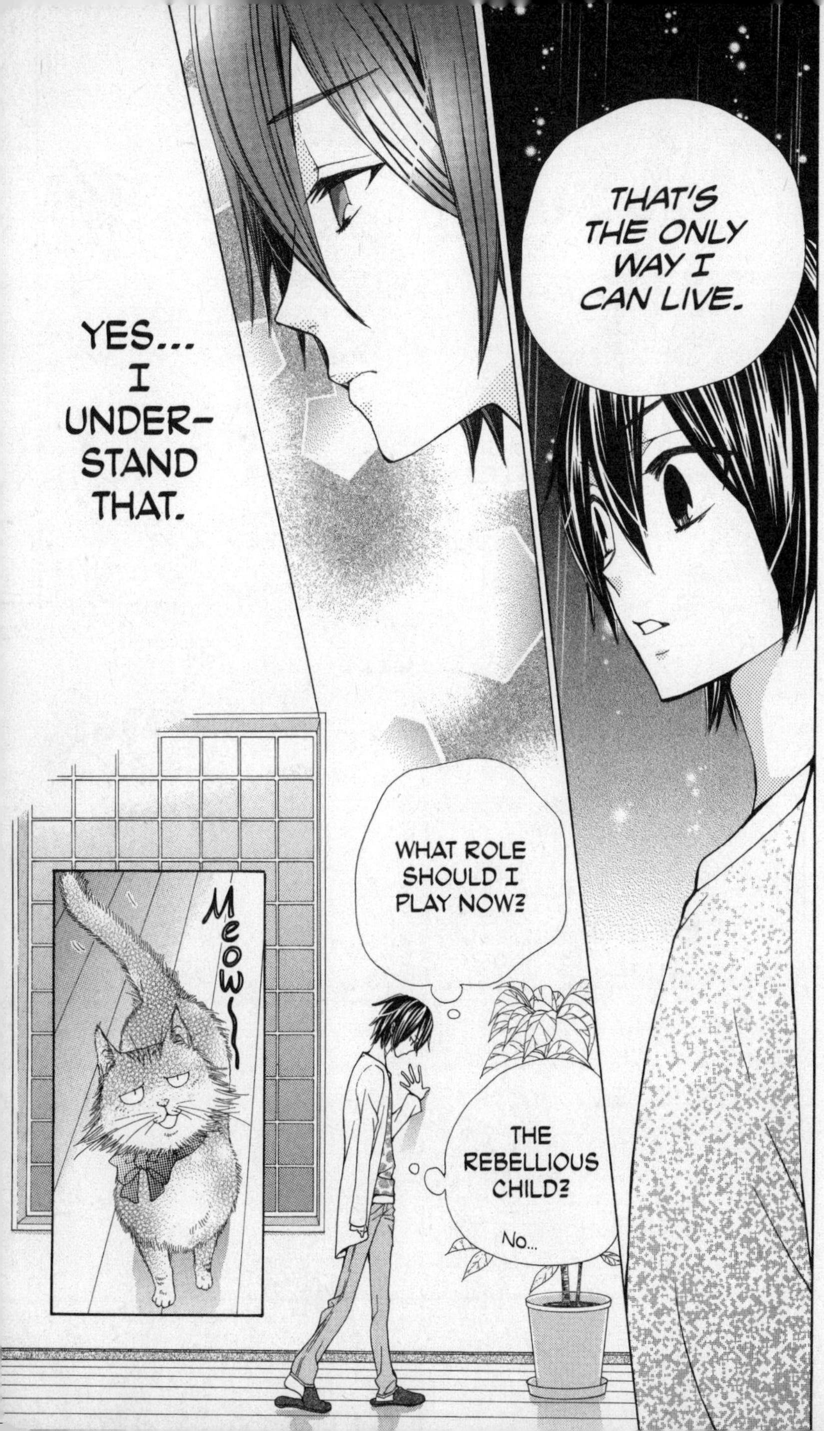
THAT'S THE ONLY WAY I CAN LIVE.
YES... I UNDER-STAND THAT.
WHAT ROLE SHOULD I PLAY NOW?
THE REBELLIOUS CHILD?
No...
Meow~

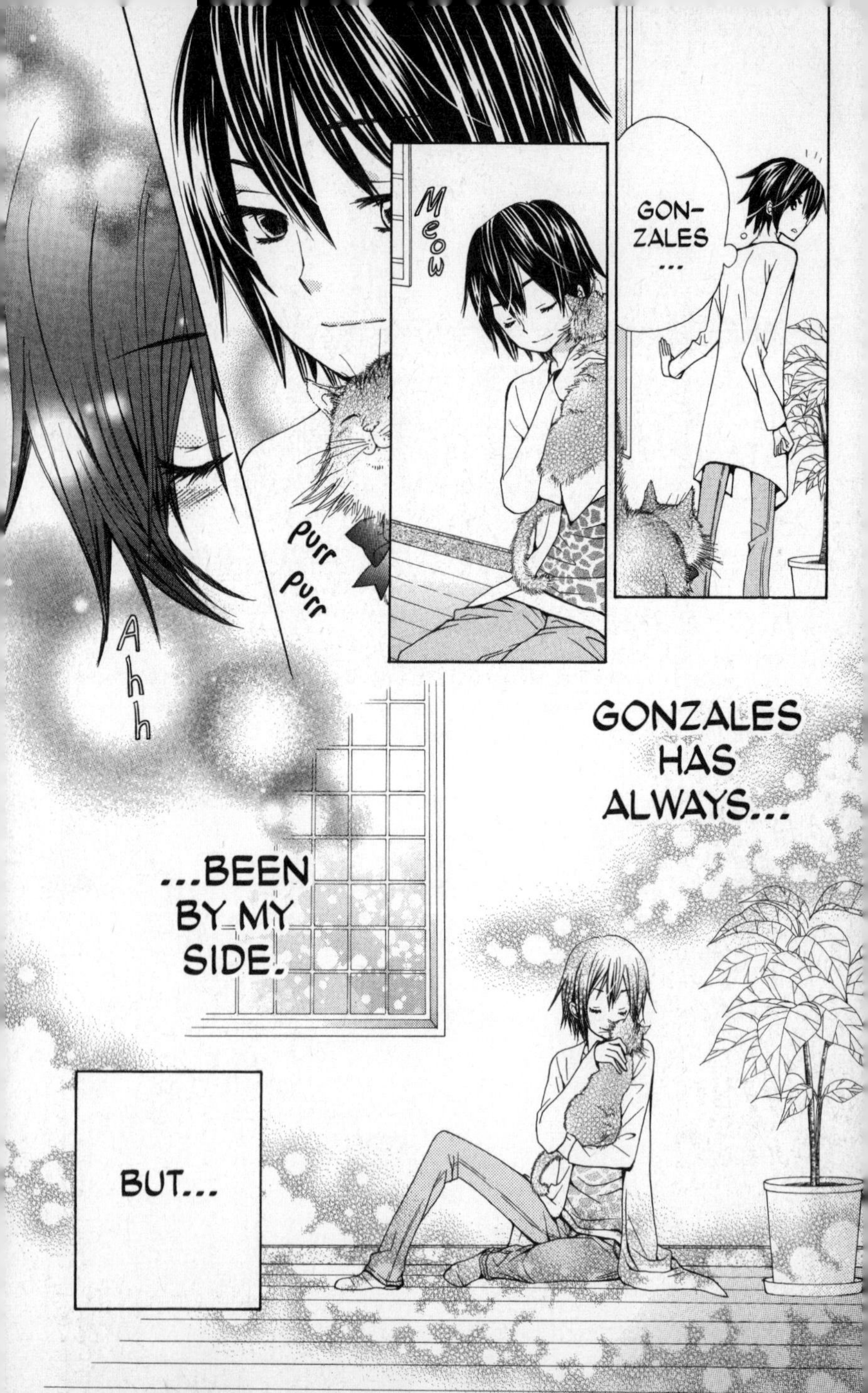
GON-ZALES ...
Meow
Purr purr
Ahh
GONZALES HAS ALWAYS...
...BEEN BY MY SIDE.
BUT...

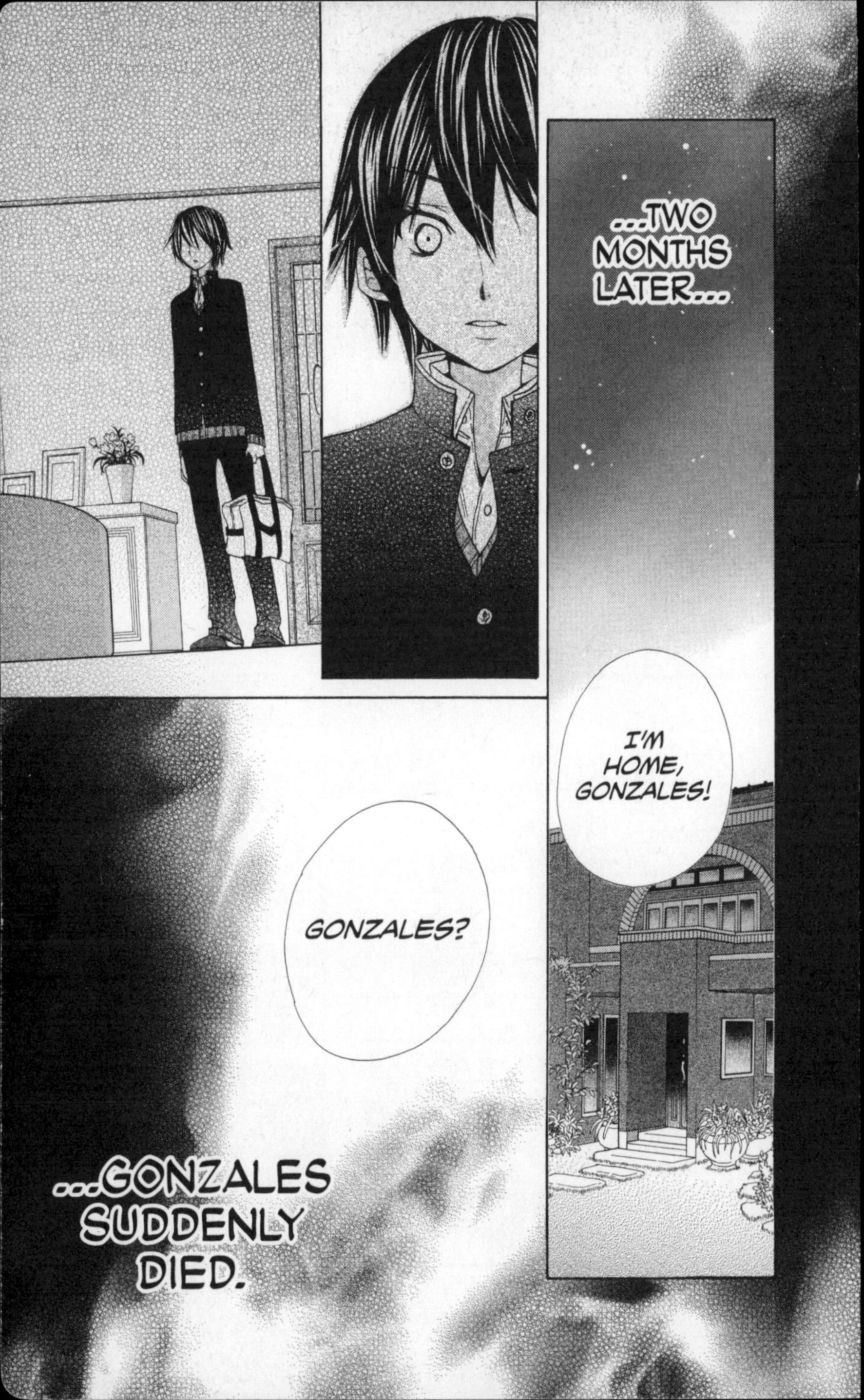
...TWO MONTHS LATER...
I'M HOME, GONZALES!
GONZALES?
...GONZALES SUDDENLY DIED.

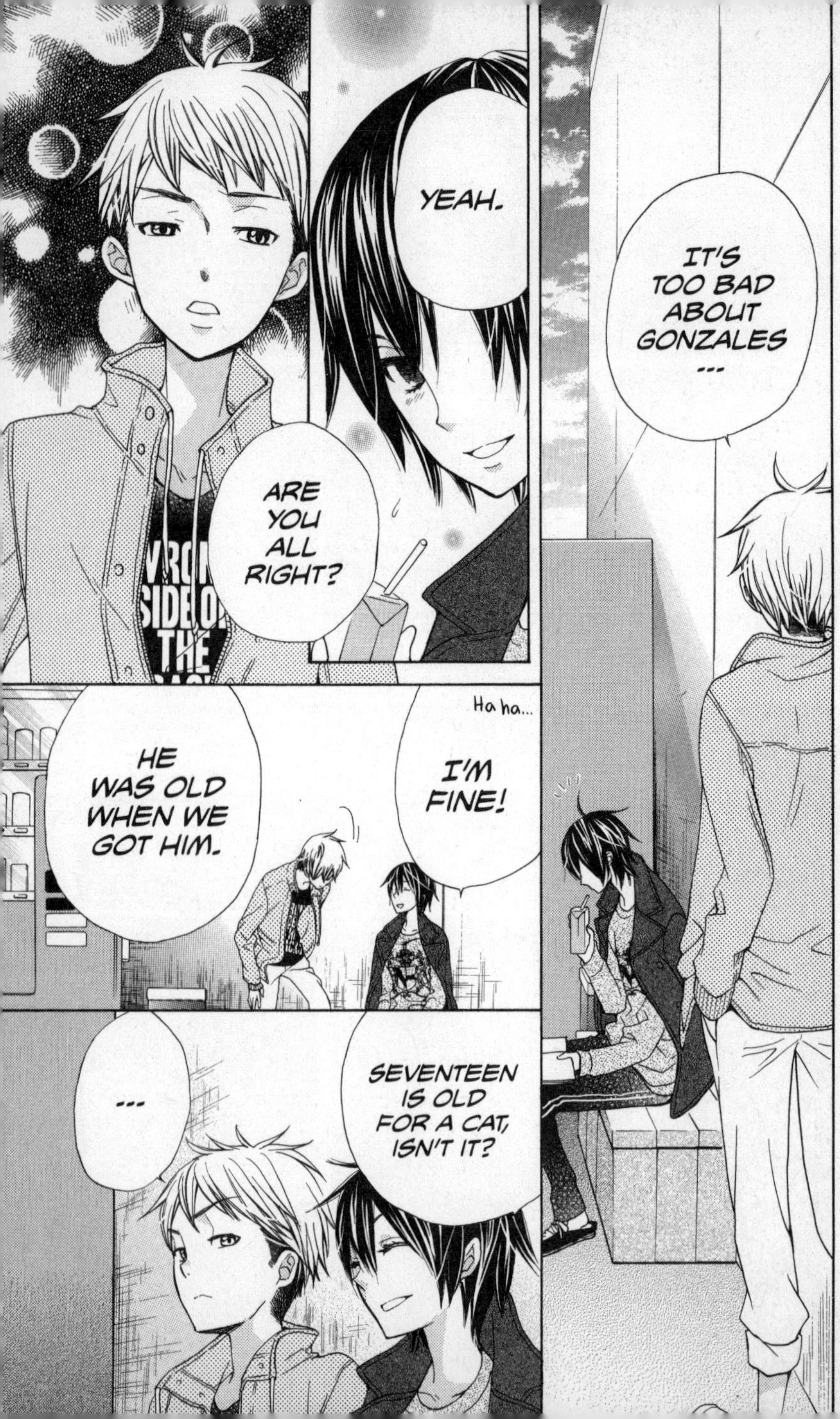
IT'S TOO BAD ABOUT GONZALES...
YEAH.
ARE YOU ALL RIGHT?
Ha ha...
I'M FINE!
HE WAS OLD WHEN WE GOT HIM.
SEVENTEEN IS OLD FOR A CAT, ISN'T IT?
...

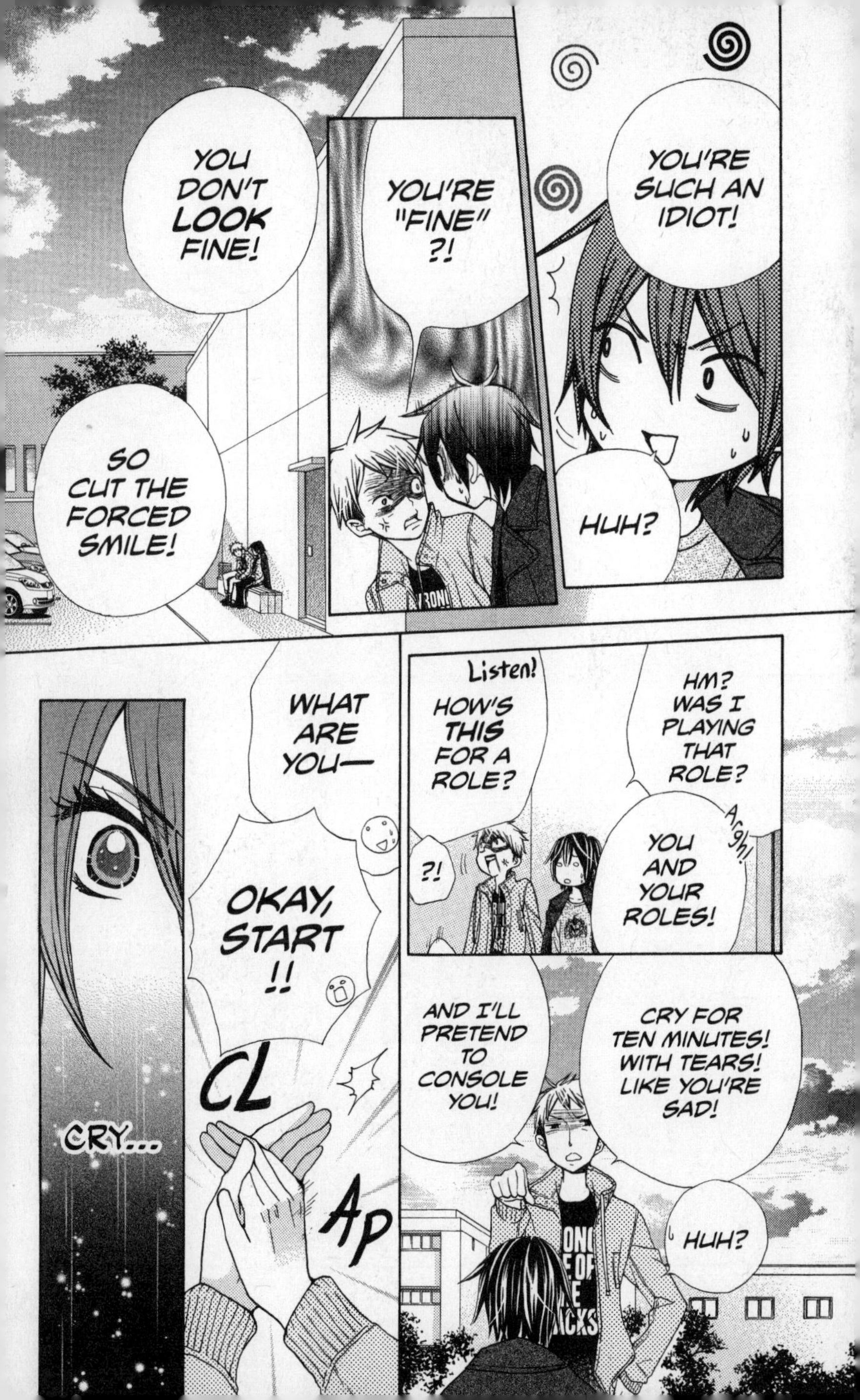
YOU'RE SUCH AN IDIOT!
HUH?
YOU'RE "FINE" ?!
YOU DON'T LOOK FINE!
SO CUT THE FORCED SMILE!
HM? WAS I PLAYING THAT ROLE?
Argh!
YOU AND YOUR ROLES!
Listen!
HOW'S THIS FOR A ROLE?
?!
CRY FOR TEN MINUTES! WITH TEARS! LIKE YOU'RE SAD!
AND I'LL PRETEND TO CONSOLE YOU!
HUH?
WHAT ARE YOU—
OKAY, START !!
CL
AP
CRY...

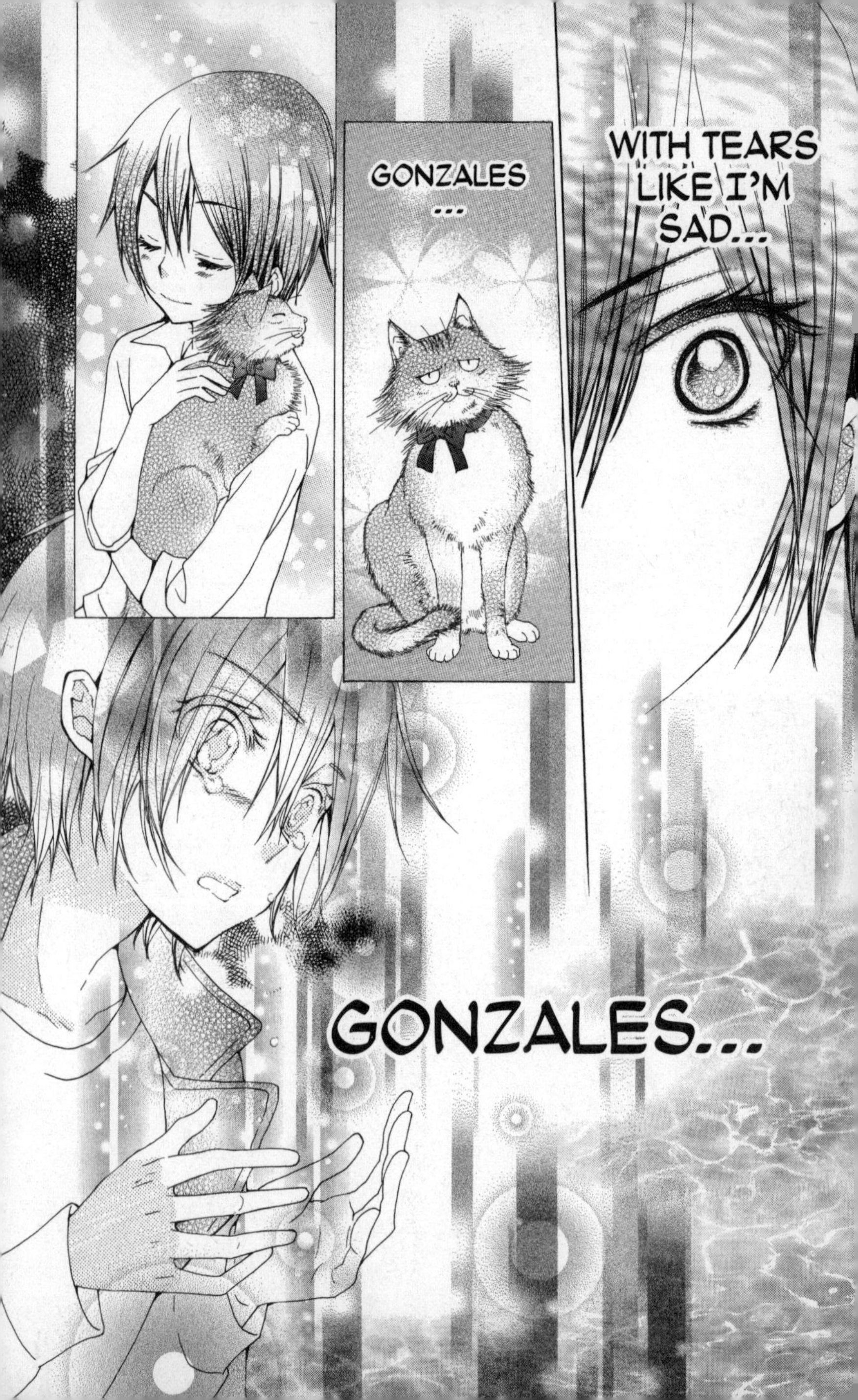
WITH TEARS LIKE I'M SAD...
GONZALES ...
GONZALES...

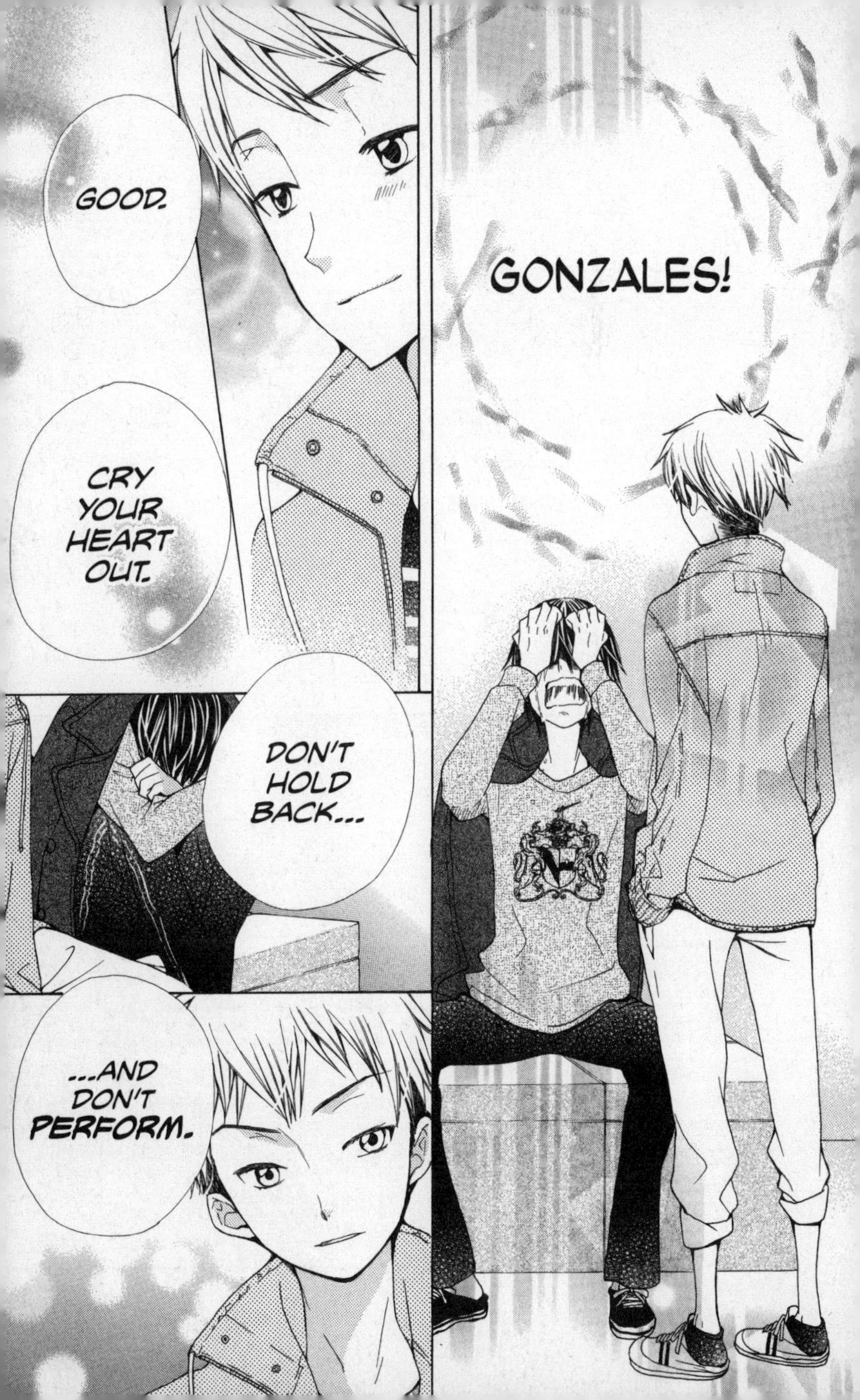
GONZALES!
GOOD.
CRY YOUR HEART OUT.
DON'T HOLD BACK...
...AND DON'T PERFORM.

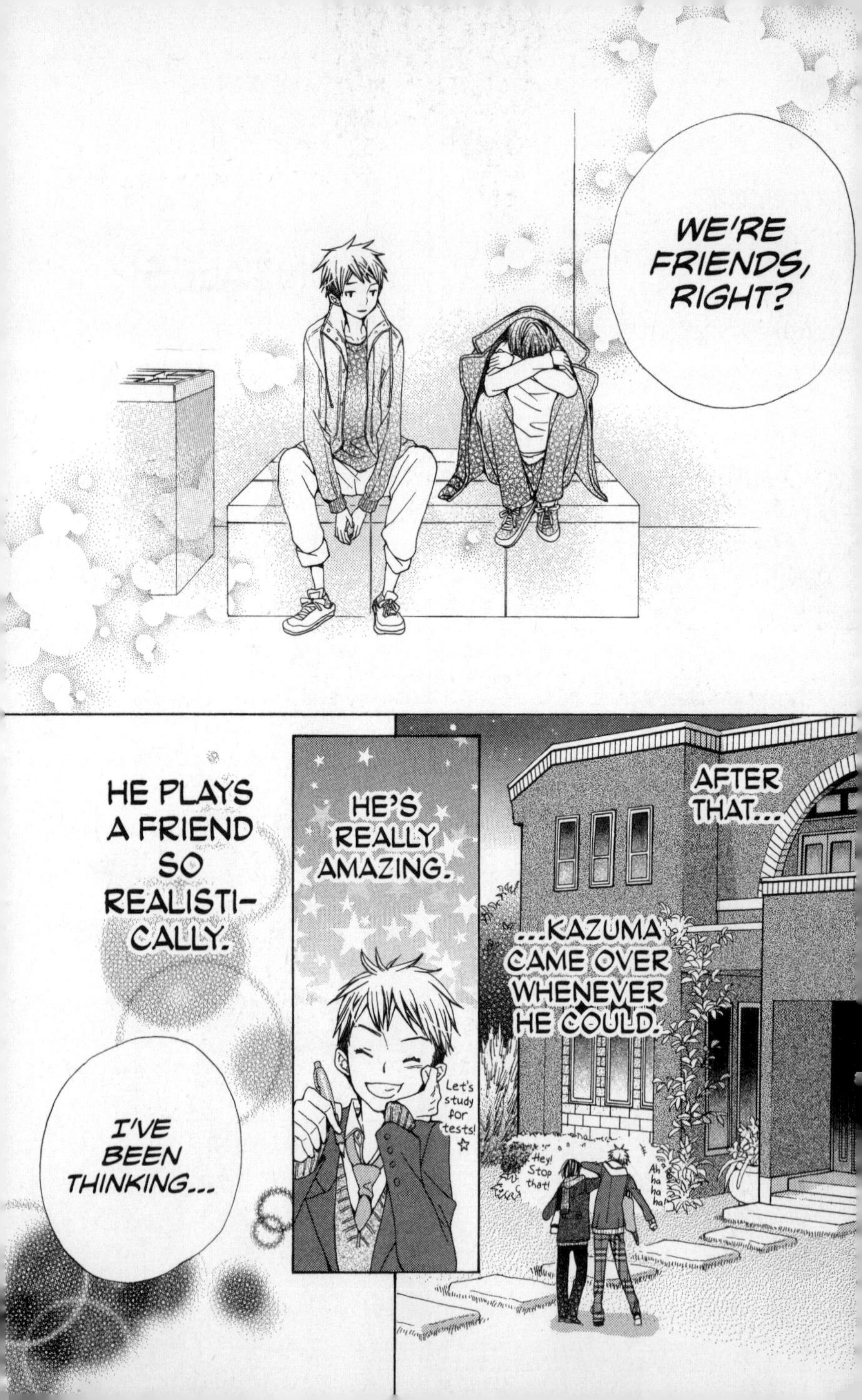

WE'RE FRIENDS, RIGHT?
AFTER THAT...
...KAZUMA CAME OVER WHENEVER HE COULD.
Ah ha ha ha!
Hey! Stop that!
HE'S REALLY AMAZING.
Let's study for tests! ☆
HE PLAYS A FRIEND SO REALISTI-CALLY.
I'VE BEEN THINKING...

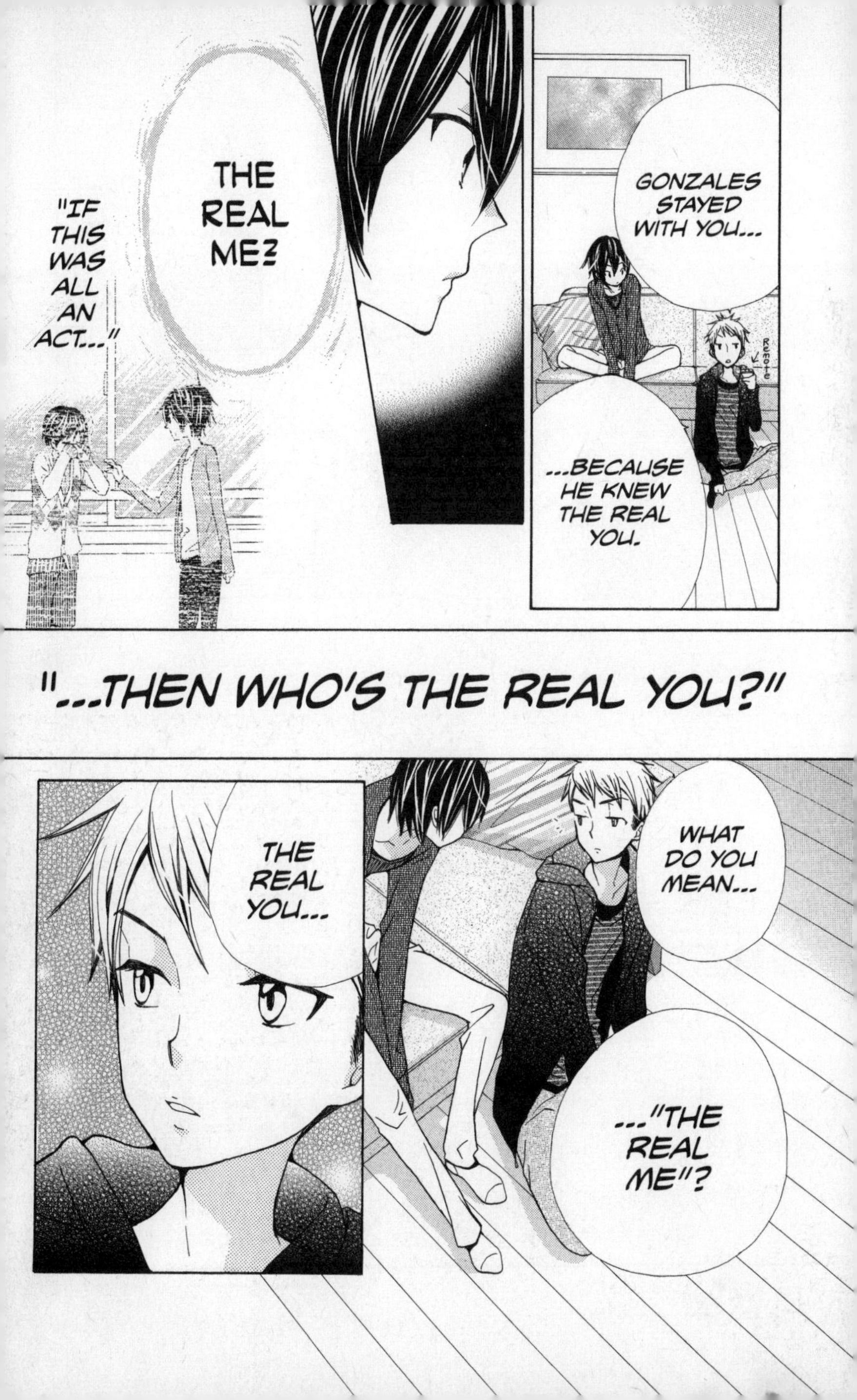
GONZALES STAYED WITH YOU...
Remote
...BECAUSE HE KNEW THE REAL YOU.
THE REAL ME?
"IF THIS WAS ALL AN ACT..."
"...THEN WHO'S THE REAL YOU?"
WHAT DO YOU MEAN...
..."THE REAL ME"?
THE REAL YOU...

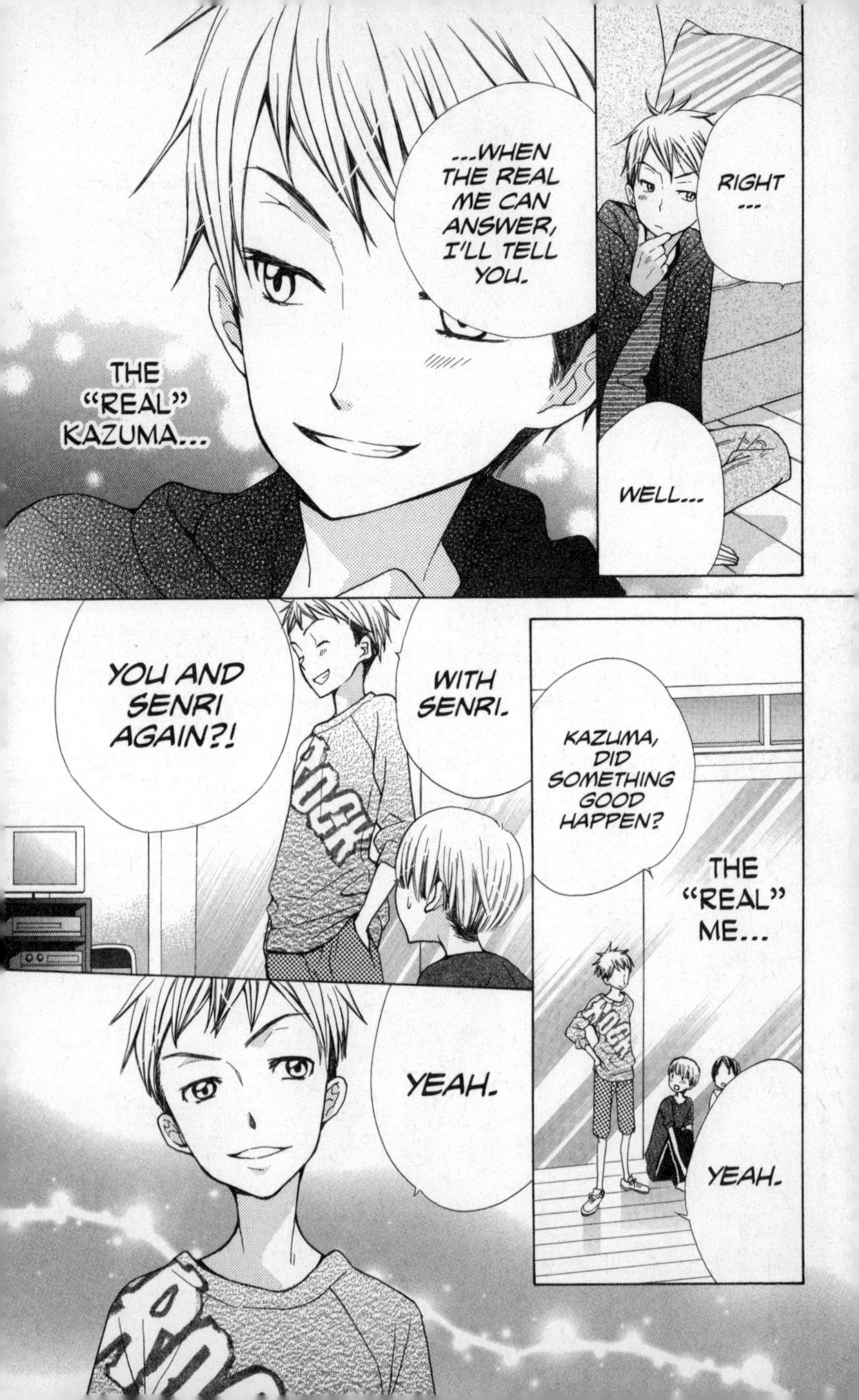
RIGHT ...
WELL...
...WHEN THE REAL ME CAN ANSWER, I'LL TELL YOU.
THE "REAL" KAZUMA...
KAZUMA, DID SOMETHING GOOD HAPPEN?
THE "REAL" ME...
YEAH.
WITH SENRI.
YOU AND SENRI AGAIN?!
YEAH.

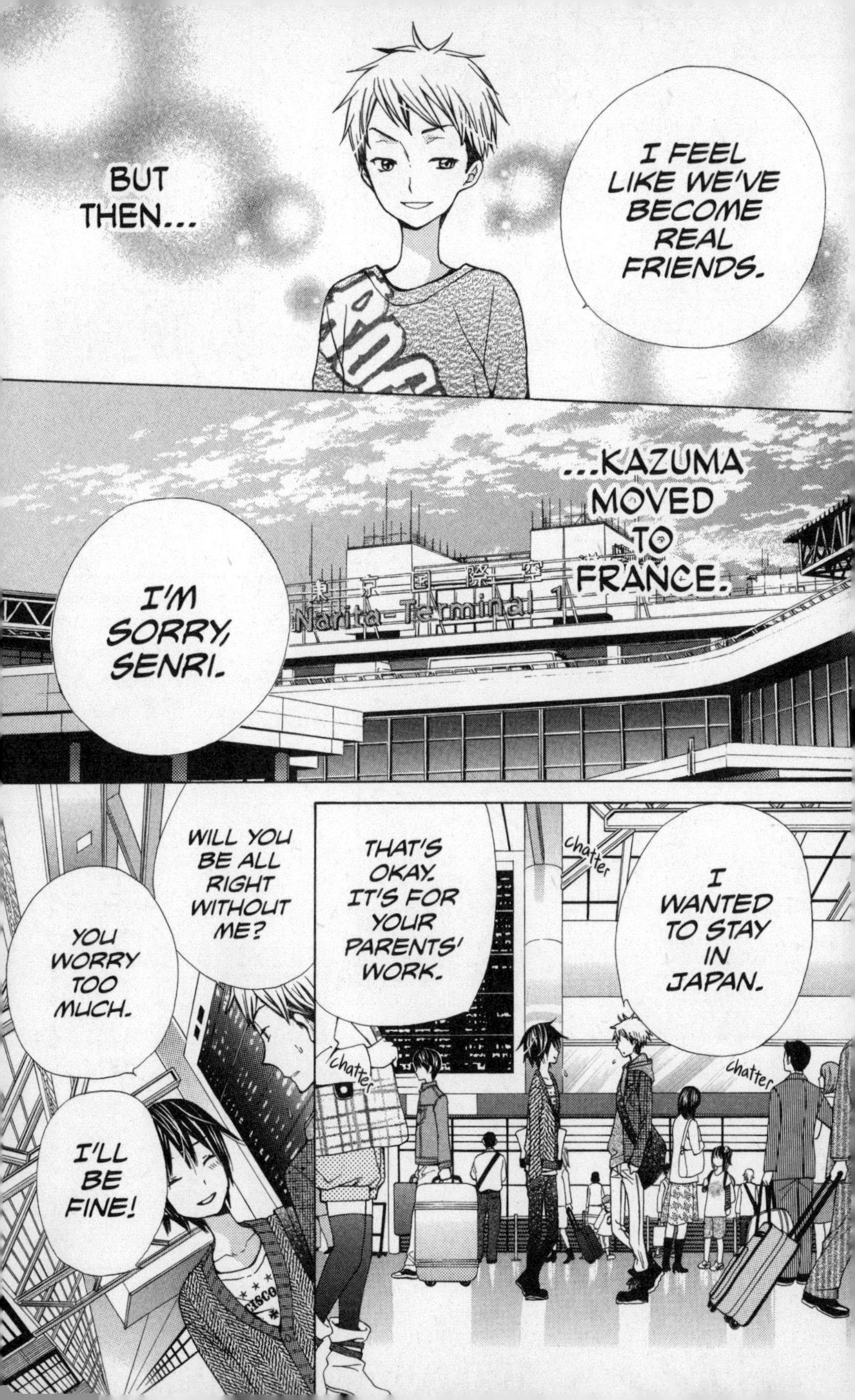
I FEEL LIKE WE'VE BECOME REAL FRIENDS.
BUT THEN...
...KAZUMA MOVED TO FRANCE.
I'M SORRY, SENRI.
I WANTED TO STAY IN JAPAN.
chatter
THAT'S OKAY. IT'S FOR YOUR PARENTS' WORK.
chatter
chatter
WILL YOU BE ALL RIGHT WITHOUT ME?
YOU WORRY TOO MUCH.
I'LL BE FINE!

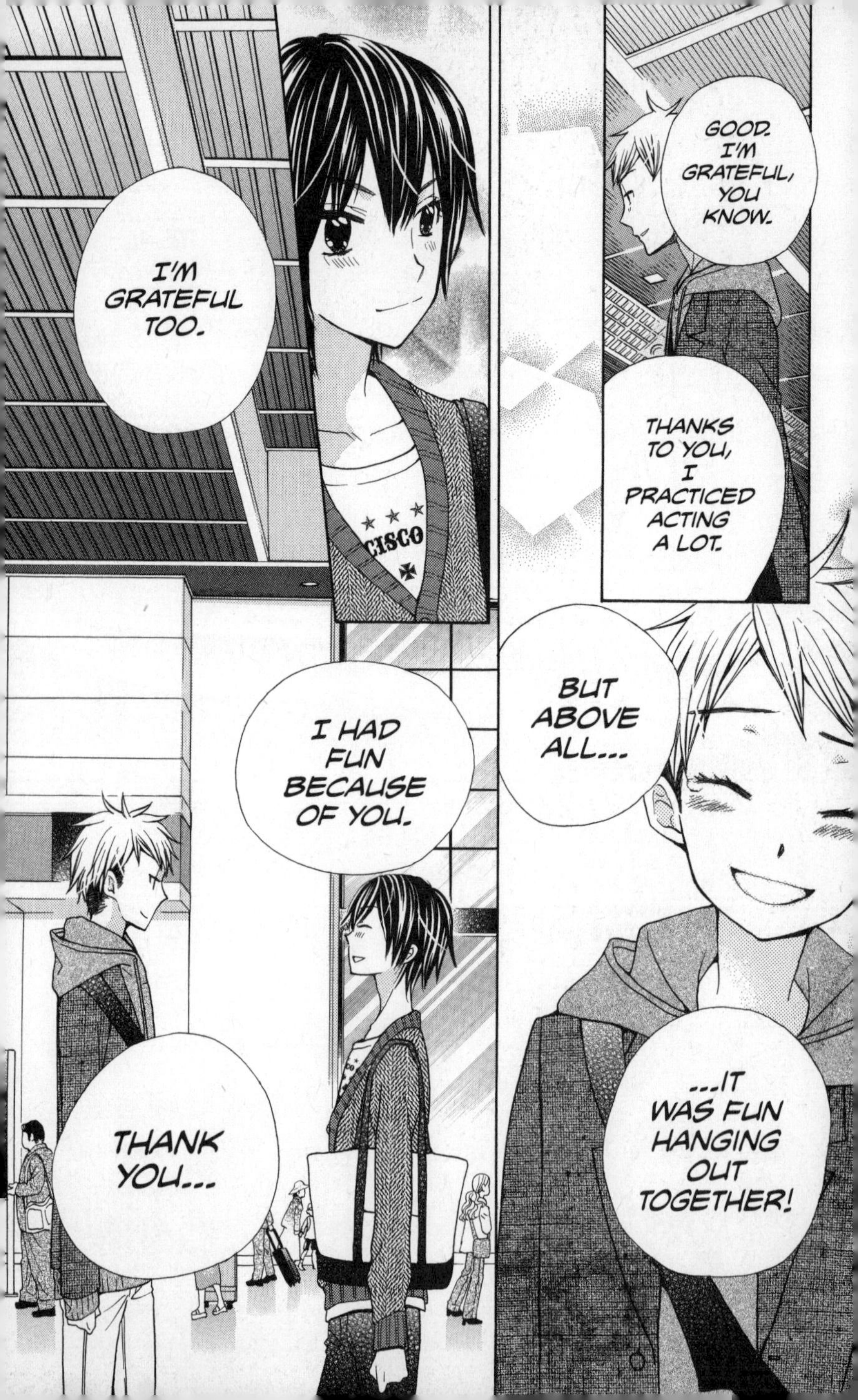
GOOD. I'M GRATEFUL, YOU KNOW.
THANKS TO YOU, I PRACTICED ACTING A LOT.
I'M GRATEFUL TOO.
CISCO
BUT ABOVE ALL...
...IT WAS FUN HANGING OUT TOGETHER!
I HAD FUN BECAUSE OF YOU.
THANK YOU...

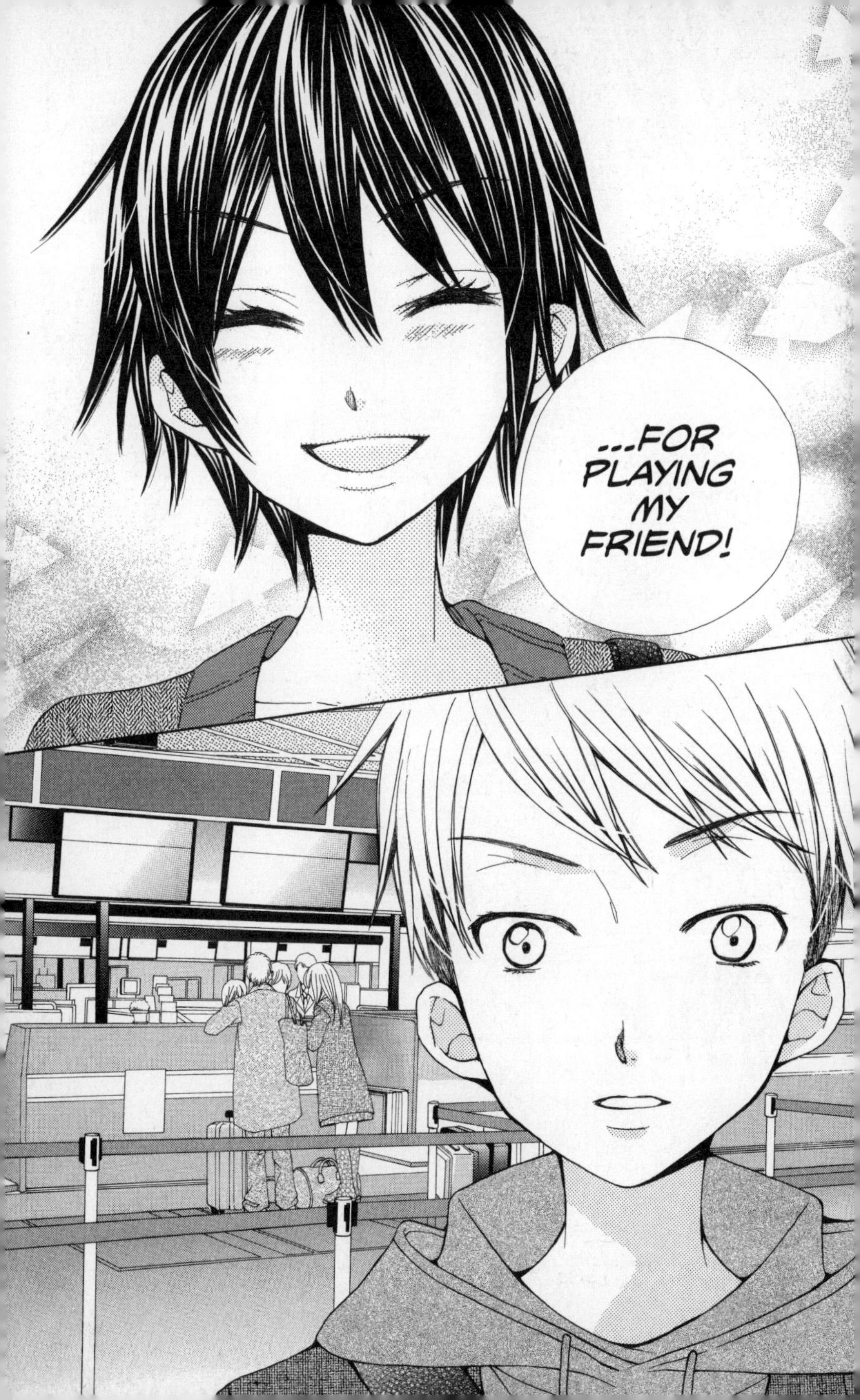
...FOR PLAYING MY FRIEND!

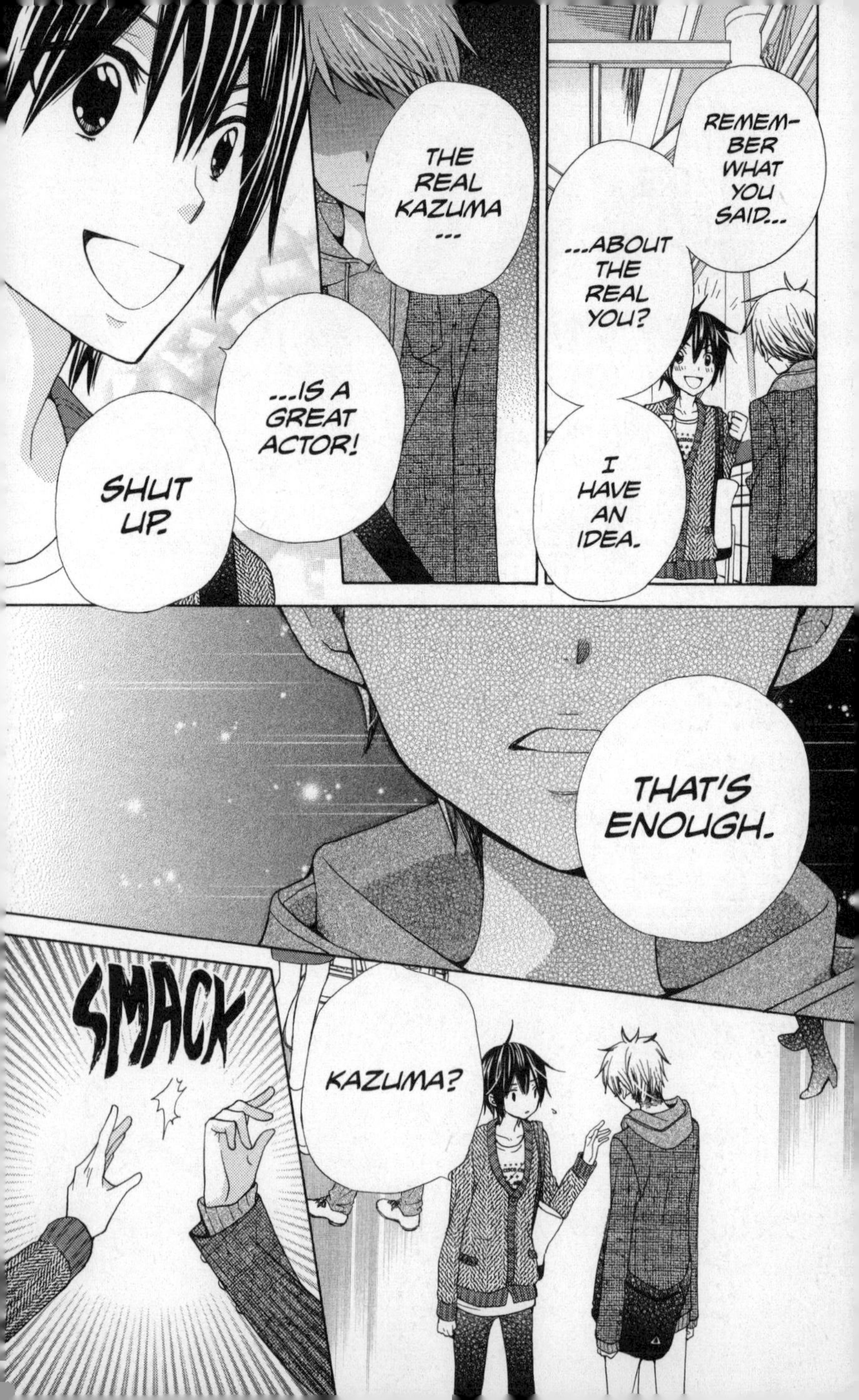
REMEMBER WHAT YOU SAID...
...ABOUT THE REAL YOU?
I HAVE AN IDEA.
THE REAL KAZUMA...
...IS A GREAT ACTOR!
SHUT UP.
THAT'S ENOUGH.
KAZUMA?
SMACK

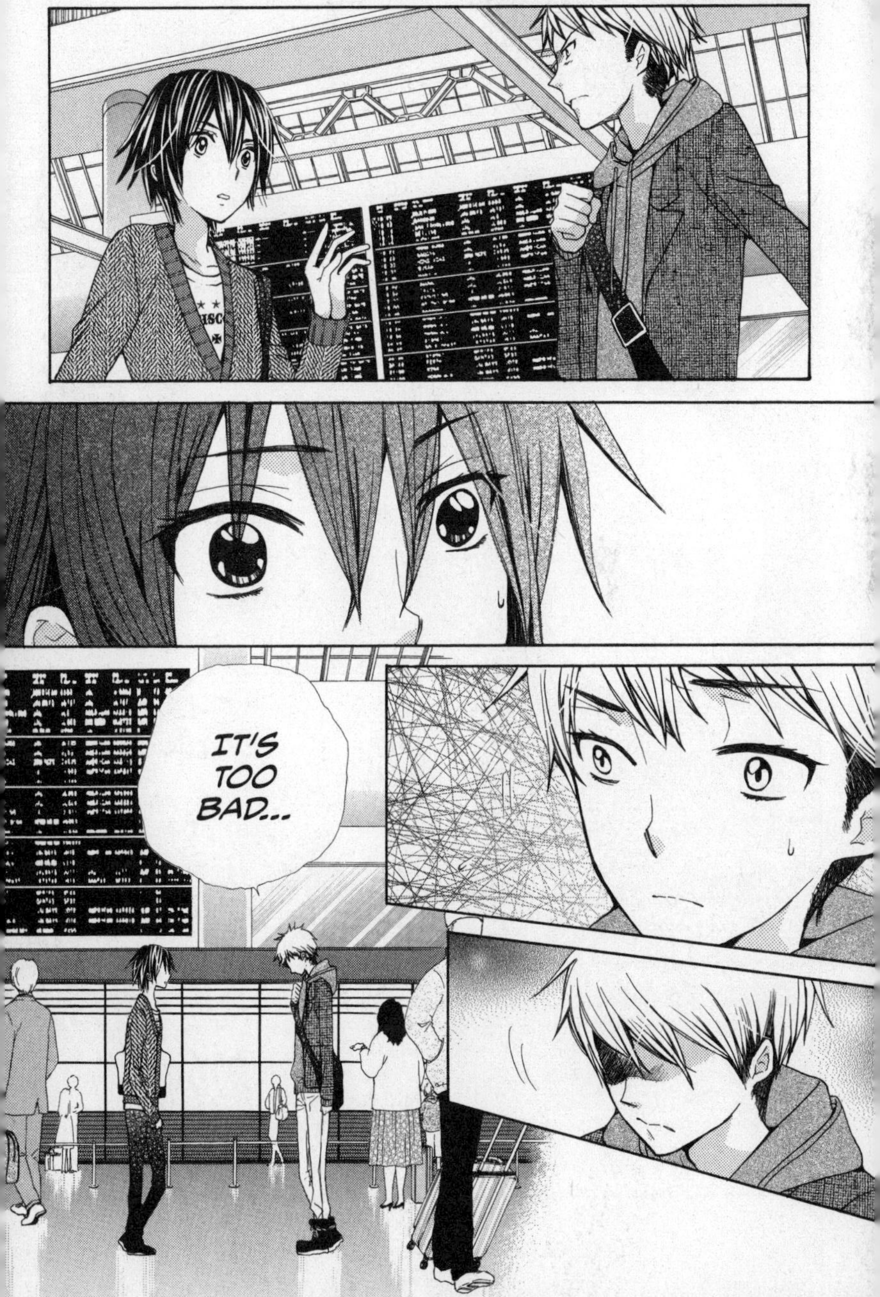
IT'S TOO BAD...

YOU ONLY CARE ABOUT ACTING.
I HAD A DIFFERENT IDEA ABOUT THE REAL YOU...
...BUT I WAS WRONG.
THE REAL YOU...
...IS EMPTY.

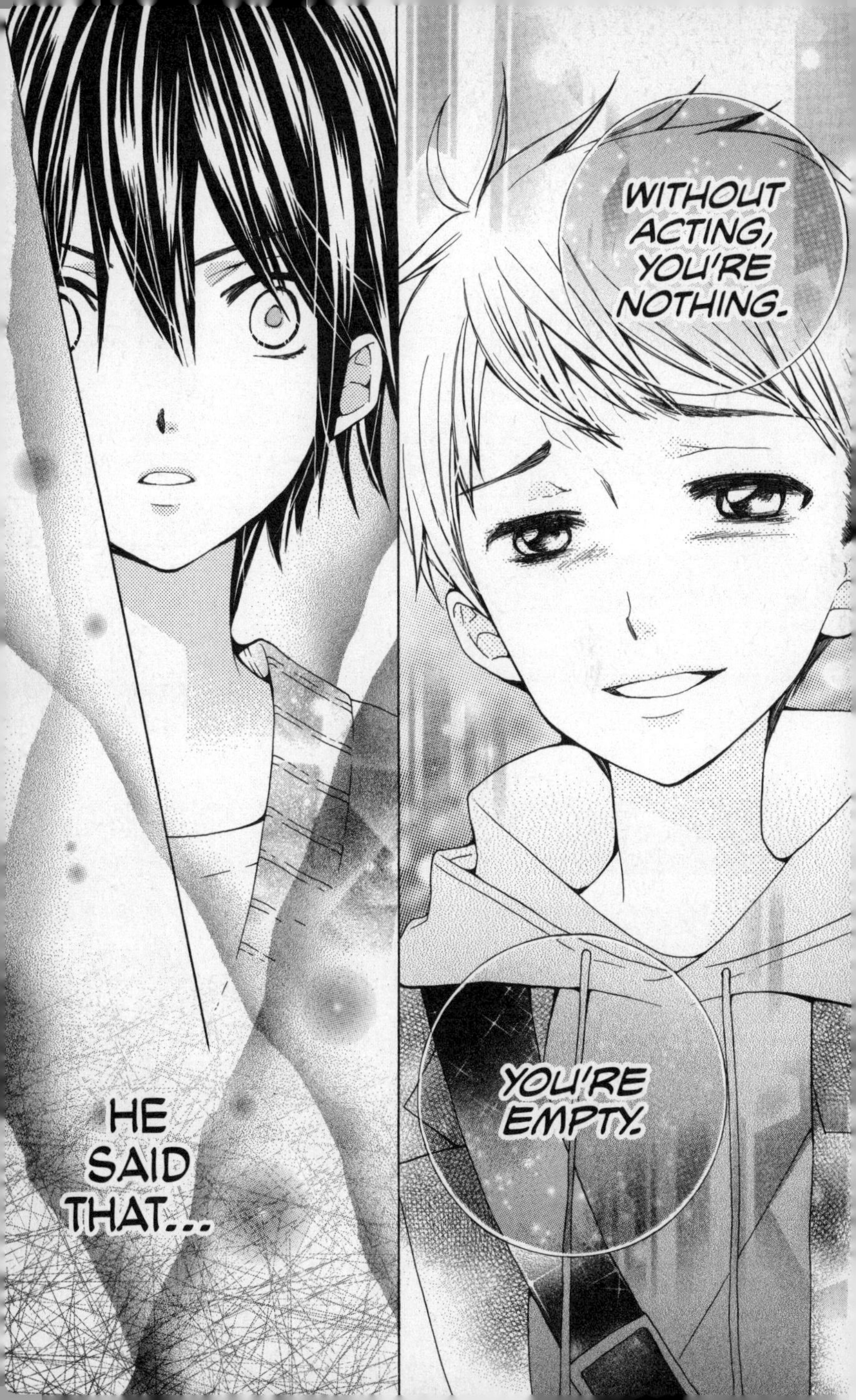
WITHOUT ACTING, YOU'RE NOTHING.
YOU'RE EMPTY.
HE SAID THAT...

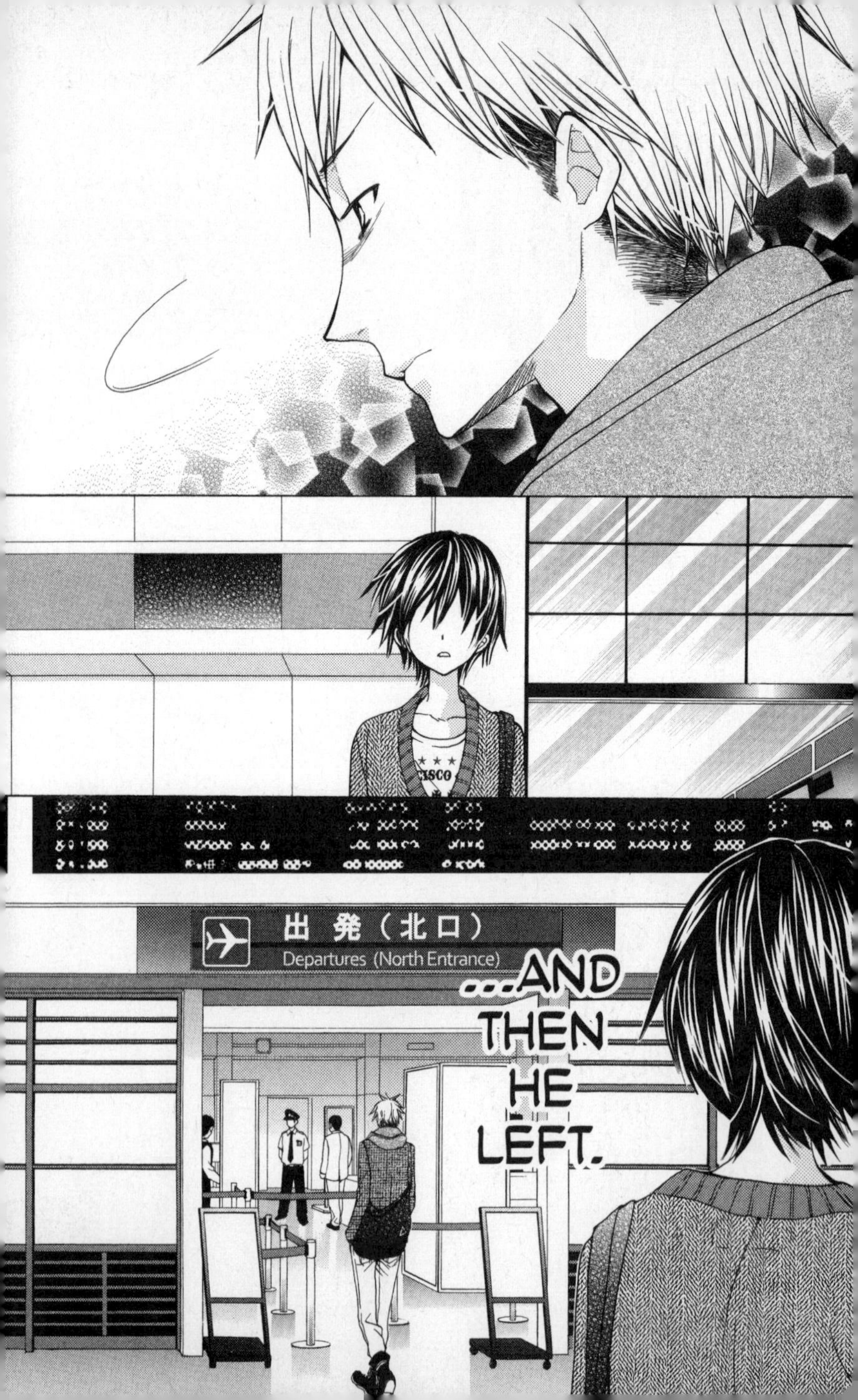
CISCO
出発（北口）
Departures (North Entrance)
...AND THEN HE LEFT.

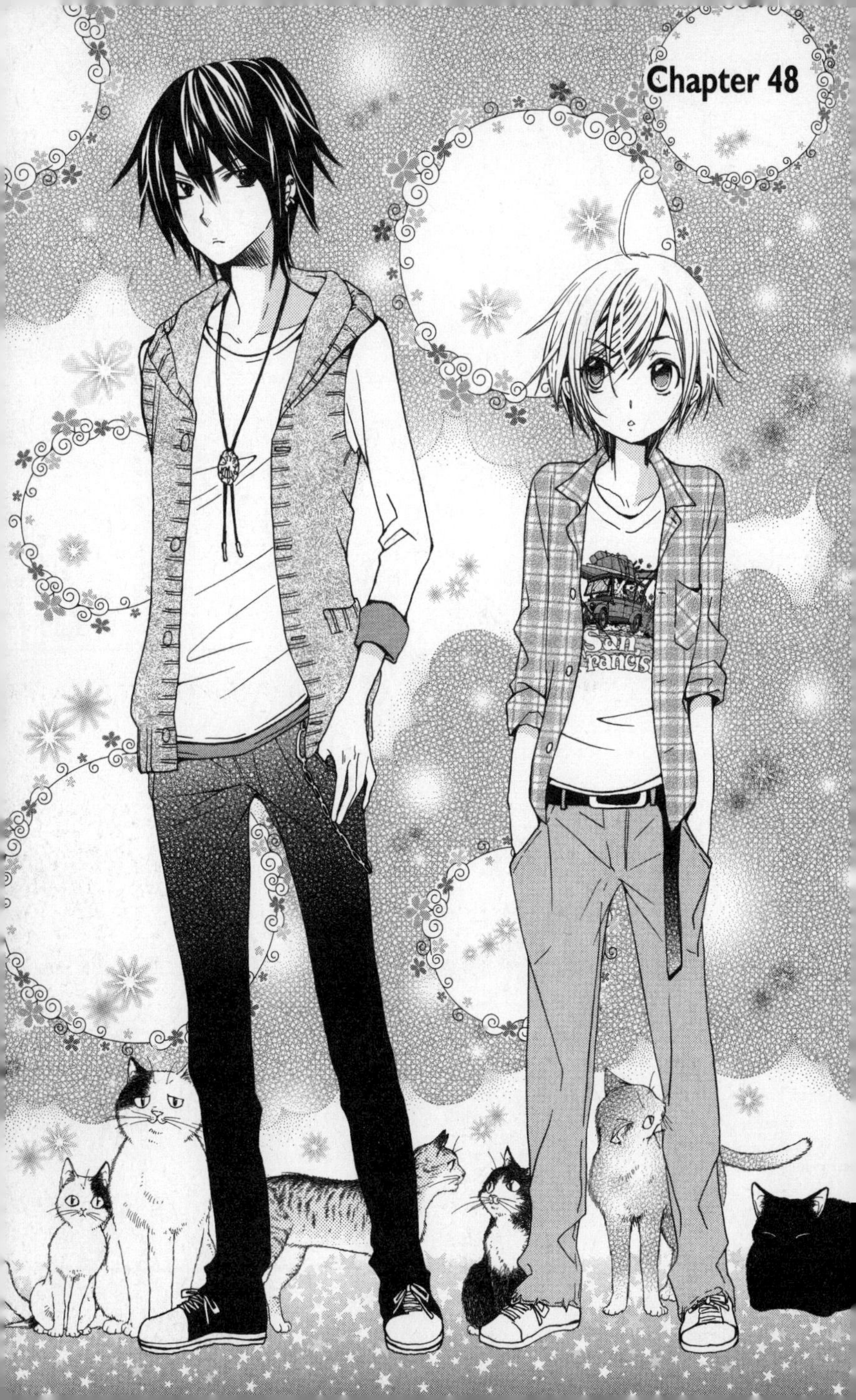
Chapter 48

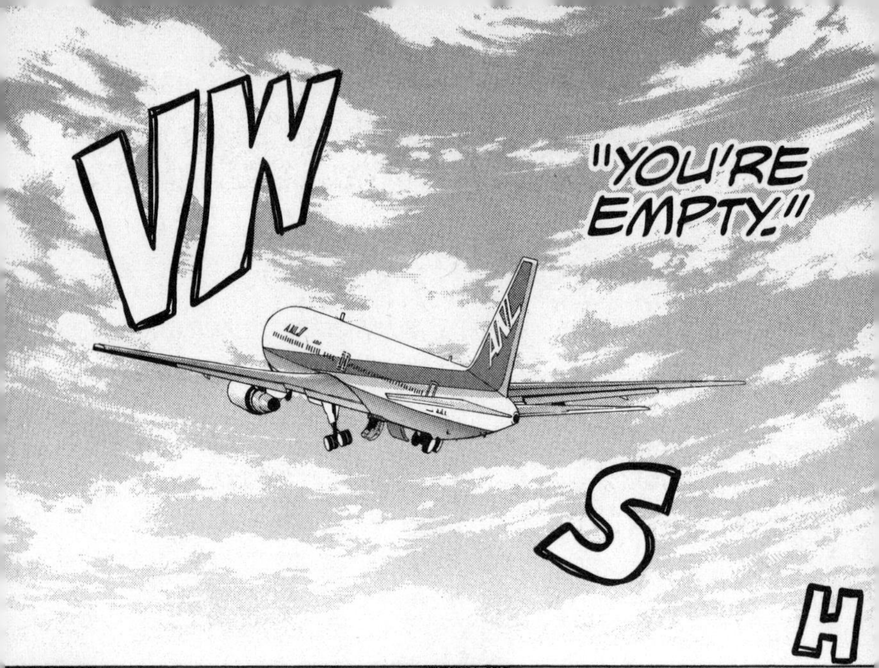
VW
"YOU'RE EMPTY."
SH

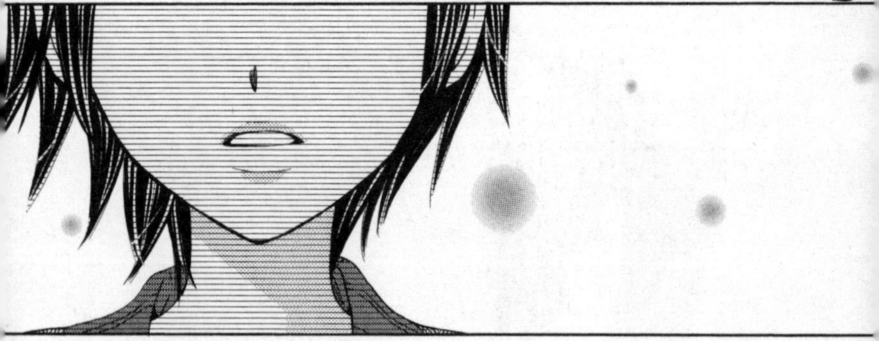

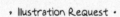

• Illustration Request •

• The request this time was Catherine as a human. She's got a lot of sense!! That was fun to draw. Thank you, everyone, for always sending in requests. I'm sorry I can't draw them all. If you have any more ideas, send 'em my way!

(2)

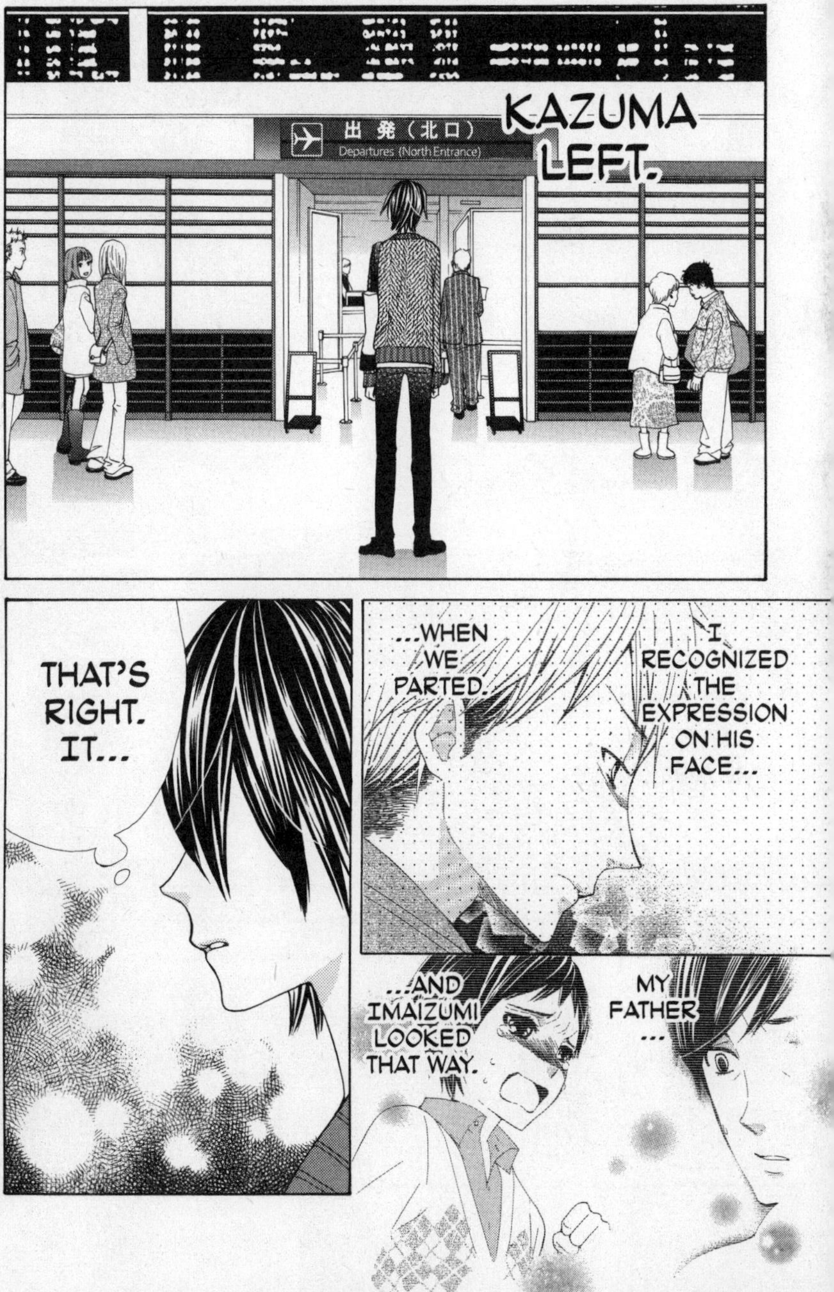
出発（北口）
Departures (North Entrance)
KAZUMA LEFT.
I RECOGNIZED THE EXPRESSION ON HIS FACE...
...WHEN WE PARTED.
MY FATHER...
...AND IMAIZUMI LOOKED THAT WAY.
THAT'S RIGHT. IT...

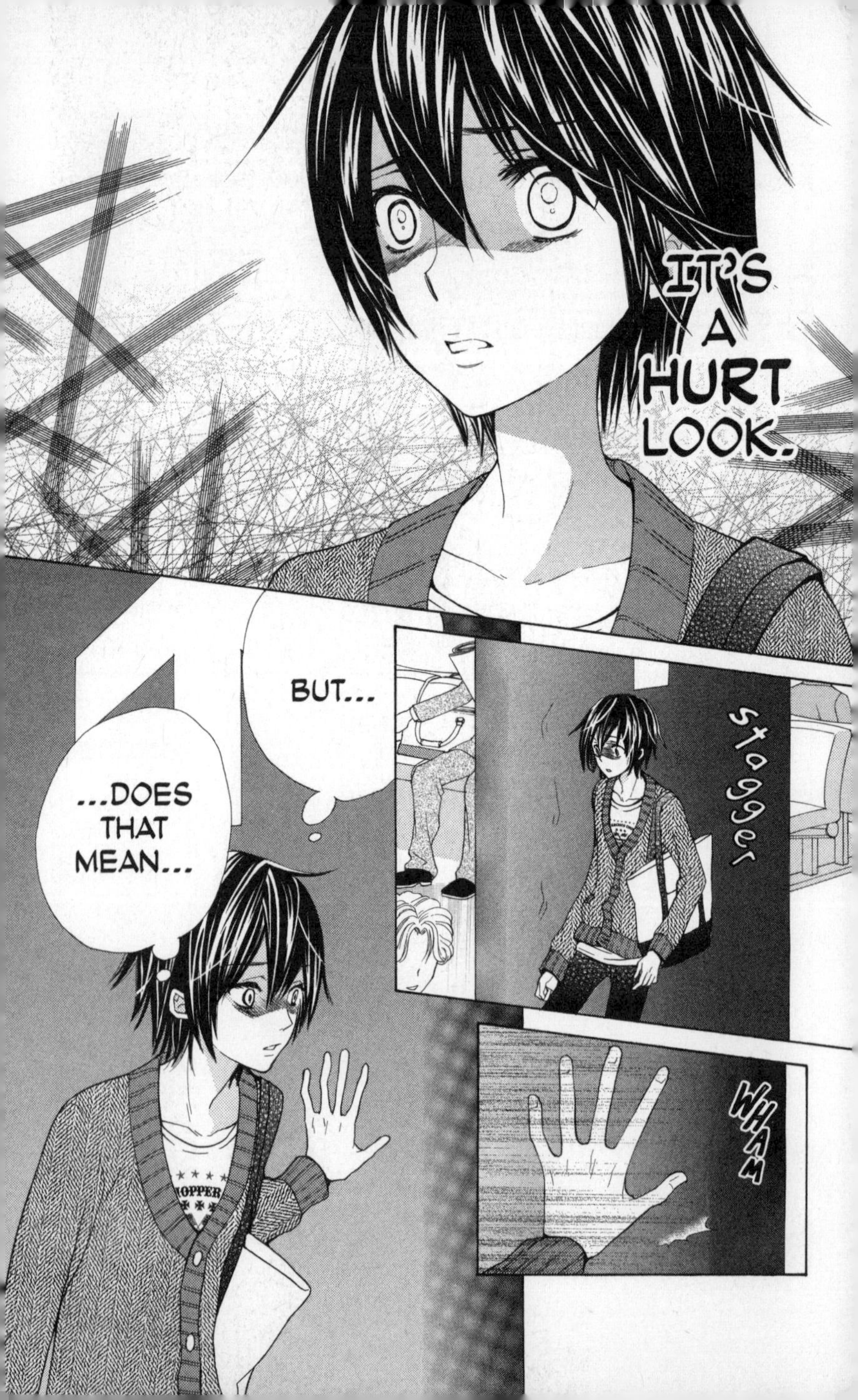
IT'S A HURT LOOK.
stagger
WHAM
BUT...
...DOES THAT MEAN...

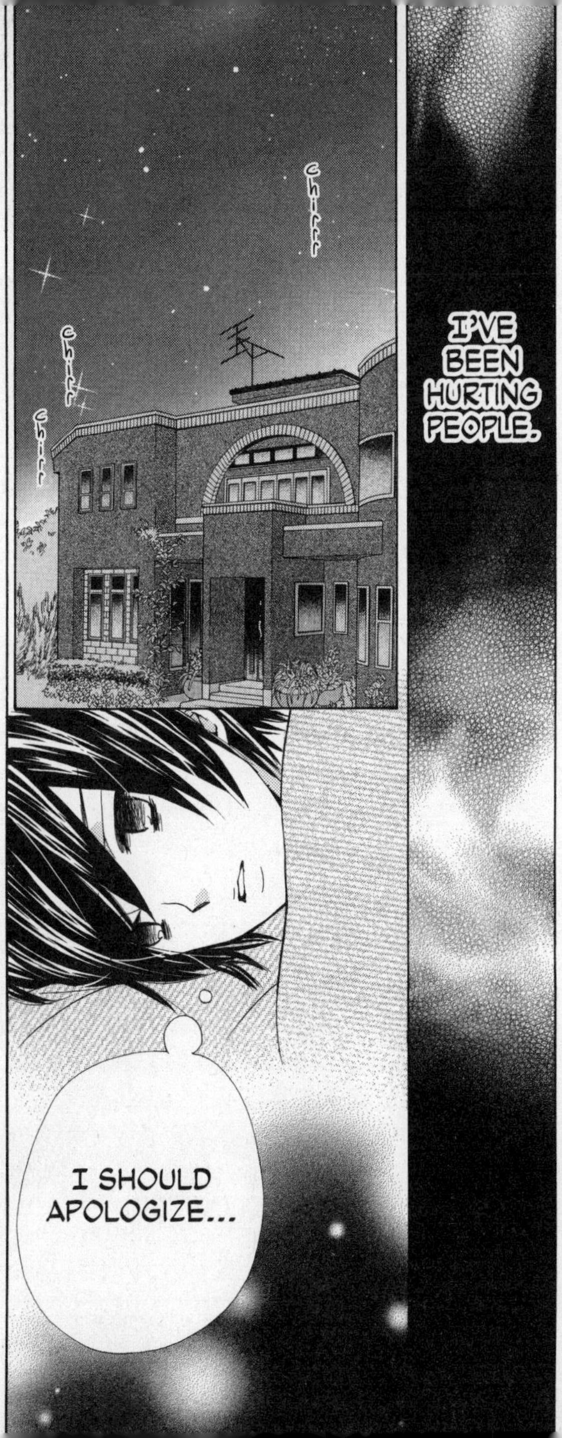
I'VE BEEN HURTING PEOPLE.
Chirrr
Chirr
Chirr
I SHOULD APOLOGIZE...

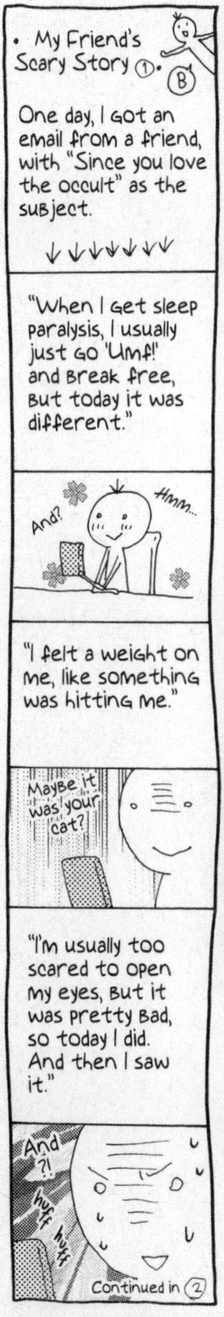
• My Friend's Scary Story ①•
B
One day, I got an email from a friend, with "Since you love the occult" as the subject.
"When I get sleep paralysis, I usually just go 'Umf!' and break free, but today it was different."
Hmm...
And?
"I felt a weight on me, like something was hitting me."
Maybe it was your cat?
"I'm usually too scared to open my eyes, but it was pretty bad, so today I did. And then I saw it."
And ?!
huff huff
Continued in ②

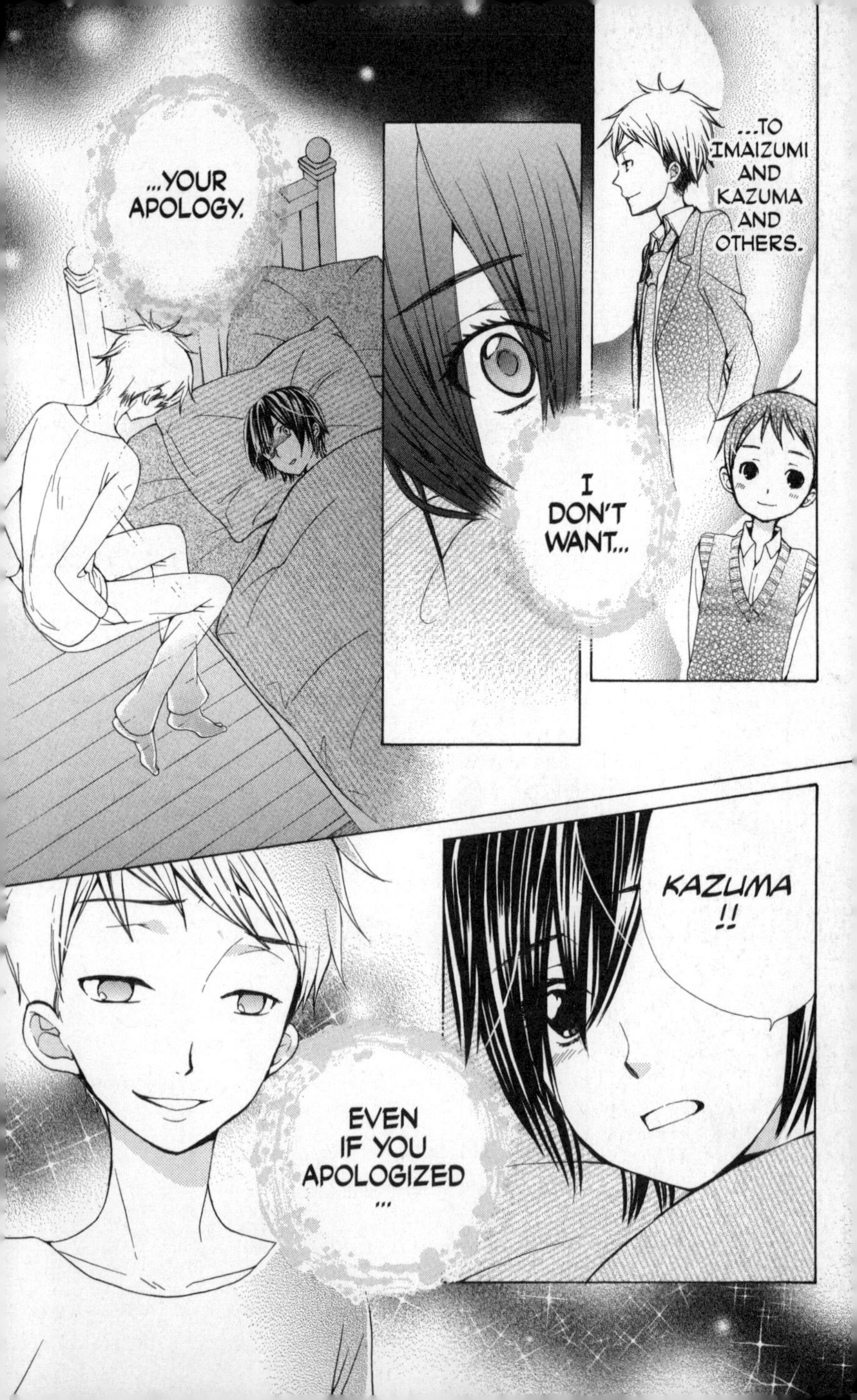
...TO IMAIZUMI AND KAZUMA AND OTHERS.
I DON'T WANT...
...YOUR APOLOGY.
KAZUMA !!
EVEN IF YOU APOLOGIZED ...

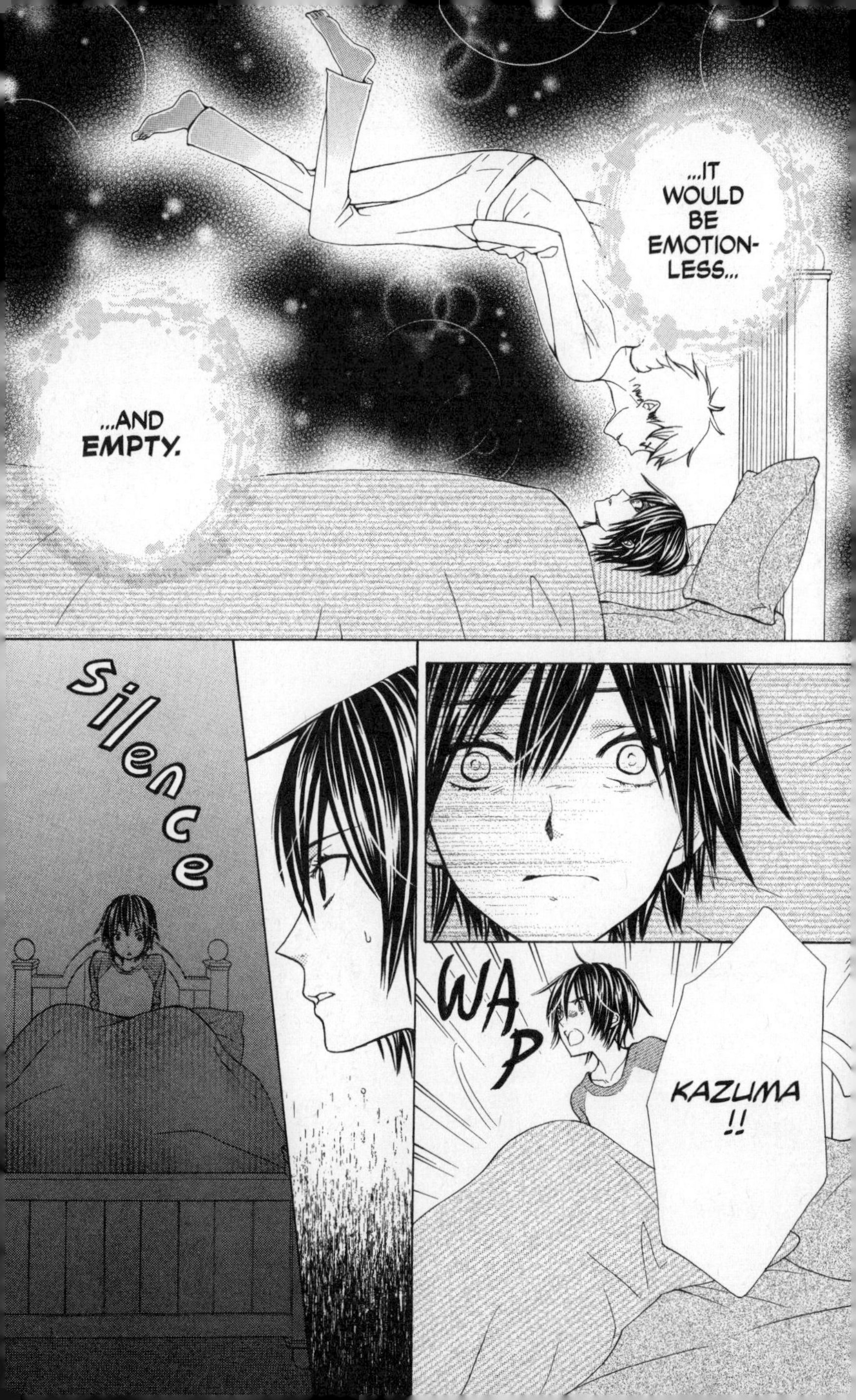
...IT WOULD BE EMOTION-LESS...
...AND EMPTY.
WAP
KAZUMA !!
Silence

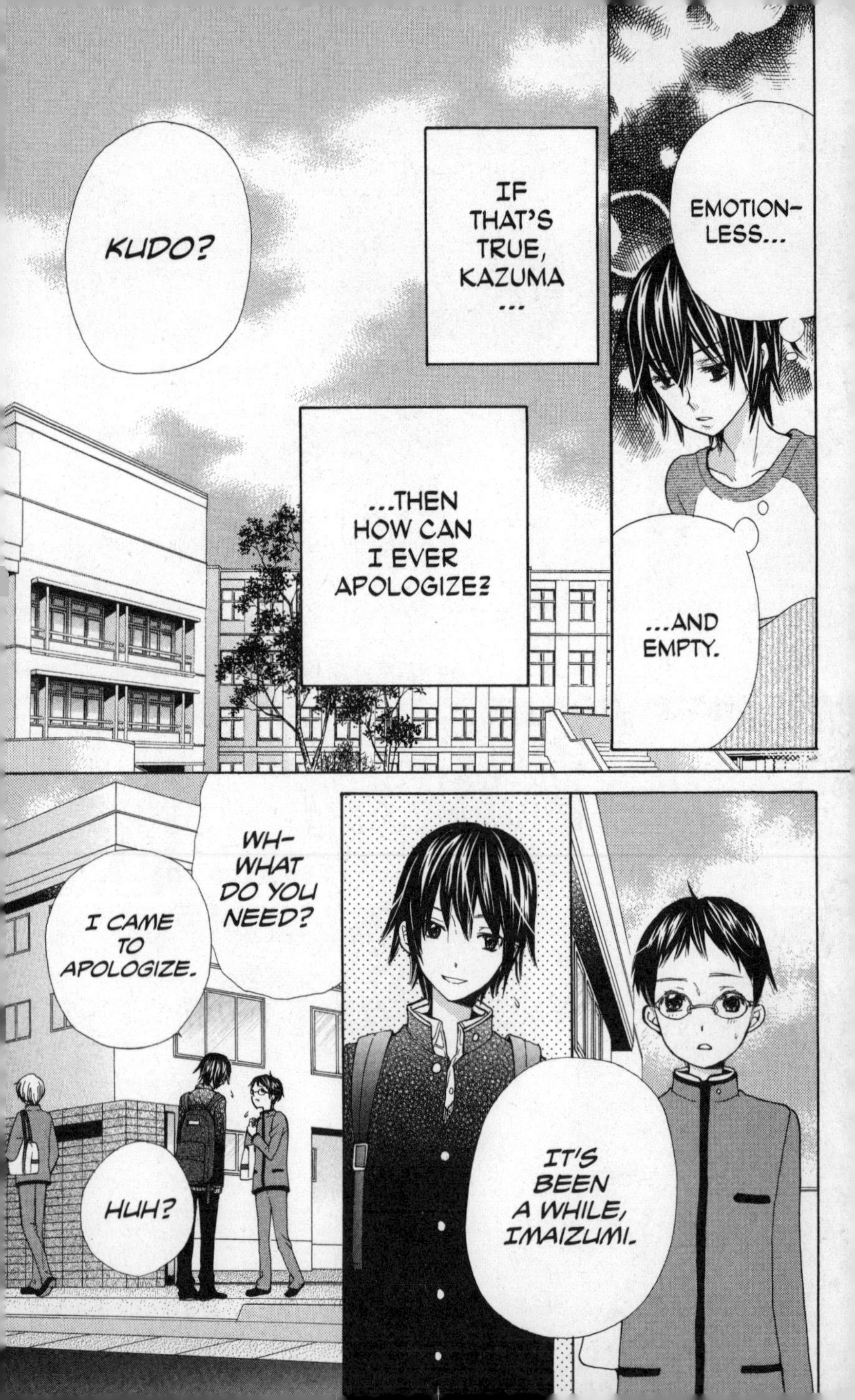
EMOTION-LESS...
...AND EMPTY.
IF THAT'S TRUE, KAZUMA...
...THEN HOW CAN I EVER APOLOGIZE?
KUDO?
IT'S BEEN A WHILE, IMAIZUMI.
WH-WHAT DO YOU NEED?
I CAME TO APOLOGIZE.
HUH?

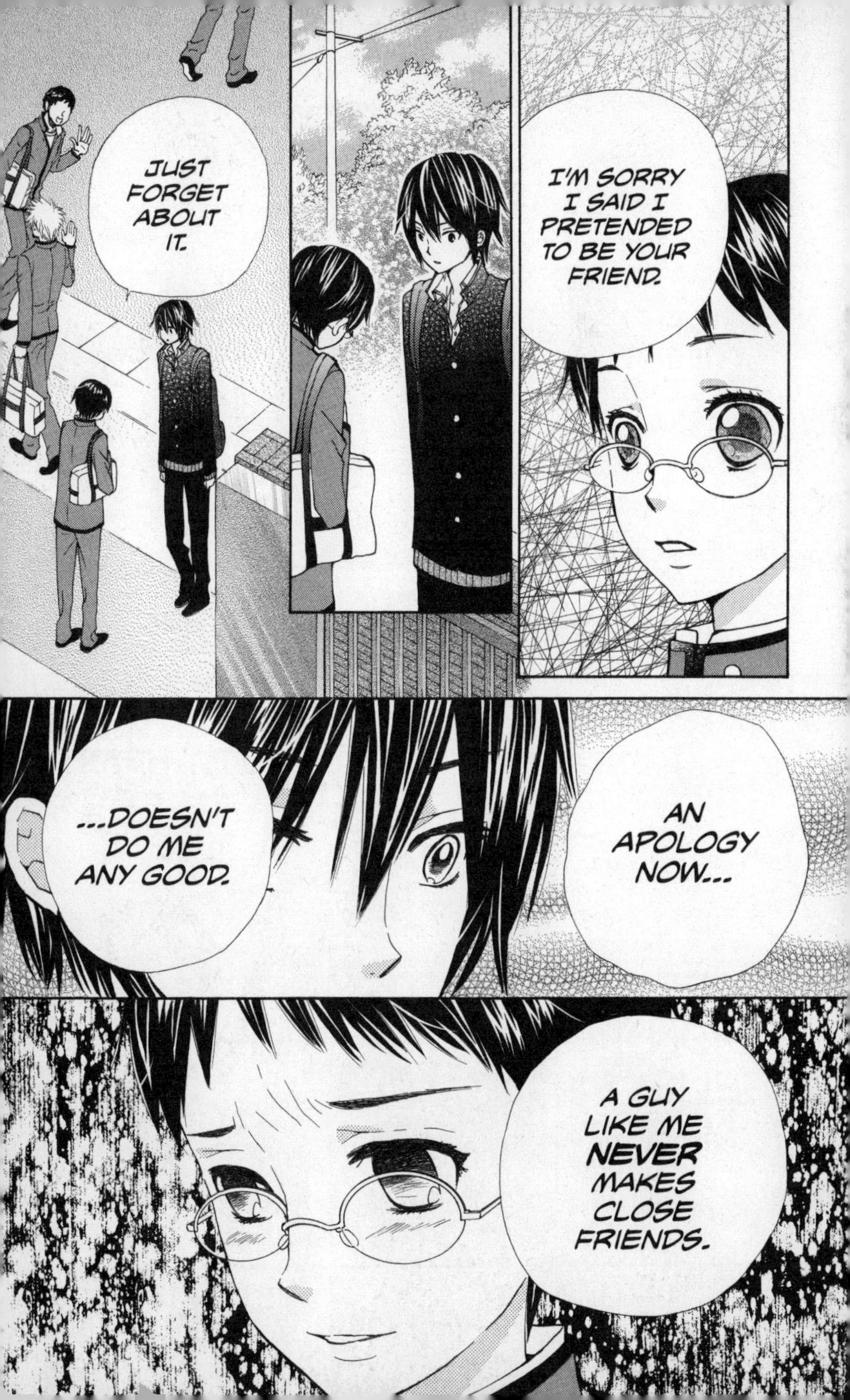
I'M SORRY I SAID I PRETENDED TO BE YOUR FRIEND.
JUST FORGET ABOUT IT.
AN APOLOGY NOW...
...DOESN'T DO ME ANY GOOD.
A GUY LIKE ME **NEVER** MAKES CLOSE FRIENDS.

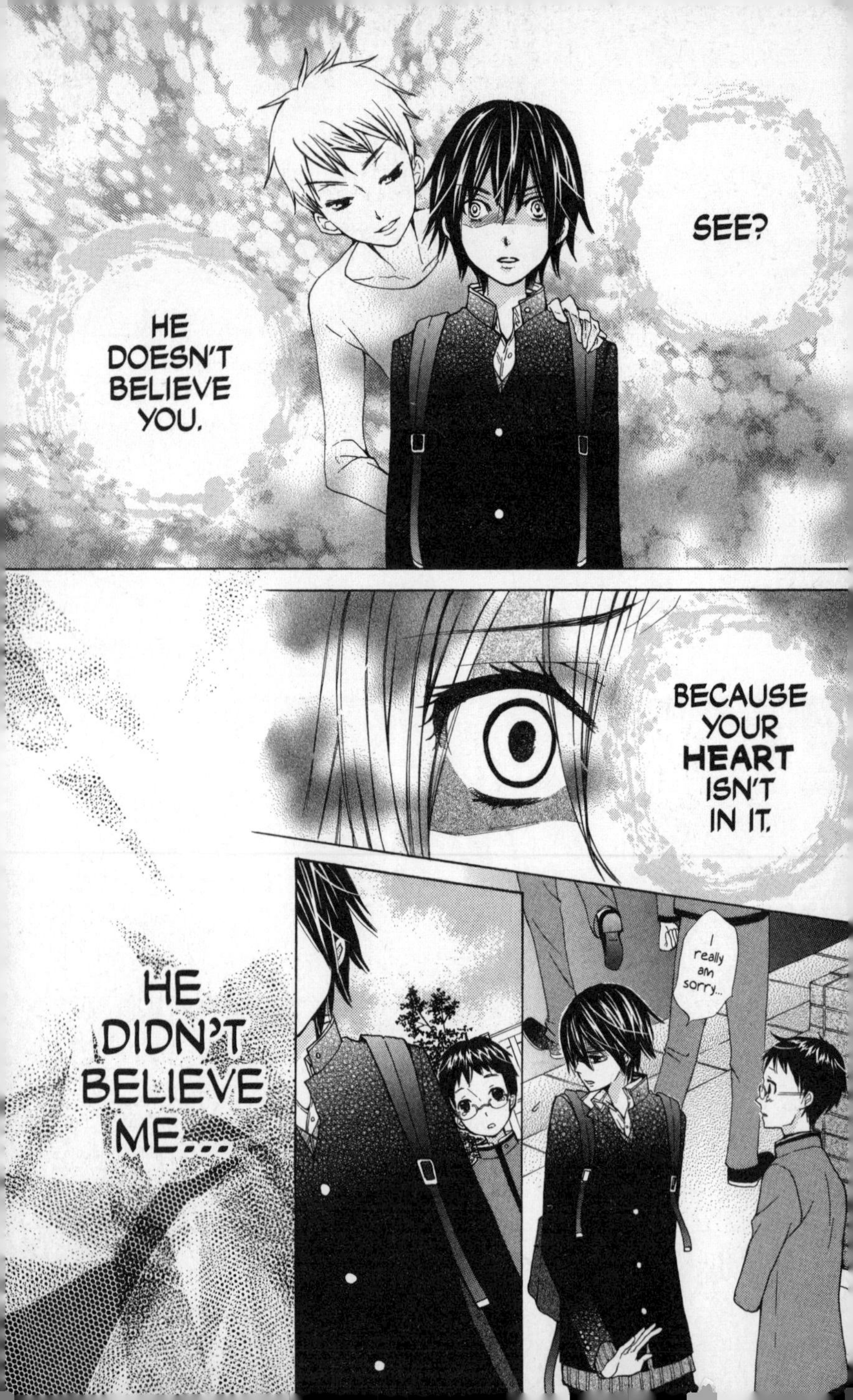
SEE?
HE DOESN'T BELIEVE YOU.
BECAUSE YOUR HEART ISN'T IN IT.
I really am sorry...
HE DIDN'T BELIEVE ME...

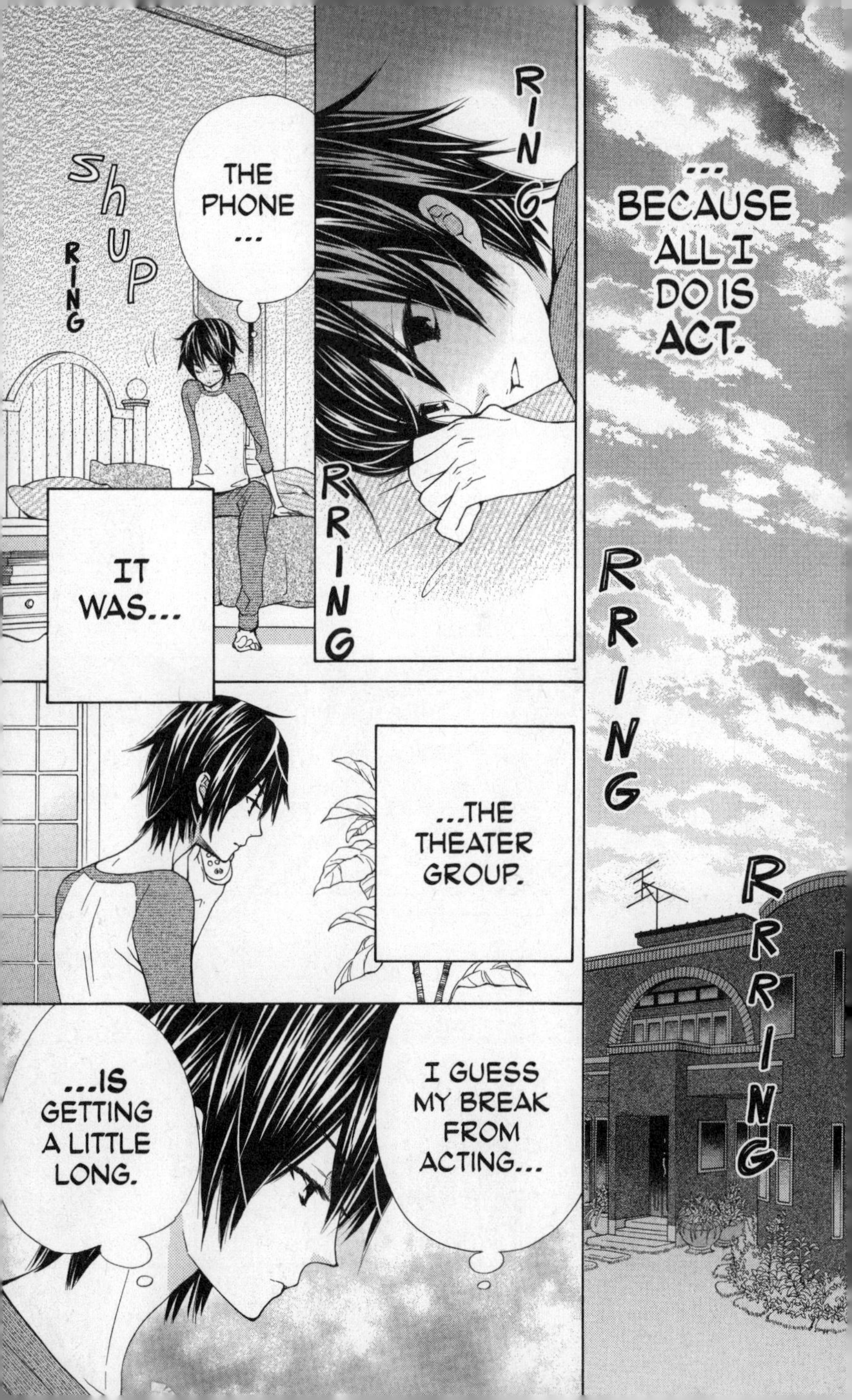
...BECAUSE ALL I DO IS ACT.
RRING
RRRING
RING
RRING
THE PHONE...
SHUP
RING
IT WAS...
...THE THEATER GROUP.
I GUESS MY BREAK FROM ACTING...
...IS GETTING A LITTLE LONG.

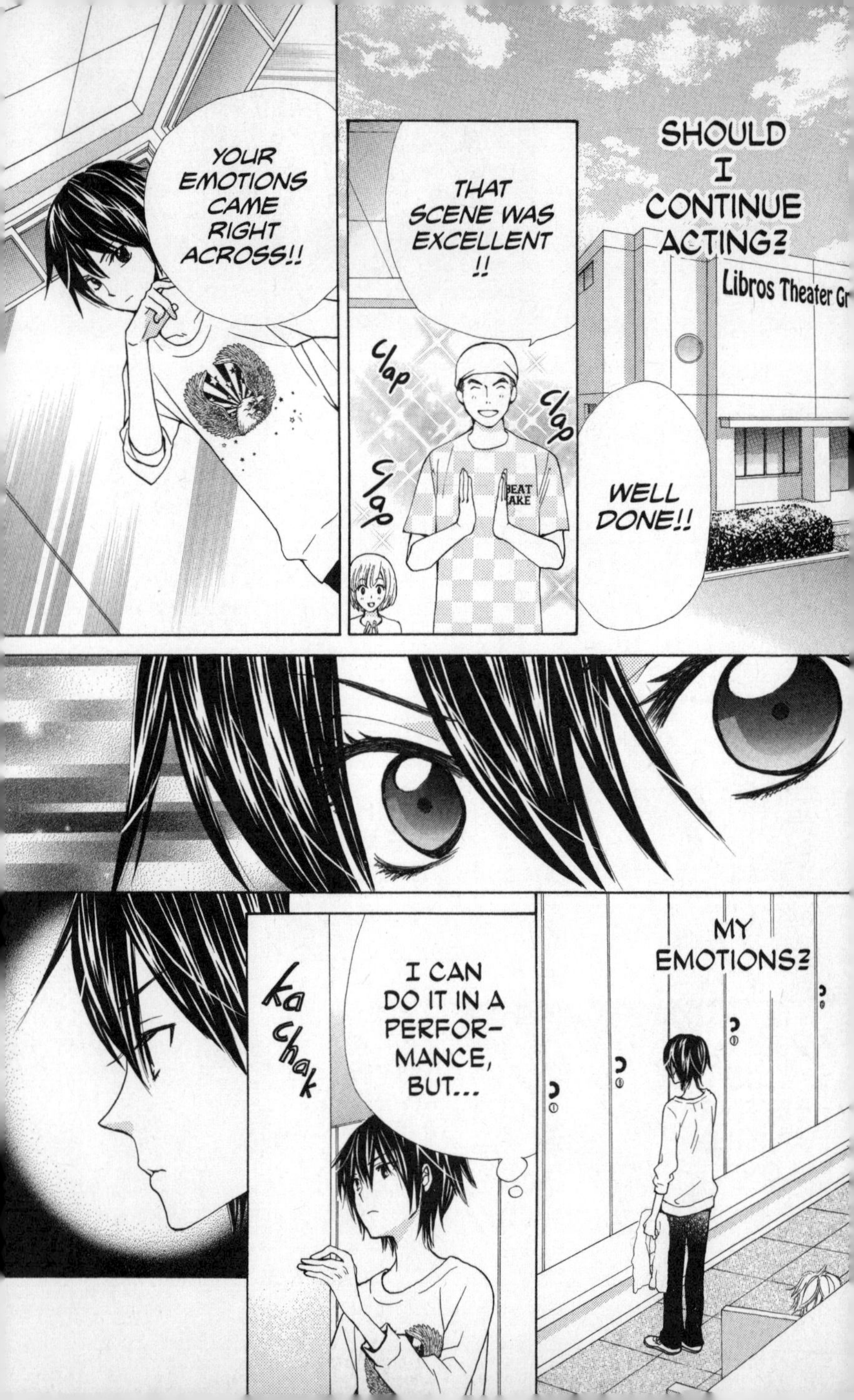
SHOULD I CONTINUE ACTING?
Libros Theater Gr
WELL DONE!!
THAT SCENE WAS EXCELLENT!!
clap clap
clap clap
YOUR EMOTIONS CAME RIGHT ACROSS!!
MY EMOTIONS?
I CAN DO IT IN A PERFORMANCE, BUT...
ka chak

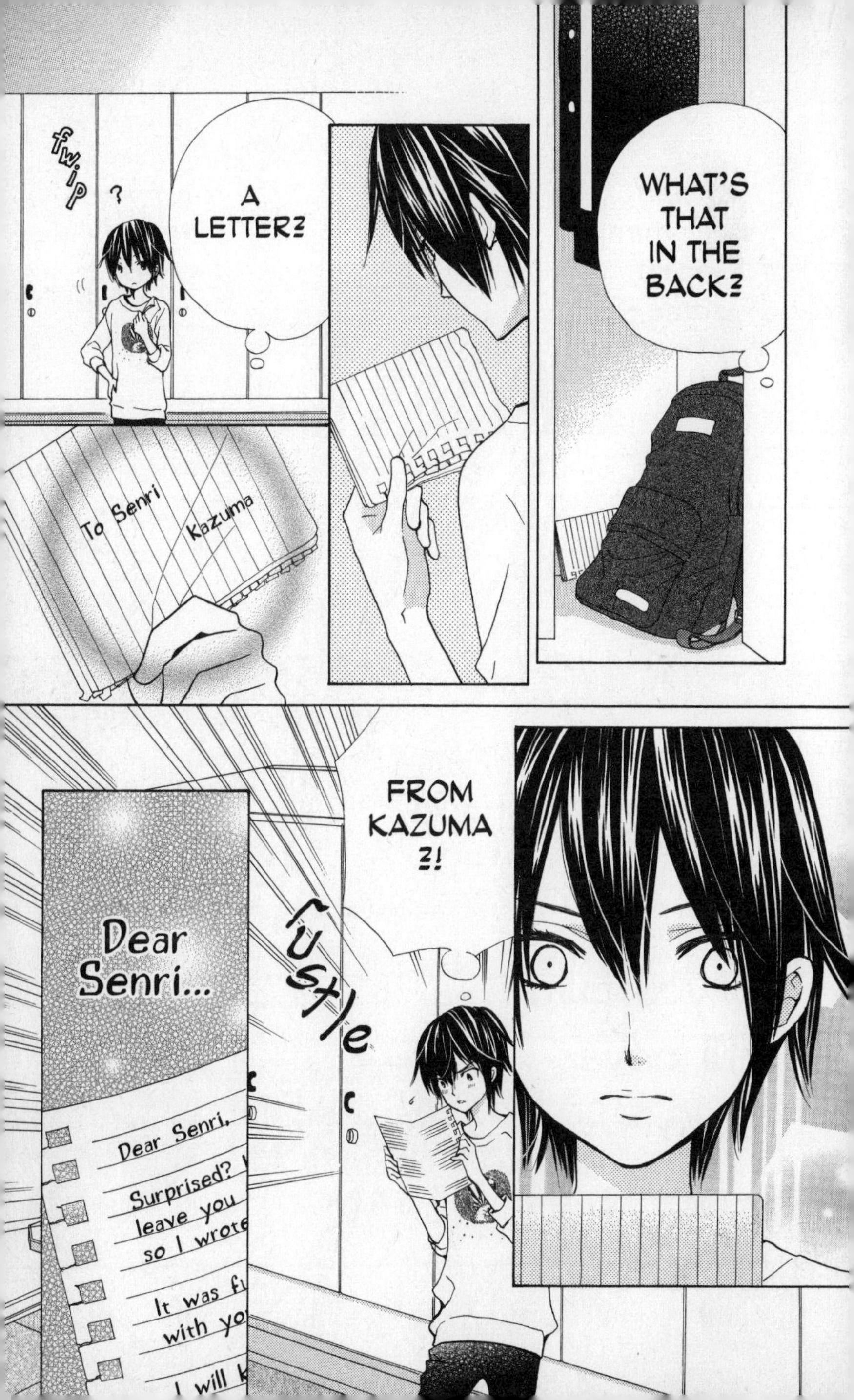
WHAT'S THAT IN THE BACK?
fwip
?
A LETTER?
To Senri Kazuma
FROM KAZUMA ?!
rustle
Dear Senri...
Dear Senri,
Surprised?
leave you
so I wrote
It was
with
I will

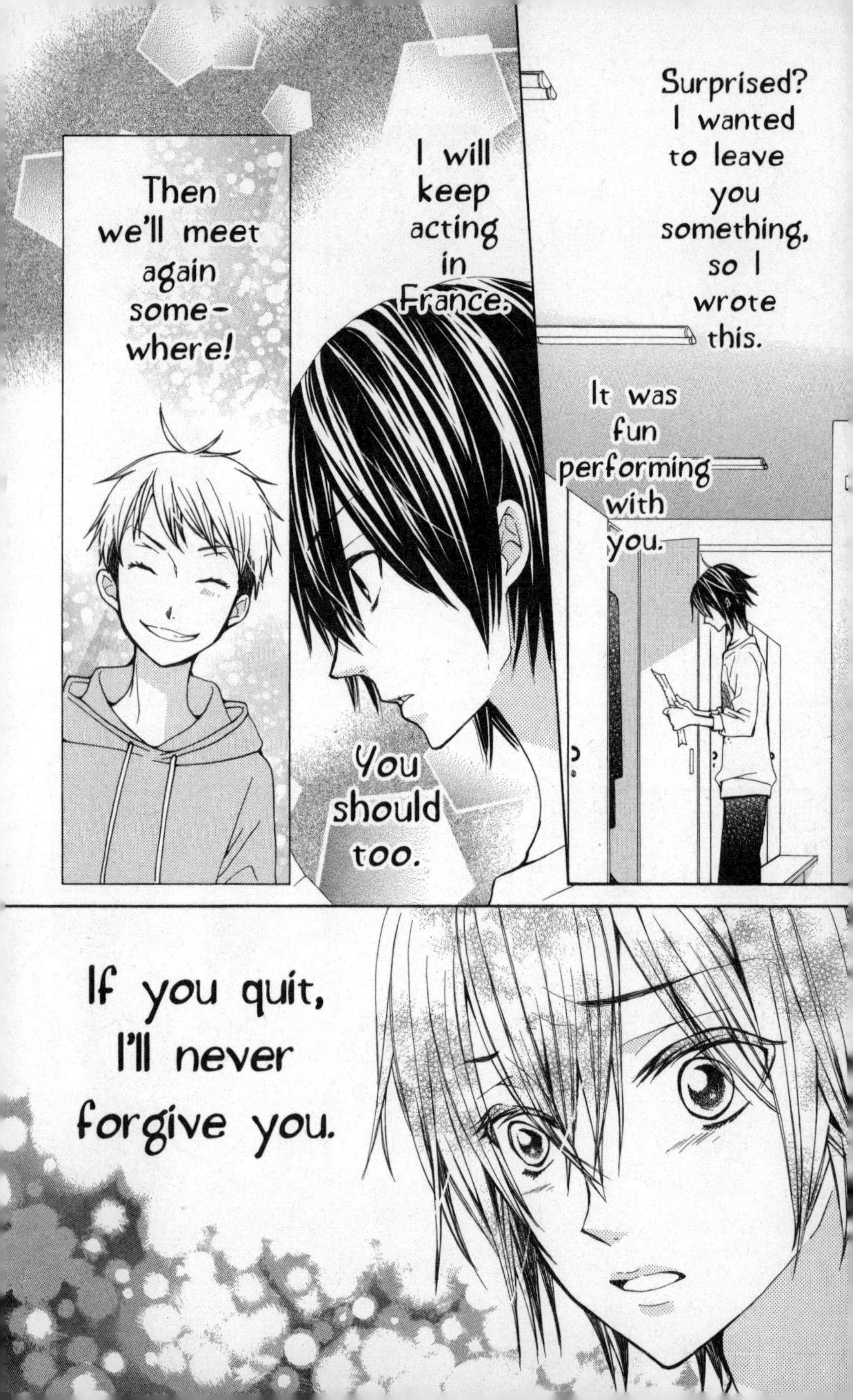
Surprised? I wanted to leave you something, so I wrote this.
It was fun performing with you.
I will keep acting in France.
You should too.
Then we'll meet again some-where!
If you quit, I'll never forgive you.

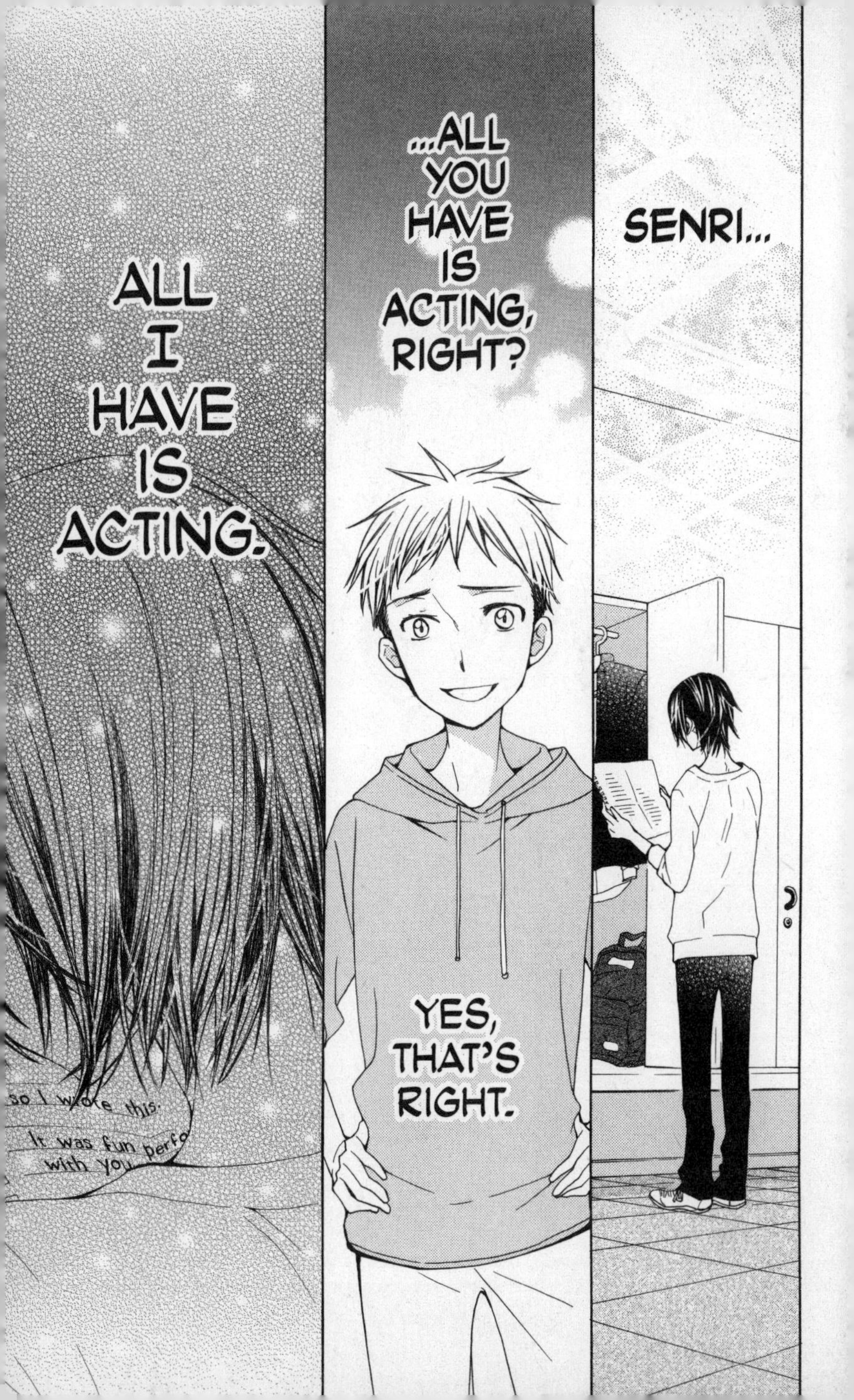
SENRI...
...ALL YOU HAVE IS ACTING, RIGHT?
YES, THAT'S RIGHT.
ALL I HAVE IS ACTING.
so I wrote this.
It was fun perfo
with you

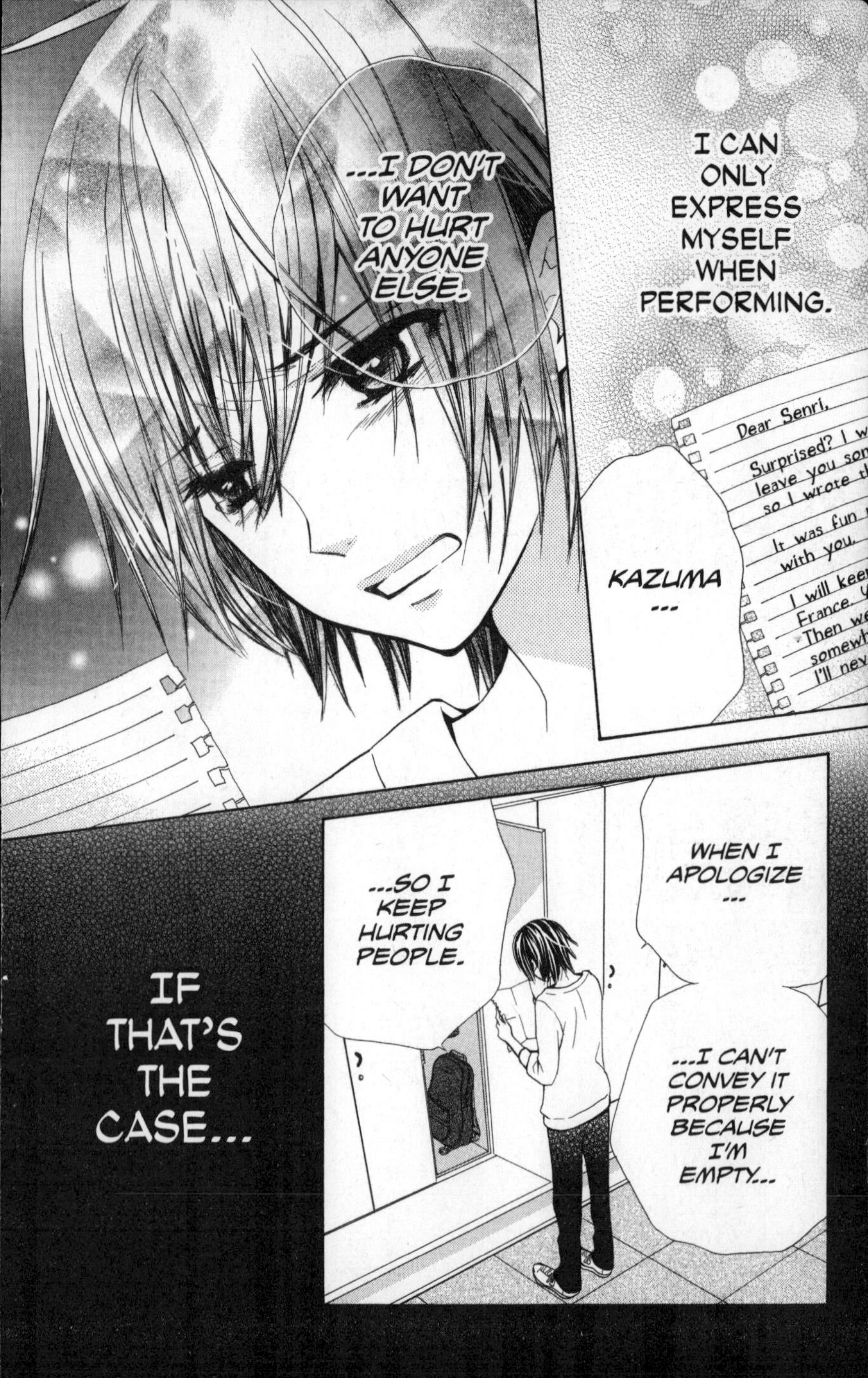
I CAN ONLY EXPRESS MYSELF WHEN PERFORMING.
Dear Senri,
Surprised? I w
leave you son
so I wrote th
It was fun
with you.
I will kee
France.
Then we
somewh
I'll nev
KAZUMA...
...I DON'T WANT TO HURT ANYONE ELSE.
WHEN I APOLOGIZE...
...I CAN'T CONVEY IT PROPERLY BECAUSE I'M EMPTY...
...SO I KEEP HURTING PEOPLE.
IF THAT'S THE CASE...

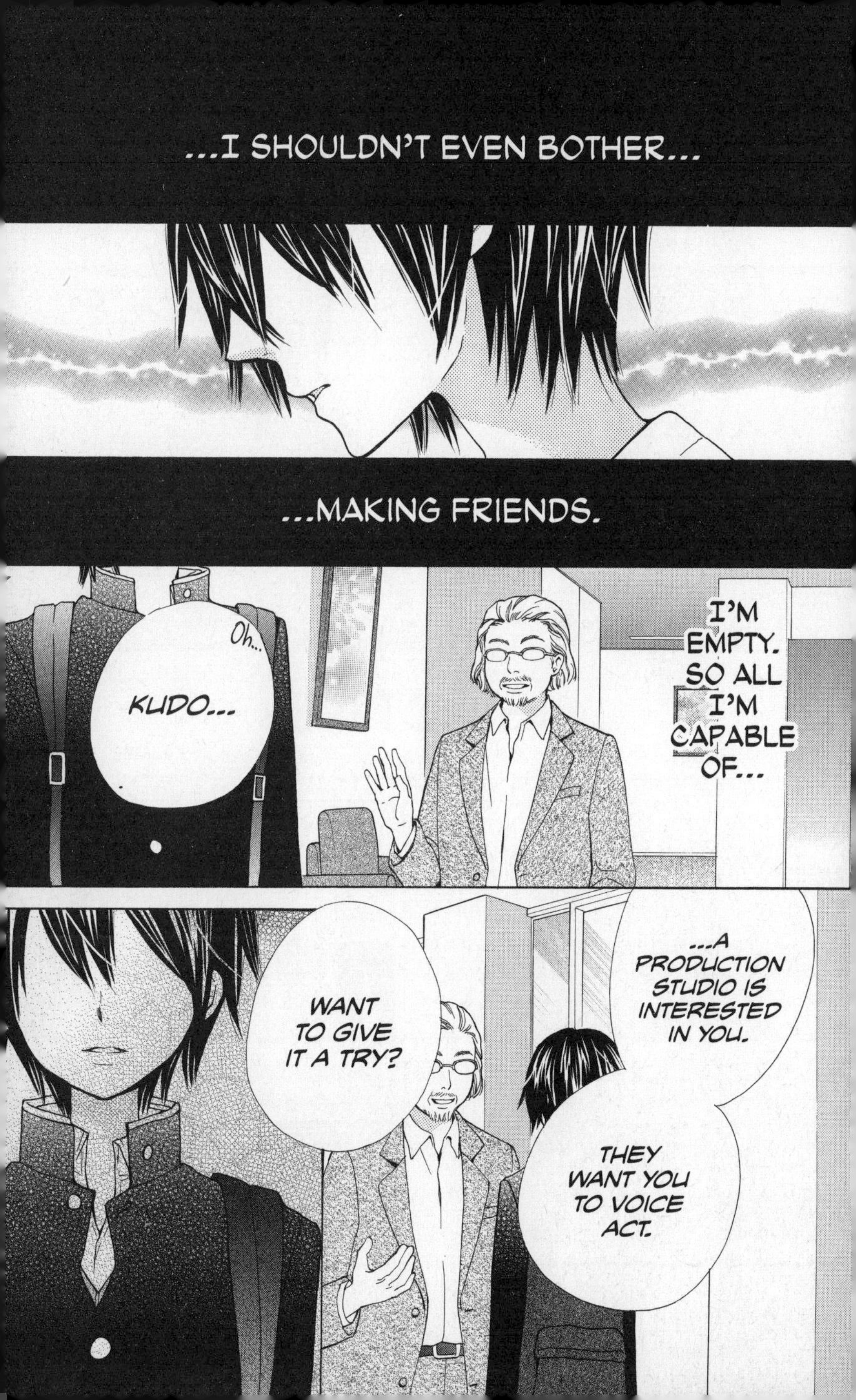
...I SHOULDN'T EVEN BOTHER...
...MAKING FRIENDS.
I'M EMPTY. SO ALL I'M CAPABLE OF...
Oh...
KUDO...
...A PRODUCTION STUDIO IS INTERESTED IN YOU.
THEY WANT YOU TO VOICE ACT.
WANT TO GIVE IT A TRY?

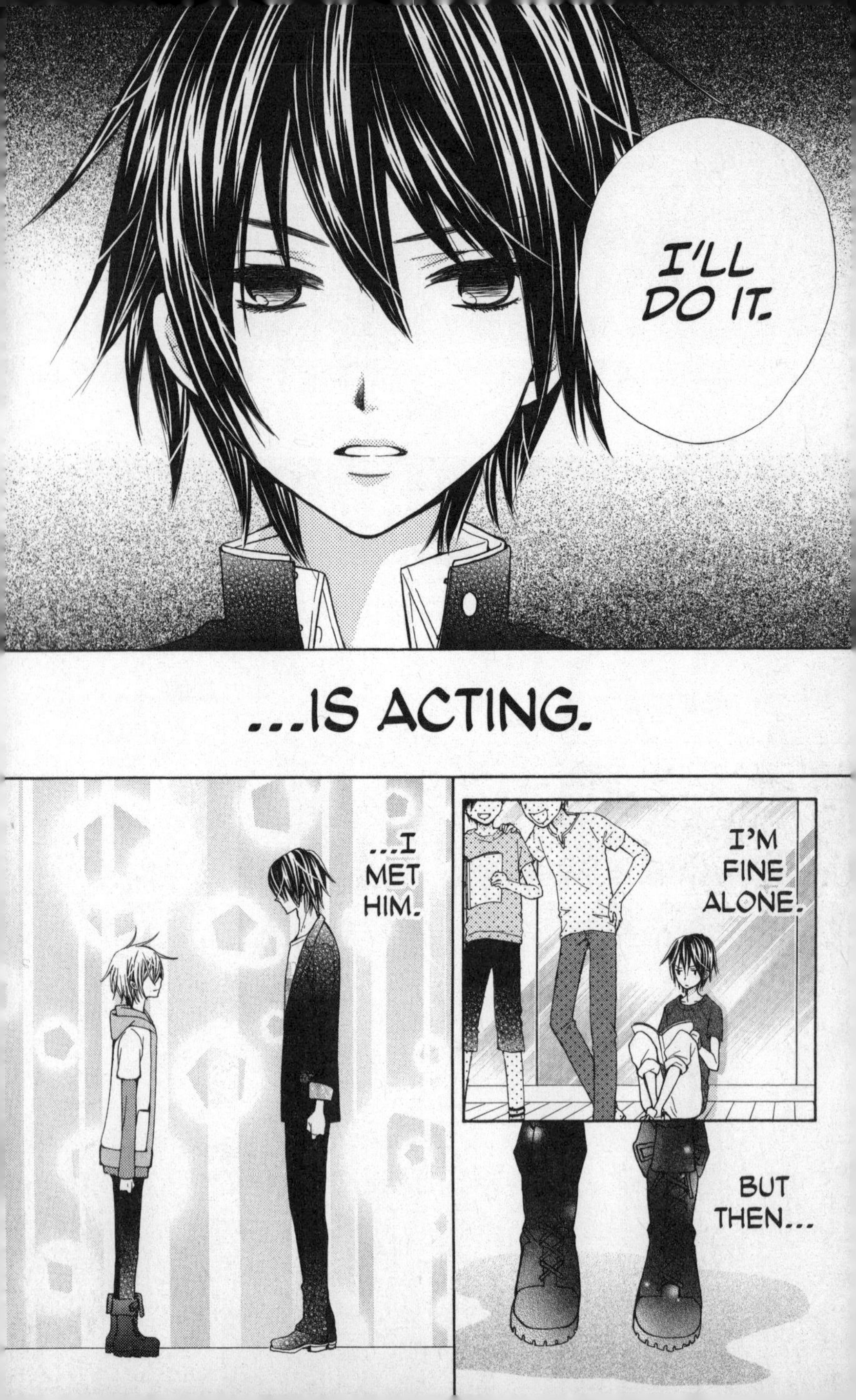
I'LL DO IT.
...IS ACTING.
I'M FINE ALONE.
BUT THEN...
...I MET HIM.

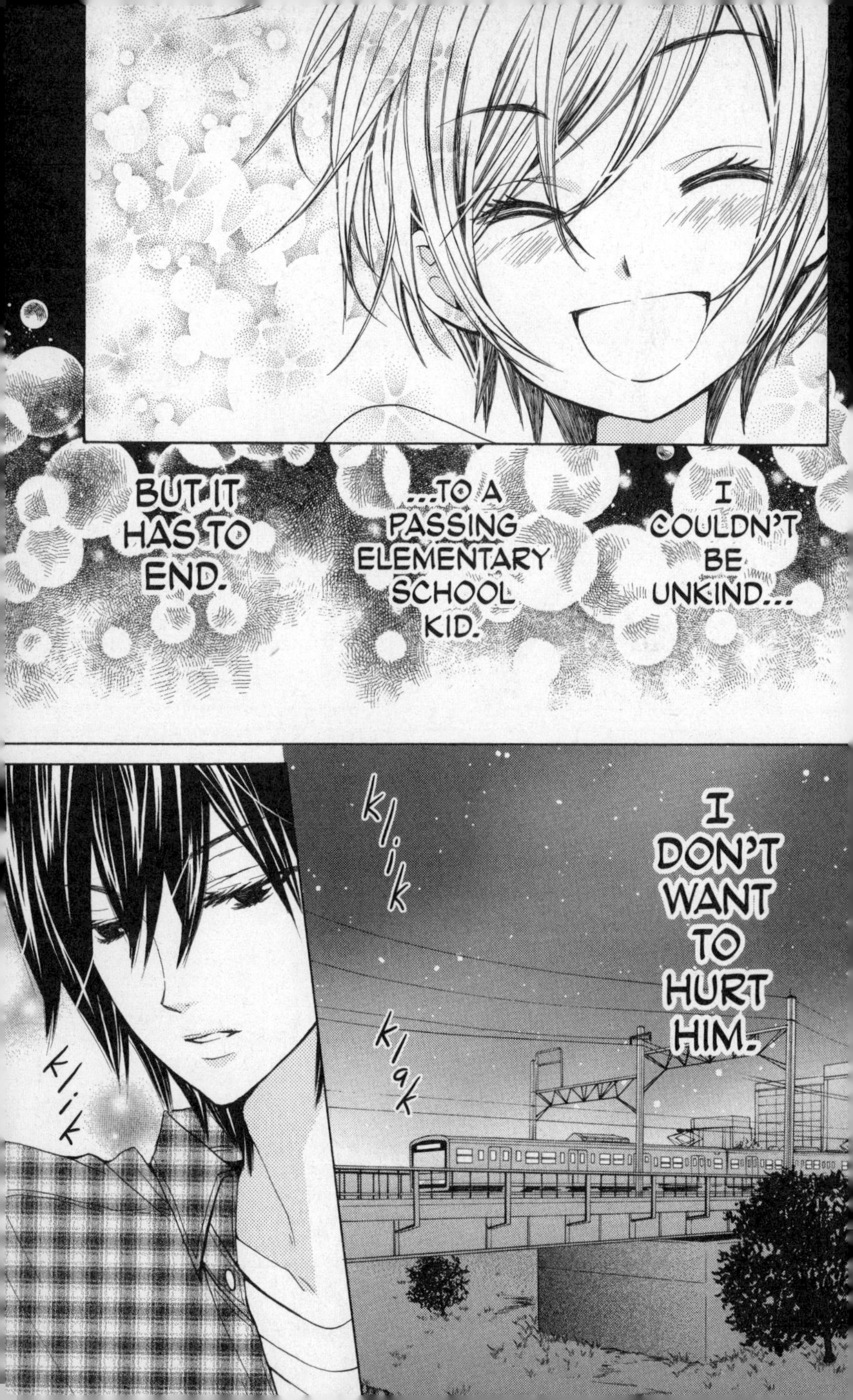
I COULDN'T BE UNKIND...
...TO A PASSING ELEMENTARY SCHOOL KID.
BUT IT HAS TO END.
I DON'T WANT TO HURT HIM.
klik
klak
klik

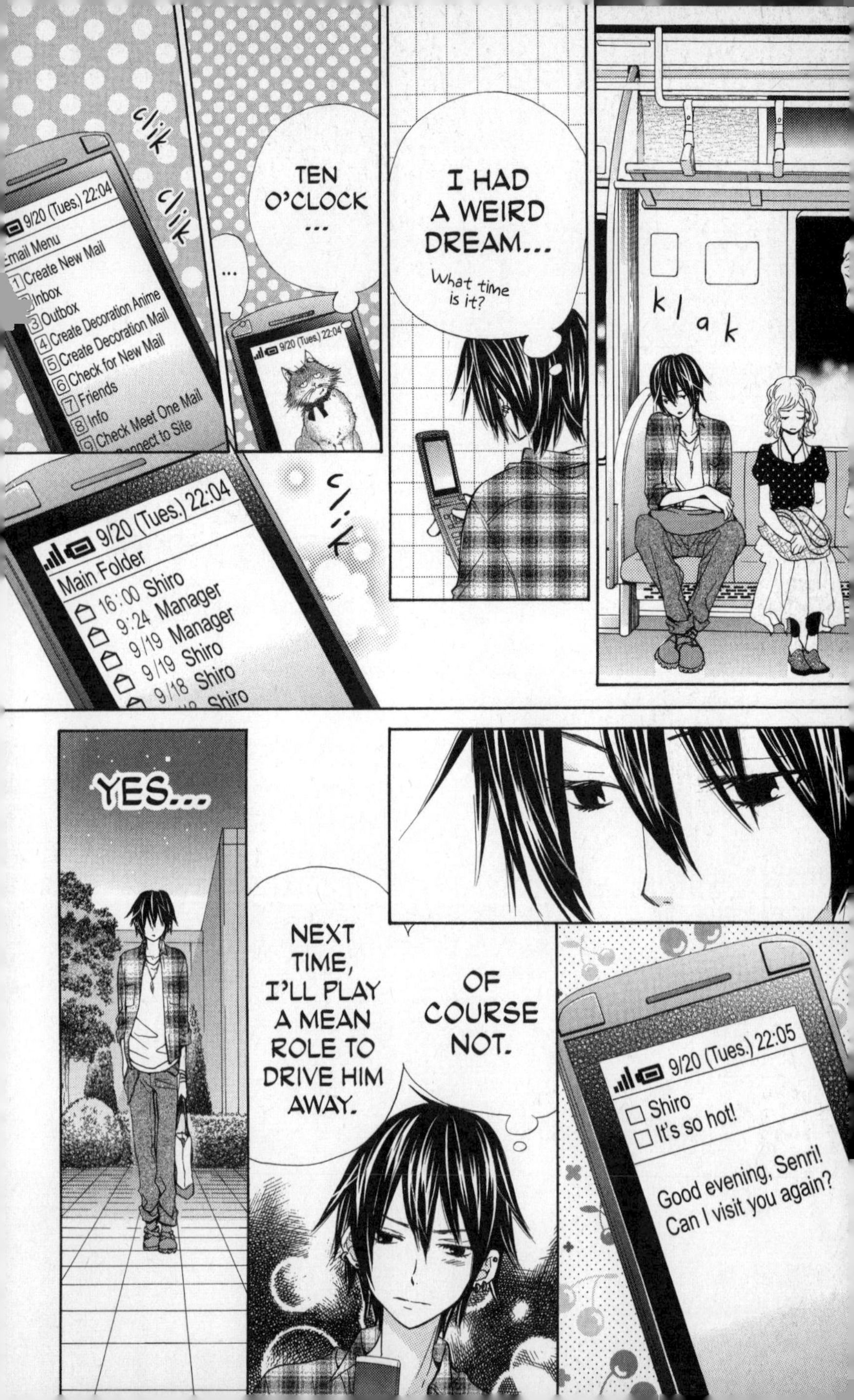
klak
I HAD A WEIRD DREAM...
What time is it?
TEN O'CLOCK ...
...
9/20 (Tues.) 22:04
clik clik
9/20 (Tues.) 22:04
Email Menu
1 Create New Mail
2 Inbox
3 Outbox
4 Create Decoration Anime
5 Create Decoration Mail
6 Check for New Mail
7 Friends
8 Info
9 Check Meet One Mail
Connect to Site
clik
9/20 (Tues.) 22:04
Main Folder
16:00 Shiro
9:24 Manager
9/19 Manager
9/19 Shiro
9/18 Shiro
Shiro
9/20 (Tues.) 22:05
Shiro
It's so hot!
Good evening, Senri! Can I visit you again?
OF COURSE NOT.
NEXT TIME, I'LL PLAY A MEAN ROLE TO DRIVE HIM AWAY.
YES...

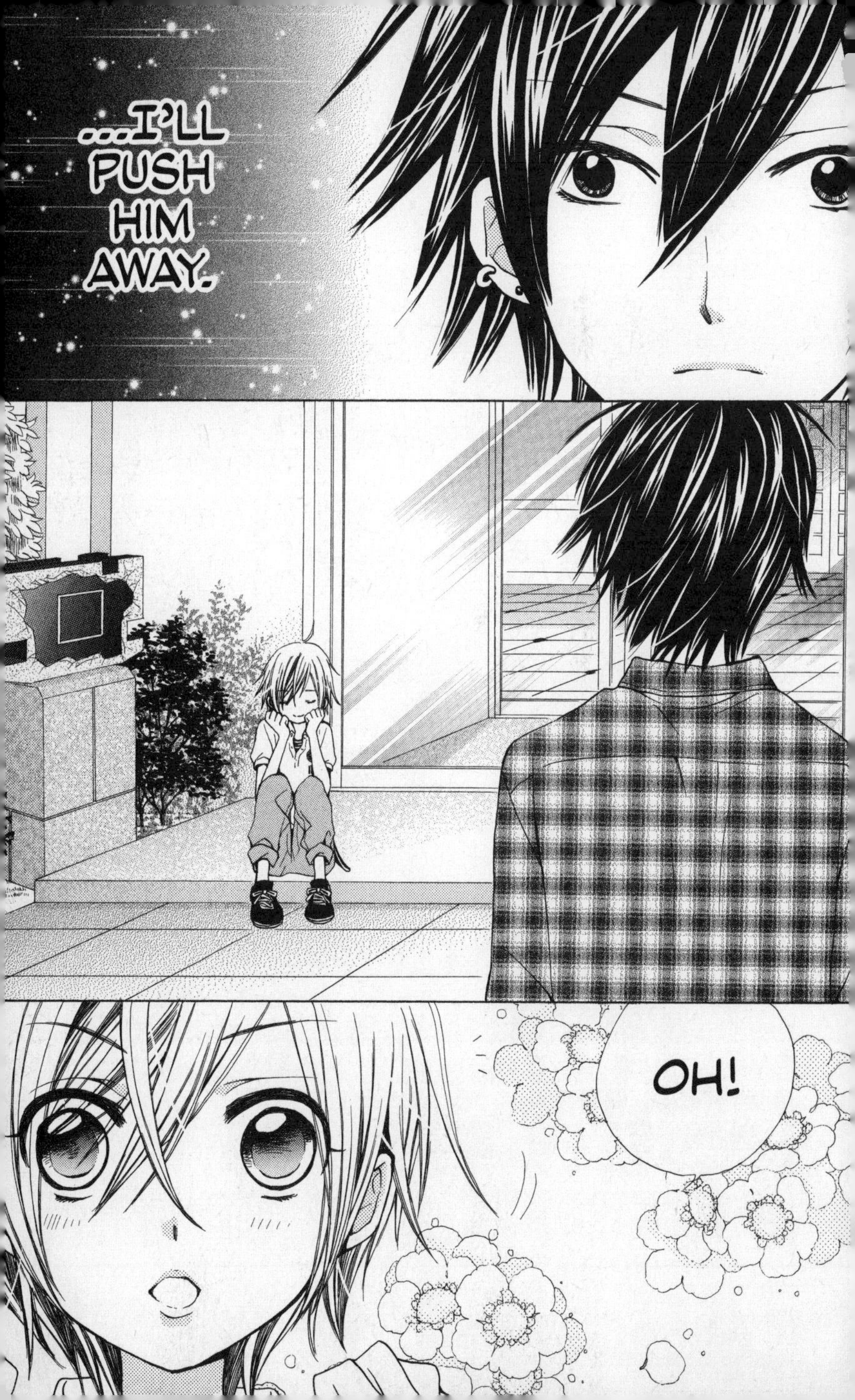
...I'LL PUSH HIM AWAY.
OH!

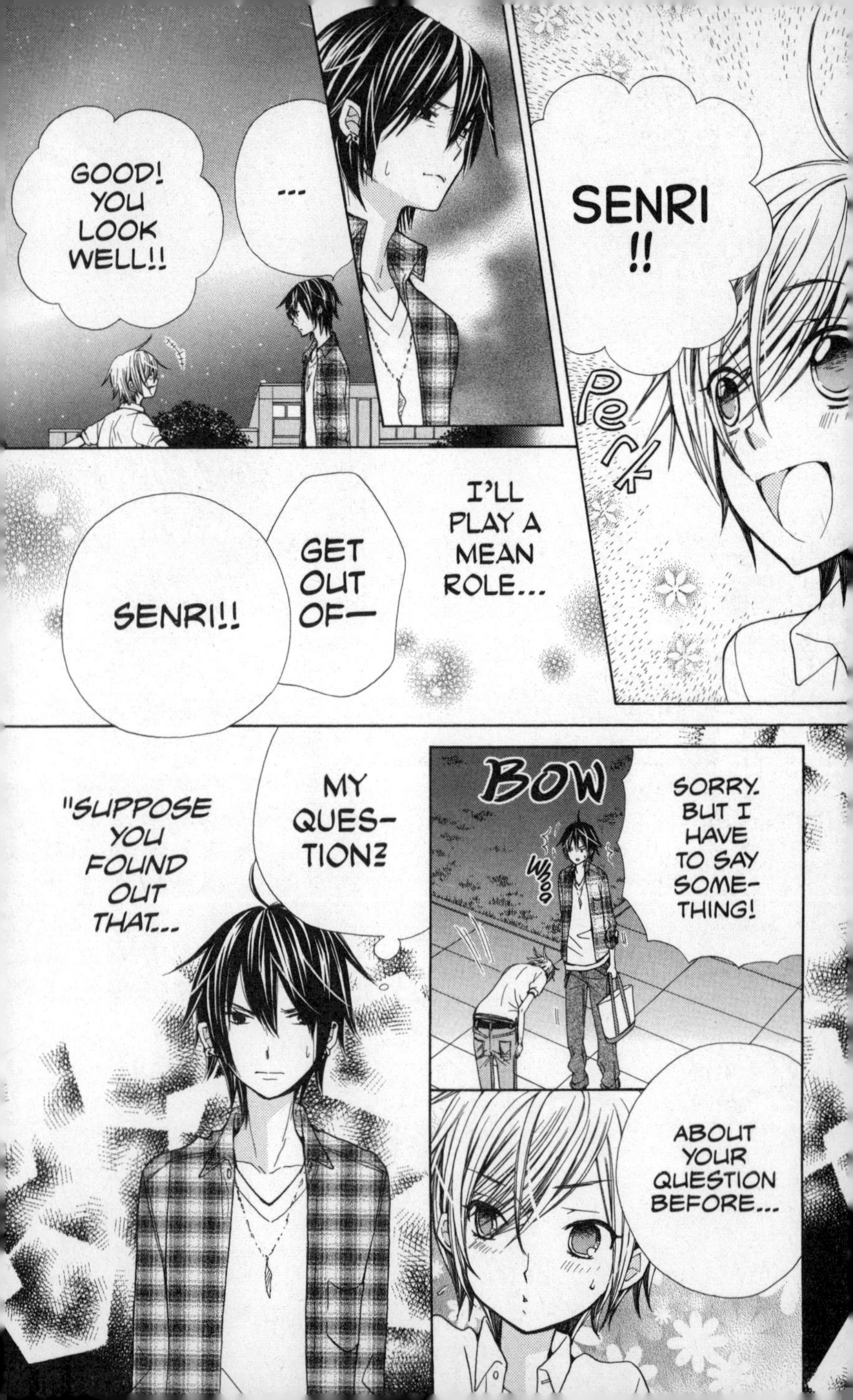
SENRI!!
Perk
...
GOOD! YOU LOOK WELL!!
I'LL PLAY A MEAN ROLE...
GET OUT OF—
SENRI!!
BOW
Whoa
SORRY. BUT I HAVE TO SAY SOMETHING!
ABOUT YOUR QUESTION BEFORE...
MY QUESTION?
"SUPPOSE YOU FOUND OUT THAT...

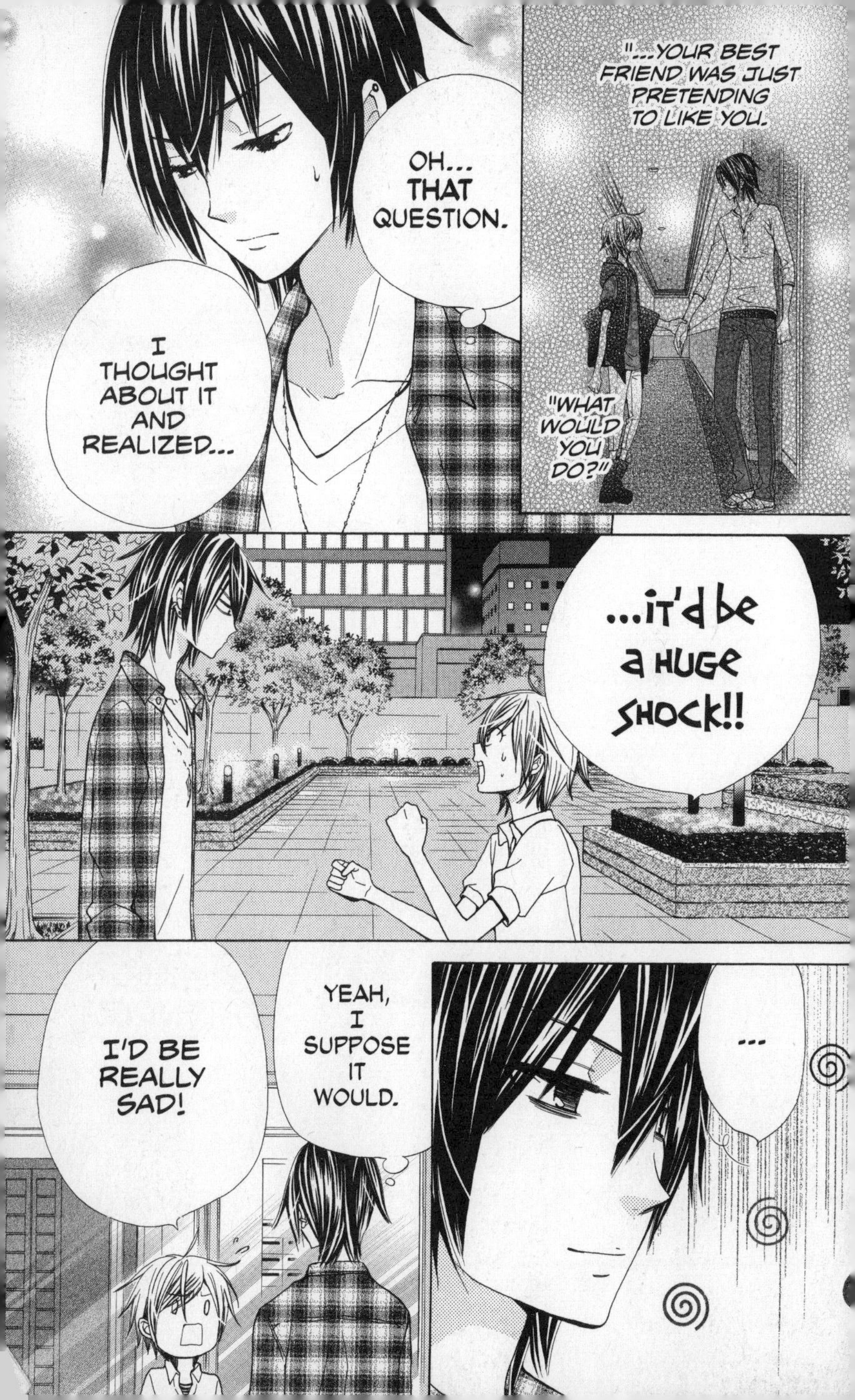
"...YOUR BEST FRIEND WAS JUST PRETENDING TO LIKE YOU.
"WHAT WOULD YOU DO?"
OH... THAT QUESTION.
I THOUGHT ABOUT IT AND REALIZED...
...it'd be a HUGE SHOCK!!
...
YEAH, I SUPPOSE IT WOULD.
I'D BE REALLY SAD!

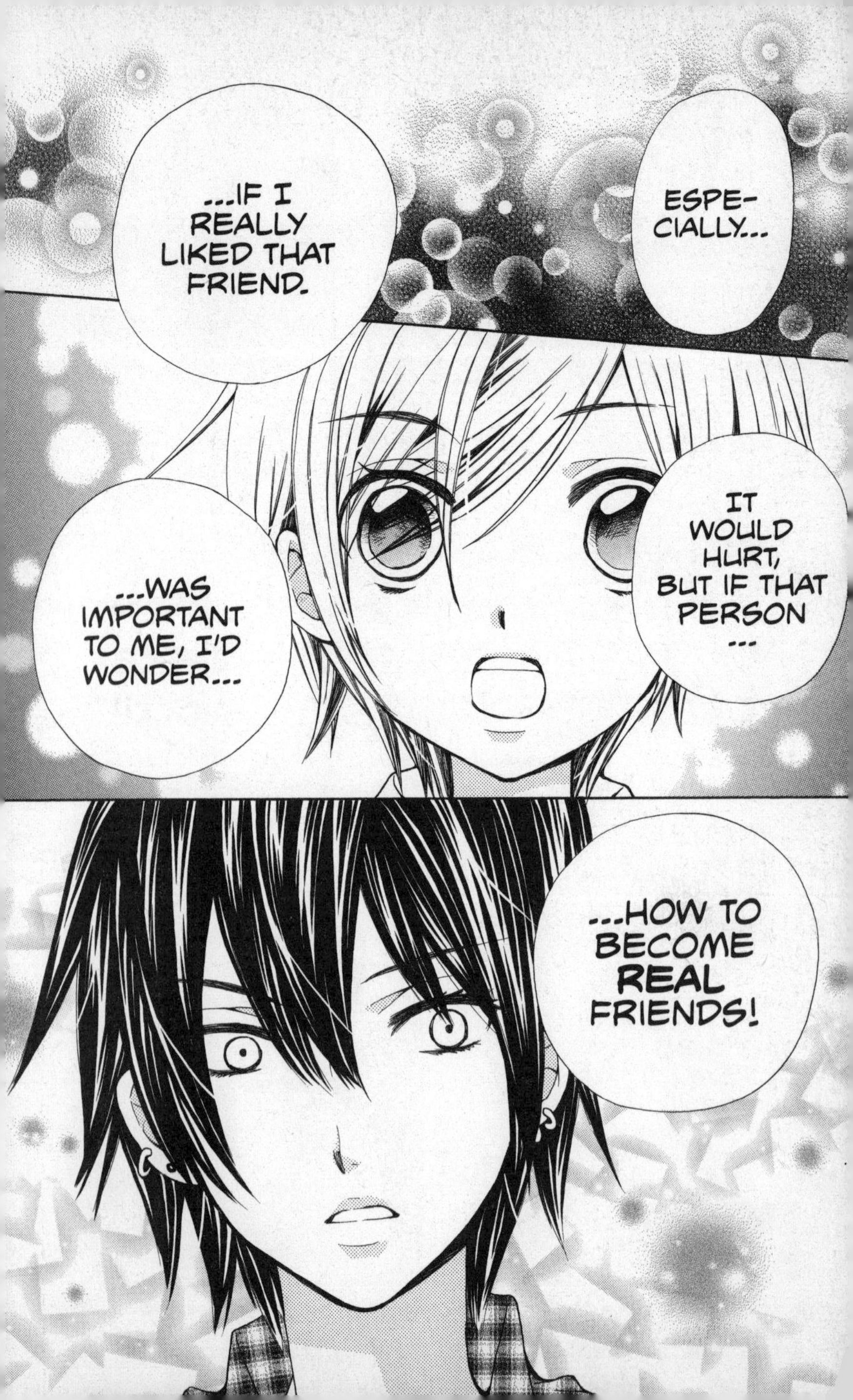
ESPE-
CIALLY...
...IF I REALLY LIKED THAT FRIEND.
IT WOULD HURT, BUT IF THAT PERSON...
...WAS IMPORTANT TO ME, I'D WONDER...
...HOW TO BECOME **REAL** FRIENDS!

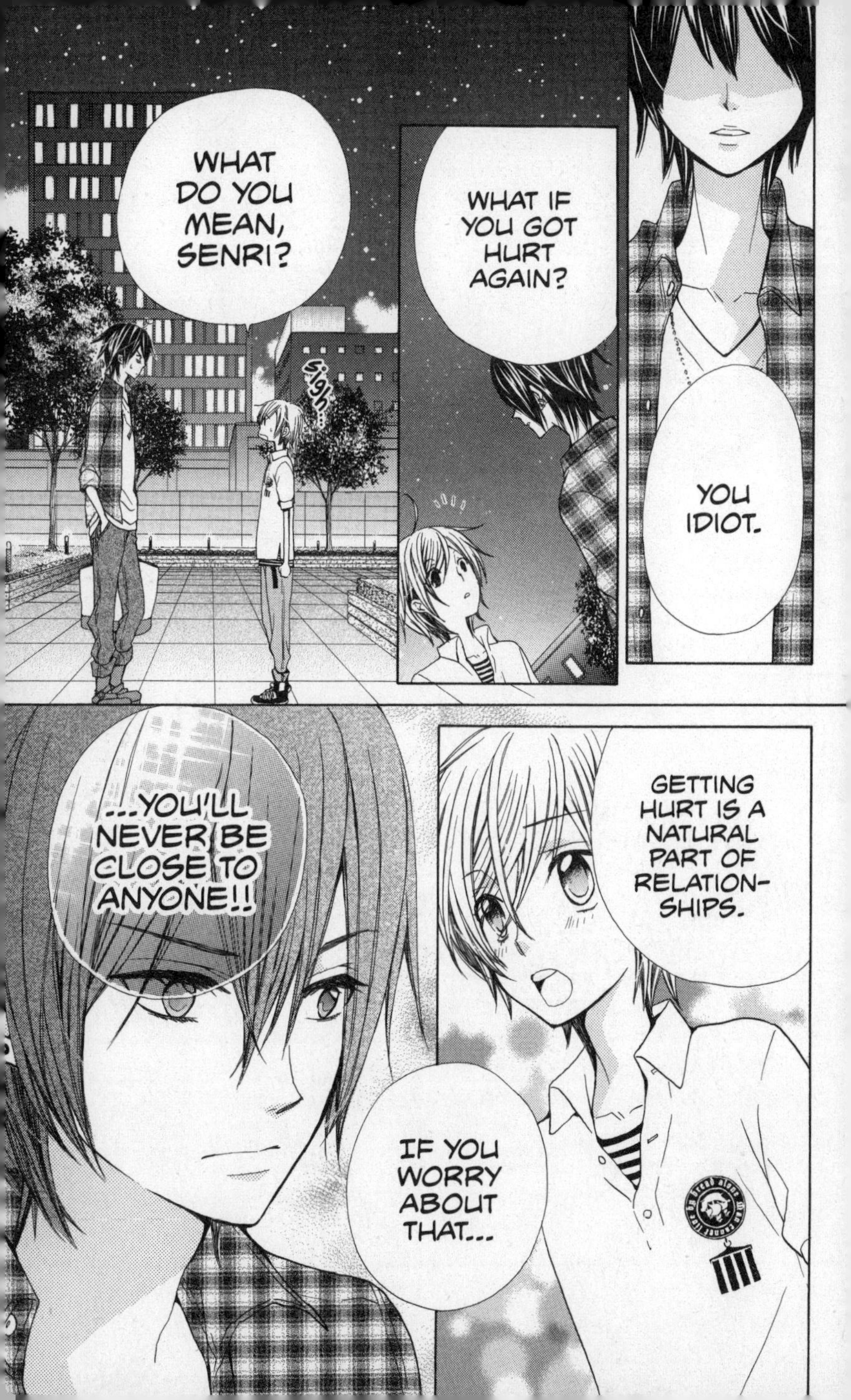
YOU IDIOT.
WHAT IF YOU GOT HURT AGAIN?
WHAT DO YOU MEAN, SENRI?
sigh...
GETTING HURT IS A NATURAL PART OF RELATION-SHIPS.
IF YOU WORRY ABOUT THAT...
...YOU'LL NEVER BE CLOSE TO ANYONE!!

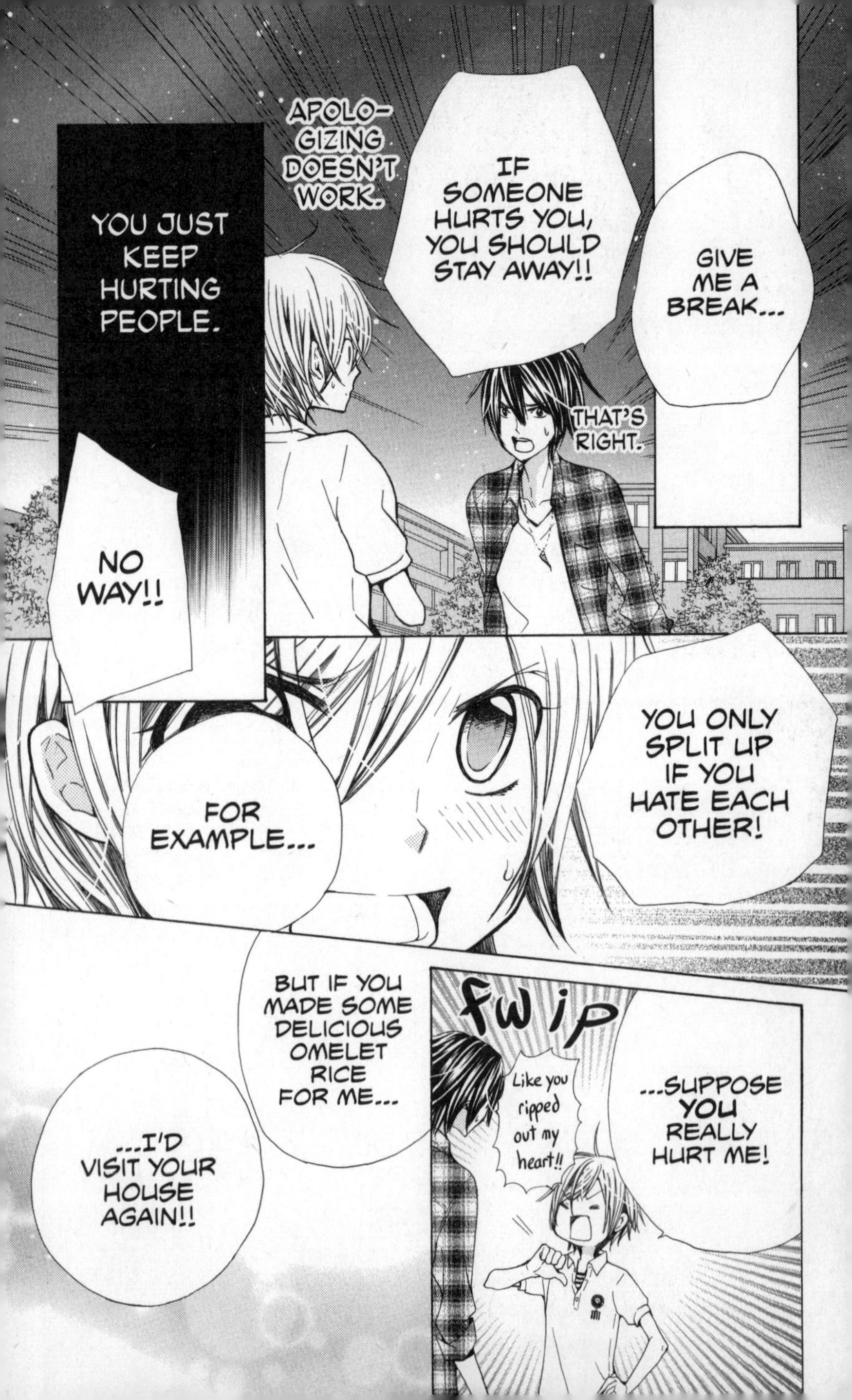
GIVE ME A BREAK...
THAT'S RIGHT.
IF SOMEONE HURTS YOU, YOU SHOULD STAY AWAY!!
APOLO-GIZING DOESN'T WORK.
YOU JUST KEEP HURTING PEOPLE.
NO WAY!!
YOU ONLY SPLIT UP IF YOU HATE EACH OTHER!
FOR EXAMPLE...
fwip
...SUPPOSE YOU REALLY HURT ME!
Like you ripped out my heart!!
BUT IF YOU MADE SOME DELICIOUS OMELET RICE FOR ME...
...I'D VISIT YOUR HOUSE AGAIN!!

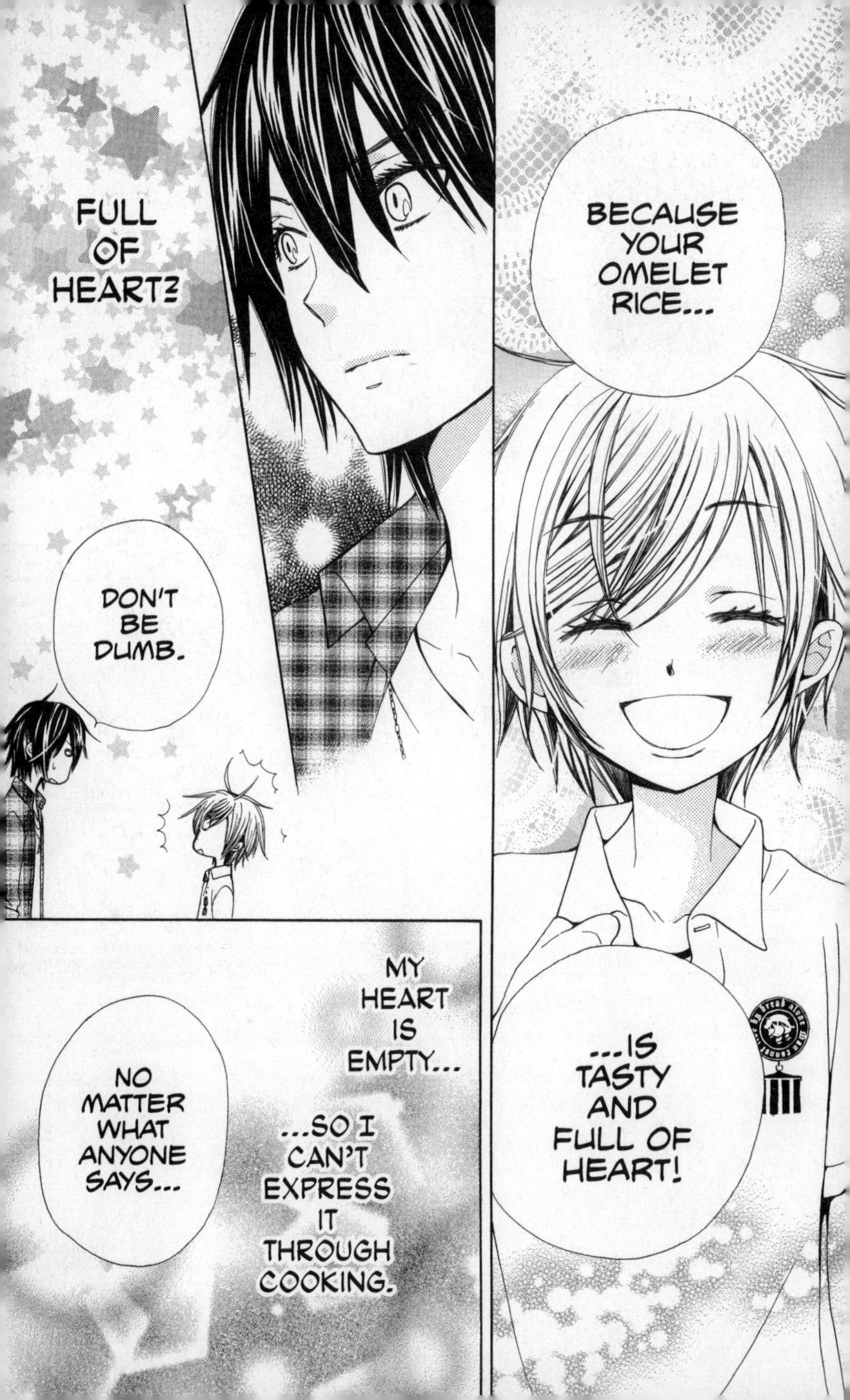
BECAUSE YOUR OMELET RICE...
...IS TASTY AND FULL OF HEART!
FULL OF HEART?
DON'T BE DUMB.
MY HEART IS EMPTY...
...SO I CAN'T EXPRESS IT THROUGH COOKING.
NO MATTER WHAT ANYONE SAYS...

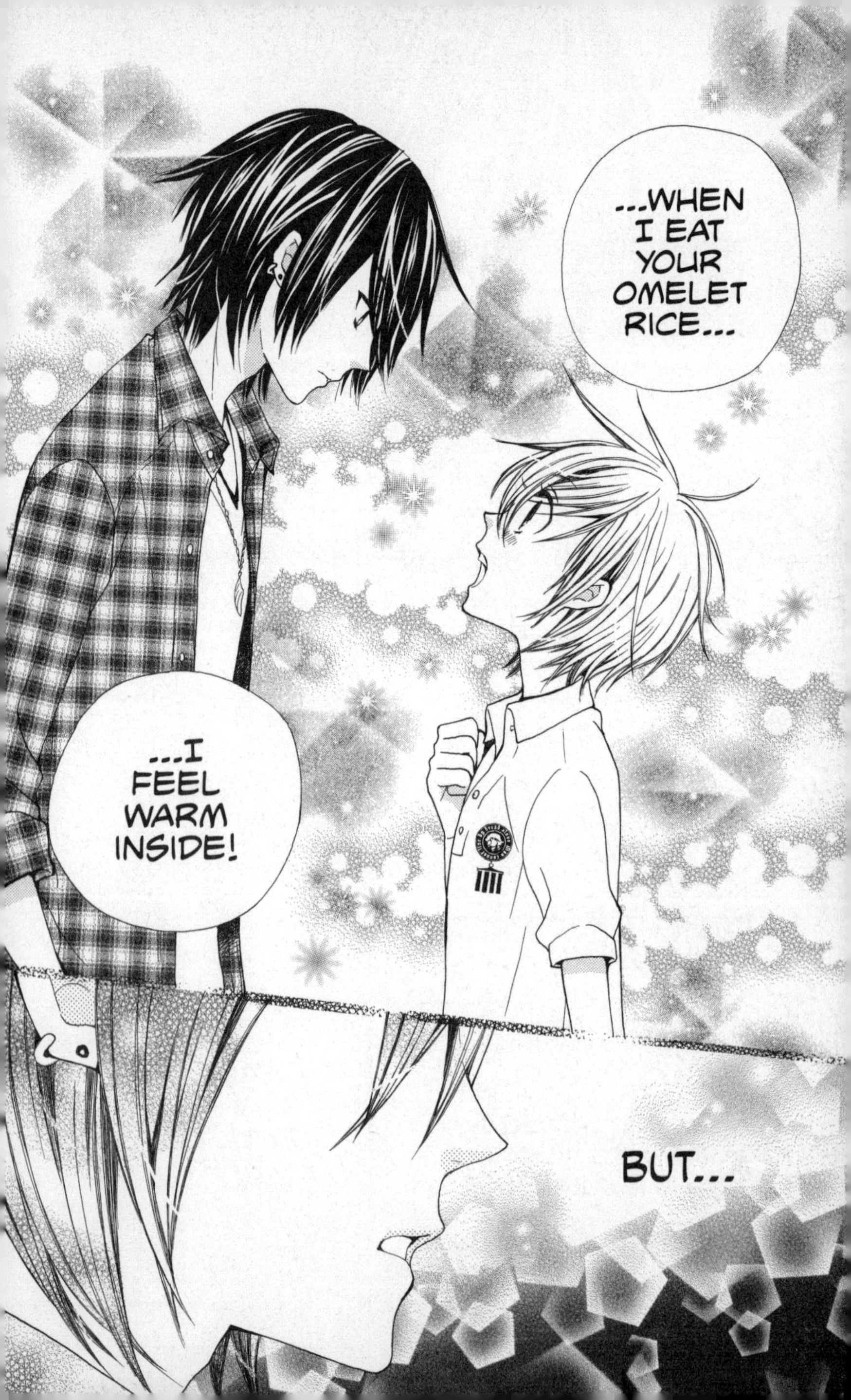
...WHEN I EAT YOUR OMELET RICE...
...I FEEL WARM INSIDE!
BUT...

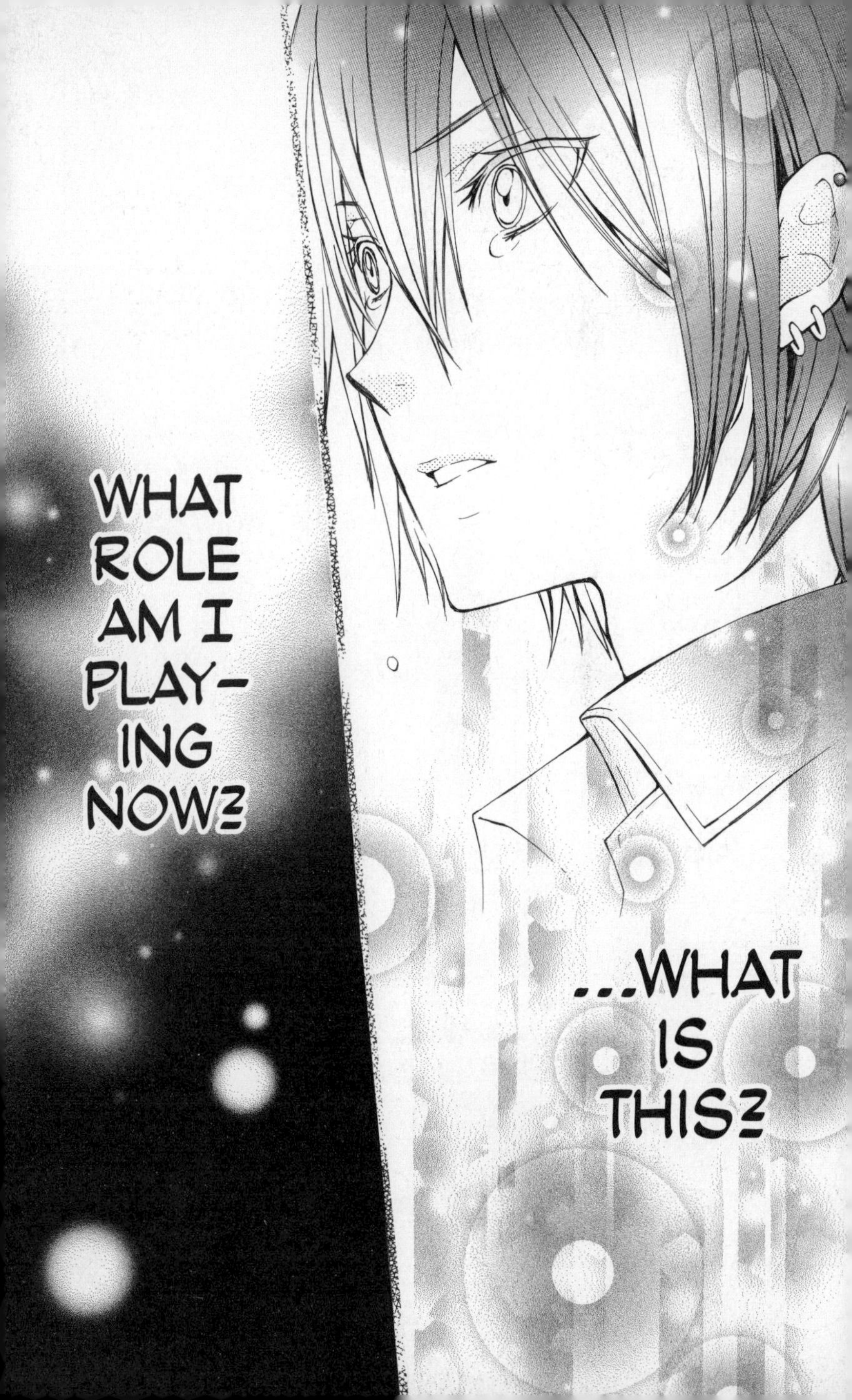
...WHAT IS THIS?
WHAT ROLE AM I PLAYING NOW?

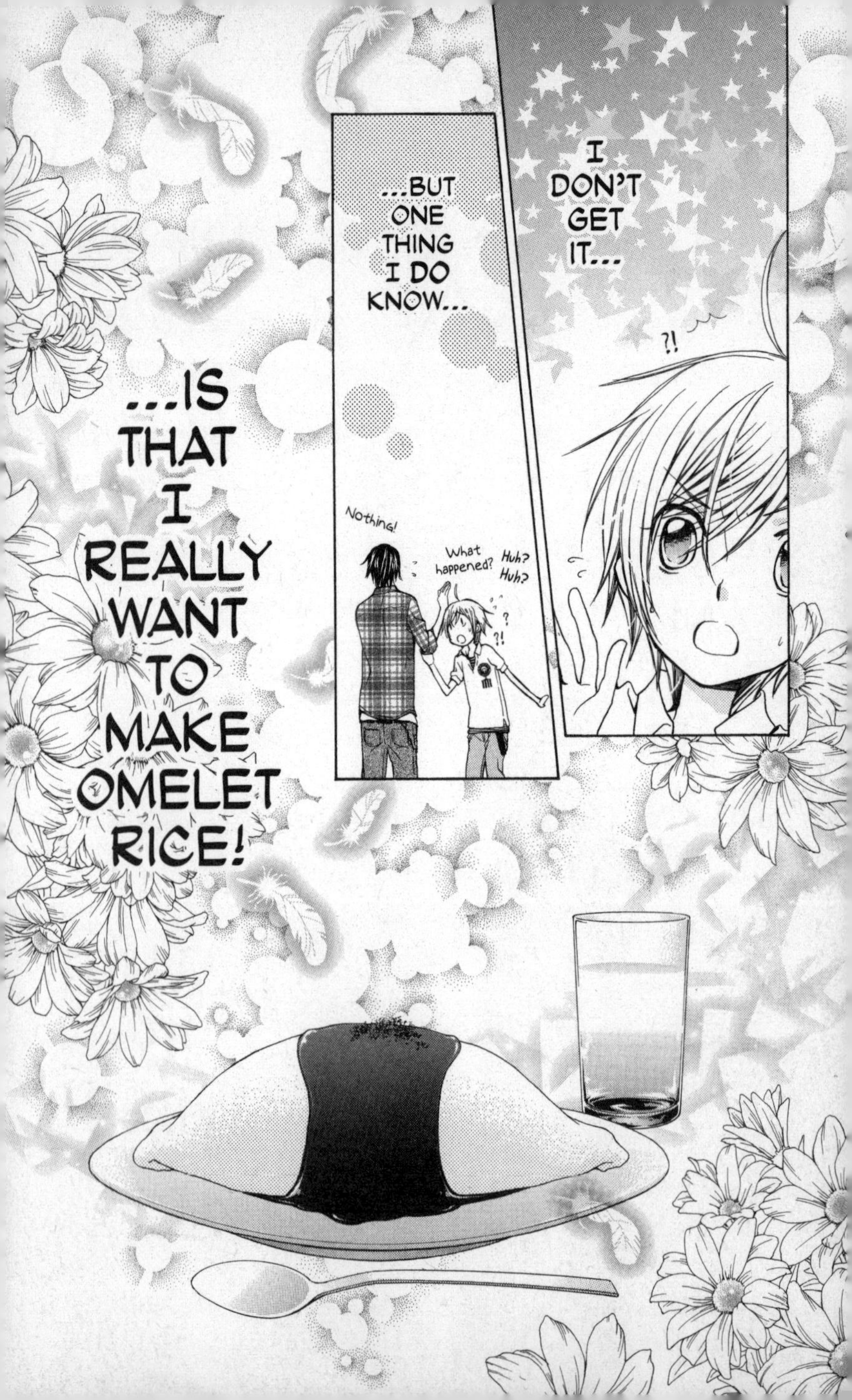
I DON'T GET IT...
?!
...BUT ONE THING I DO KNOW...
Nothing!
What happened?
Huh? Huh?
?
?!
...IS THAT I REALLY WANT TO MAKE OMELET RICE!

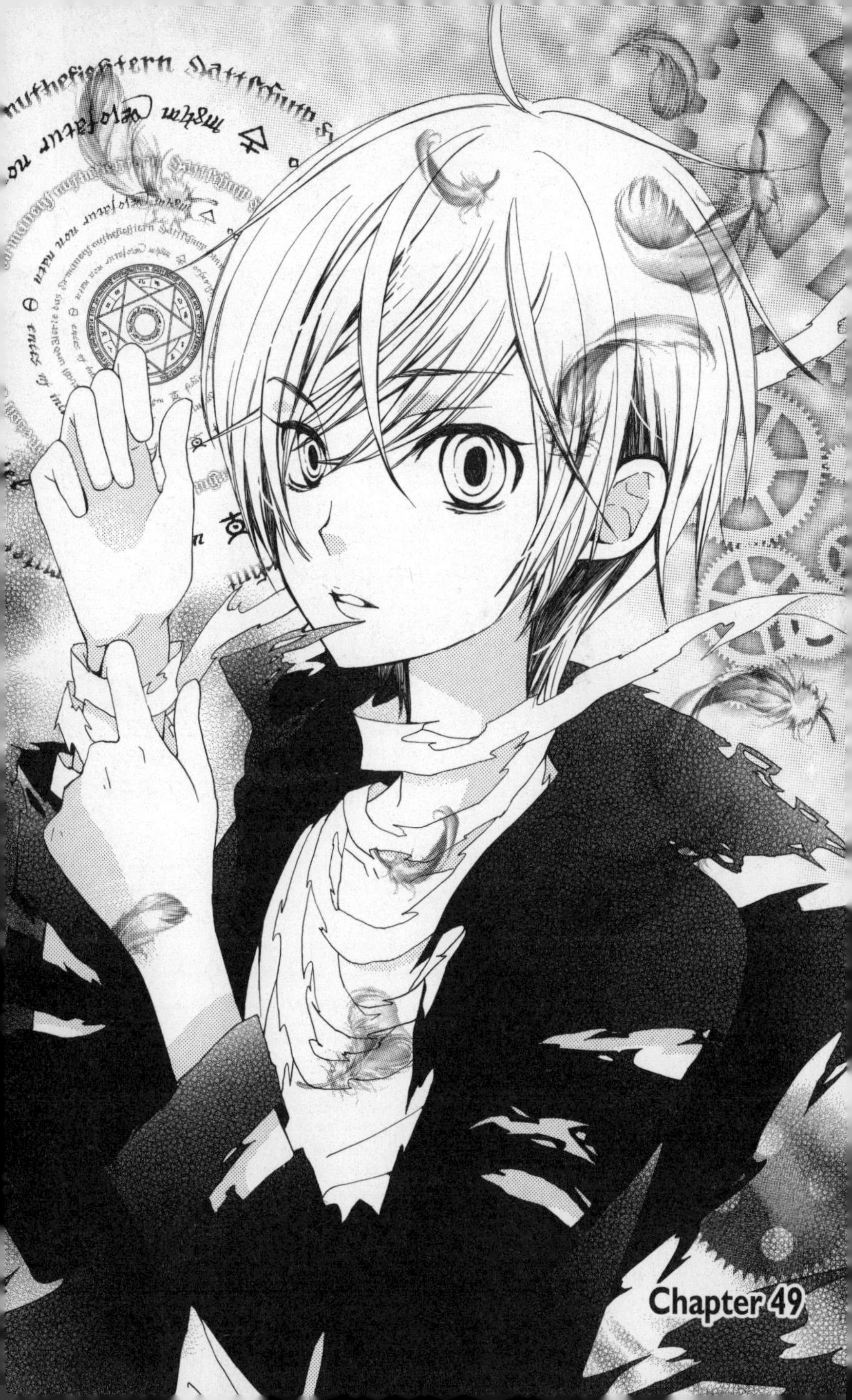
Chapter 49

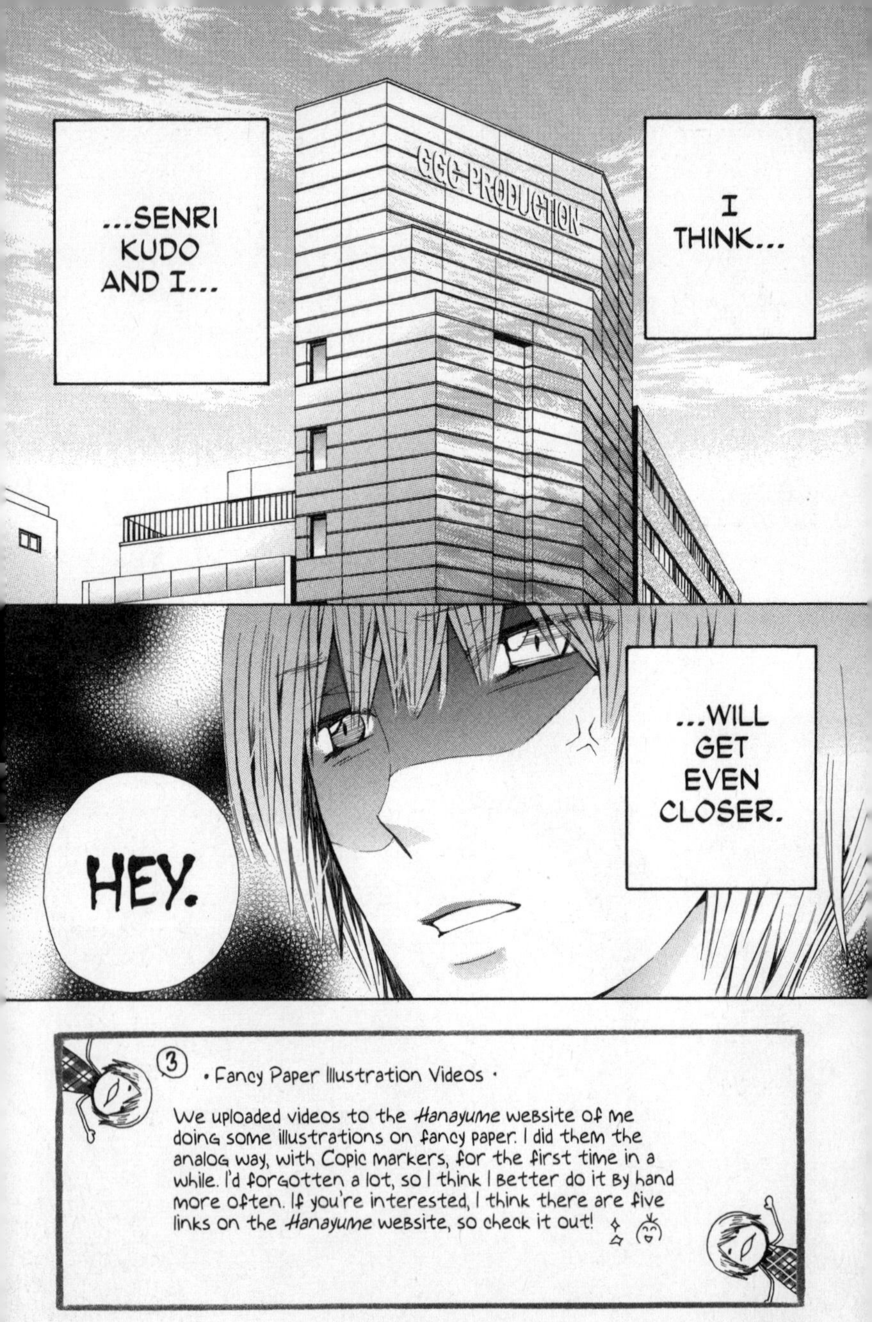
I THINK...
GGC PRODUCTION
...SENRI KUDO AND I...
...WILL GET EVEN CLOSER.
HEY.

③ • Fancy Paper Illustration Videos •

We uploaded videos to the *Hanayume* website of me doing some illustrations on fancy paper. I did them the analog way, with Copic markers, for the first time in a while. I'd forgotten a lot, so I think I better do it by hand more often. If you're interested, I think there are five links on the *Hanayume* website, so check it out!

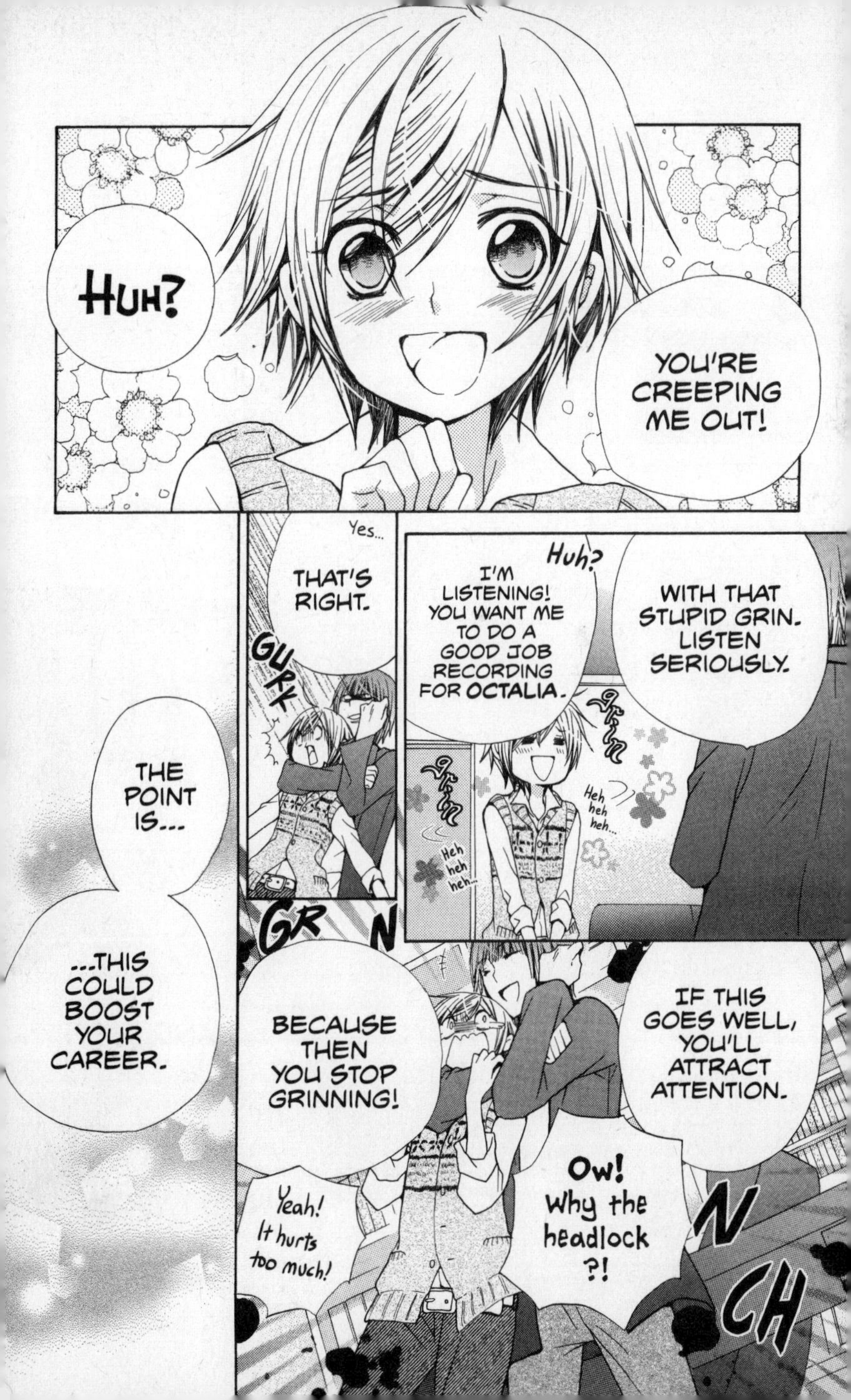
YOU'RE CREEPING ME OUT!
HUH?
WITH THAT STUPID GRIN. LISTEN SERIOUSLY.
Huh?
I'M LISTENING! YOU WANT ME TO DO A GOOD JOB RECORDING FOR OCTALIA.
grin
Heh heh heh...
grin
Heh heh heh...
Yes...
THAT'S RIGHT.
GURK
IF THIS GOES WELL, YOU'LL ATTRACT ATTENTION.
BECAUSE THEN YOU STOP GRINNING!
GRNNCH
Ow! Why the headlock?!
Yeah! It hurts too much!
THE POINT IS...
...THIS COULD BOOST YOUR CAREER.

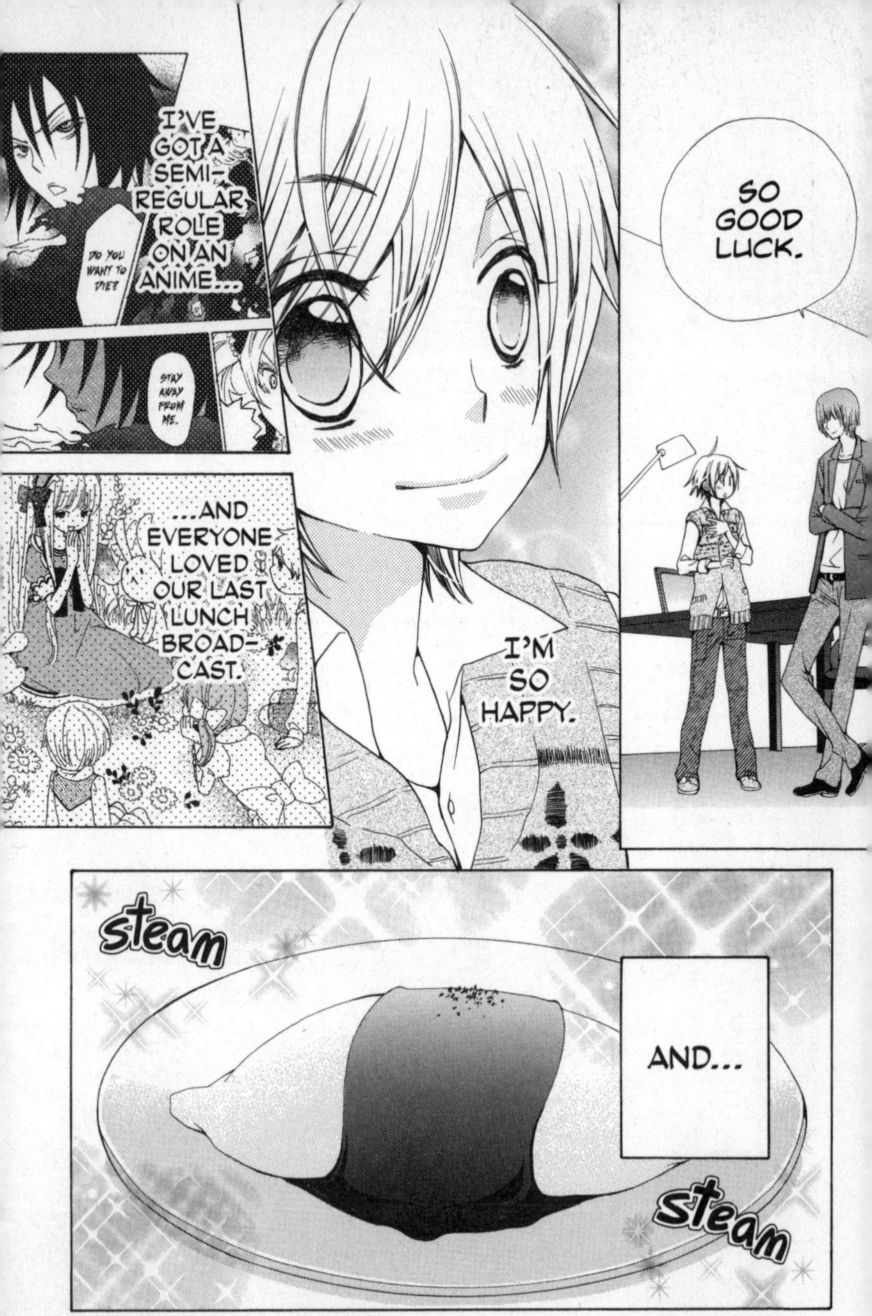
SO GOOD LUCK.
I'M SO HAPPY.
I'VE GOT A SEMI-REGULAR ROLE ON AN ANIME...
DO YOU WANT TO DIE?
STAY AWAY FROM ME.
...AND EVERYONE LOVED OUR LAST LUNCH BROAD-CAST.
steam
AND...
steam

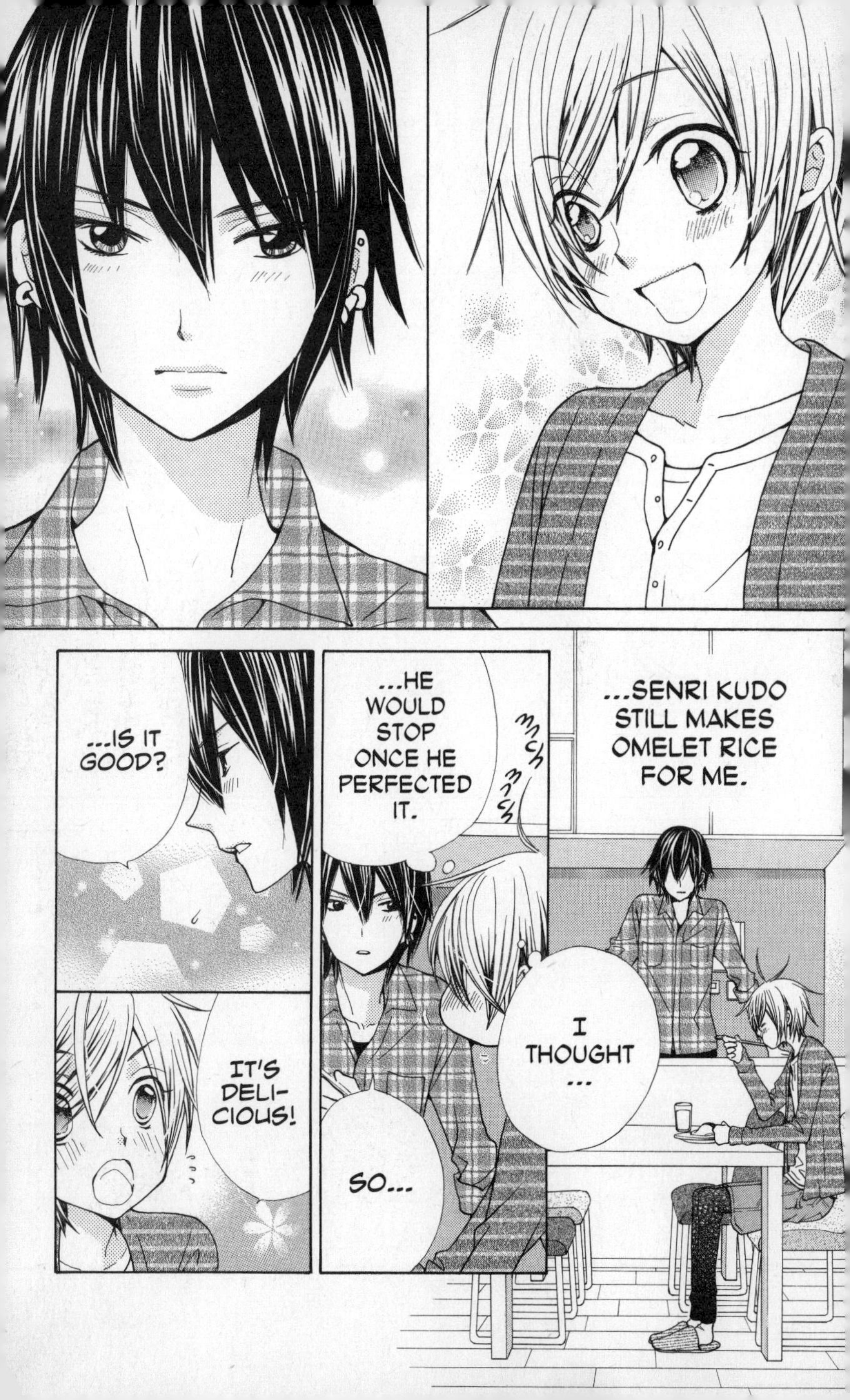
...SENRI KUDO STILL MAKES OMELET RICE FOR ME.
I THOUGHT ...
...HE WOULD STOP ONCE HE PERFECTED IT.
SO...
...IS IT GOOD?
IT'S DELICIOUS!

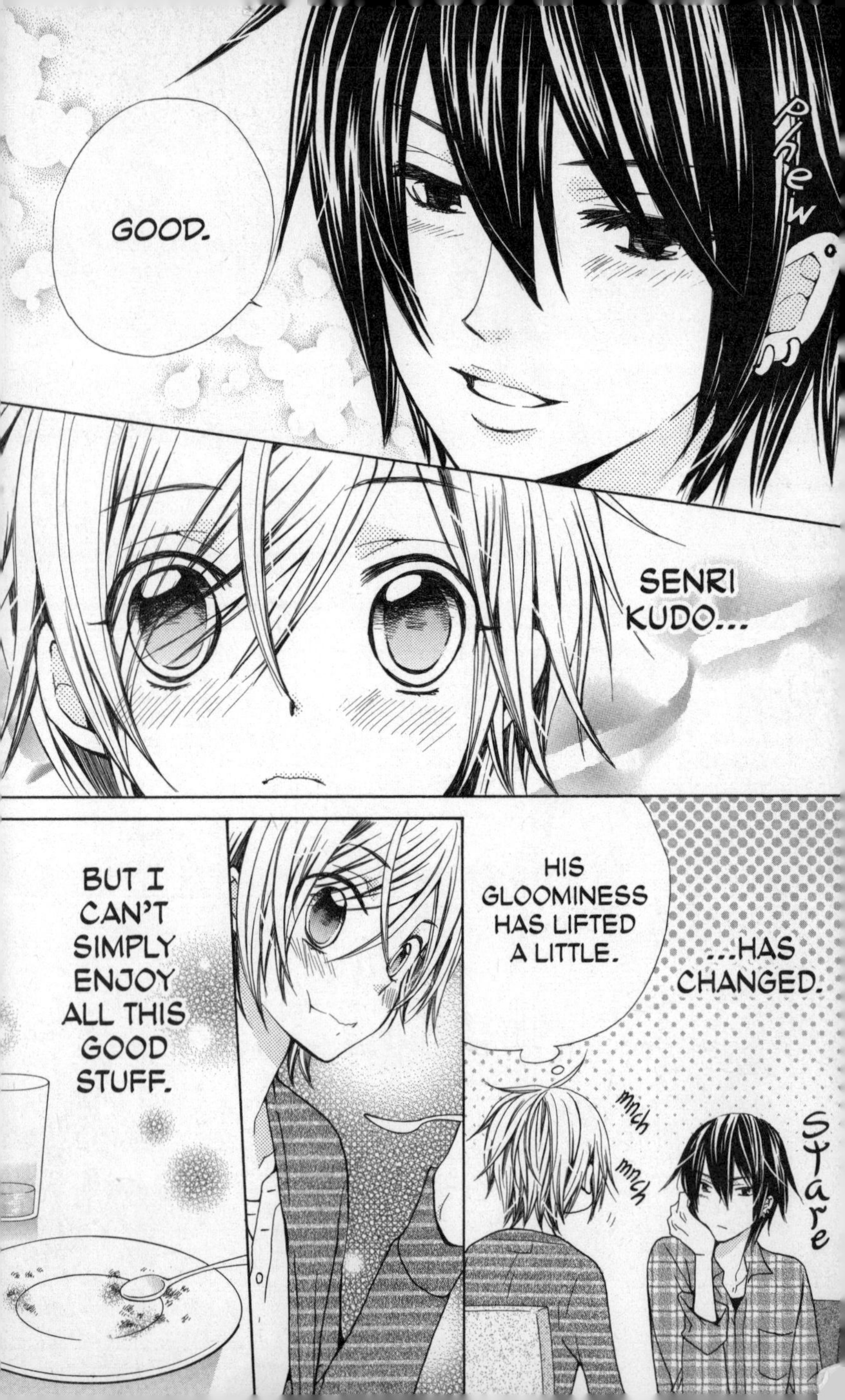
Phew
GOOD.
SENRI KUDO...
...HAS CHANGED.
HIS GLOOMINESS HAS LIFTED A LITTLE.
Stare
mnch
mnch
BUT I CAN'T SIMPLY ENJOY ALL THIS GOOD STUFF.

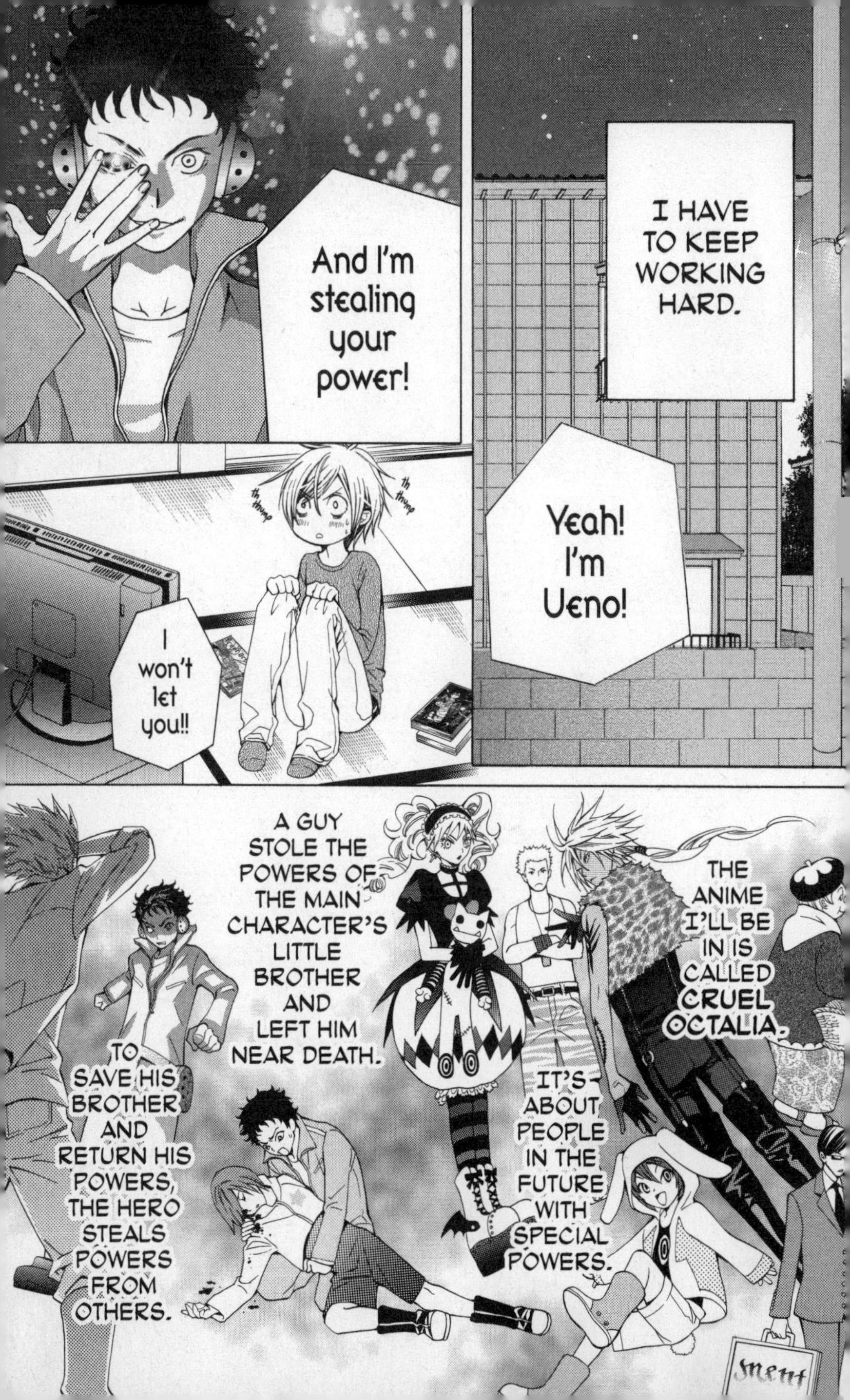
I HAVE TO KEEP WORKING HARD.
Yeah! I'm Ueno!
And I'm stealing your power!
th thump
th thump
I won't let you!!
THE ANIME I'LL BE IN IS CALLED CRUEL OCTALIA.
A GUY STOLE THE POWERS OF THE MAIN CHARACTER'S LITTLE BROTHER AND LEFT HIM NEAR DEATH.
IT'S ABOUT PEOPLE IN THE FUTURE WITH SPECIAL POWERS.
TO SAVE HIS BROTHER AND RETURN HIS POWERS, THE HERO STEALS POWERS FROM OTHERS.

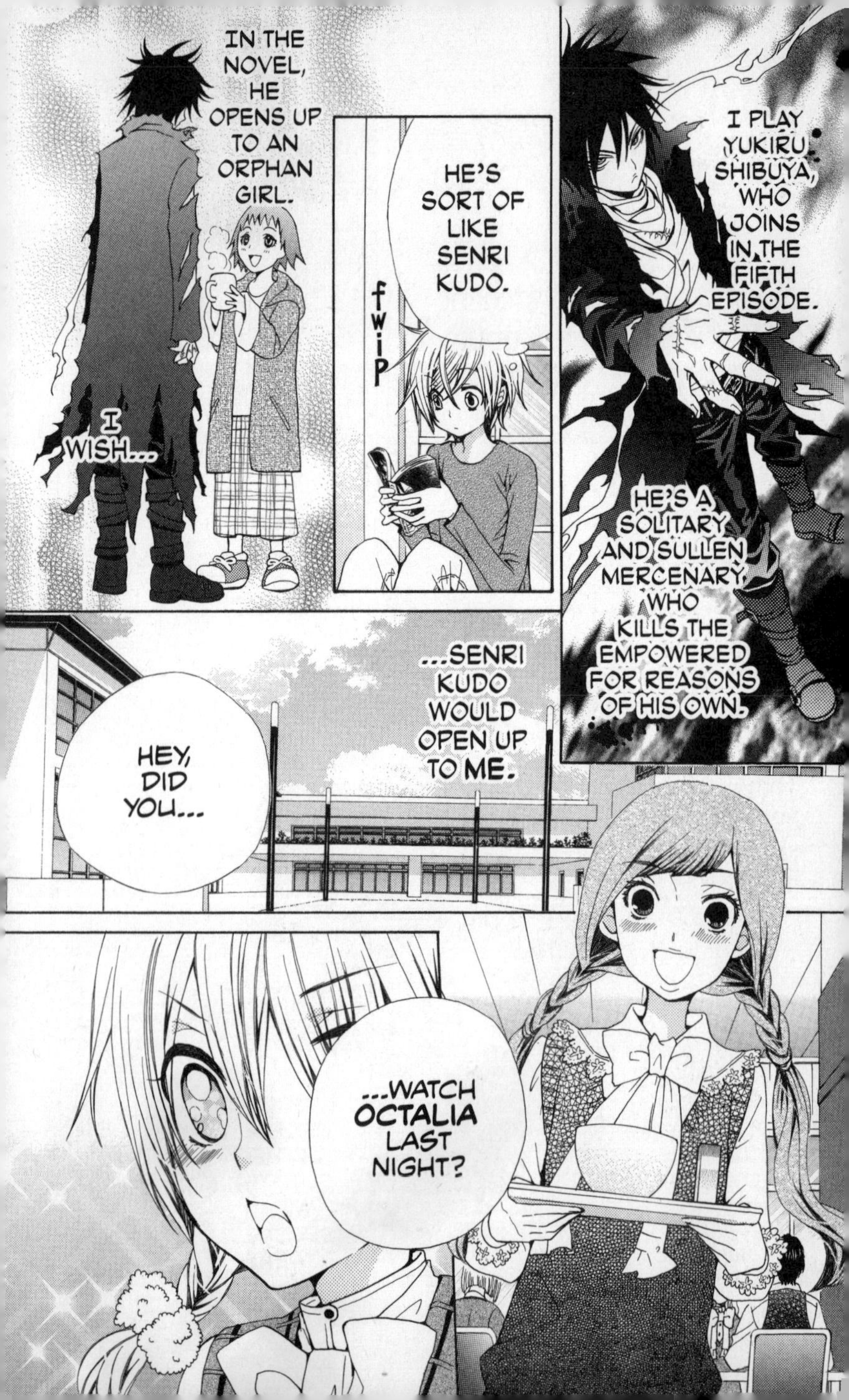
I PLAY YUKIRU SHIBUYA, WHO JOINS IN THE FIFTH EPISODE.
HE'S A SOLITARY AND SULLEN MERCENARY WHO KILLS THE EMPOWERED FOR REASONS OF HIS OWN.
HE'S SORT OF LIKE SENRI KUDO.
fwip
IN THE NOVEL, HE OPENS UP TO AN ORPHAN GIRL.
I WISH...
...SENRI KUDO WOULD OPEN UP TO ME.
HEY, DID YOU...
...WATCH OCTALIA LAST NIGHT?

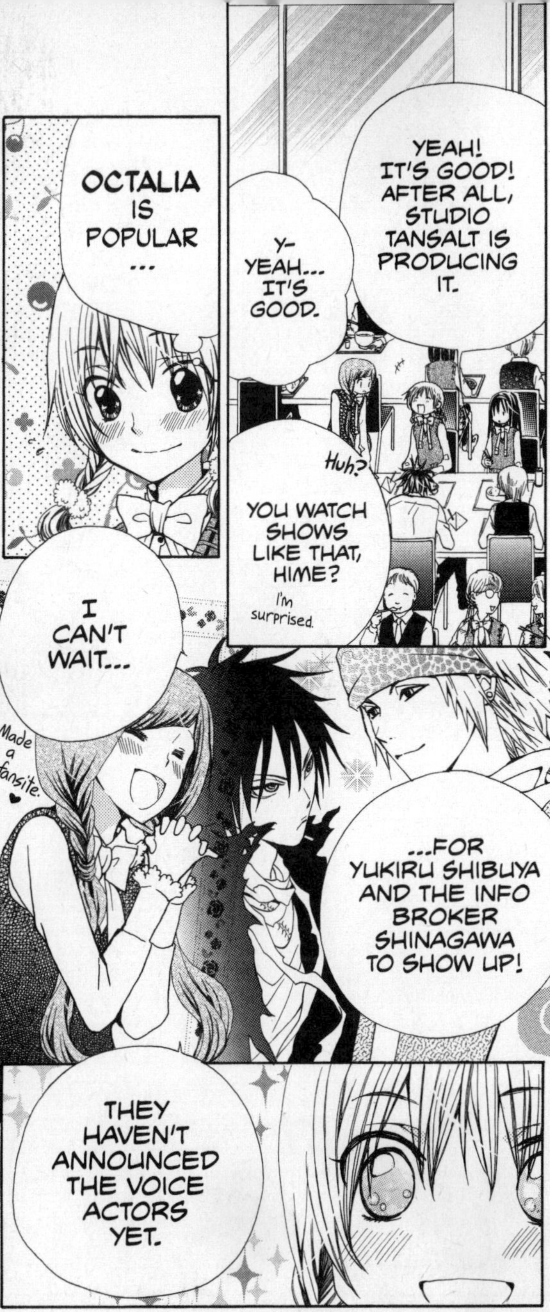
YEAH! IT'S GOOD! AFTER ALL, STUDIO TANSALT IS PRODUCING IT.
Y-YEAH... IT'S GOOD.
Huh?
YOU WATCH SHOWS LIKE THAT, HIME?
I'm surprised.
OCTALIA IS POPULAR...
I CAN'T WAIT...
...FOR YUKIRU SHIBUYA AND THE INFO BROKER SHINAGAWA TO SHOW UP!
Made a fansite.
THEY HAVEN'T ANNOUNCED THE VOICE ACTORS YET.

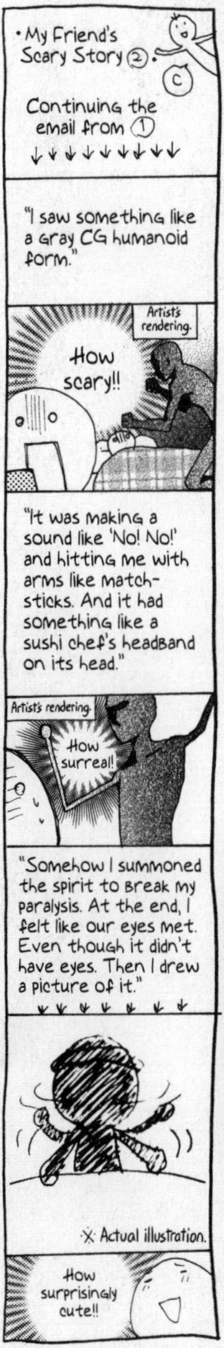
• My Friend's Scary Story ②.
Continuing the email from ①
↓↓↓↓↓↓↓↓↓
"I saw something like a gray CG humanoid form."
Artist's rendering.
How scary!!
"It was making a sound like 'No! No!' and hitting me with arms like matchsticks. And it had something like a sushi chef's headband on its head."
Artist's rendering.
How surreal!
"Somehow I summoned the spirit to break my paralysis. At the end, I felt like our eyes met. Even though it didn't have eyes. Then I drew a picture of it."
↓↓↓↓↓↓↓
※ Actual illustration.
How surprisingly cute!!

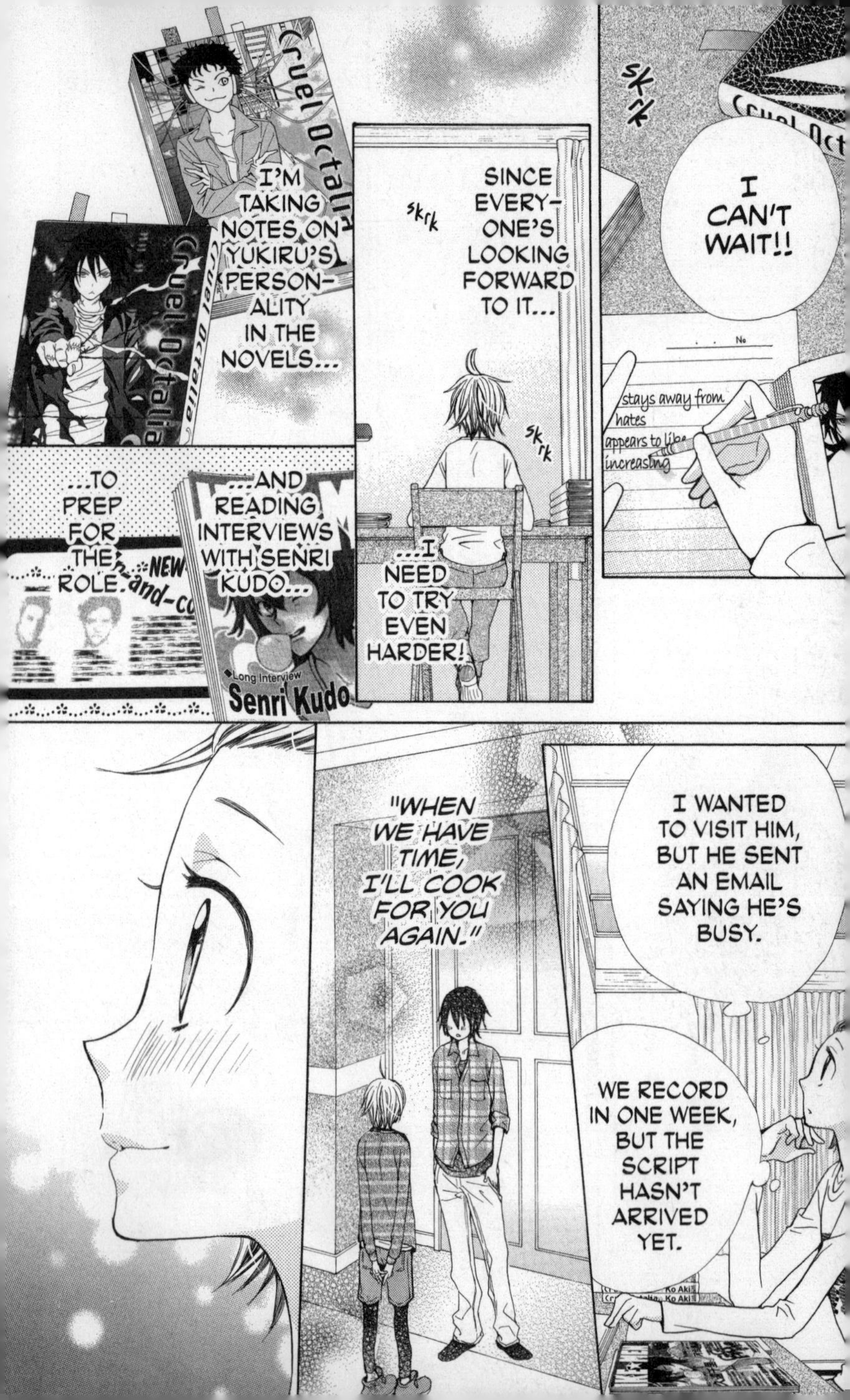
SKRK
Cruel Oct
I CAN'T WAIT!!
No
stays away from
hates
appears to like
increasing
SINCE EVERYONE'S LOOKING FORWARD TO IT...
SKRK
SKRK
...I NEED TO TRY EVEN HARDER!
Cruel Octalia
I'M TAKING NOTES ON YUKIRU'S PERSONALITY IN THE NOVELS...
Cruel Octalia
...AND READING INTERVIEWS WITH SENRI KUDO...
Long Interview
Senri Kudo
...TO PREP FOR THE ROLE.
NEW
I WANTED TO VISIT HIM, BUT HE SENT AN EMAIL SAYING HE'S BUSY.
WE RECORD IN ONE WEEK, BUT THE SCRIPT HASN'T ARRIVED YET.
Ko Aki
Ko Aki
"WHEN WE HAVE TIME, I'LL COOK FOR YOU AGAIN."

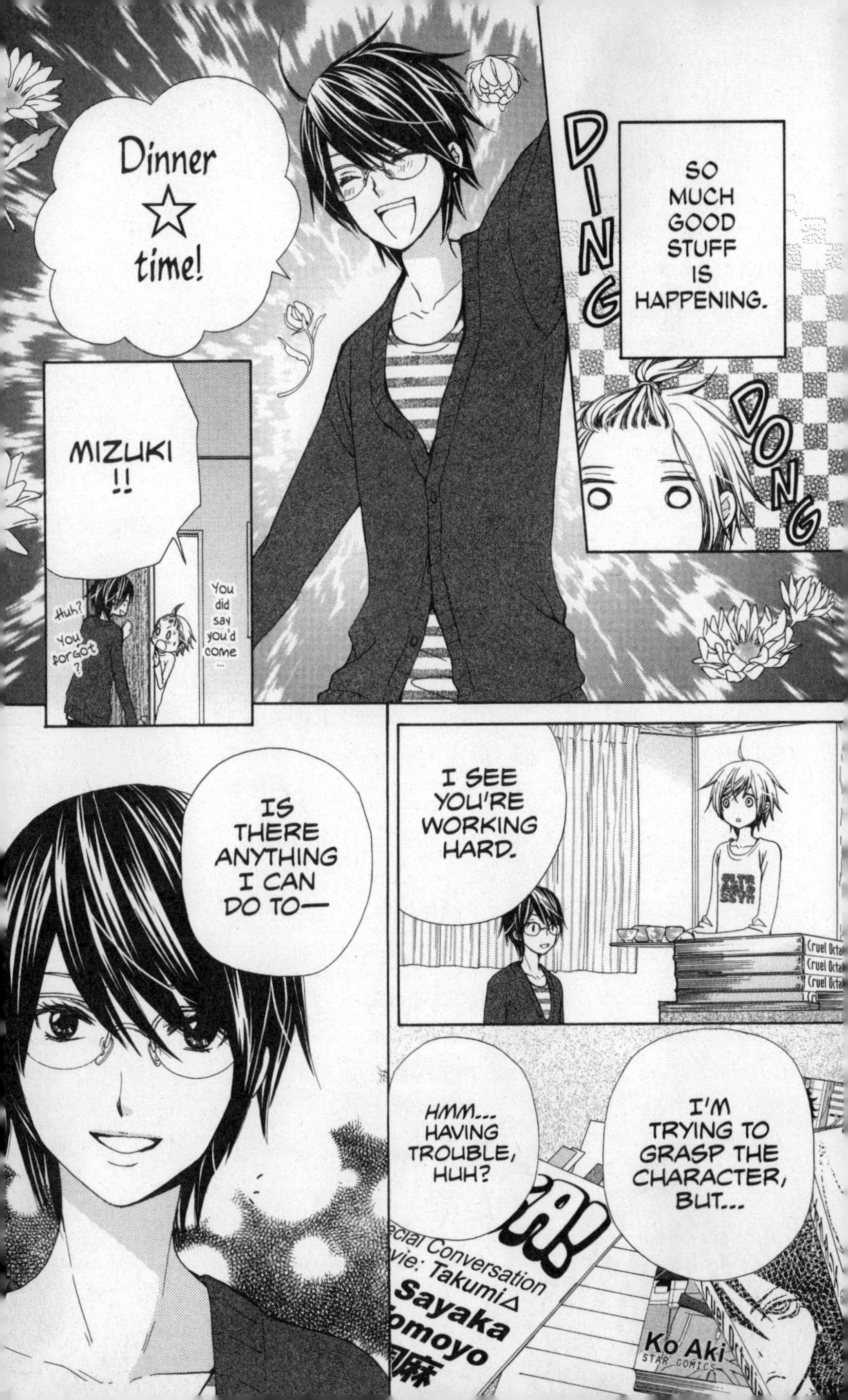
DING
DONG
SO MUCH GOOD STUFF IS HAPPENING.
Dinner ☆ time!
MIZUKI !!
You did say you'd come ...
Huh? You forgot?
I SEE YOU'RE WORKING HARD.
Cruel Octa
I'M TRYING TO GRASP THE CHARACTER, BUT...
HMM... HAVING TROUBLE, HUH?
Conversation
Takumi△
Sayaka
Ko Aki
STAR COMICS
IS THERE ANYTHING I CAN DO TO—

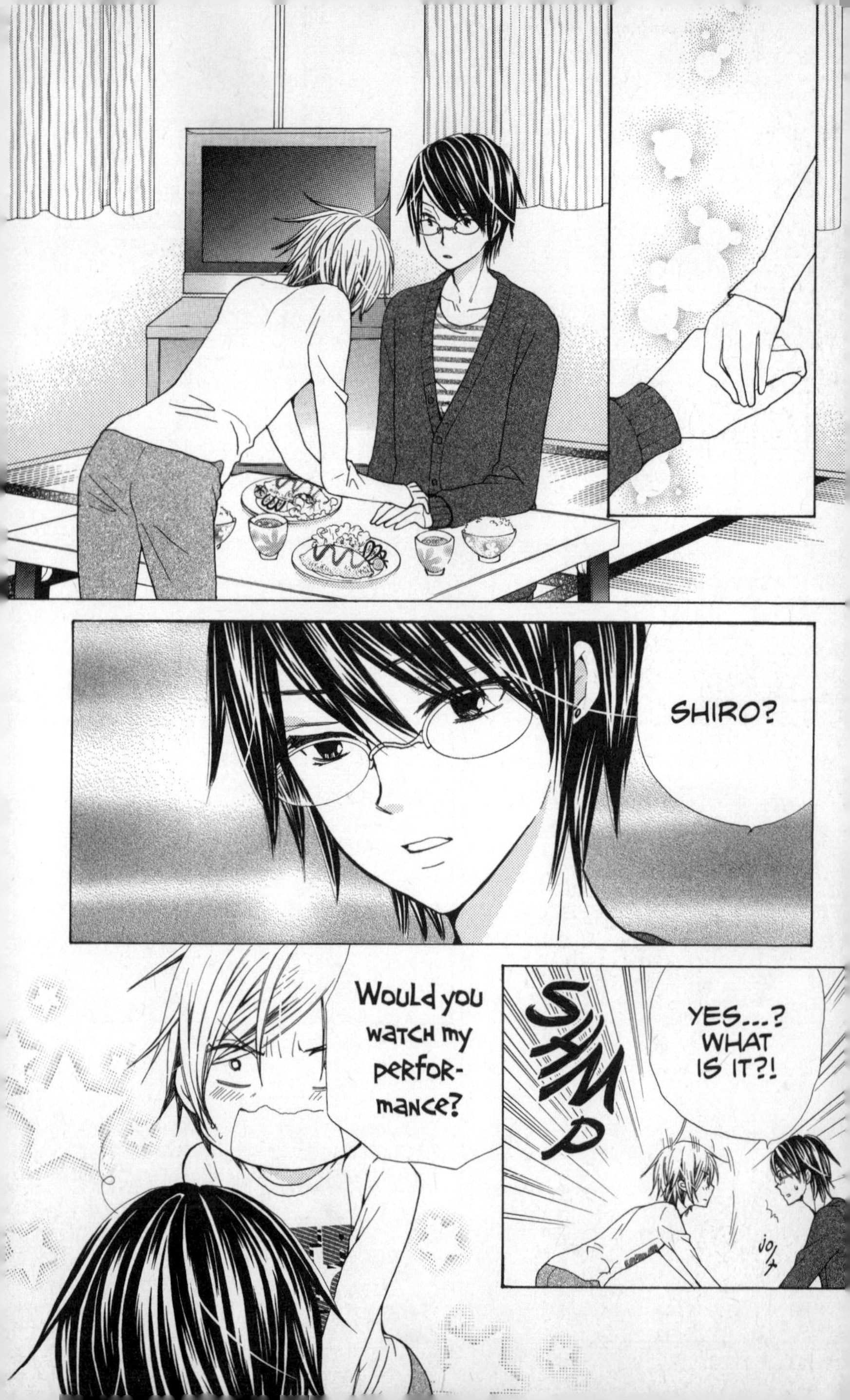
SHIRO?
SHMP
YES...? WHAT IS IT?!
jolt
Would you watch my perfor-mance?

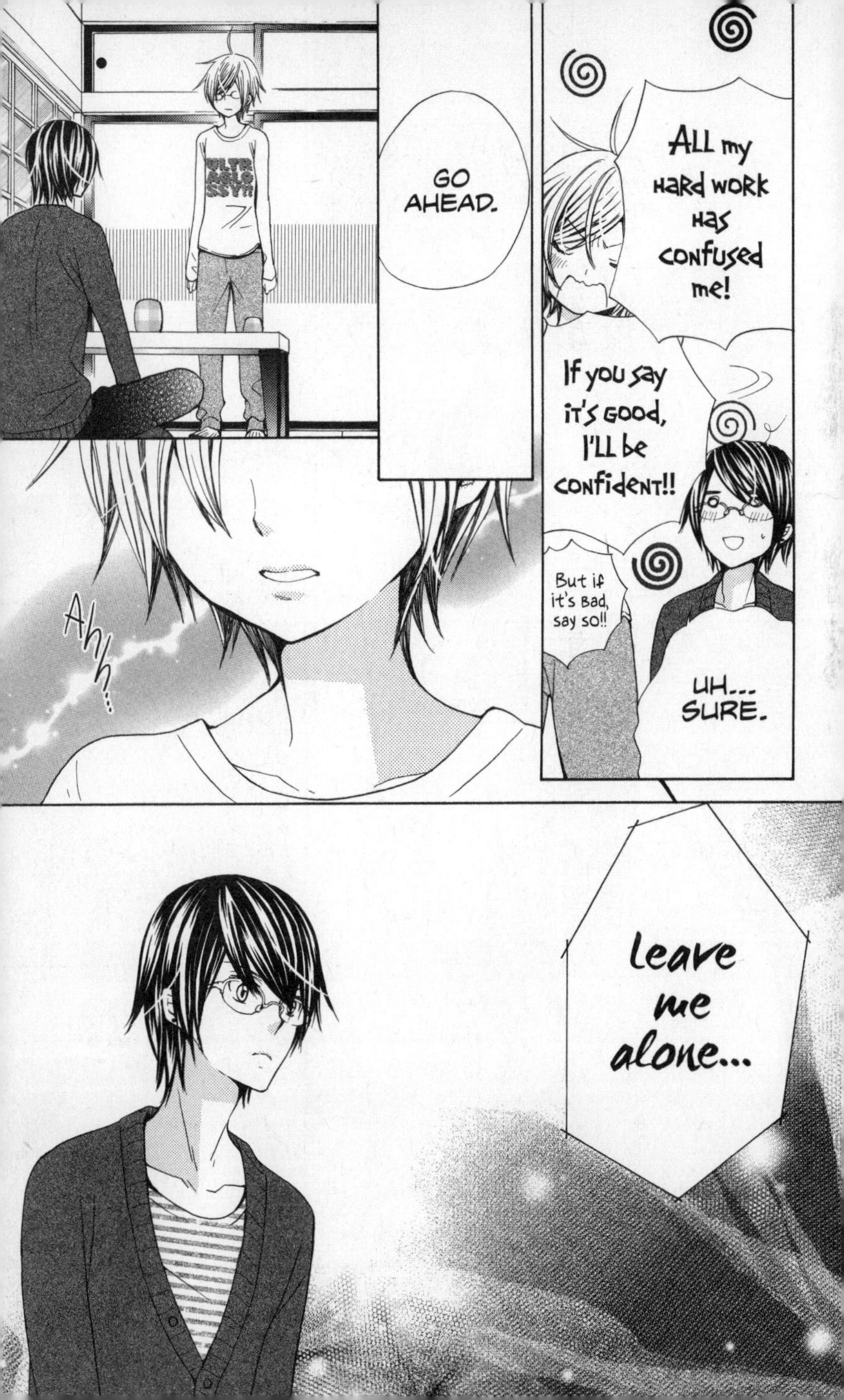
ALL my hard work has confused me!
If you say it's good, I'll be confident!!
But if it's bad, say so!!
UH... SURE.
GO AHEAD.
Ahh...
leave me alone...

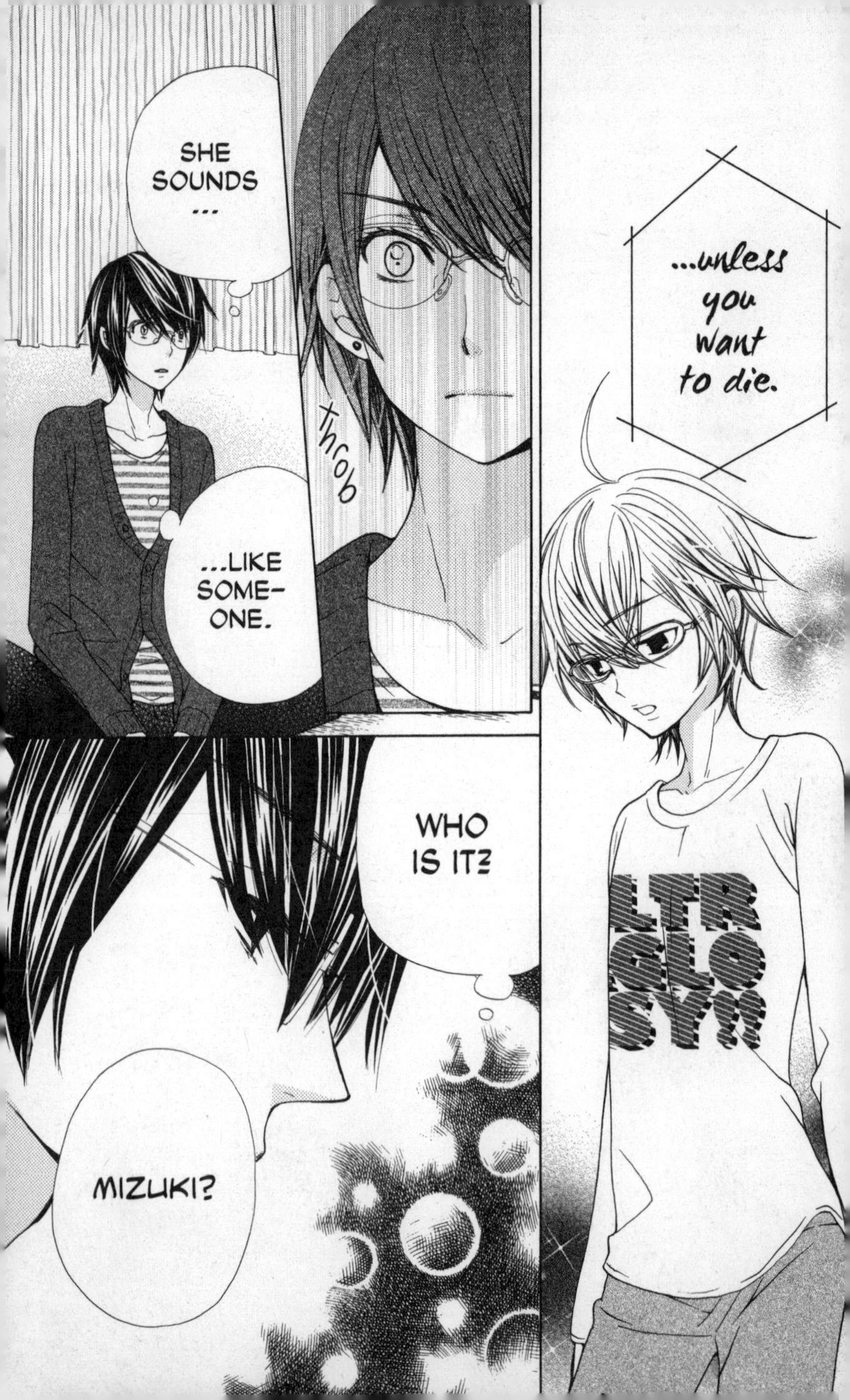
...unless you want to die.
THROB
SHE SOUNDS...
...LIKE SOMEONE.
WHO IS IT?
MIZUKI?

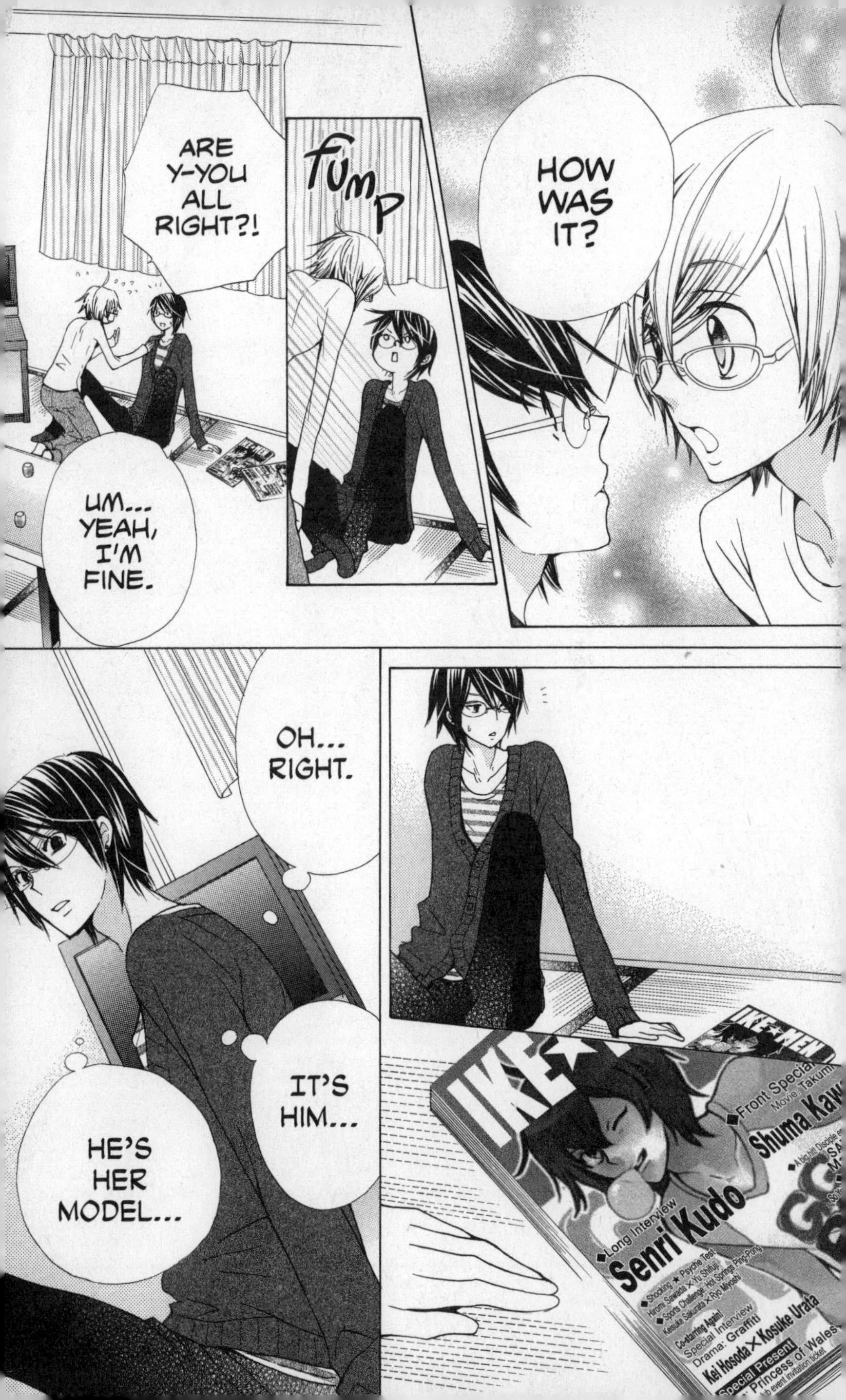
HOW WAS IT?
FUMP
ARE Y-YOU ALL RIGHT?!
UM... YEAH, I'M FINE.
IKE★MEN
Front Special
Long Interview
Senri Kudo
Drama: Graffiti
Kei Hosoda × Kosuke Urata
Special Present
OH... RIGHT.
IT'S HIM...
HE'S HER MODEL...

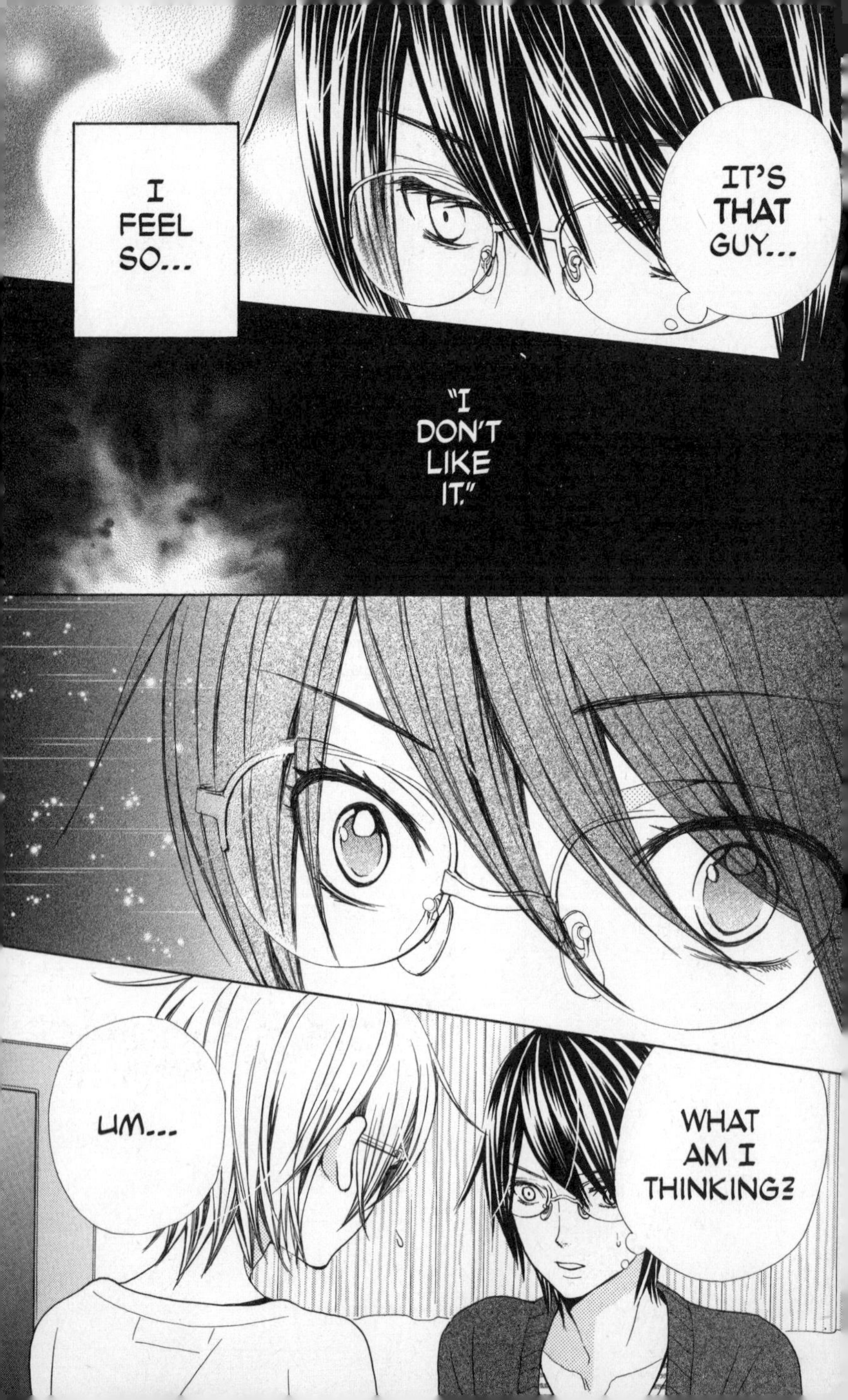
IT'S THAT GUY...
I FEEL SO...
"I DON'T LIKE IT."
WHAT AM I THINKING?
UM...

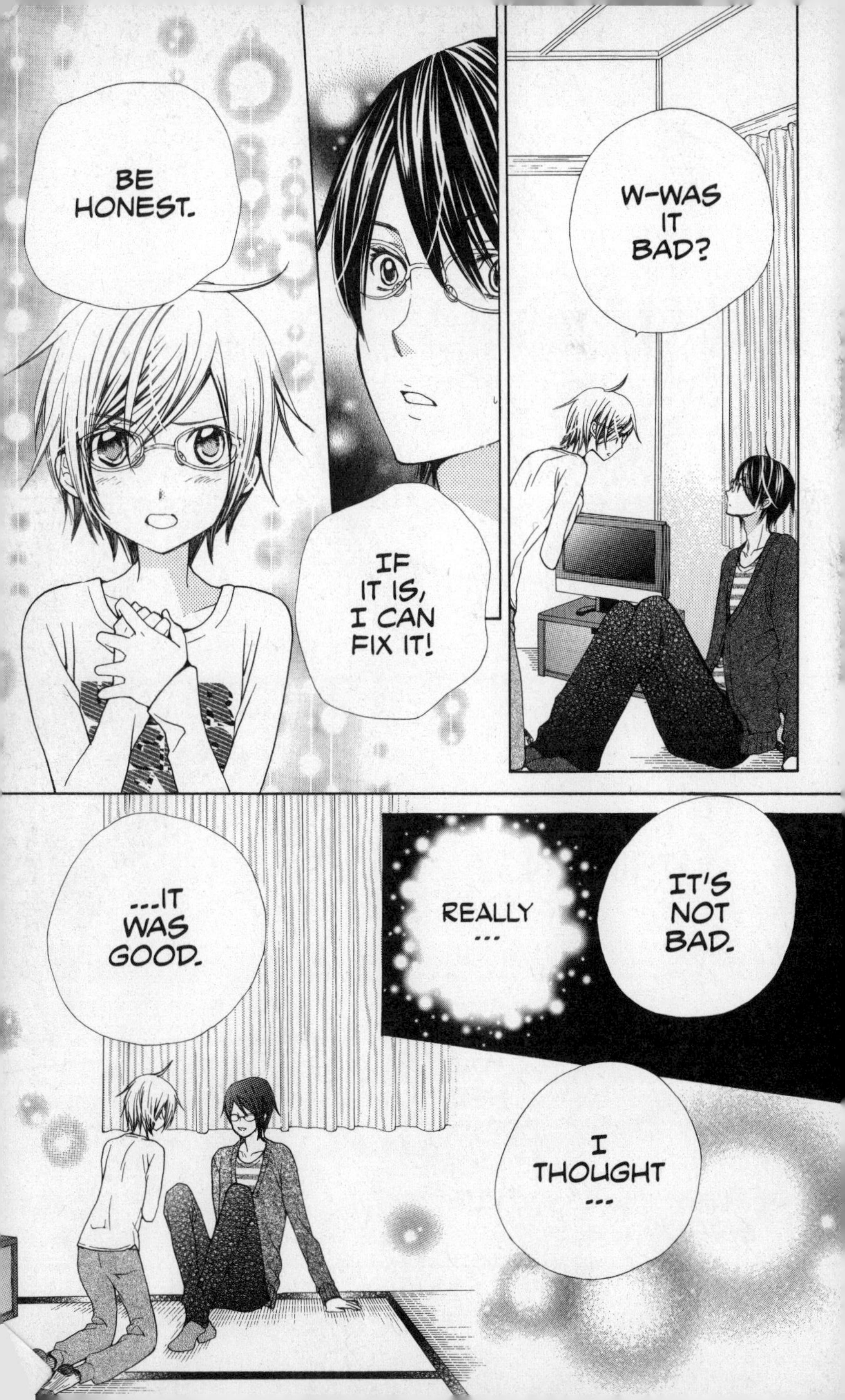
W-WAS IT BAD?
IF IT IS, I CAN FIX IT!
BE HONEST.
IT'S NOT BAD.
REALLY...
I THOUGHT...
...IT WAS GOOD.

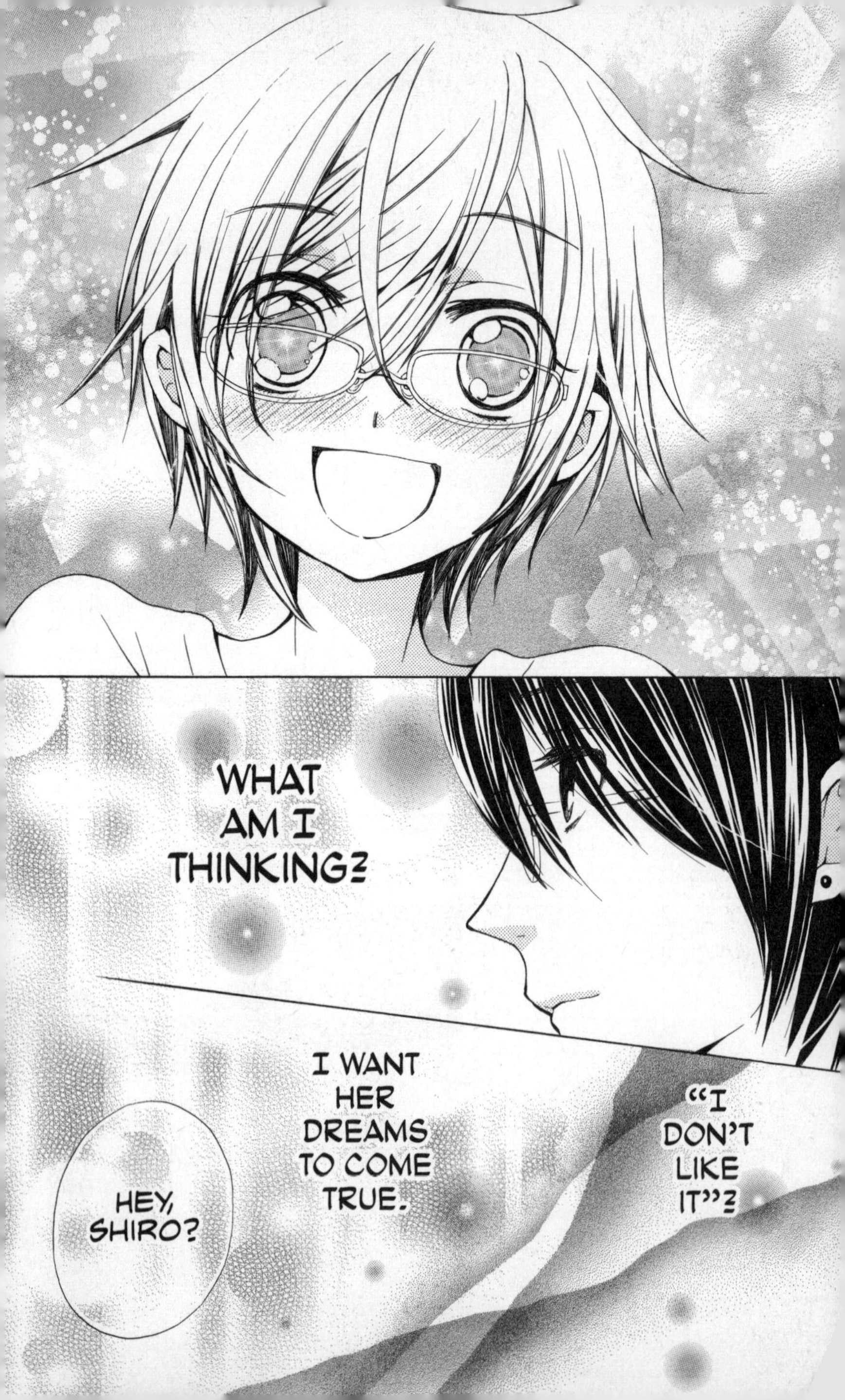
WHAT AM I THINKING?
"I DON'T LIKE IT"?
I WANT HER DREAMS TO COME TRUE.
HEY, SHIRO?

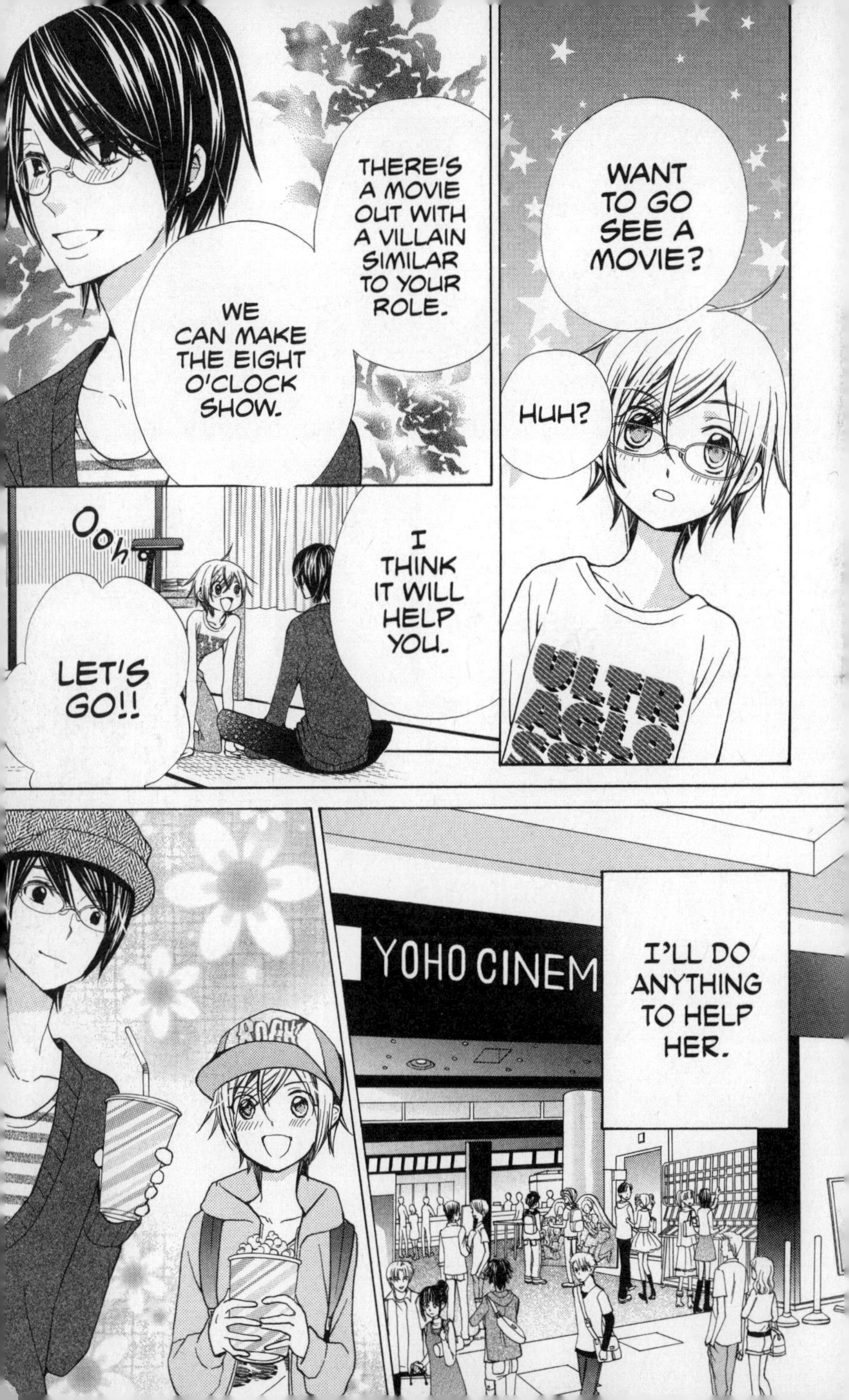
WANT TO GO SEE A MOVIE?
HUH?
THERE'S A MOVIE OUT WITH A VILLAIN SIMILAR TO YOUR ROLE.
WE CAN MAKE THE EIGHT O'CLOCK SHOW.
I THINK IT WILL HELP YOU.
Ooh
LET'S GO!!
YOHO CINEM
I'LL DO ANYTHING TO HELP HER.

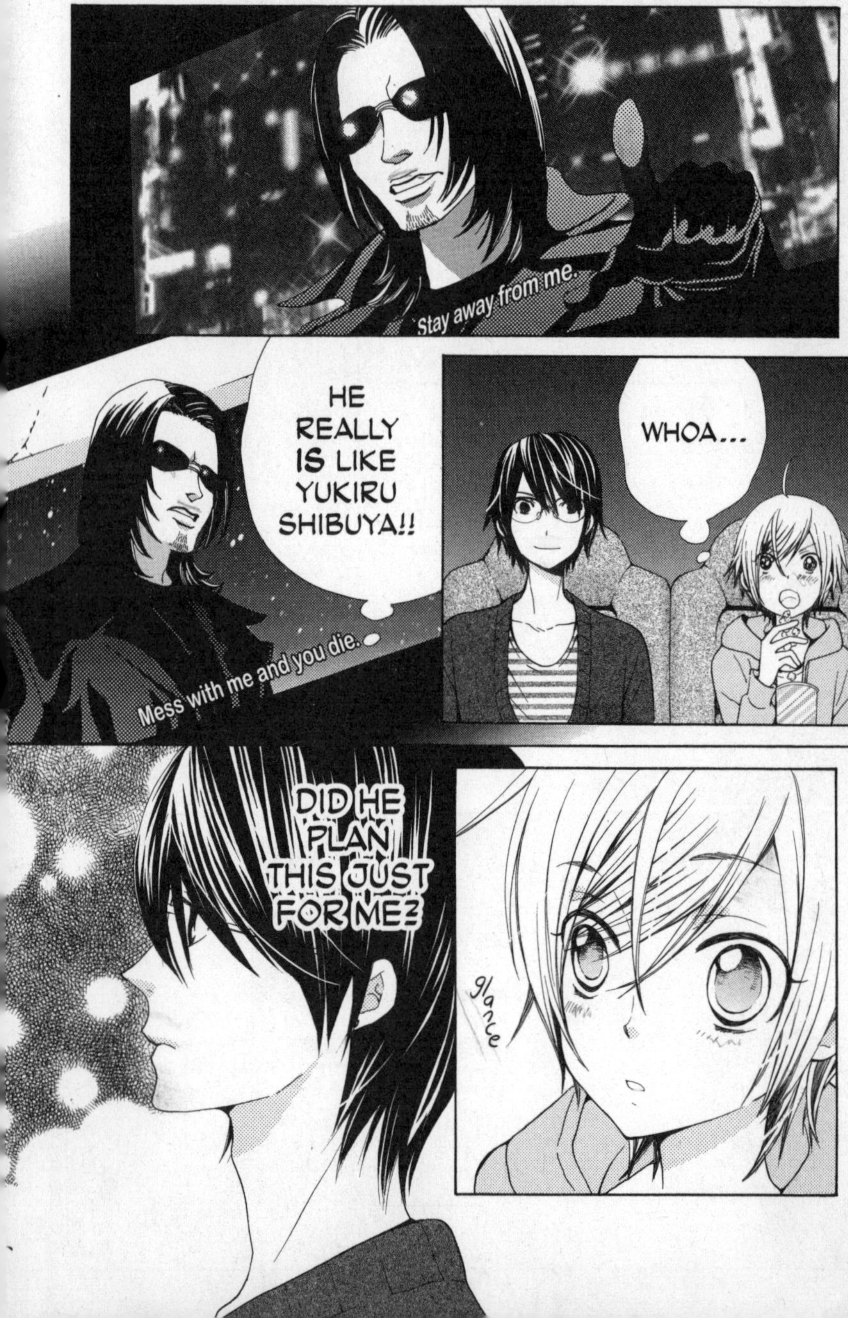
Stay away from me.
WHOA...
HE REALLY IS LIKE YUKIRU SHIBUYA!!
Mess with me and you die.
glance
DID HE PLAN THIS JUST FOR ME?

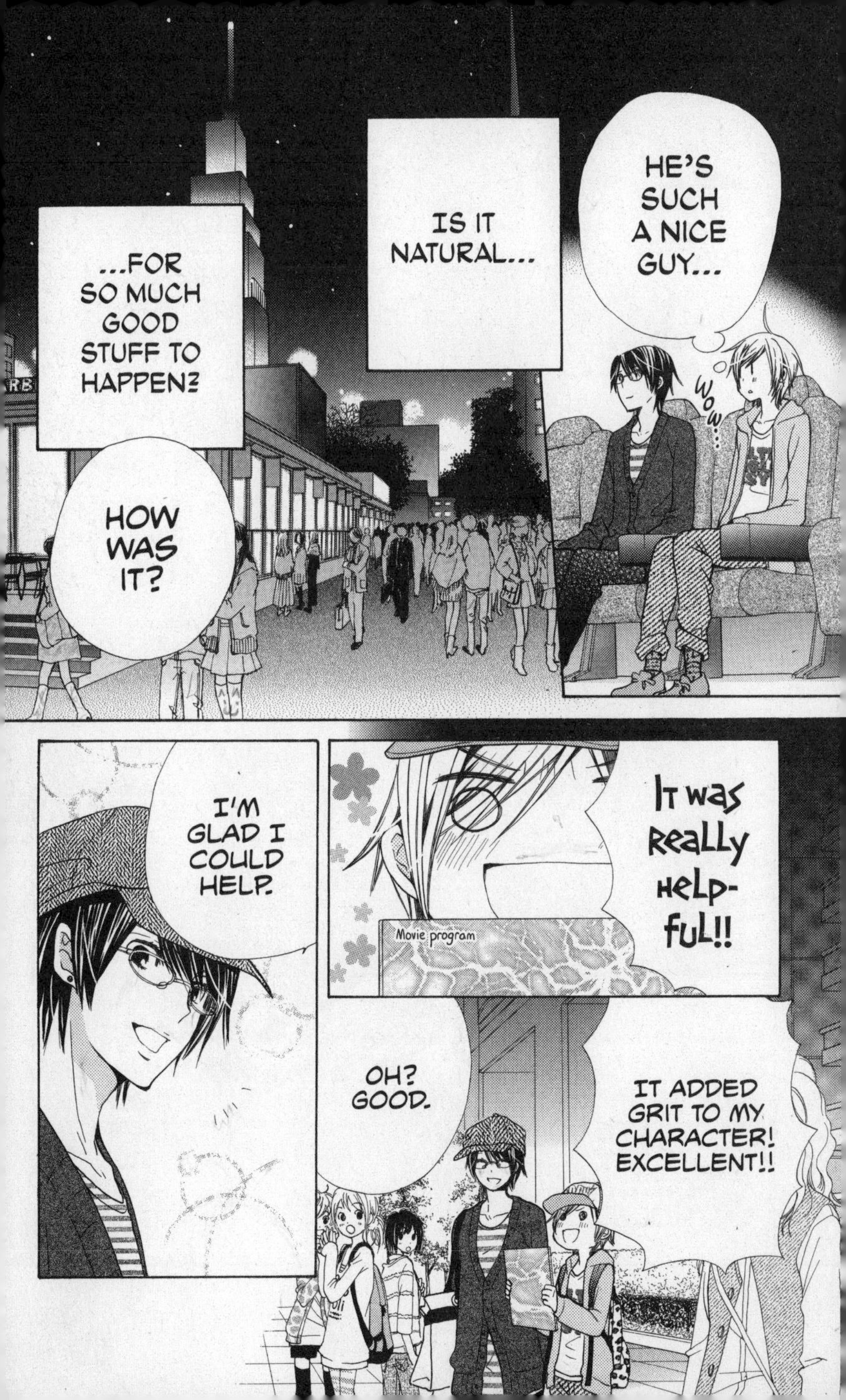
HE'S SUCH A NICE GUY...
WOW...
IS IT NATURAL...
...FOR SO MUCH GOOD STUFF TO HAPPEN?
HOW WAS IT?
It was really help-ful!!
Movie program
I'M GLAD I COULD HELP.
IT ADDED GRIT TO MY CHARACTER! EXCELLENT!!
OH? GOOD.

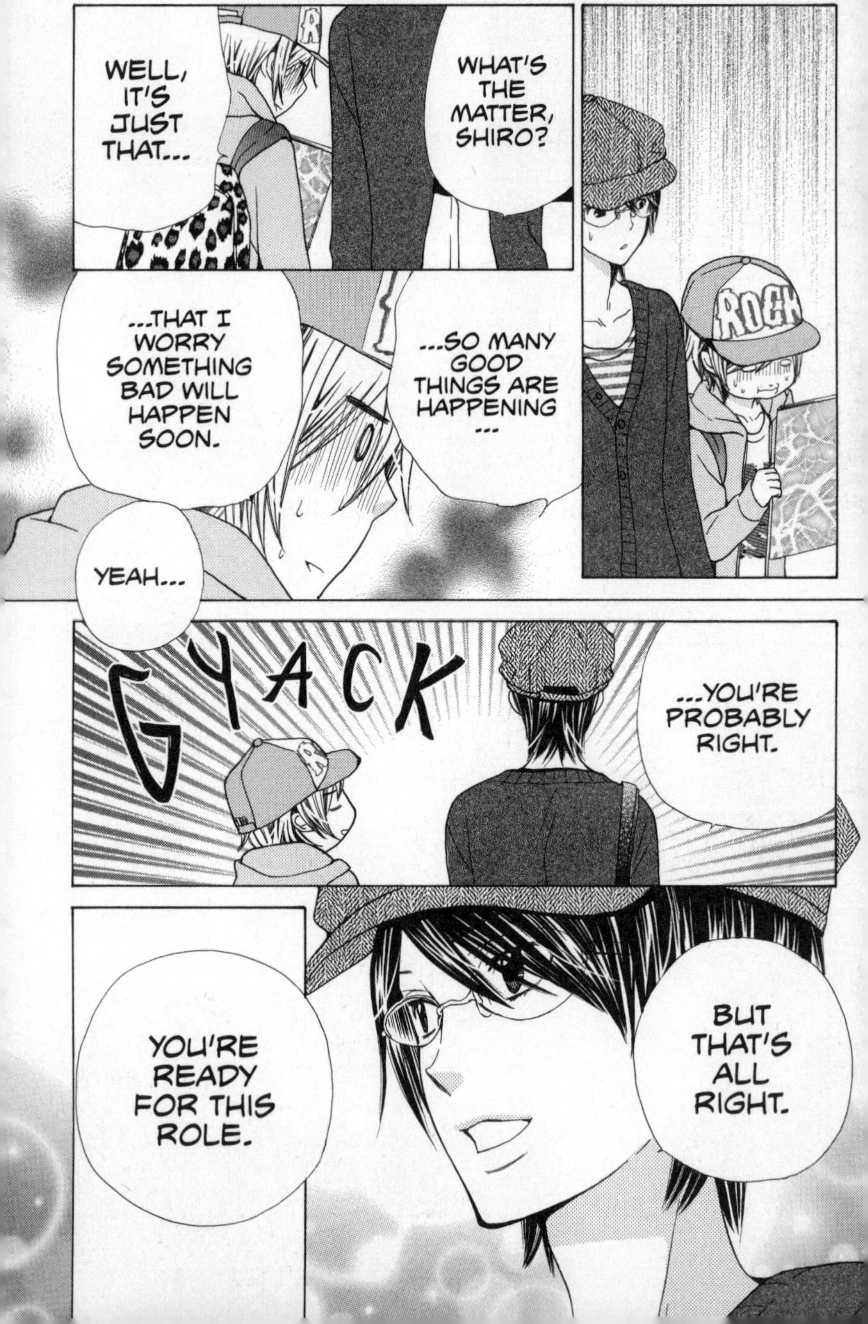
WHAT'S THE MATTER, SHIRO?
WELL, IT'S JUST THAT...
...SO MANY GOOD THINGS ARE HAPPENING...
...THAT I WORRY SOMETHING BAD WILL HAPPEN SOON.
YEAH...
...YOU'RE PROBABLY RIGHT.
GYACK
BUT THAT'S ALL RIGHT.
YOU'RE READY FOR THIS ROLE.

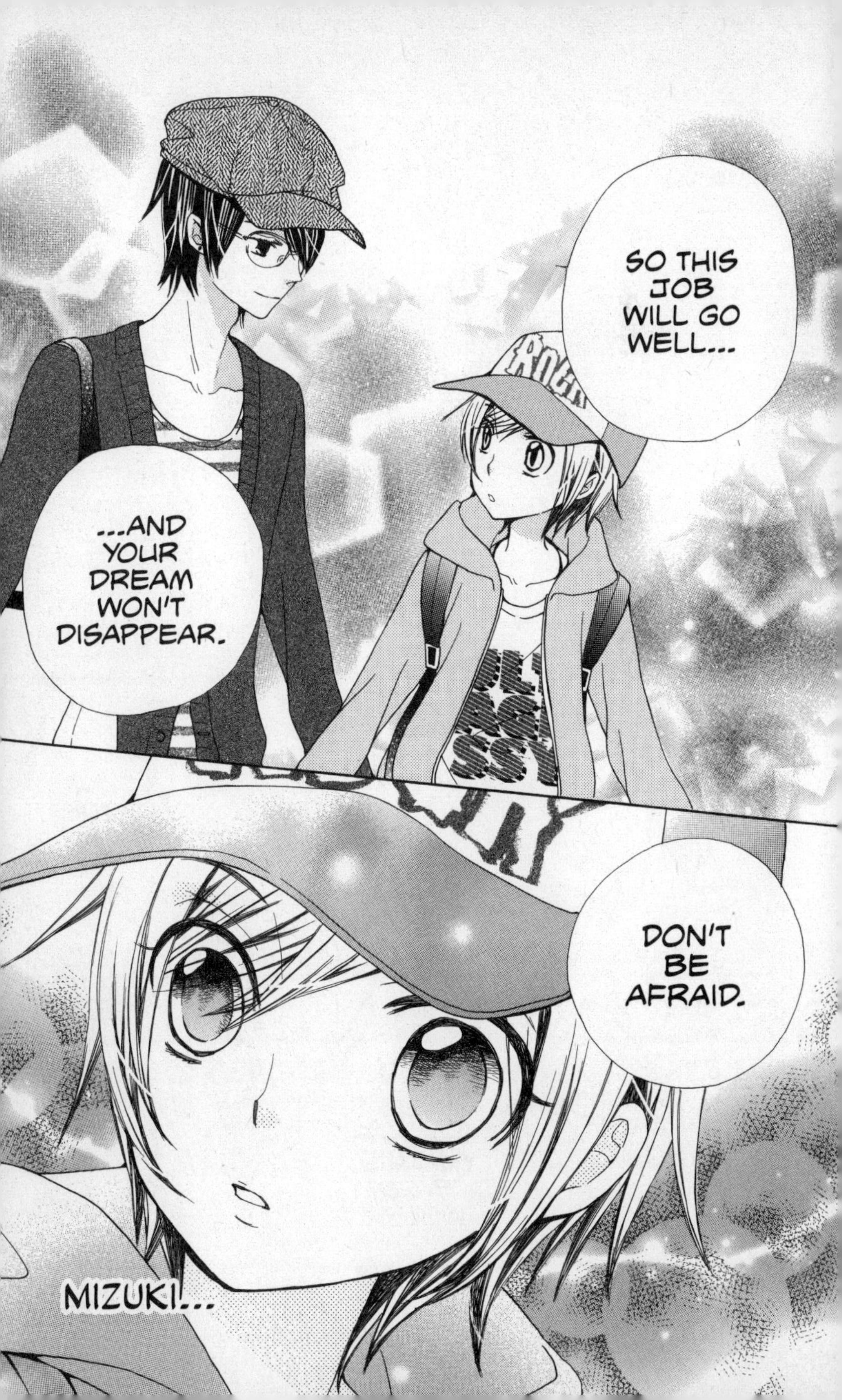
SO THIS JOB WILL GO WELL...
...AND YOUR DREAM WON'T DISAPPEAR.
DON'T BE AFRAID.
MIZUKI...

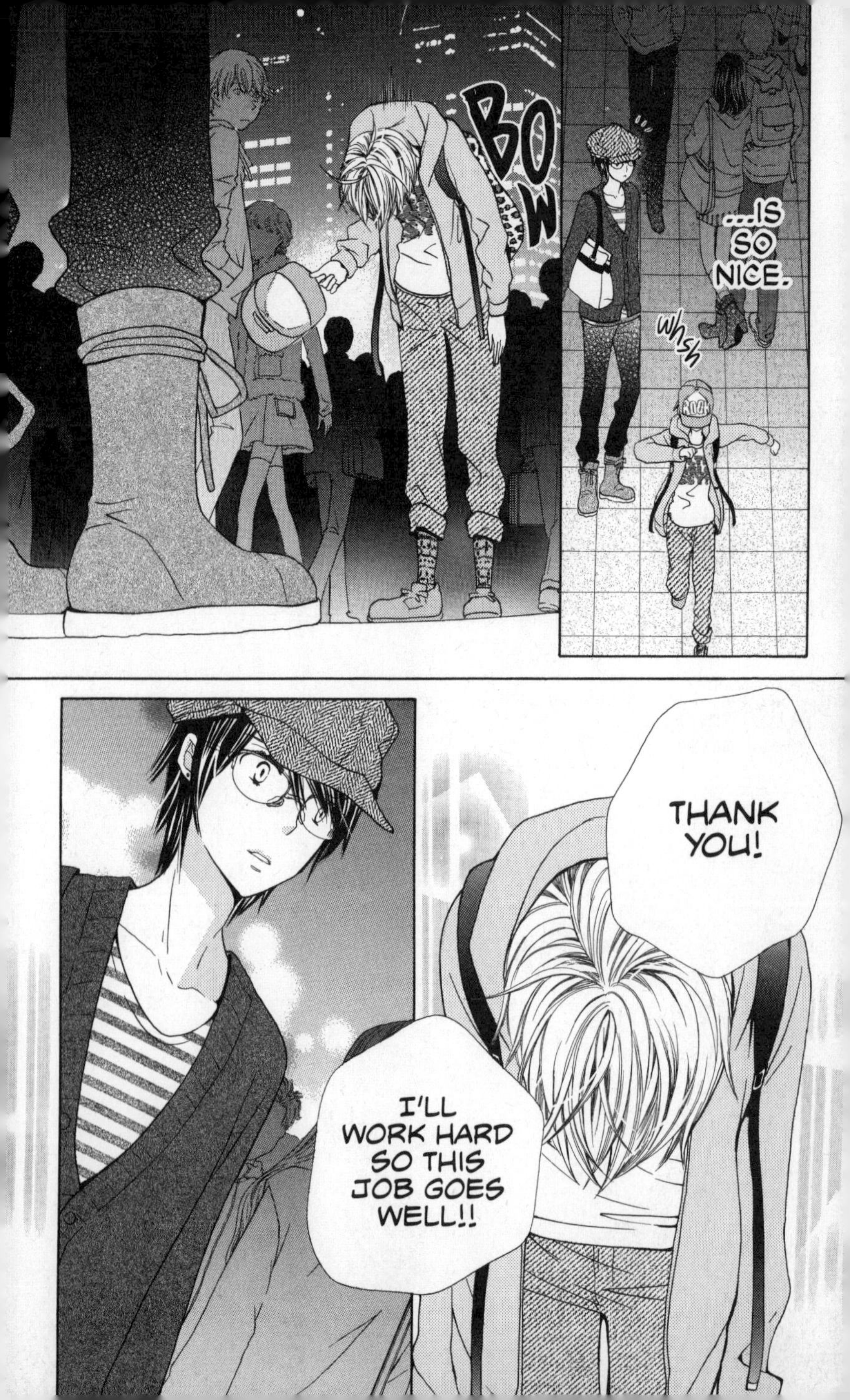
...IS SO NICE.
whsh
BOW
THANK YOU!
I'LL WORK HARD SO THIS JOB GOES WELL!!

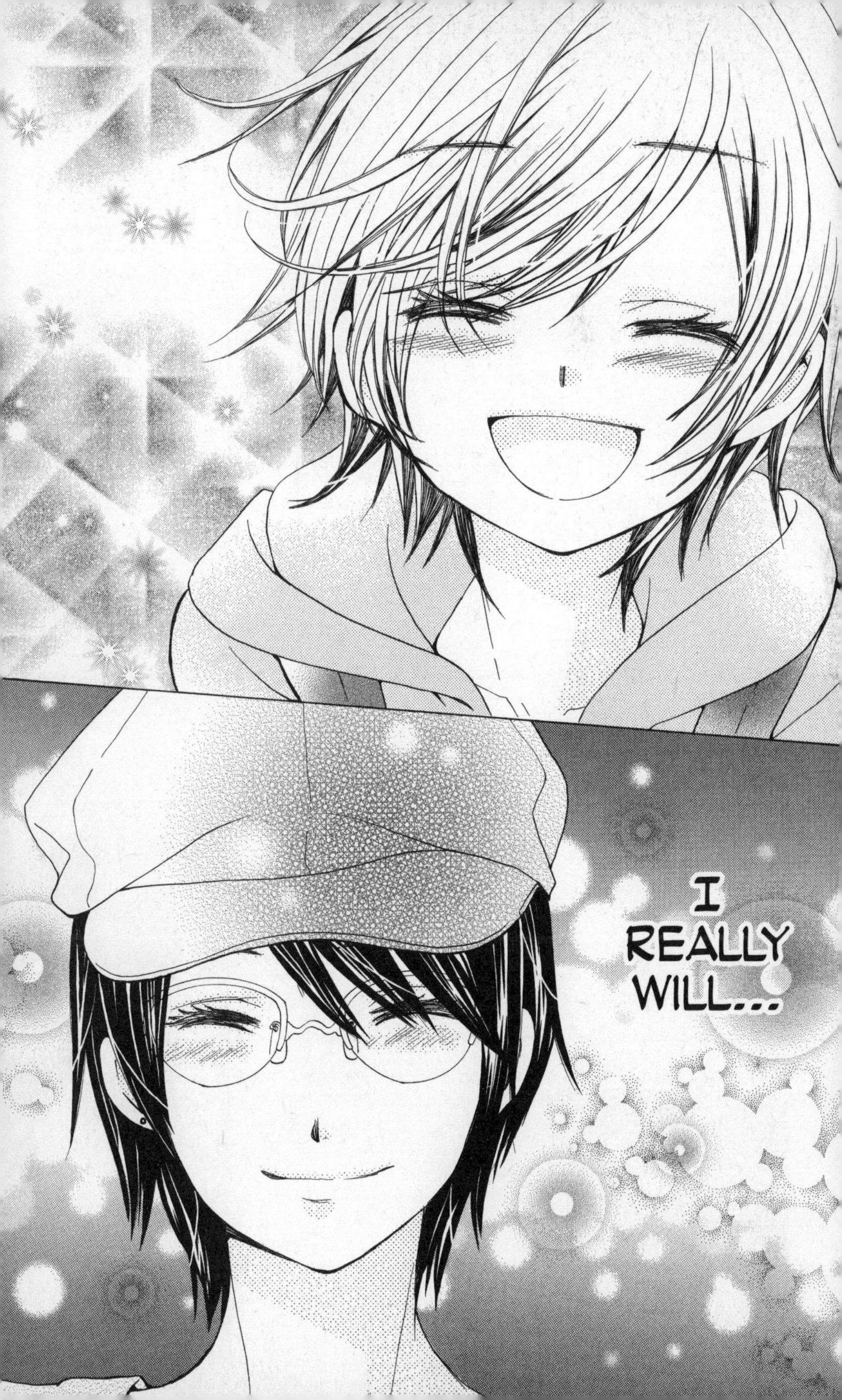
I REALLY WILL...

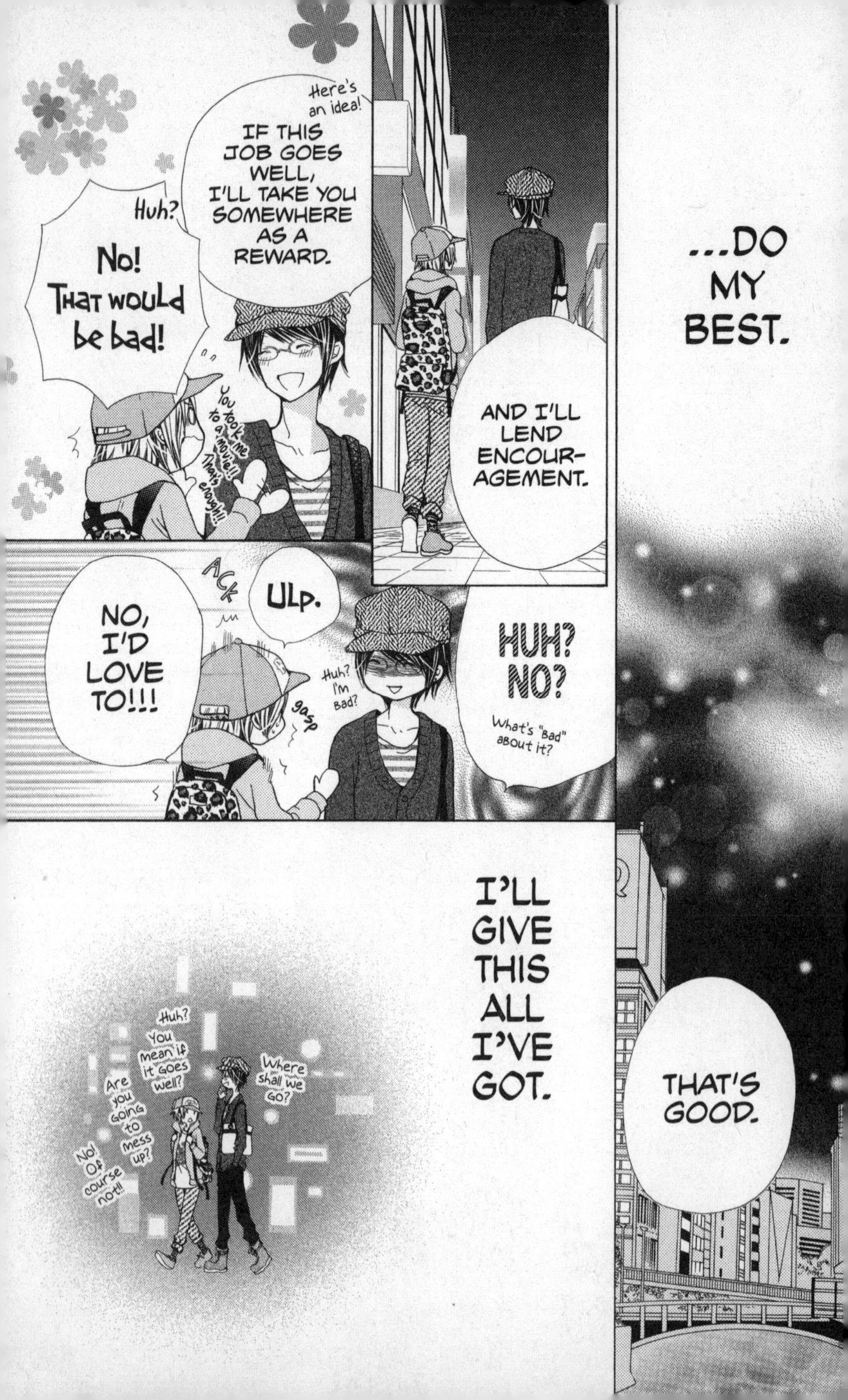
...DO MY BEST.
THAT'S GOOD.
AND I'LL LEND ENCOURAGEMENT.
Here's an idea!
IF THIS JOB GOES WELL, I'LL TAKE YOU SOMEWHERE AS A REWARD.
Huh?
No! That would be bad!
You took me to a movie!! That's enough!!
HUH? NO?
What's "Bad" about it?
Huh? I'm Bad?
ULp.
ACK
gasp
NO, I'D LOVE TO!!!
I'LL GIVE THIS ALL I'VE GOT.
Where shall we go?
Huh? You mean if it goes well?
Are you going to mess up?
No! Of course not!!

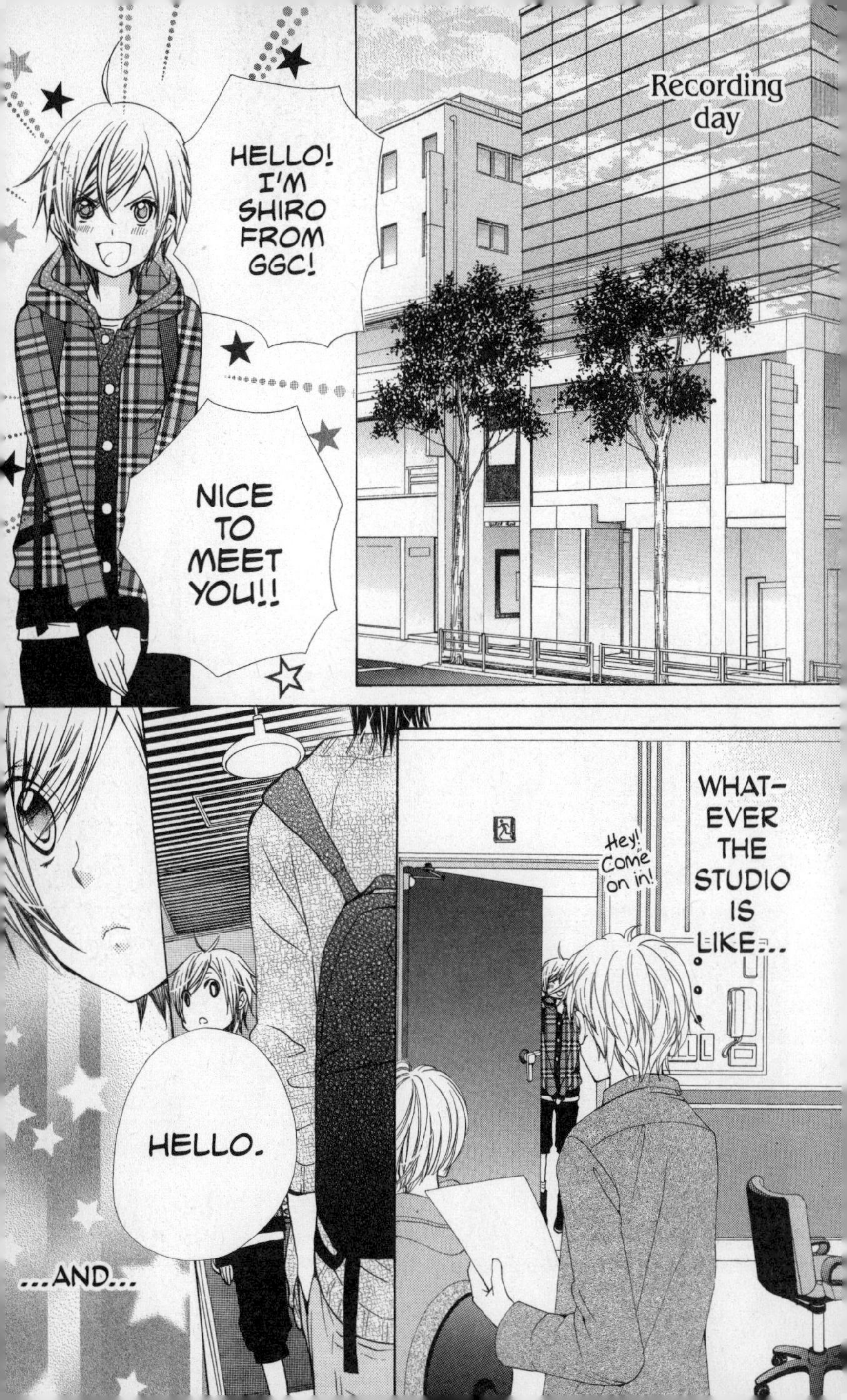
Recording day
HELLO! I'M SHIRO FROM GGC!
NICE TO MEET YOU!!
WHAT-EVER THE STUDIO IS LIKE...
Hey! Come on in!
HELLO.
...AND...

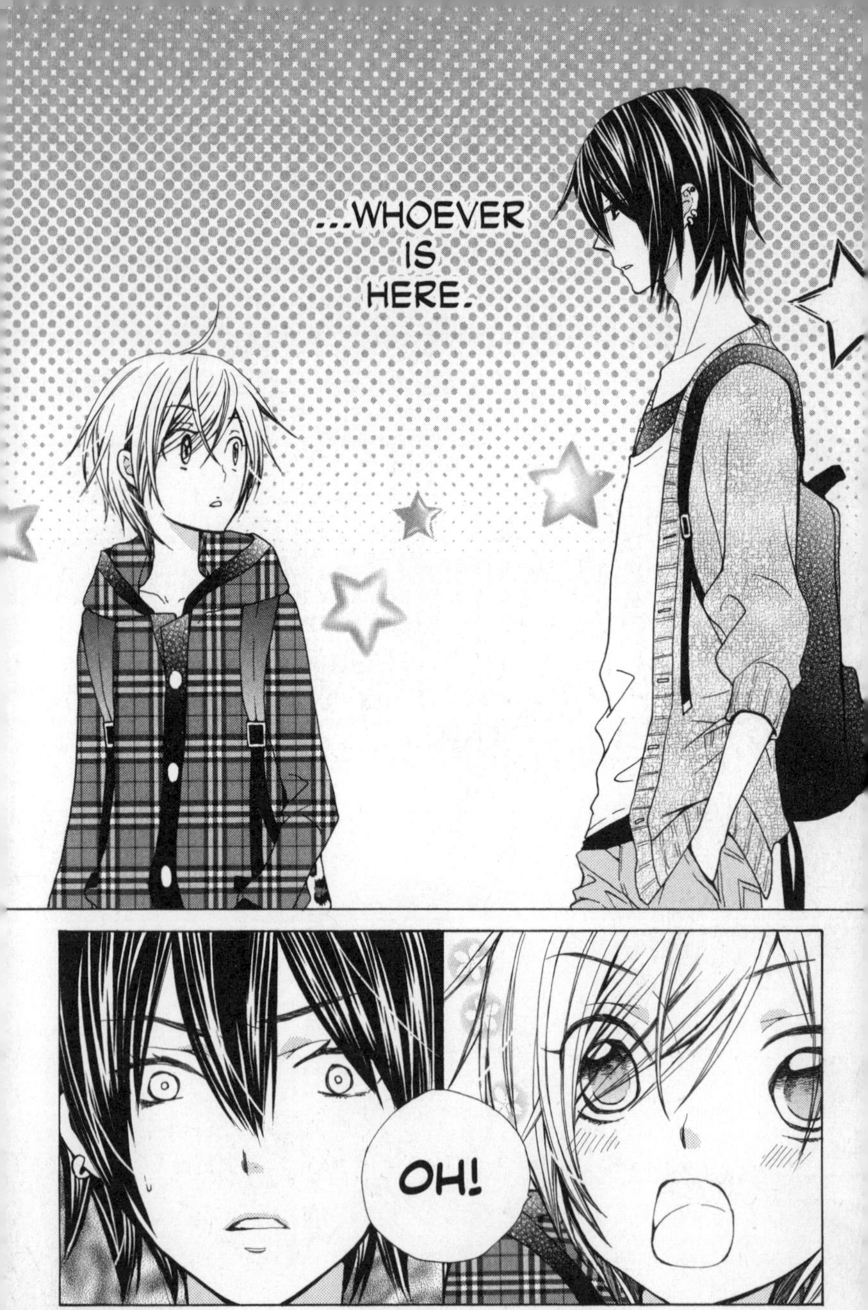
...WHOEVER IS HERE.
OH!

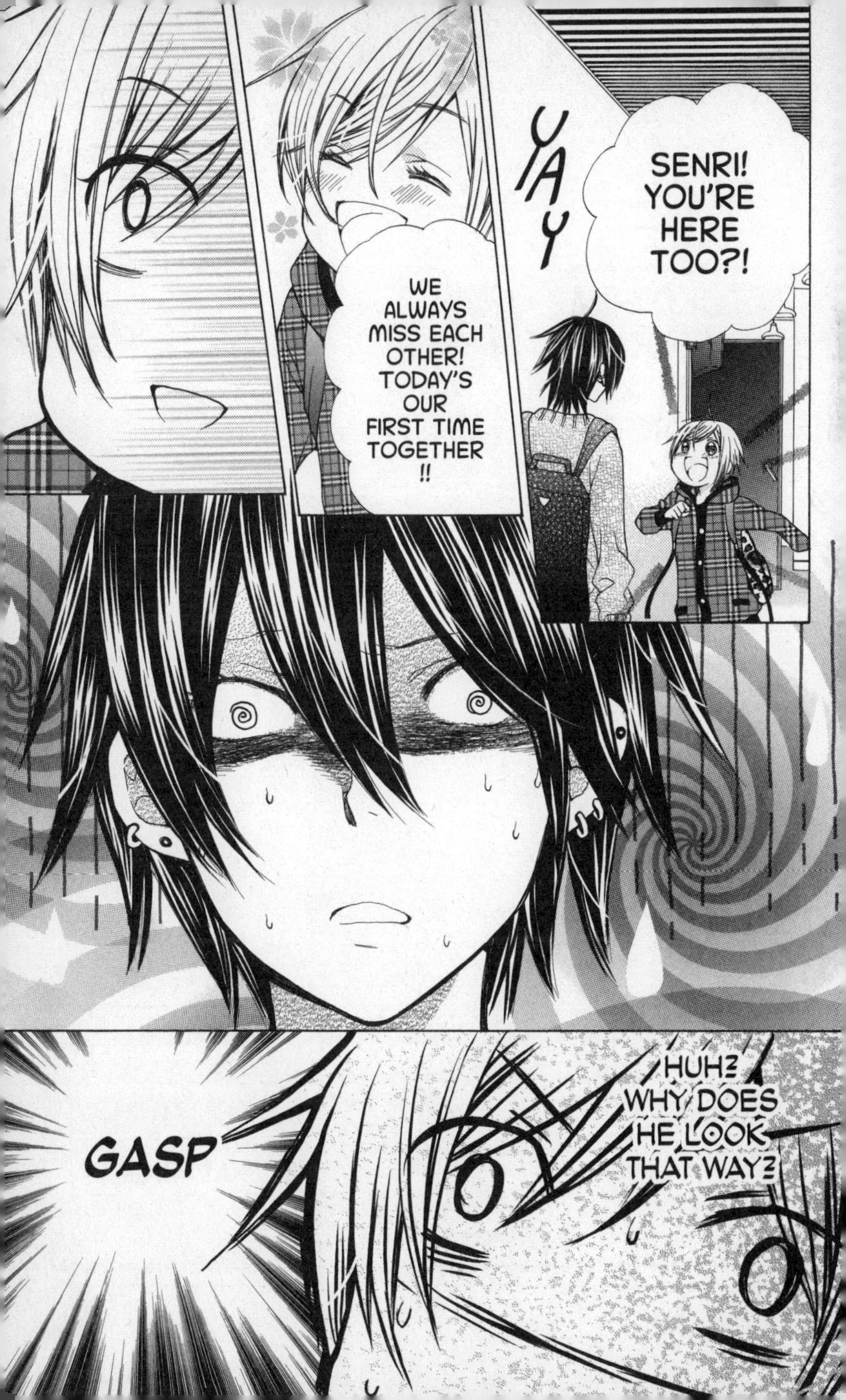
SENRI! YOU'RE HERE TOO?!
YAY
WE ALWAYS MISS EACH OTHER! TODAY'S OUR FIRST TIME TOGETHER !!
HUH? WHY DOES HE LOOK THAT WAY?
GASP

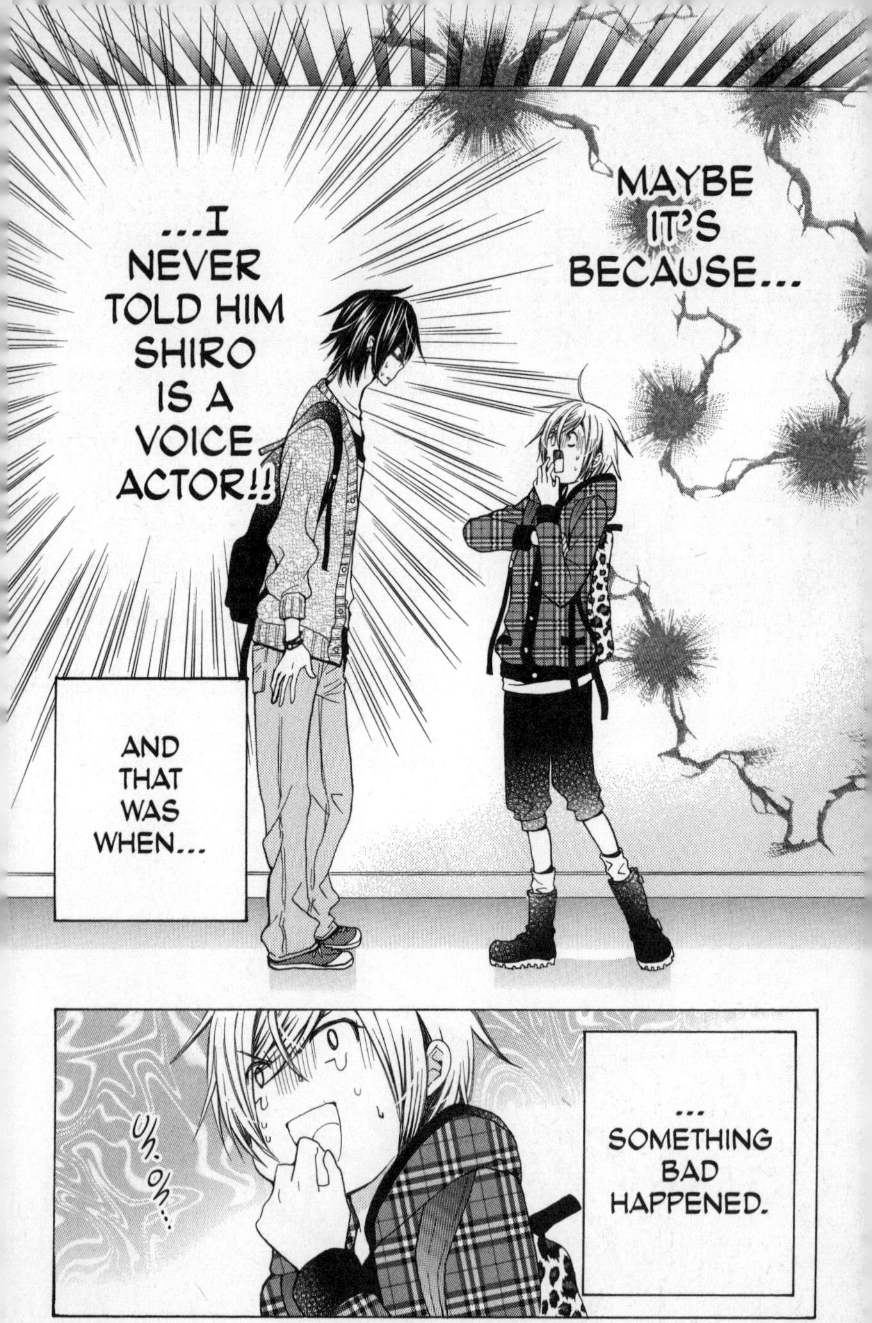
MAYBE IT'S BECAUSE...
...I NEVER TOLD HIM SHIRO IS A VOICE ACTOR!!
AND THAT WAS WHEN...
... SOMETHING BAD HAPPENED.
uh-oh...

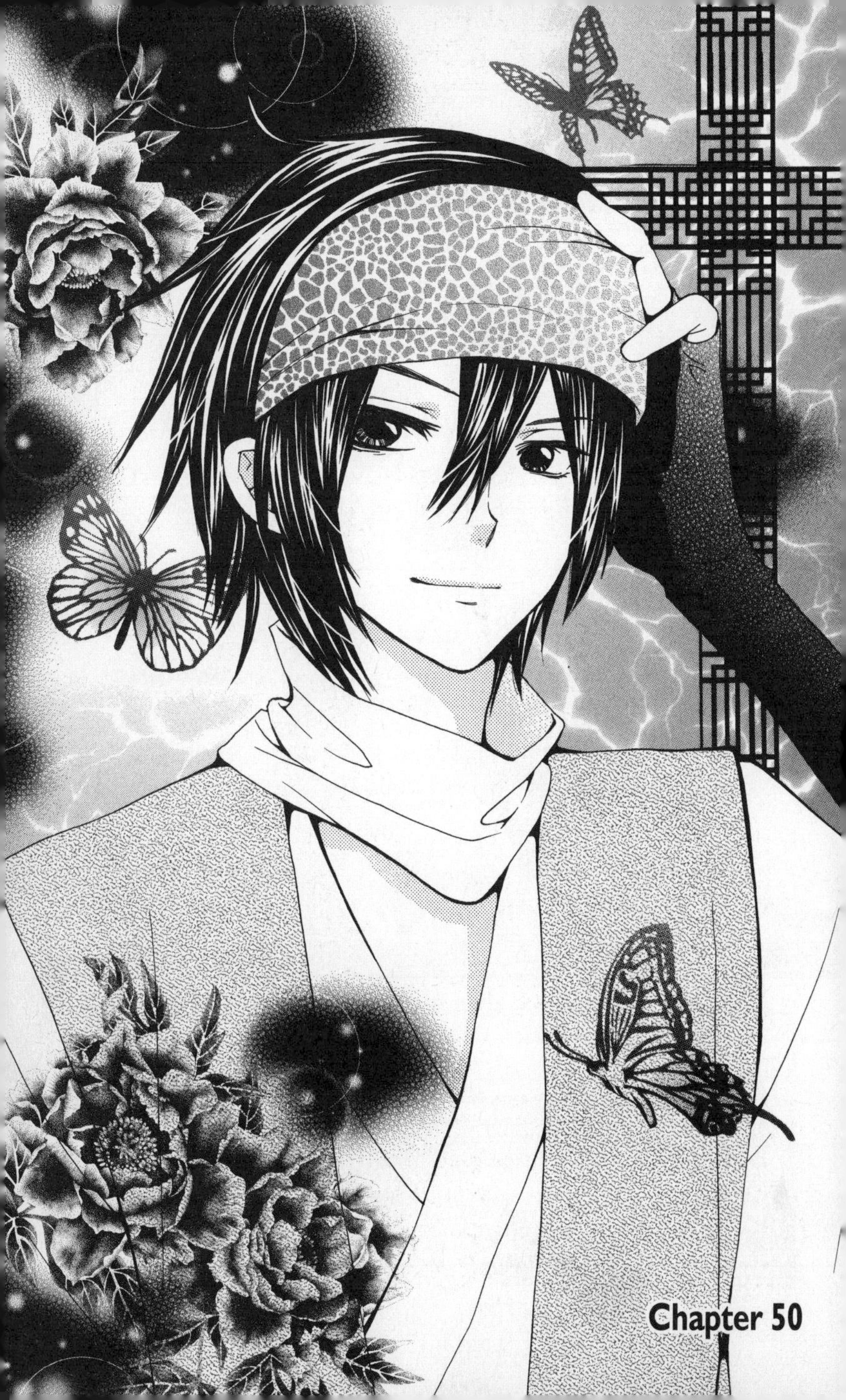
Chapter 50

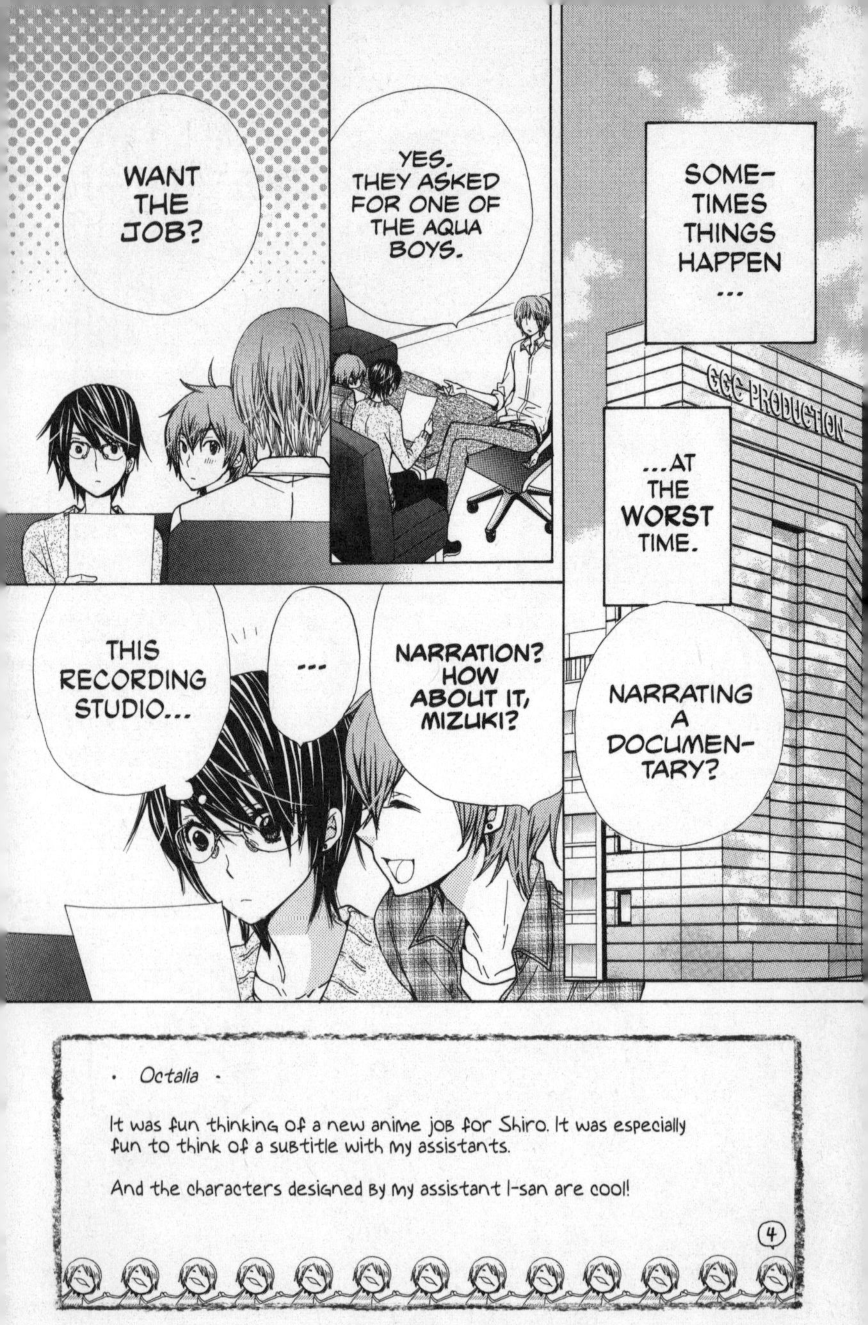
SOME-TIMES THINGS HAPPEN...
...AT THE WORST TIME.
NARRATING A DOCUMENTARY?
YES. THEY ASKED FOR ONE OF THE AQUA BOYS.
WANT THE JOB?
GGC PRODUCTION
NARRATION? HOW ABOUT IT, MIZUKI?
...
THIS RECORDING STUDIO...

· *Octalia* ·

It was fun thinking of a new anime job for Shiro. It was especially fun to think of a subtitle with my assistants.

And the characters designed by my assistant I-san are cool!

(4)

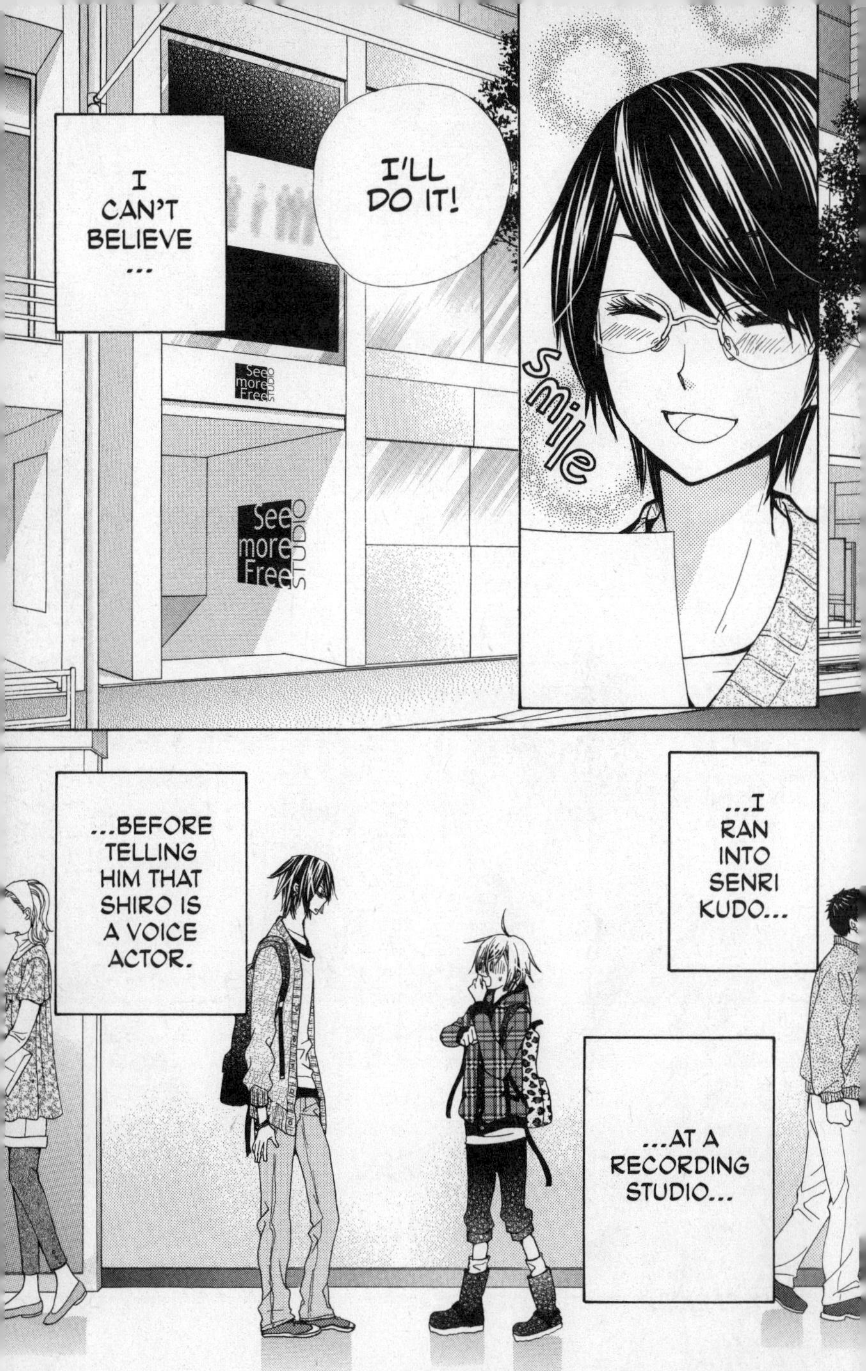
smile
I'LL DO IT!
I CAN'T BELIEVE ...
See more Free STUDIO
See more Free STUDIO
...I RAN INTO SENRI KUDO...
...AT A RECORDING STUDIO...
...BEFORE TELLING HIM THAT SHIRO IS A VOICE ACTOR.

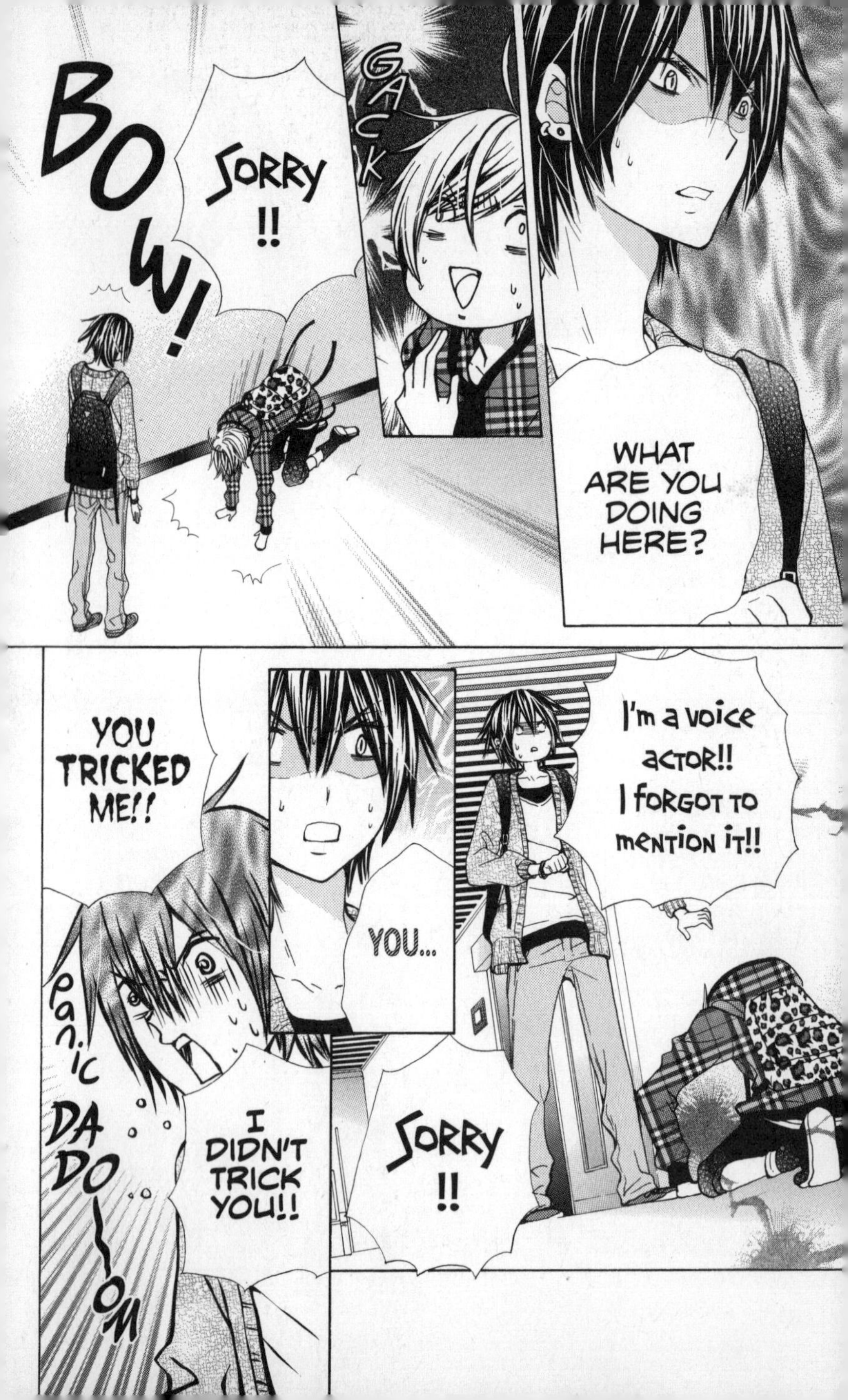
WHAT ARE YOU DOING HERE?
GACK
SORRY!!
BOW!
I'm a voice actor!! I forgot to mention it!!
SORRY!!
YOU...
YOU TRICKED ME!!
I DIDN'T TRICK YOU!!
Panic
DADO—OM

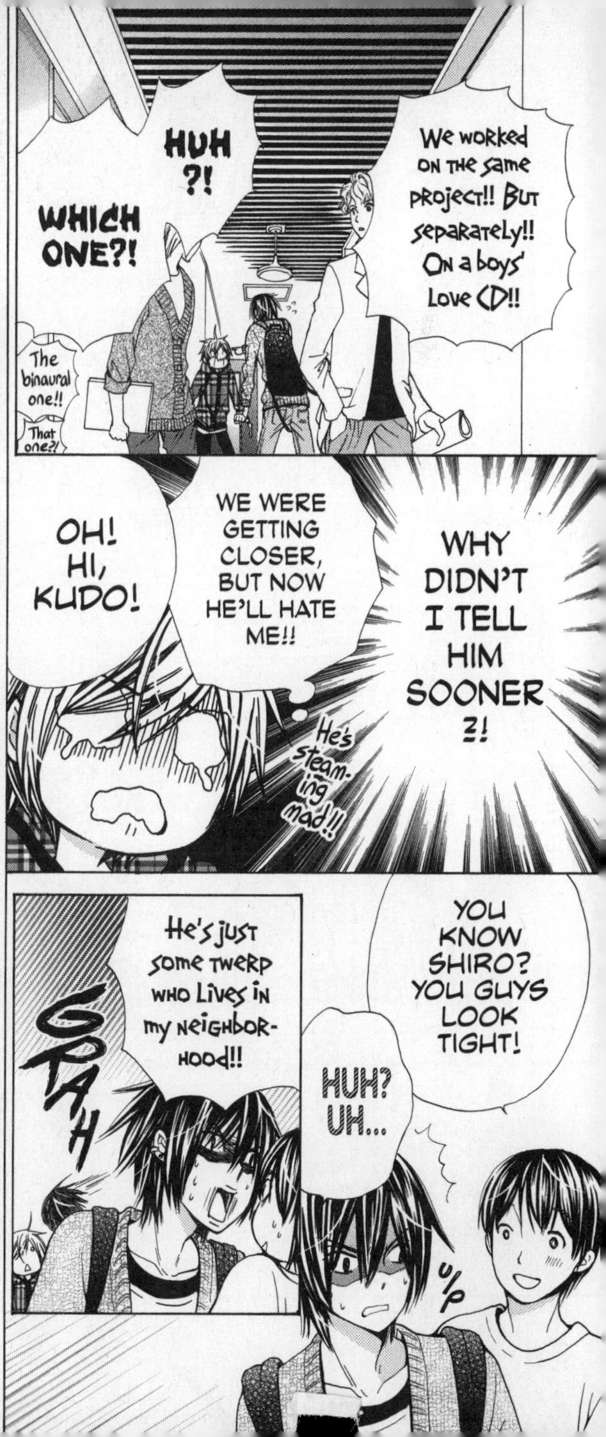
We worked on the same project!! But separately!! On a boys' Love CD!!
HUH ?!
WHICH ONE?!
The binaural one!!
That one?!
WHY DIDN'T I TELL HIM SOONER ?!
WE WERE GETTING CLOSER, BUT NOW HE'LL HATE ME!!
OH! HI, KUDO!
He's steaming mad!!
YOU KNOW SHIRO? YOU GUYS LOOK TIGHT!
HUH? UH...
He's just some twerp who lives in my neighborhood!!
GRAH

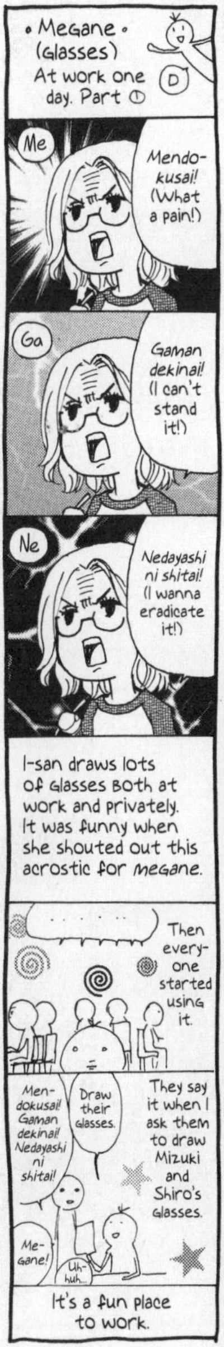
• Megane •
(Glasses)
At work one day. Part ①
D
Me
Mendokusai! (What a pain!)
Ga
Gaman dekinai! (I can't stand it!)
Ne
Nedayashi ni shitai! (I wanna eradicate it!)
I-san draws lots of glasses both at work and privately. It was funny when she shouted out this acrostic for megane.
. . . . . .
Then everyone started using it.
They say it when I ask them to draw Mizuki and Shiro's glasses.
Draw their glasses.
Mendokusai! Gaman dekinai! Nedayashi ni shitai!
Megane!
Uh-huh...
It's a fun place to work.

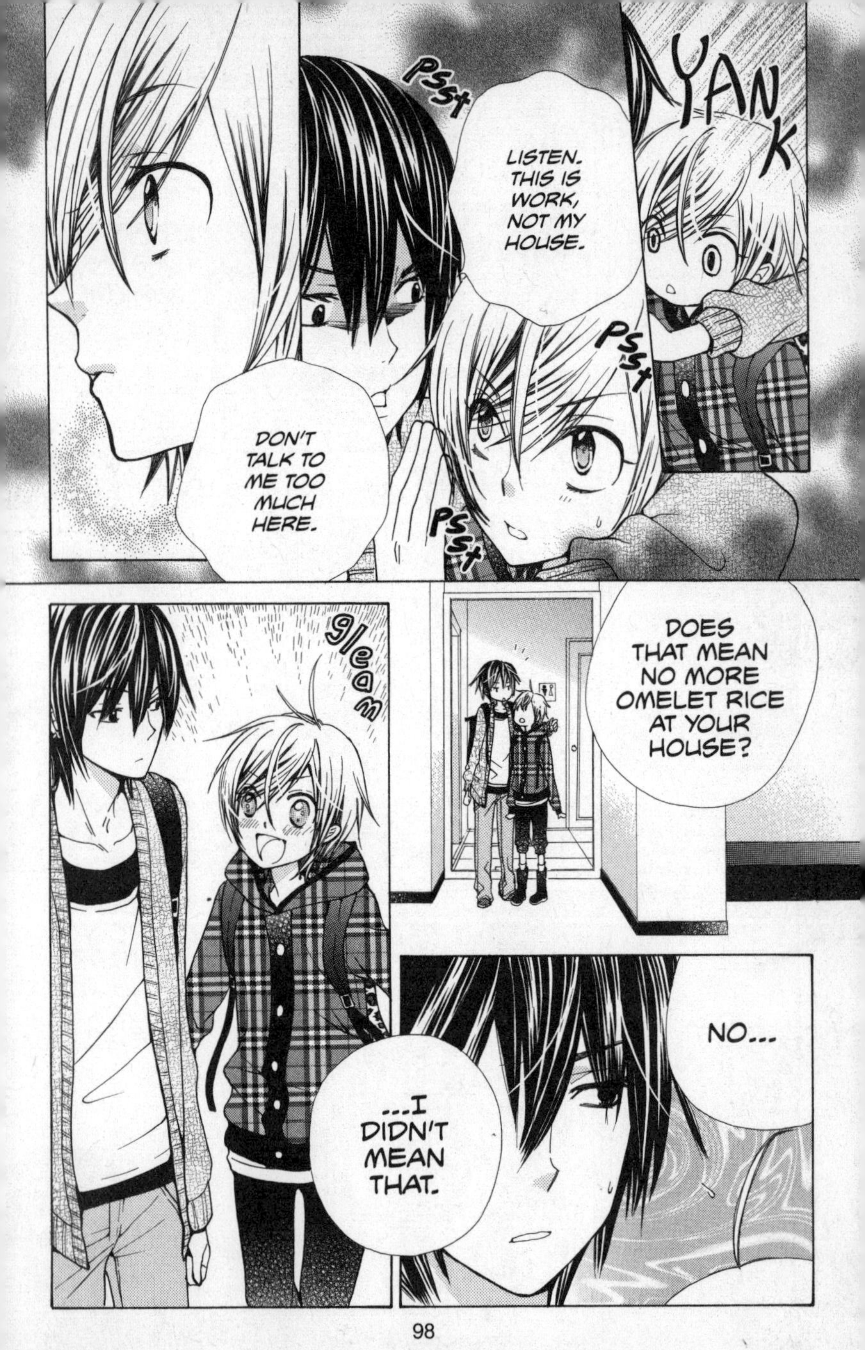
YANK
PSST
LISTEN. THIS IS WORK, NOT MY HOUSE.
PSST
DON'T TALK TO ME TOO MUCH HERE.
PSST
DOES THAT MEAN NO MORE OMELET RICE AT YOUR HOUSE?
NO...
...I DIDN'T MEAN THAT.
gleam

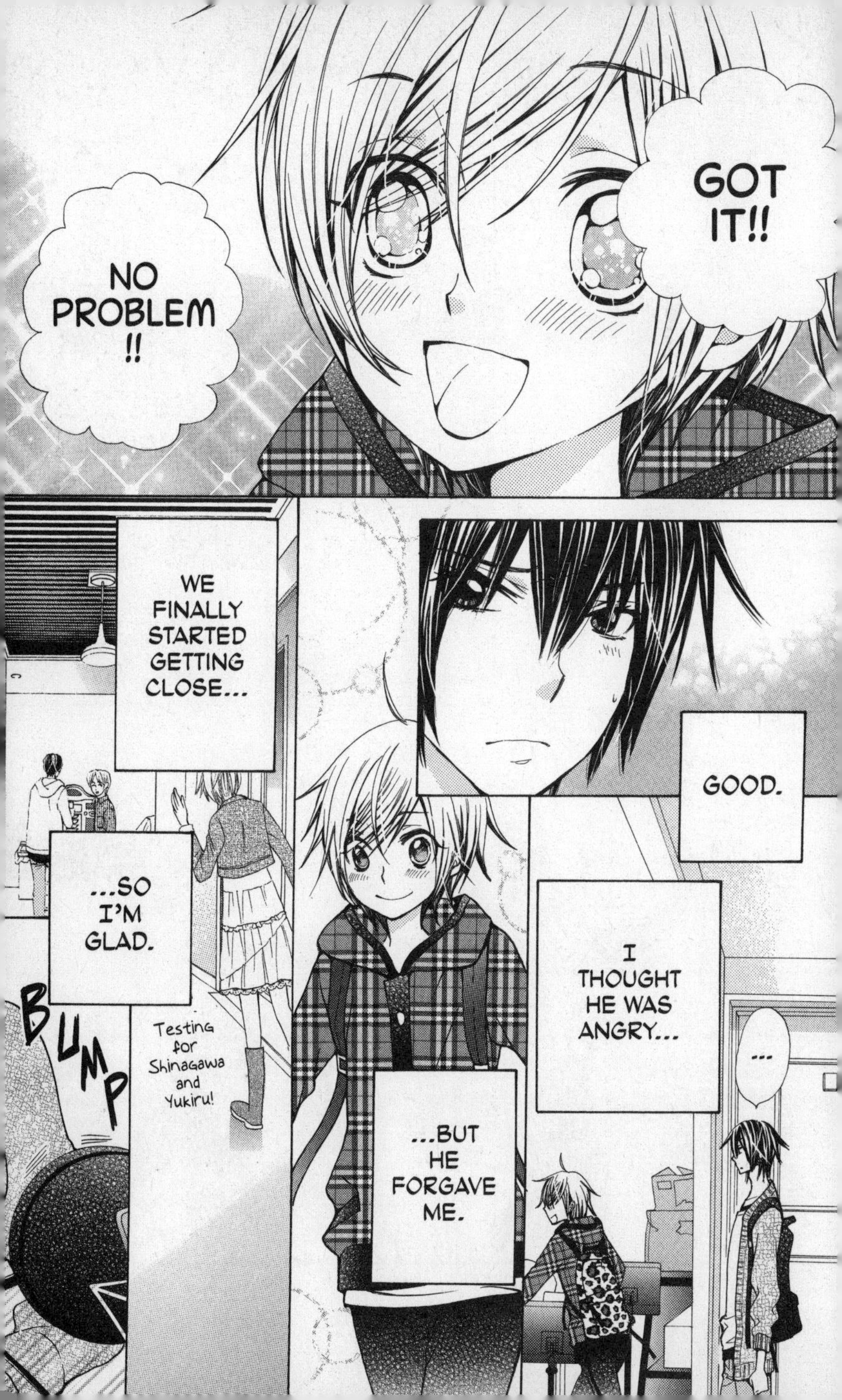
GOT IT!!
NO PROBLEM !!
GOOD.
I THOUGHT HE WAS ANGRY...
...
...BUT HE FORGAVE ME.
WE FINALLY STARTED GETTING CLOSE...
...SO I'M GLAD.
Testing for Shinagawa and Yukiru!
BUMP

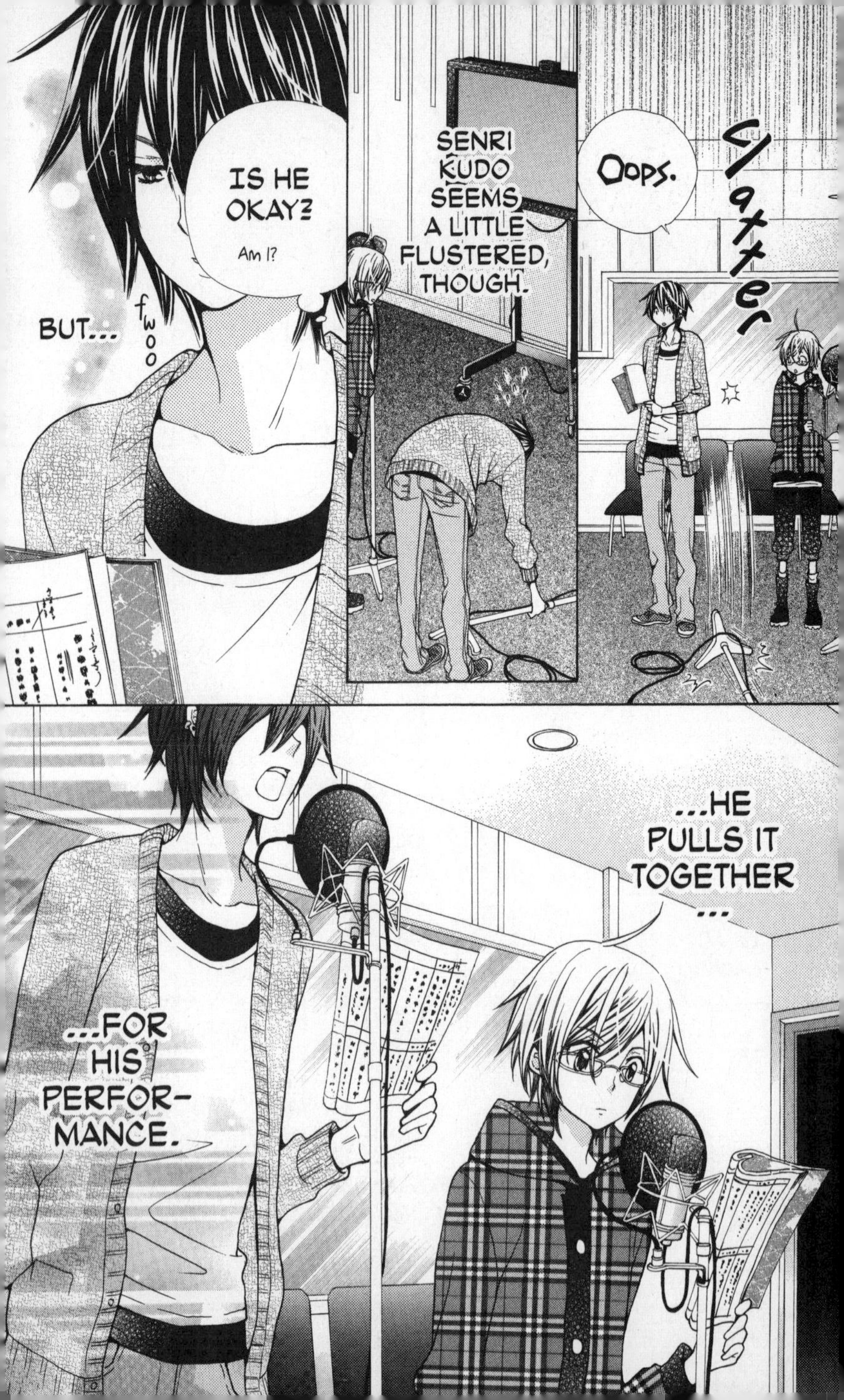
Oops.
Clatter
Senri Kudo seems a little flustered, though.
Is he okay?
Am I?
fwoo
But...
...He pulls it together...
...For his perfor-mance.

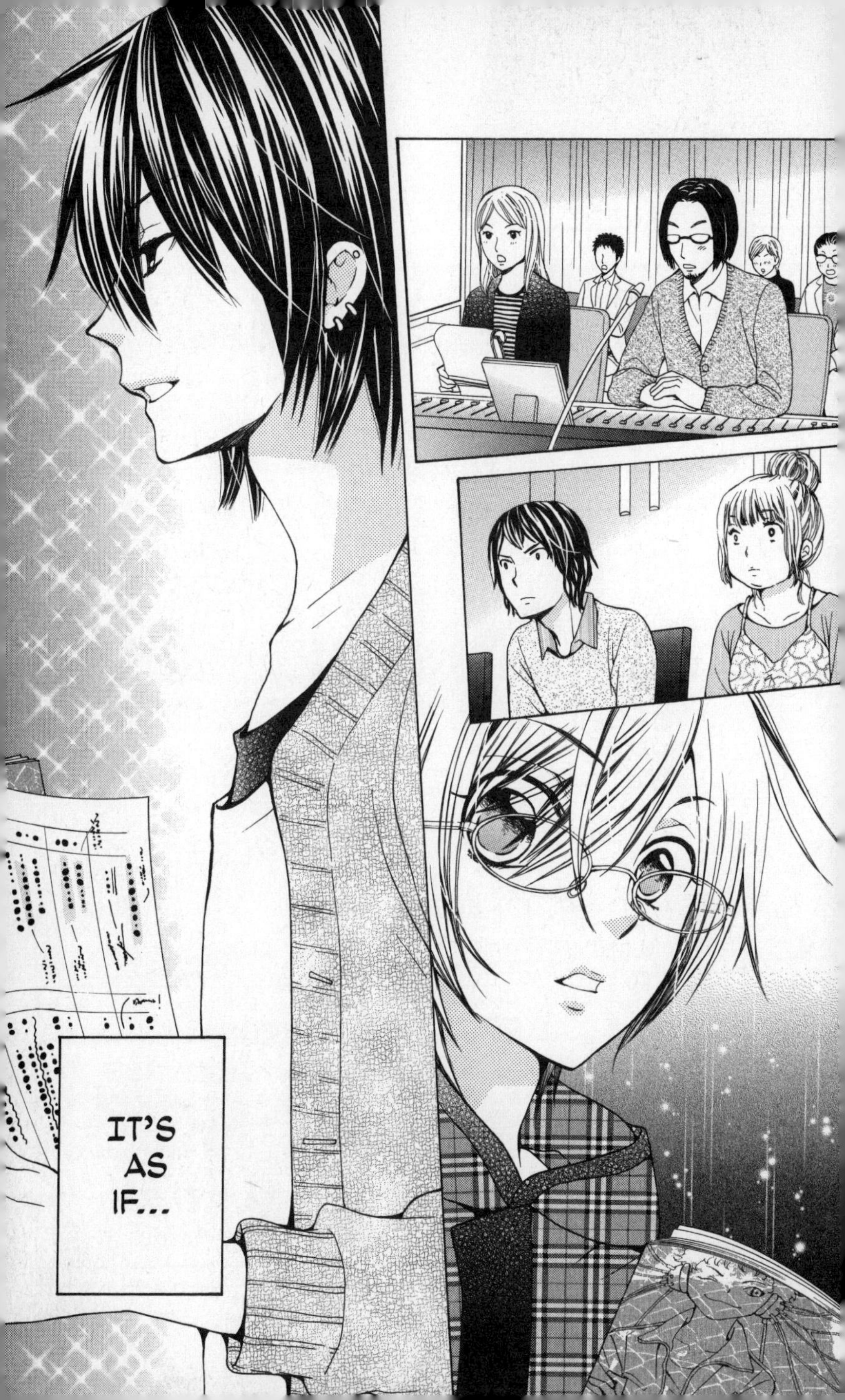
IT'S AS IF...

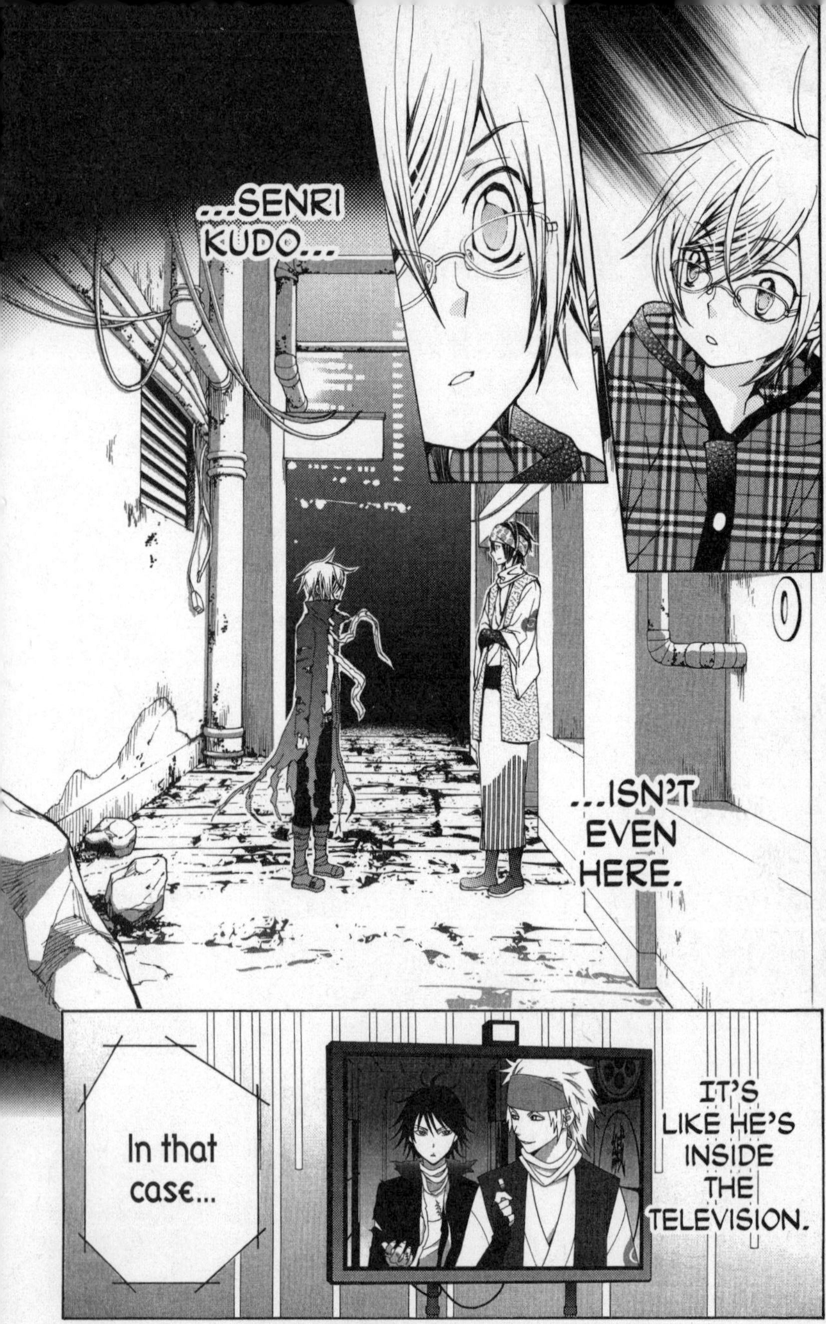
...SENRI KUDO...
...ISN'T EVEN HERE.
IT'S LIKE HE'S INSIDE THE TELEVISION.
In that case...

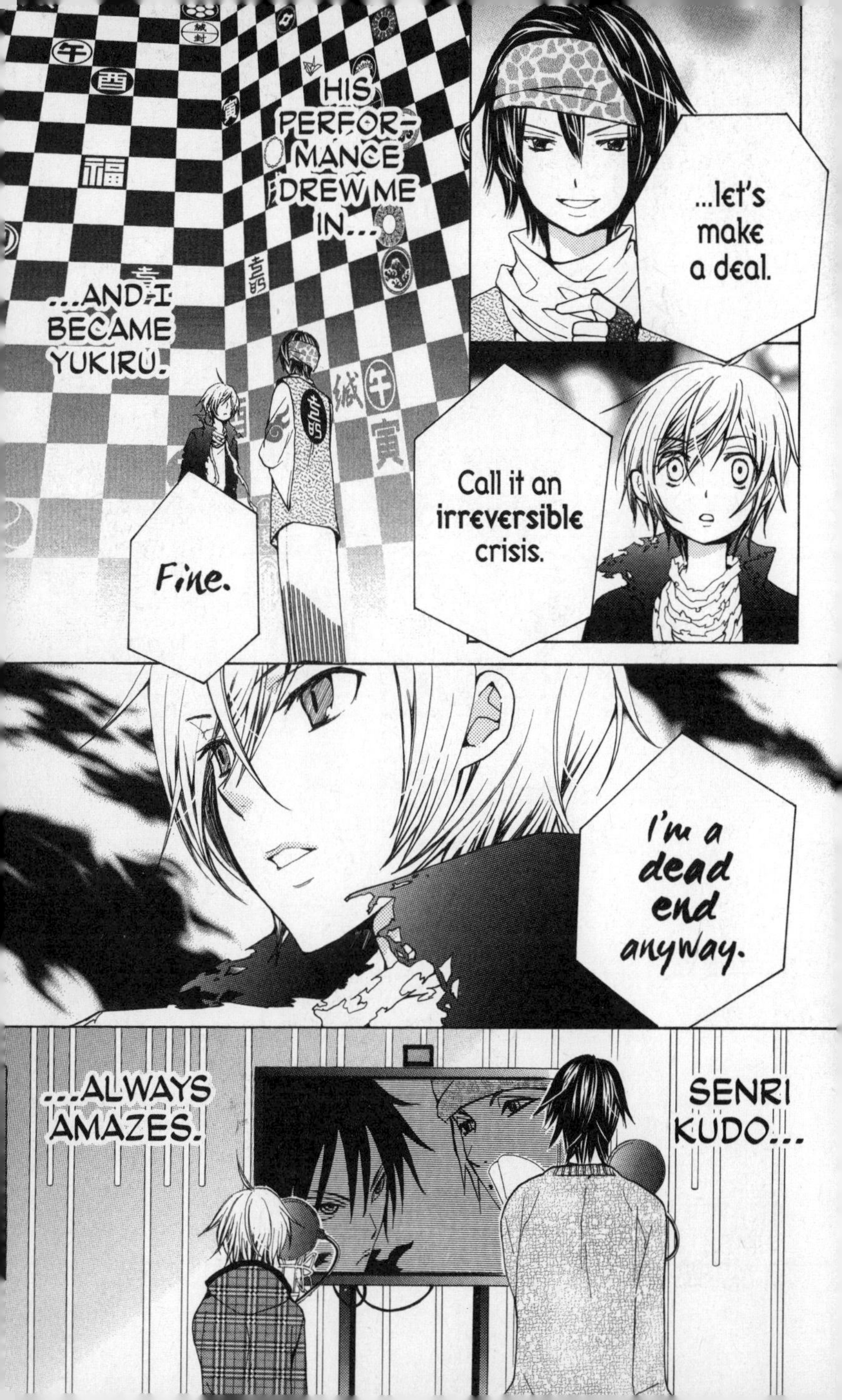
...let's make a deal.
Call it an irreversible crisis.
HIS PERFOR-MANCE DREW ME IN...
...AND I BECAME YUKIRU.
Fine.
I'm a dead end anyway.
SENRI KUDO...
...ALWAYS AMAZES.

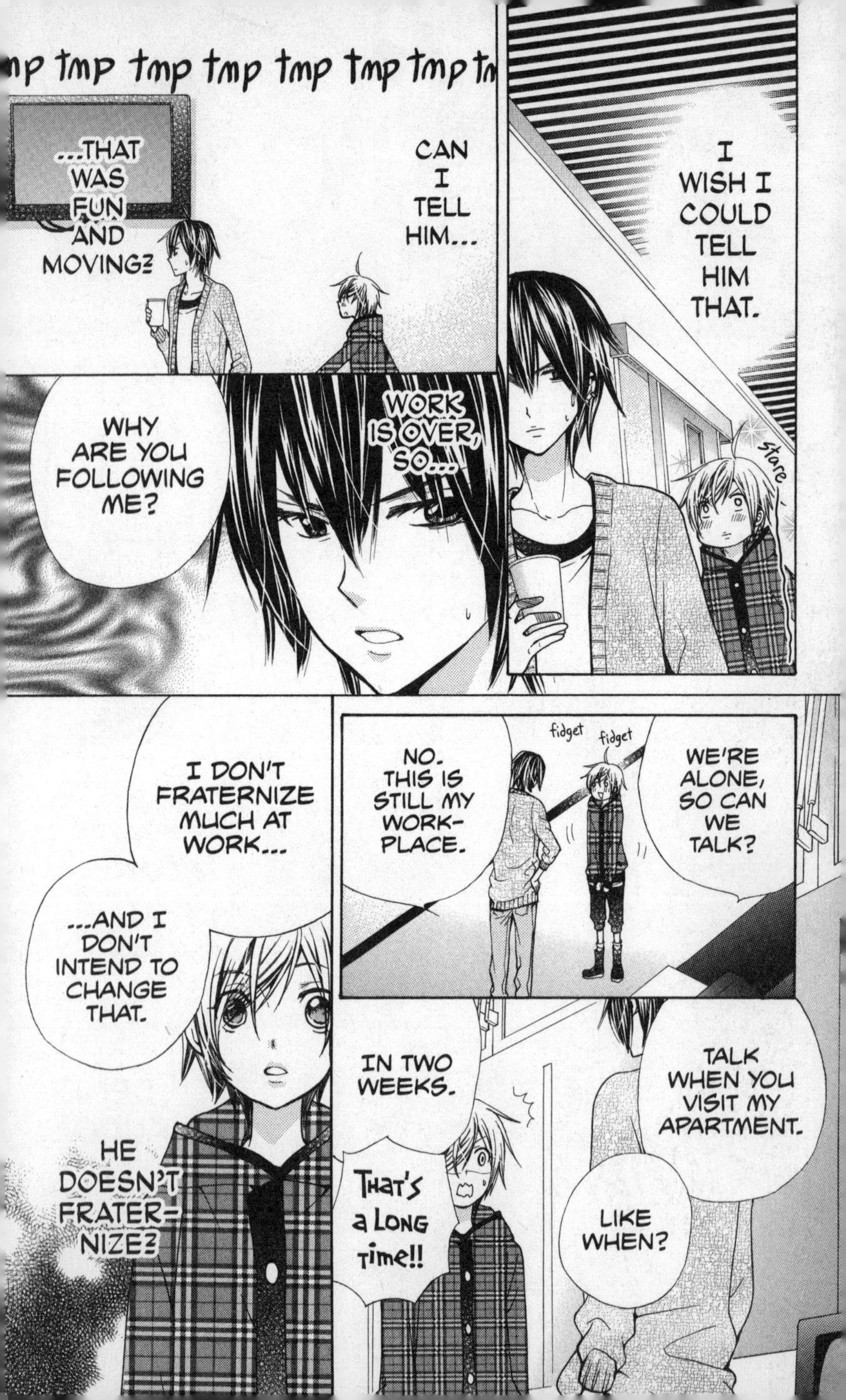

I WISH I COULD TELL HIM THAT.
stare
tmp tmp tmp tmp tmp tmp tmp tm
CAN I TELL HIM...
...THAT WAS FUN AND MOVING?
WORK IS OVER, SO...
WHY ARE YOU FOLLOWING ME?
WE'RE ALONE, SO CAN WE TALK?
fidget
fidget
NO. THIS IS STILL MY WORK-PLACE.
I DON'T FRATERNIZE MUCH AT WORK...
...AND I DON'T INTEND TO CHANGE THAT.
HE DOESN'T FRATER-NIZE?
TALK WHEN YOU VISIT MY APARTMENT.
LIKE WHEN?
IN TWO WEEKS.
That's a LONG time!!

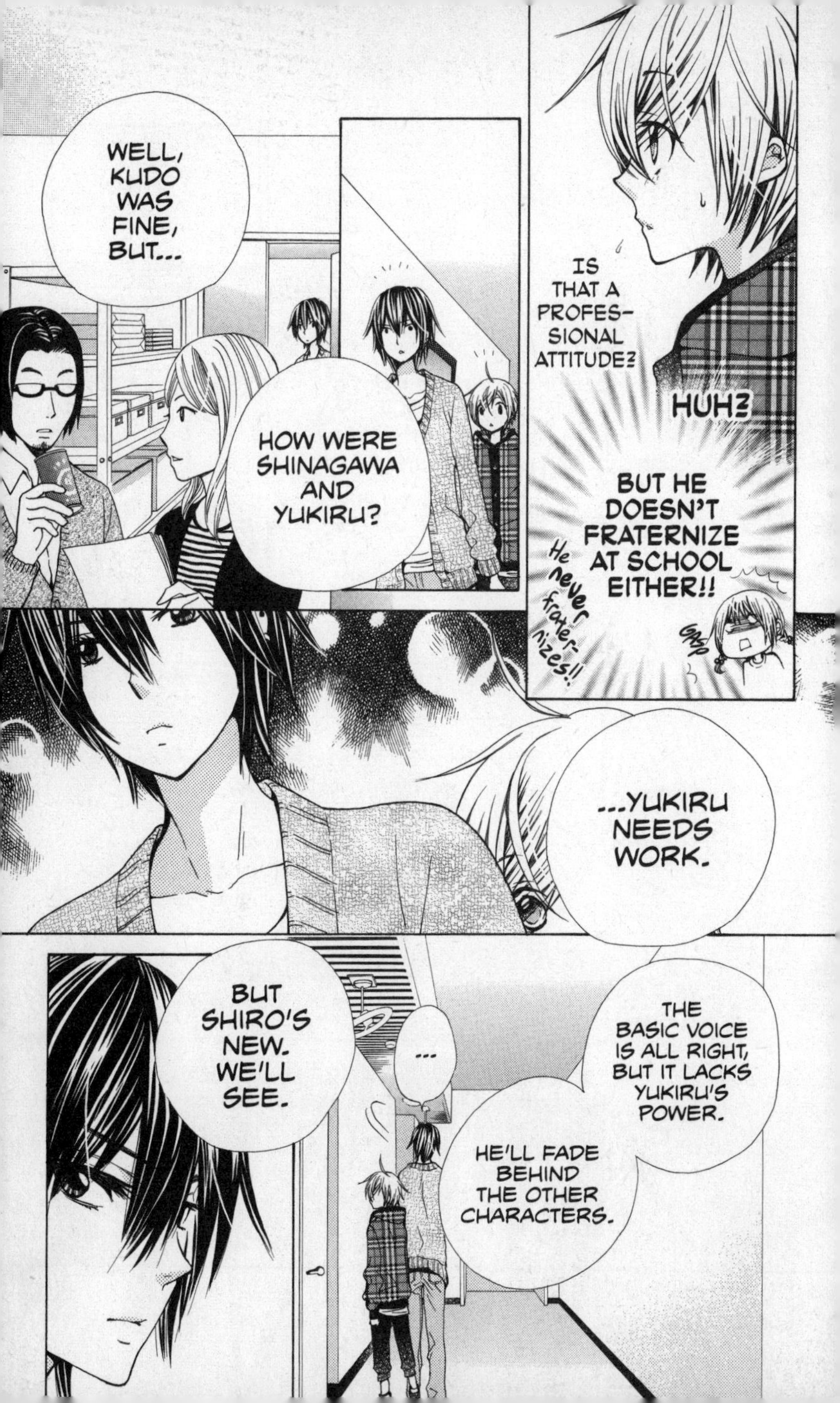
IS THAT A PROFES-SIONAL ATTITUDE?
HUH?
BUT HE DOESN'T FRATERNIZE AT SCHOOL EITHER!!
He never frater-nizes!!
GASP
HOW WERE SHINAGAWA AND YUKIRU?
WELL, KUDO WAS FINE, BUT...
...YUKIRU NEEDS WORK.
THE BASIC VOICE IS ALL RIGHT, BUT IT LACKS YUKIRU'S POWER.
HE'LL FADE BEHIND THE OTHER CHARACTERS.
...
BUT SHIRO'S NEW. WE'LL SEE.

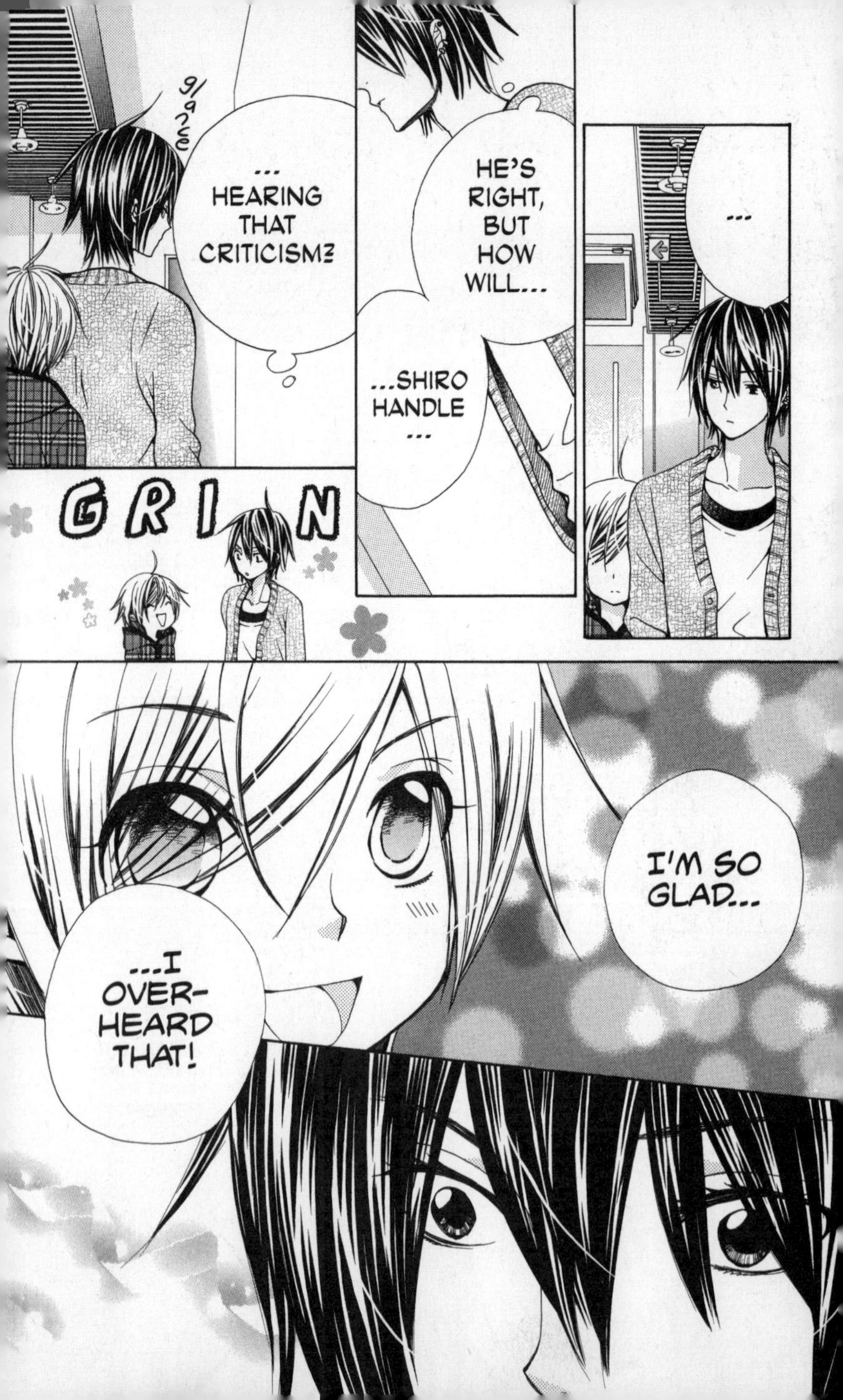
...
HE'S RIGHT, BUT HOW WILL...
...SHIRO HANDLE...
glance
...HEARING THAT CRITICISM?
GRIN
I'M SO GLAD...
...I OVERHEARD THAT!

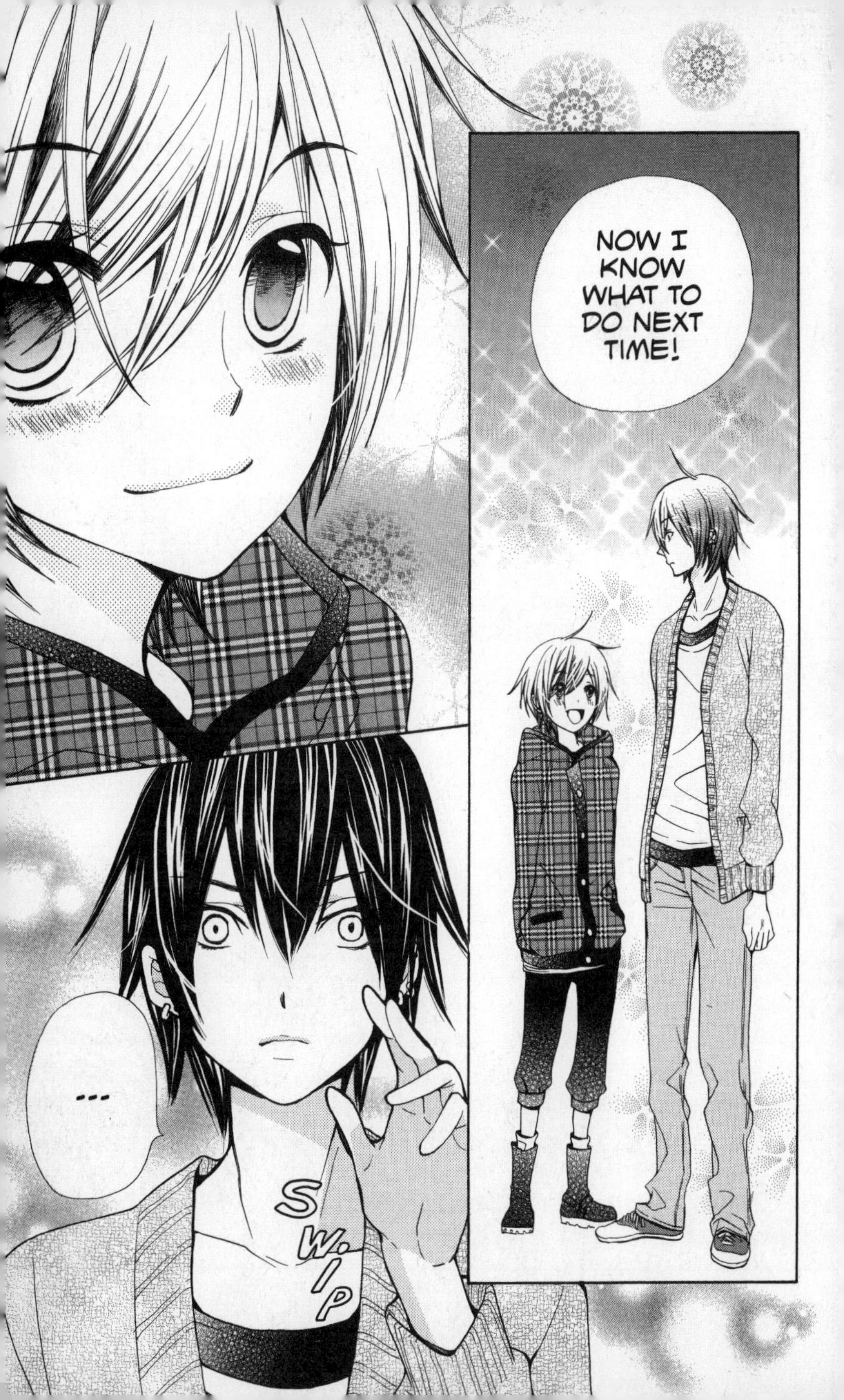
NOW I KNOW WHAT TO DO NEXT TIME!
...
SWIP

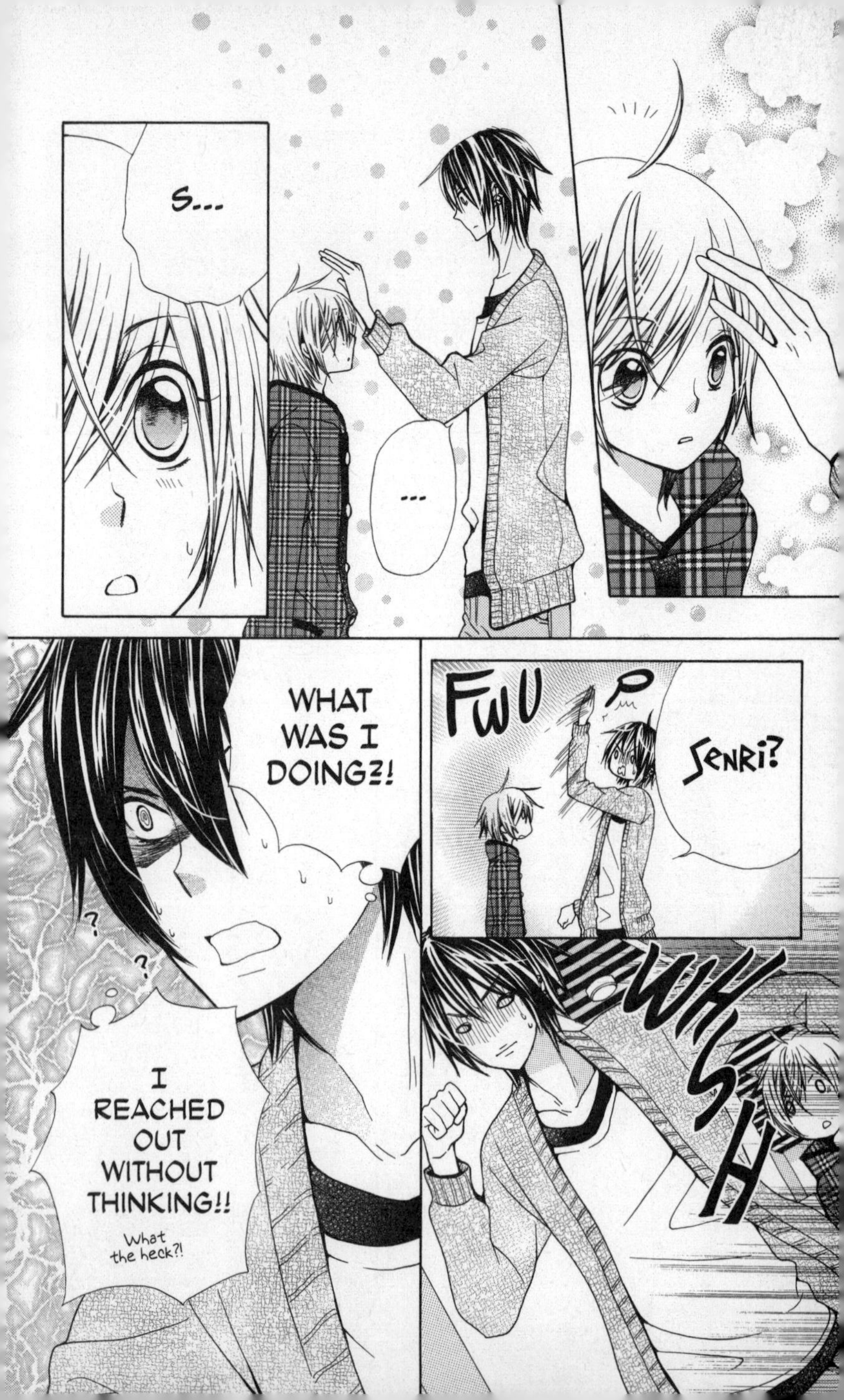
...
S...
FWU
Senri?
WHSH
WHAT WAS I DOING?!
I REACHED OUT WITHOUT THINKING!!
What the heck?!

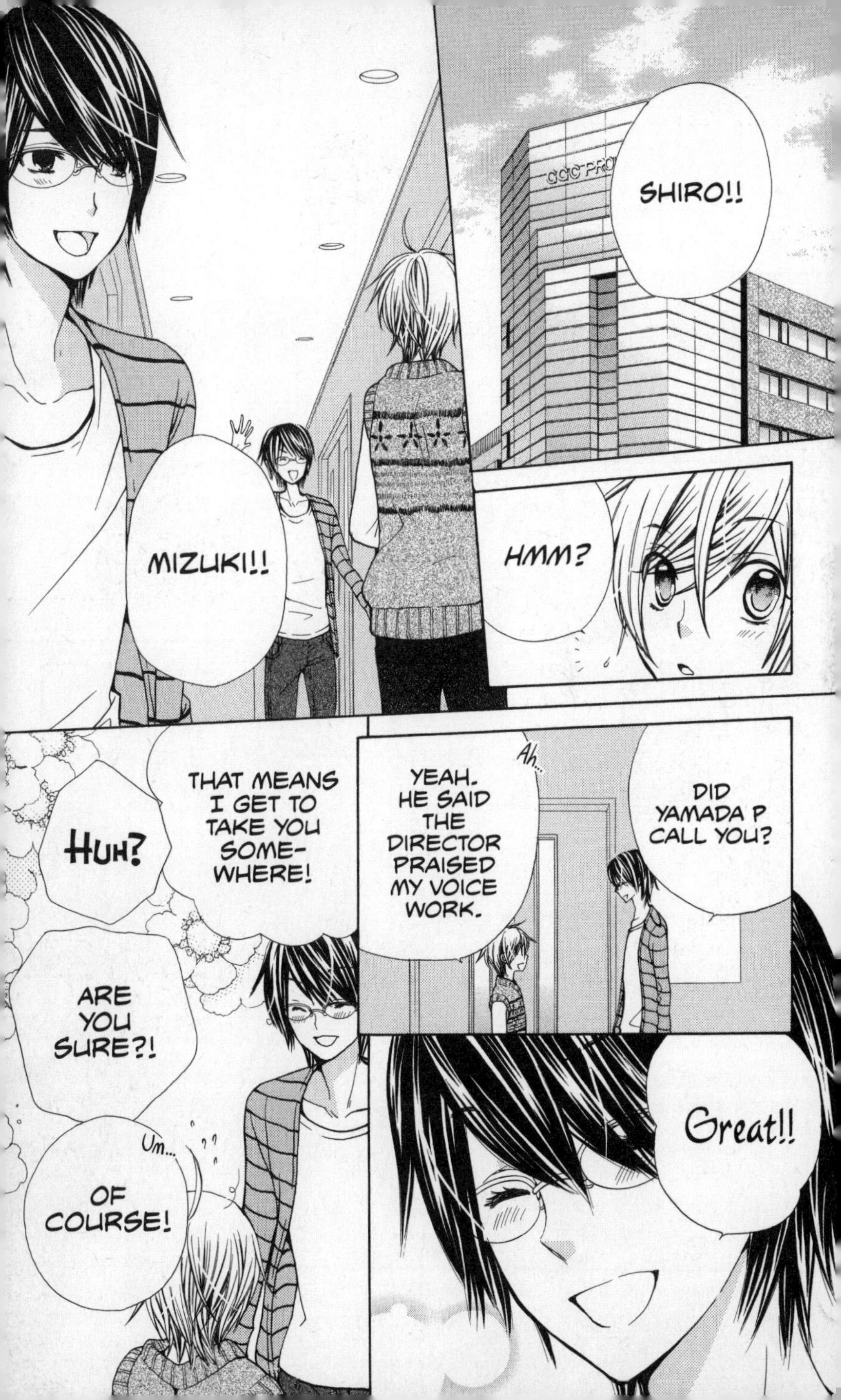
SHIRO!!
HMM?
MIZUKI!!
DID YAMADA P CALL YOU?
Ah...
YEAH. HE SAID THE DIRECTOR PRAISED MY VOICE WORK.
Great!!
THAT MEANS I GET TO TAKE YOU SOME-WHERE!
HUH?
ARE YOU SURE?!
Um...
OF COURSE!

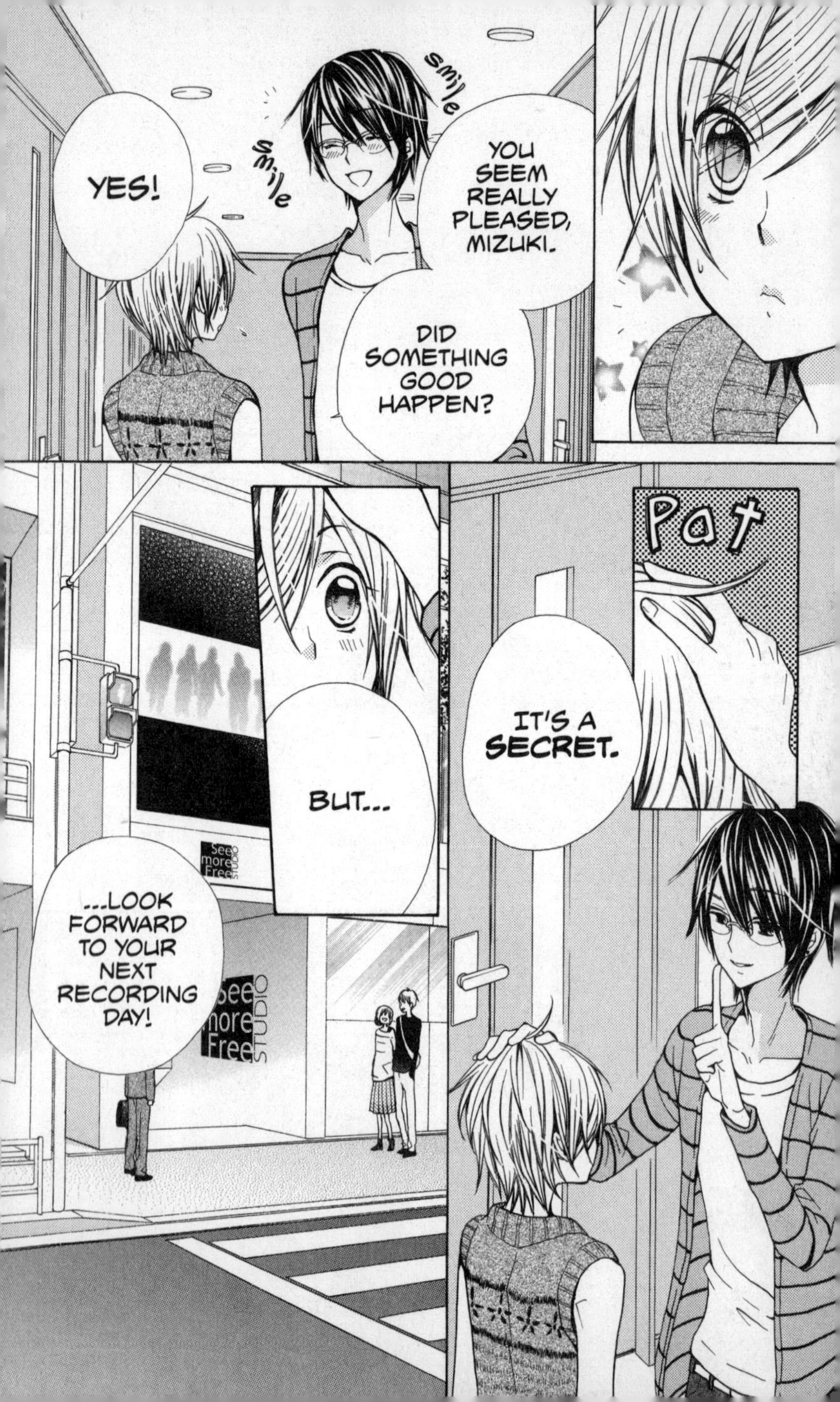
smile
YOU SEEM REALLY PLEASED, MIZUKI.
DID SOMETHING GOOD HAPPEN?
smile
YES!
Pat
IT'S A SECRET.
BUT...
See more Free STUDIO
...LOOK FORWARD TO YOUR NEXT RECORDING DAY!
See more Free STUDIO

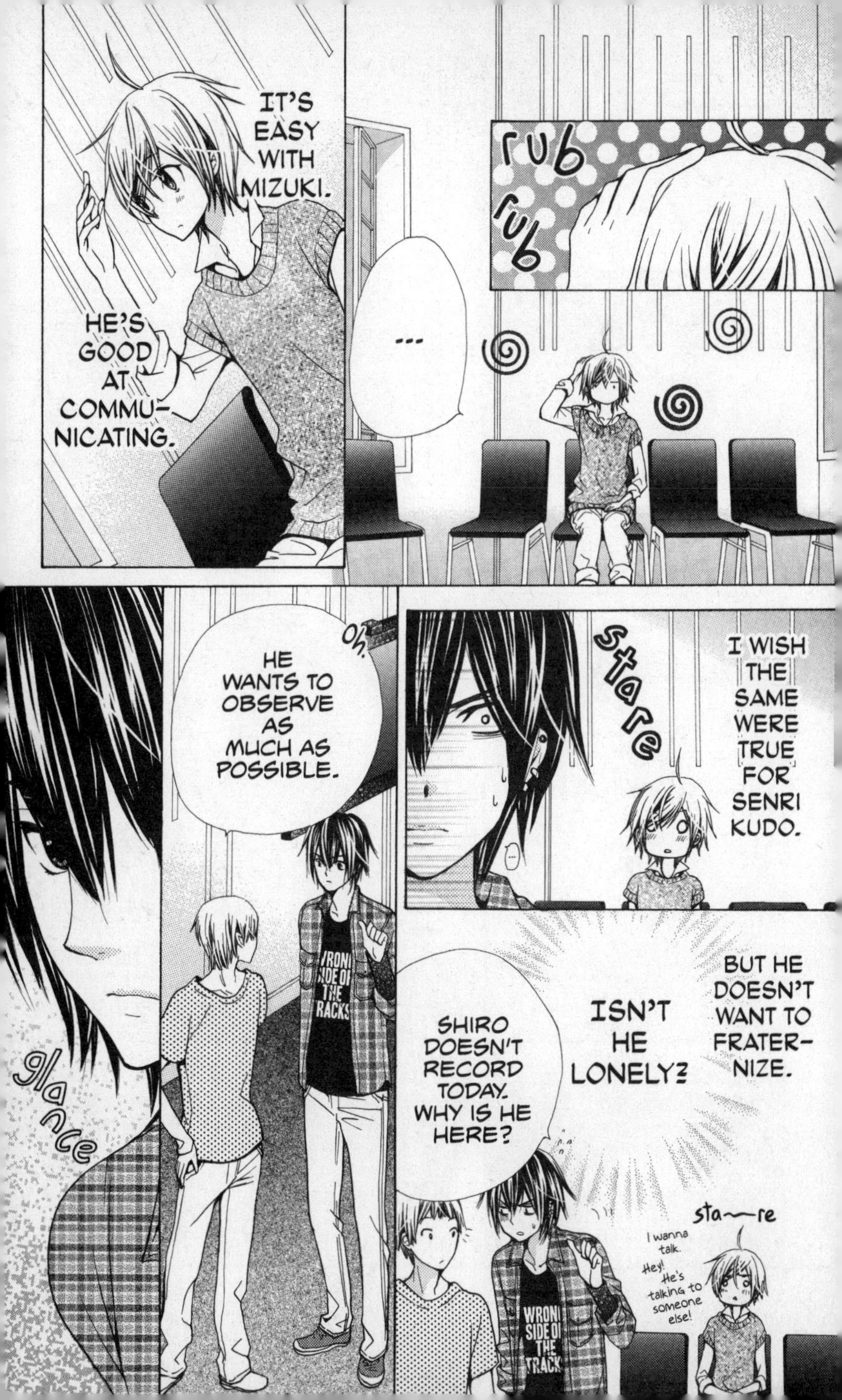
rub rub
...
IT'S EASY WITH MIZUKI.
HE'S GOOD AT COMMUNICATING.
stare
I WISH THE SAME WERE TRUE FOR SENRI KUDO.
...
BUT HE DOESN'T WANT TO FRATERNIZE.
ISN'T HE LONELY?
SHIRO DOESN'T RECORD TODAY. WHY IS HE HERE?
sta~re
I wanna talk.
Hey! He's talking to someone else!
Oh.
HE WANTS TO OBSERVE AS MUCH AS POSSIBLE.
glance

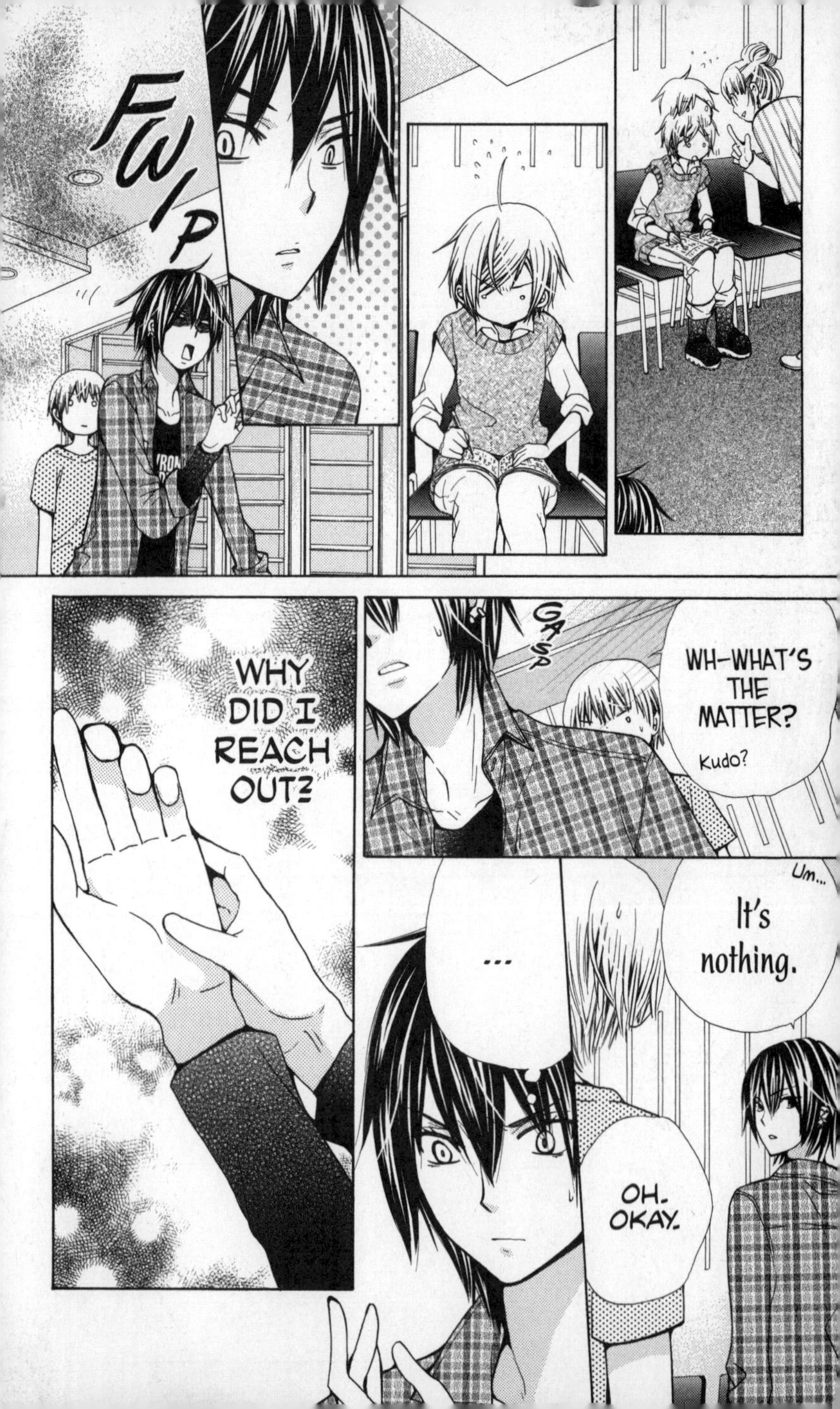
FWIP
GASP
WH-WHAT'S THE MATTER?
Kudo?
Um...
It's nothing.
...
OH. OKAY.
WHY DID I REACH OUT?

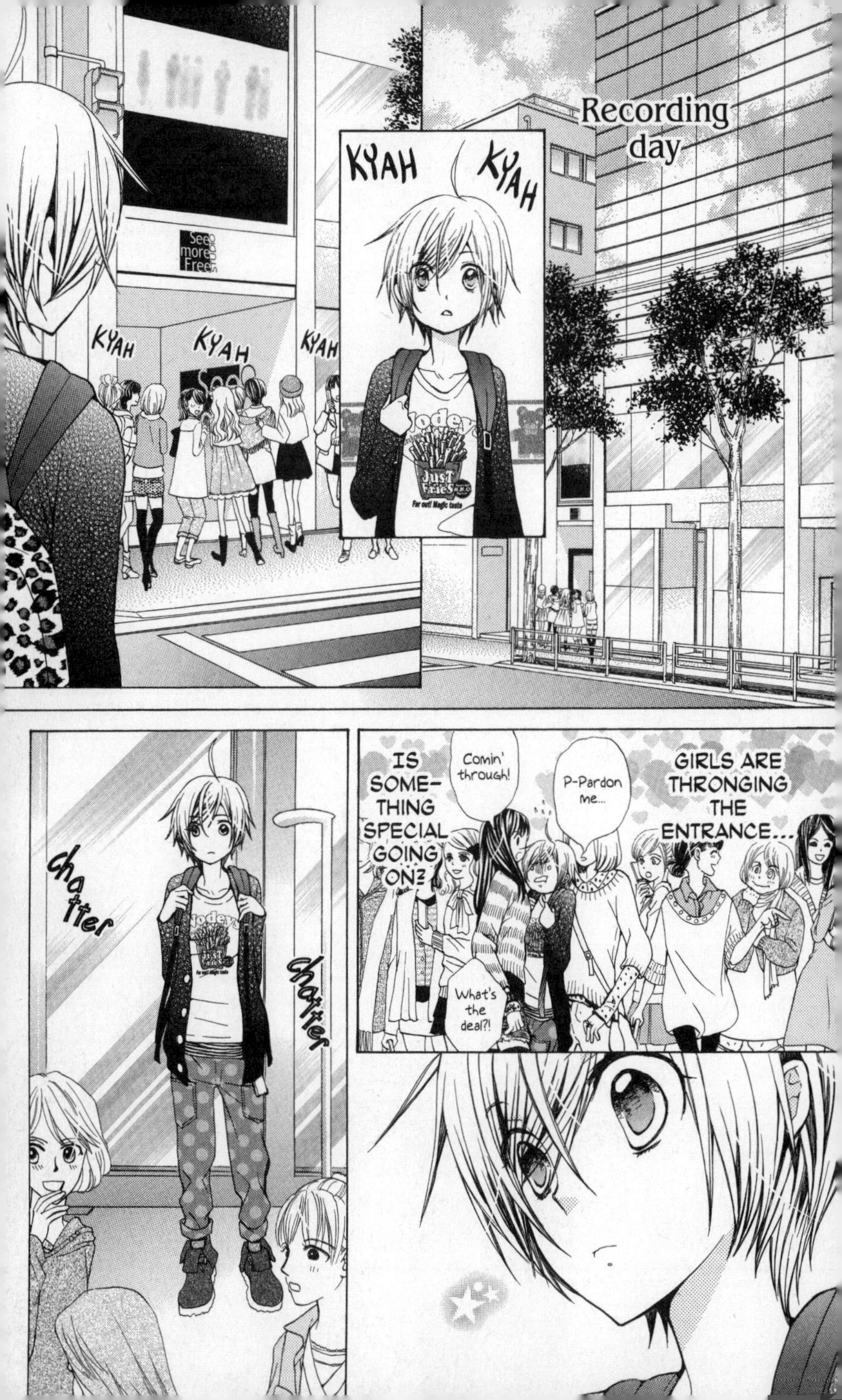
Recording day
KYAH
KYAH
KYAH
KYAH
KYAH
GIRLS ARE THRONGING THE ENTRANCE...
P-Pardon me...
Comin' through!
IS SOME-THING SPECIAL GOING ON?
What's the deal?!
chatter
chatter

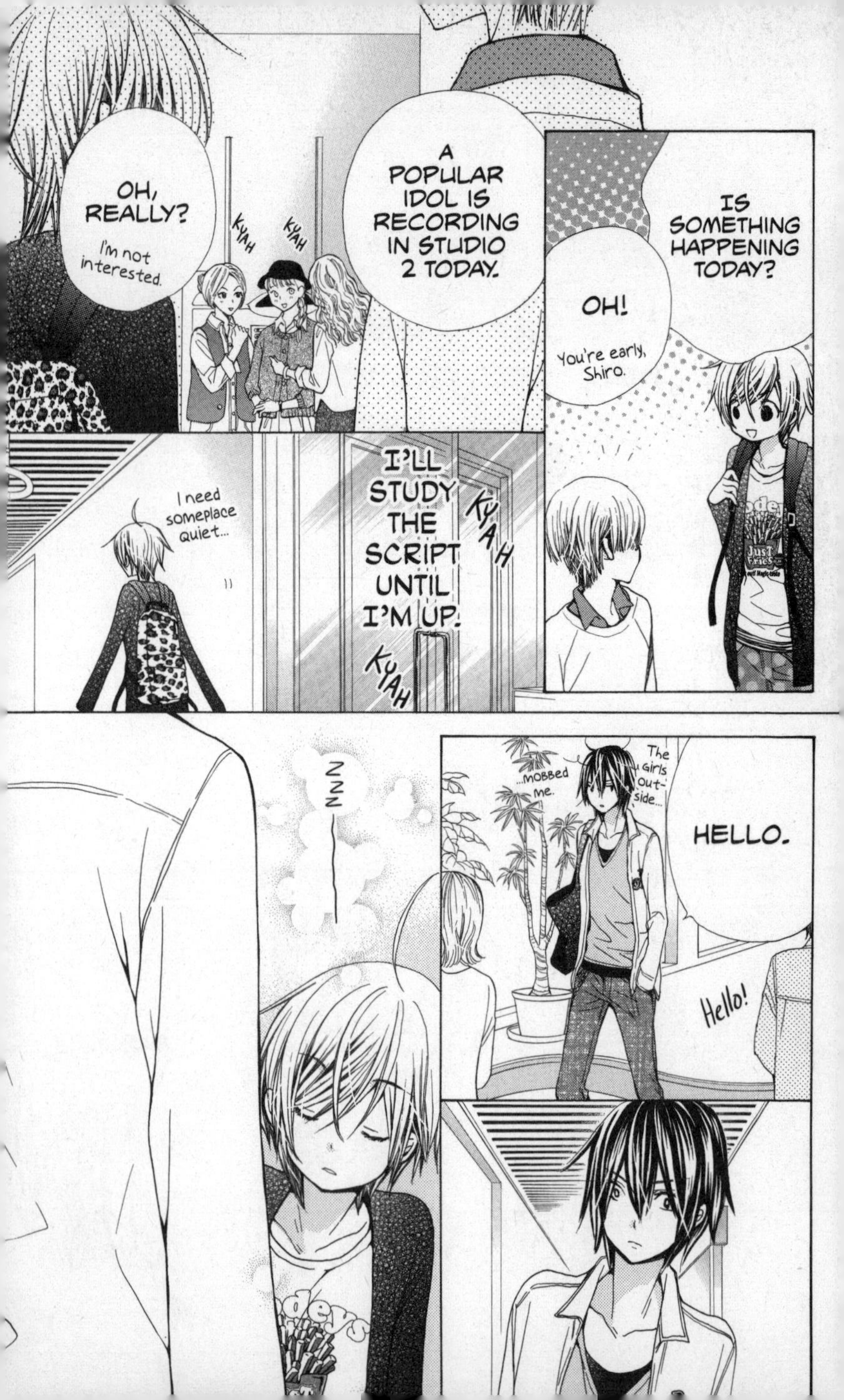
IS SOMETHING HAPPENING TODAY?
OH!
You're early, Shiro.
A POPULAR IDOL IS RECORDING IN STUDIO 2 TODAY.
KYAH
KYAH
OH, REALLY?
I'm not interested.
I'LL STUDY THE SCRIPT UNTIL I'M UP.
KYAH
KYAH
I need someplace quiet...
HELLO.
The girls out-side...
...mobbed me.
Hello!
ZZZ—

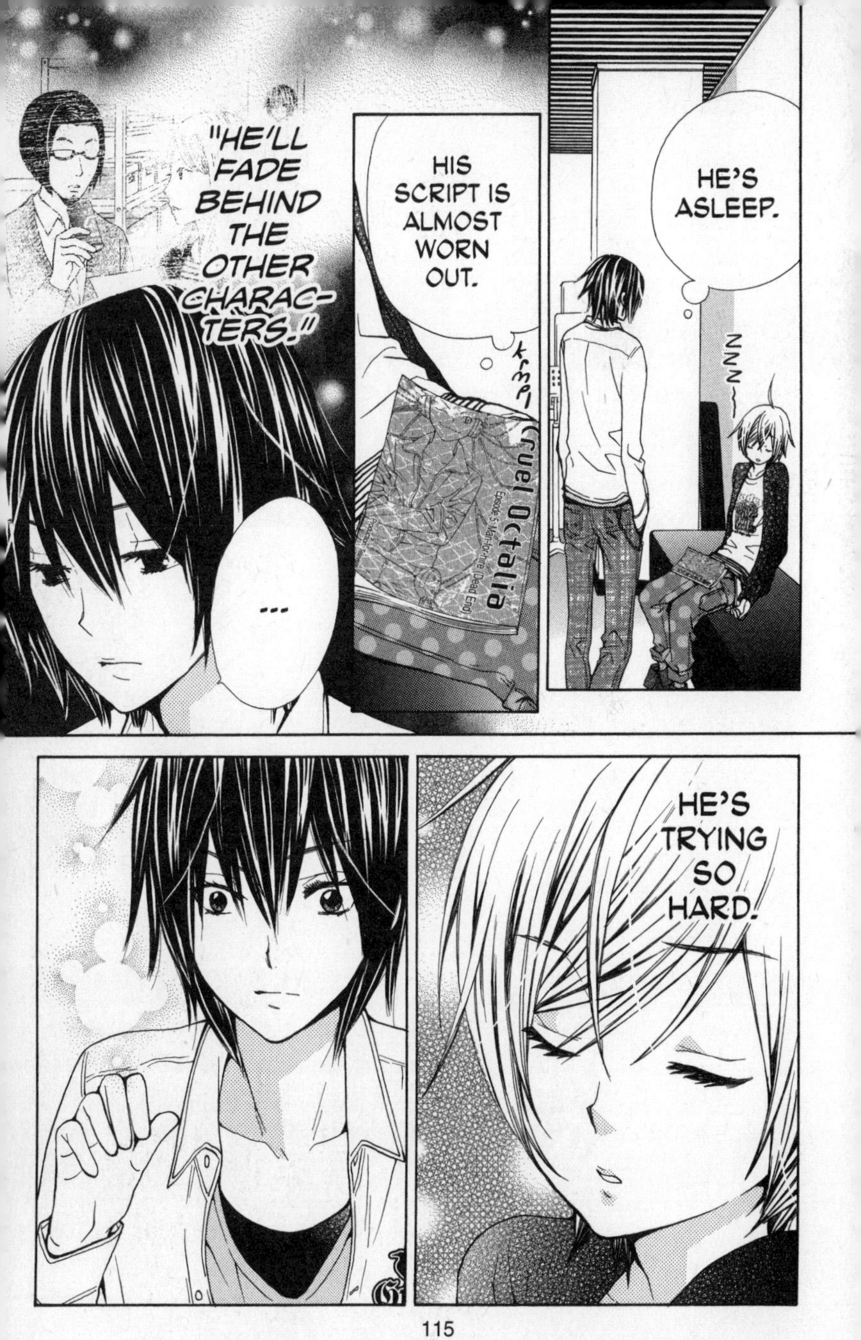
HE'S ASLEEP.
ZZZ
HIS SCRIPT IS ALMOST WORN OUT.
KRMPL
Cruel Octalia
Episode 5: Man-for-hire [Dead End]
"HE'LL FADE BEHIND THE OTHER CHARACTERS."
...
HE'S TRYING SO HARD.

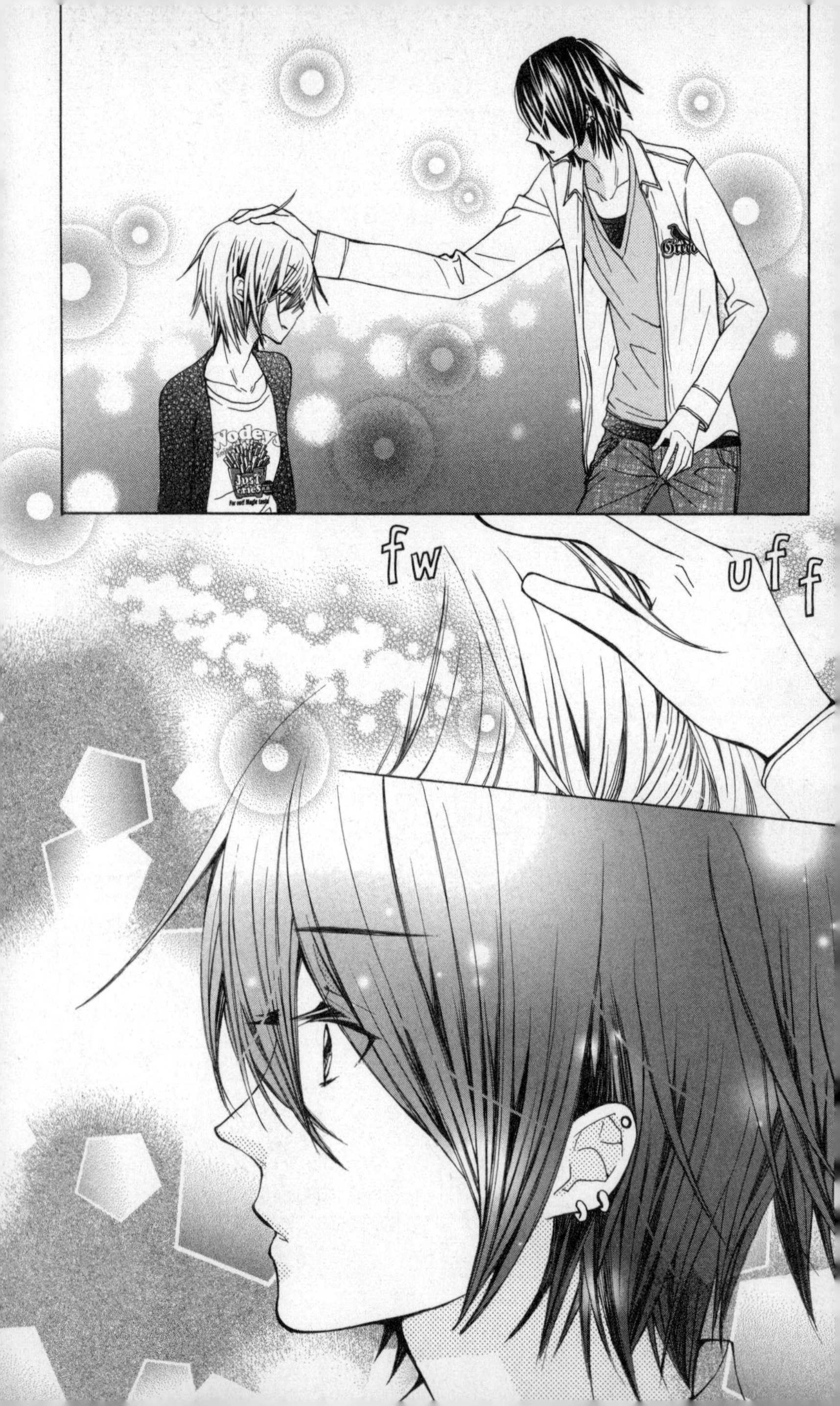
fwuff

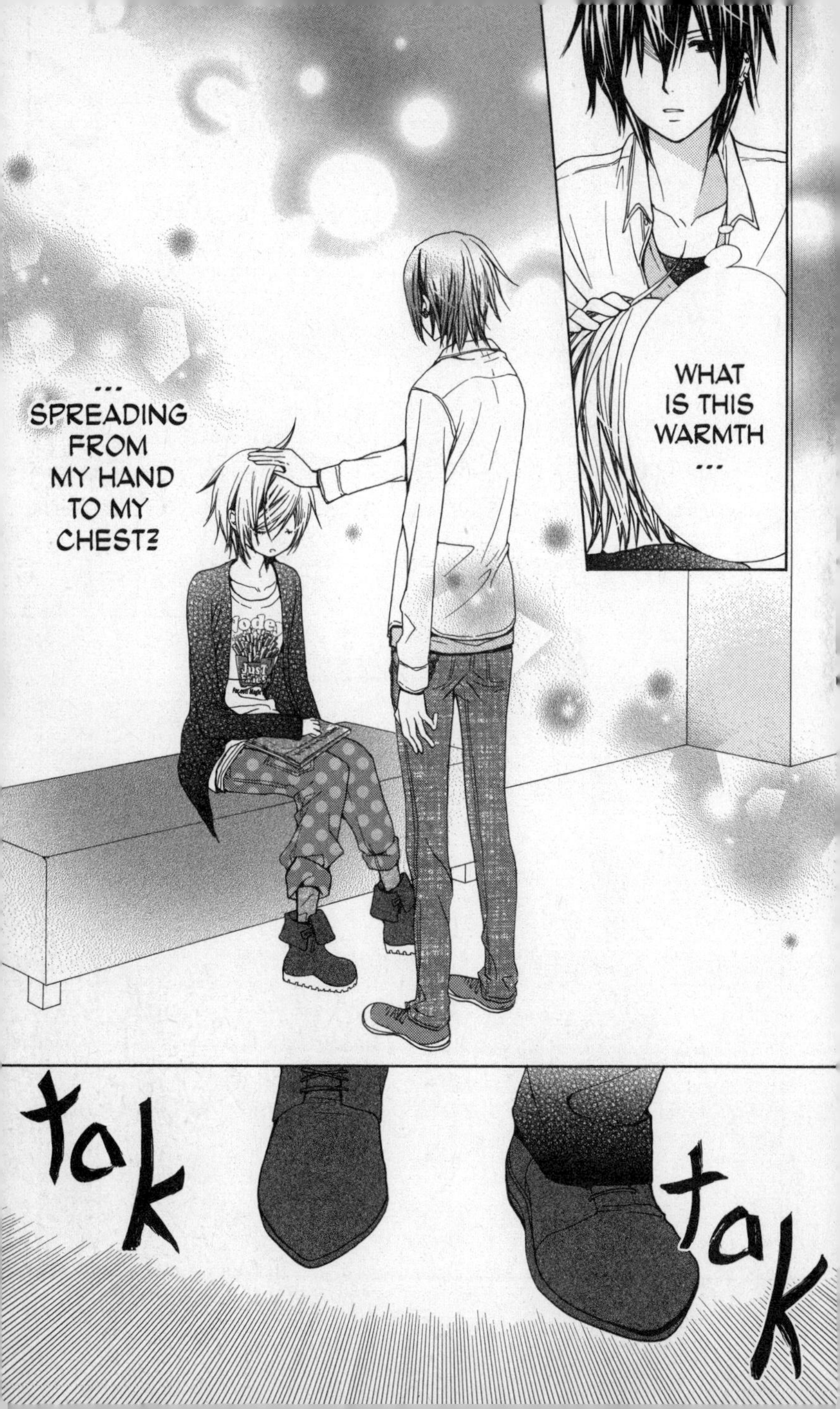
WHAT IS THIS WARMTH ...
... SPREADING FROM MY HAND TO MY CHEST?
tak
tak

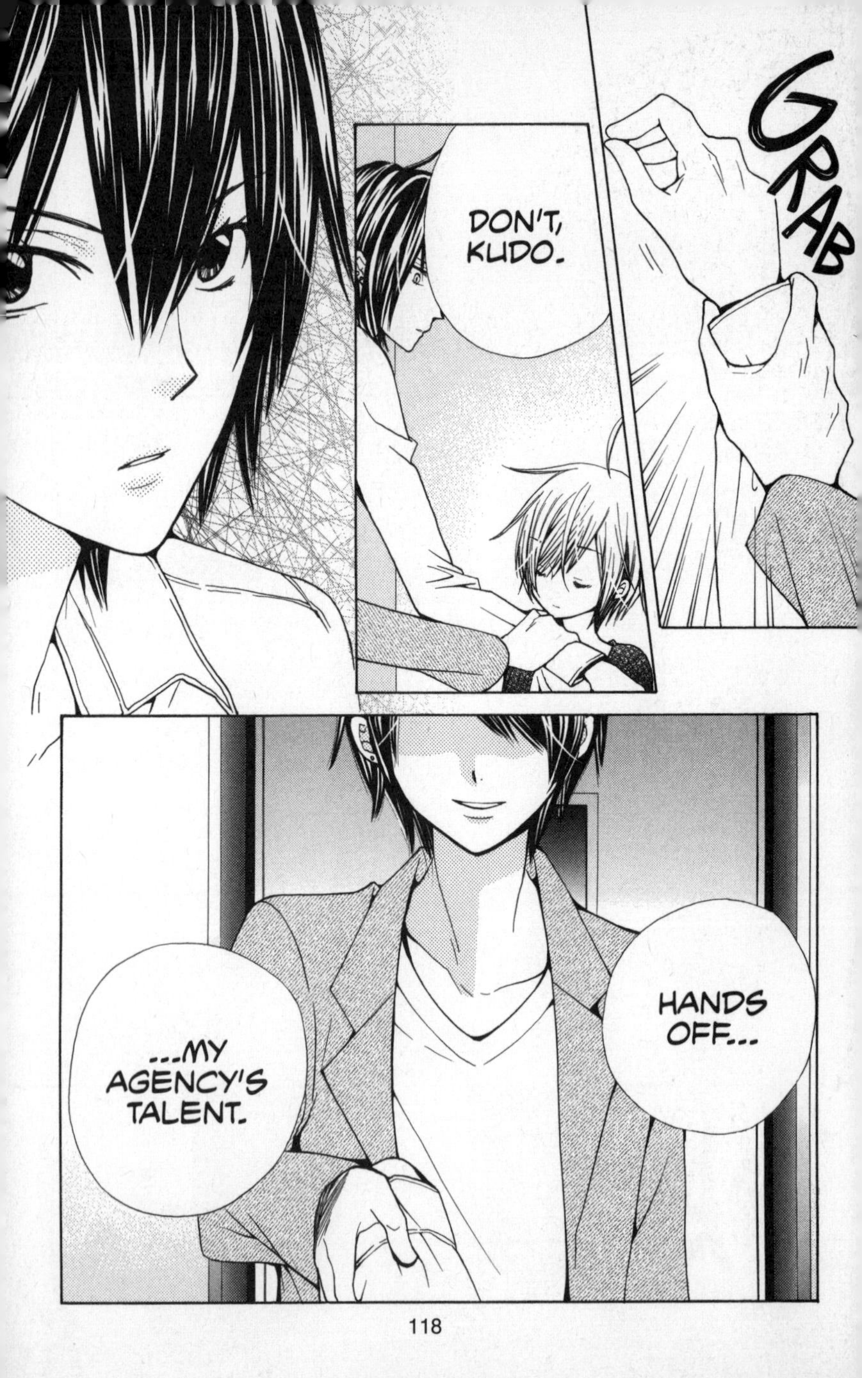
GRAB
DON'T, KUDO.
HANDS OFF...
...MY AGENCY'S TALENT.

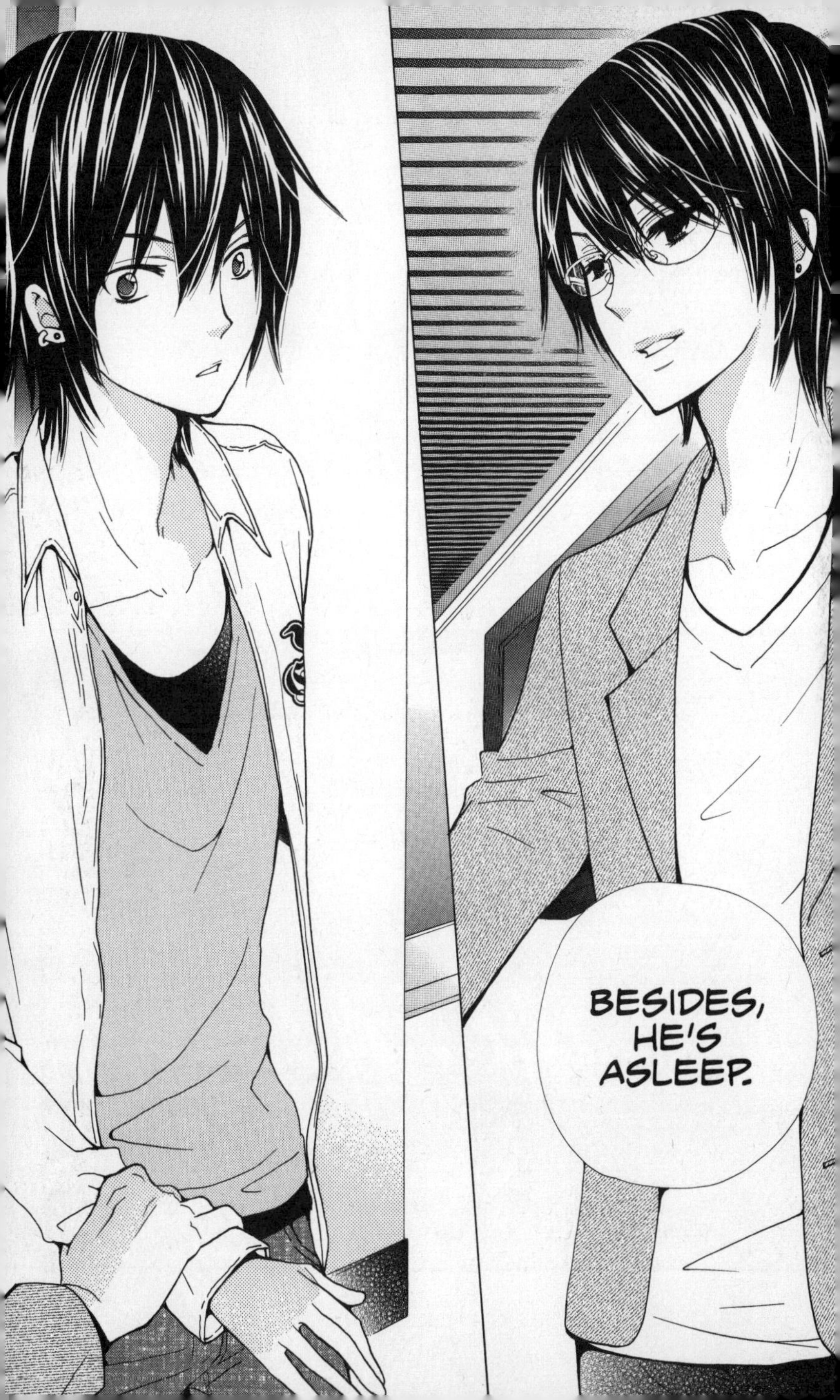
BESIDES, HE'S ASLEEP.

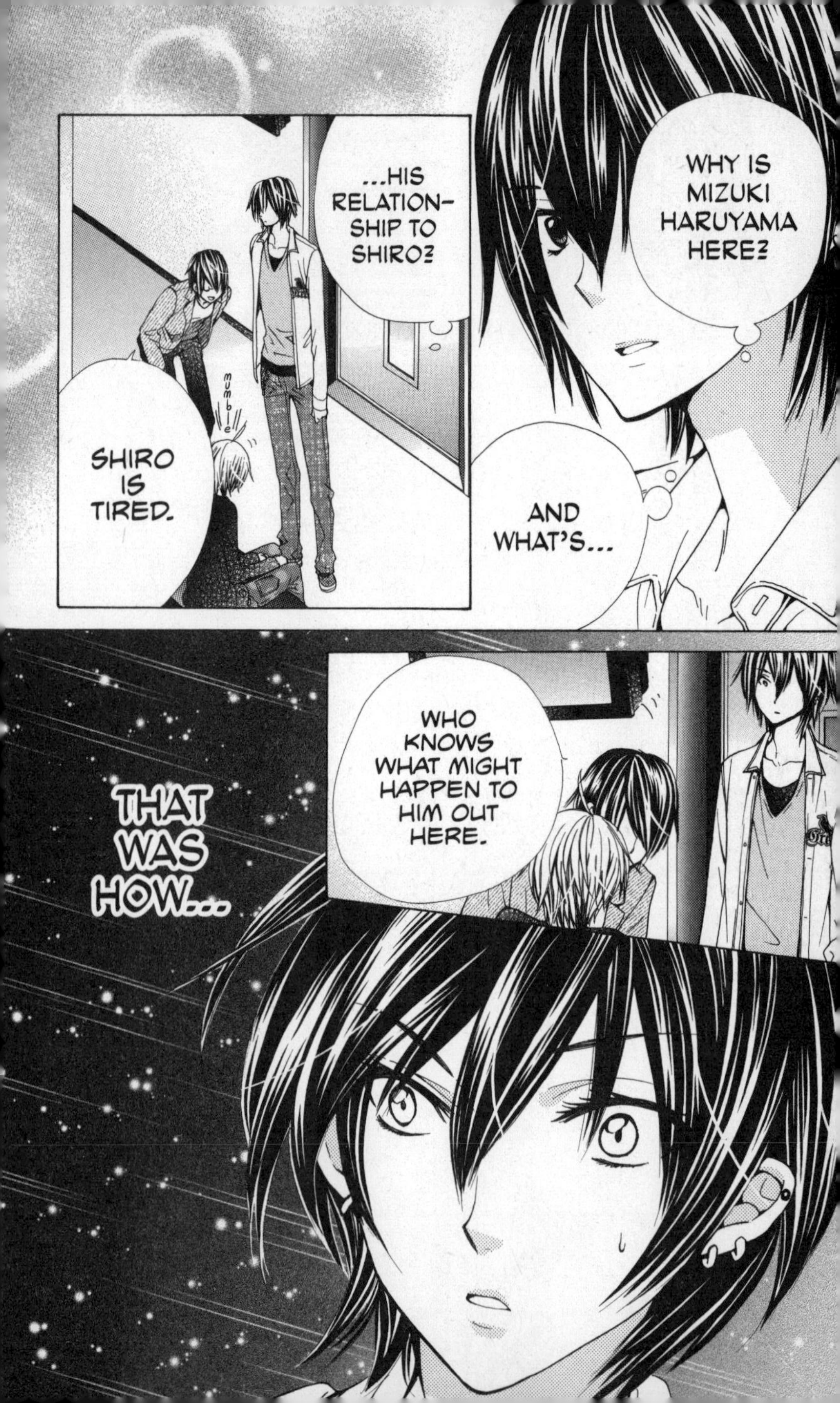
WHY IS MIZUKI HARUYAMA HERE?
AND WHAT'S...
...HIS RELATION-SHIP TO SHIRO?
mumble
SHIRO IS TIRED.
WHO KNOWS WHAT MIGHT HAPPEN TO HIM OUT HERE.
THAT WAS HOW...

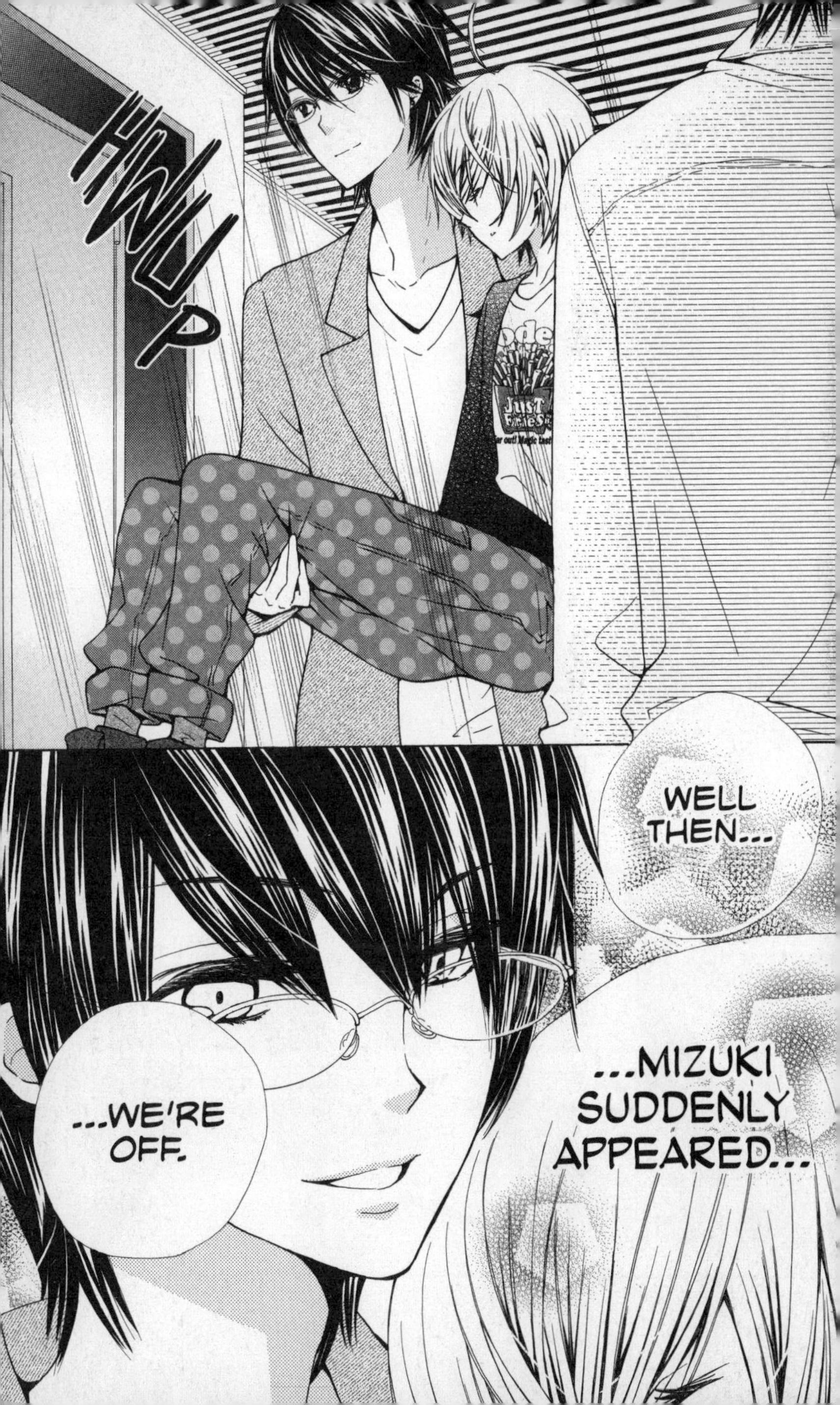
HWUP
WELL THEN...
...MIZUKI SUDDENLY APPEARED...
...WE'RE OFF.

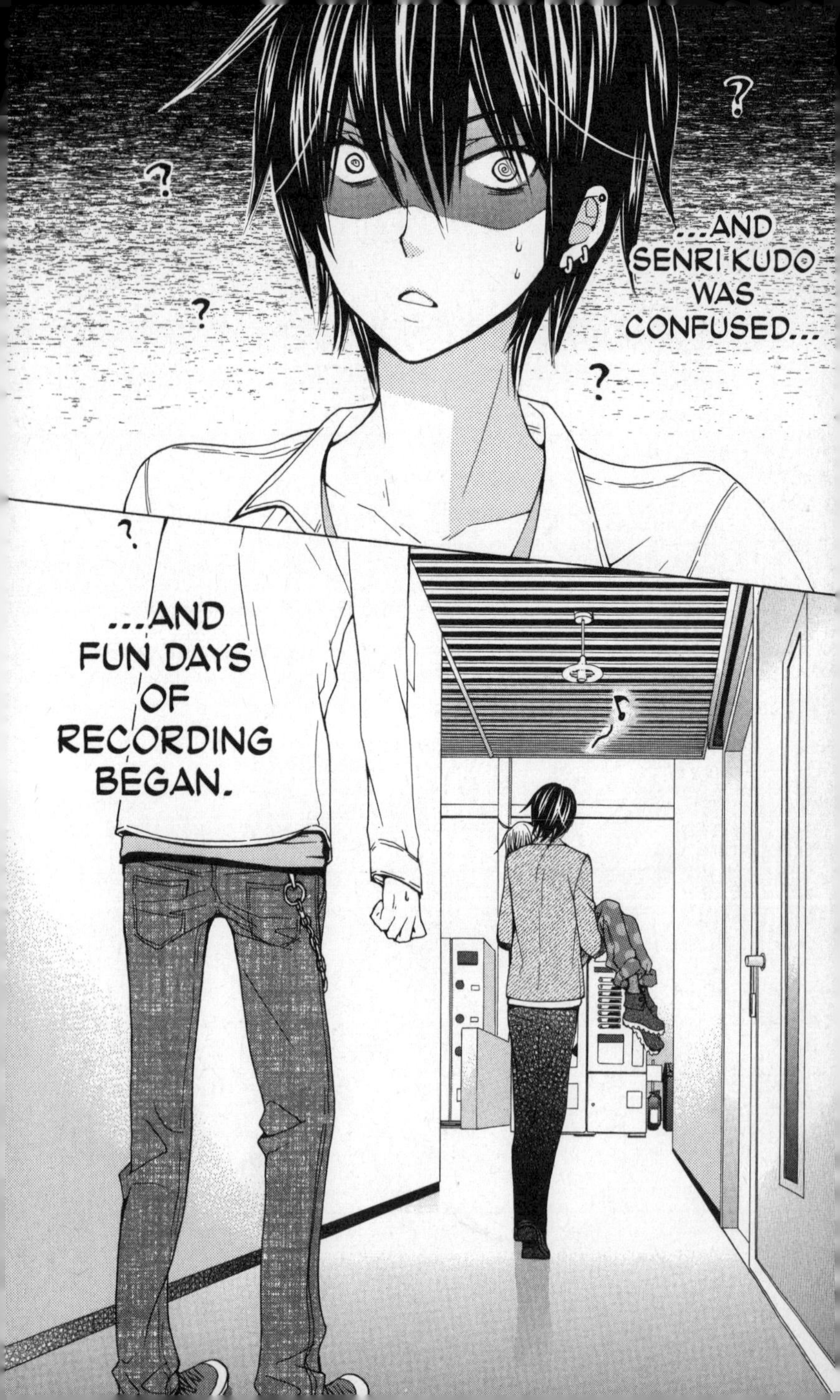
?
?
?
?
...AND SENRI KUDO WAS CONFUSED...
?
...AND FUN DAYS OF RECORDING BEGAN.

Chapter 51

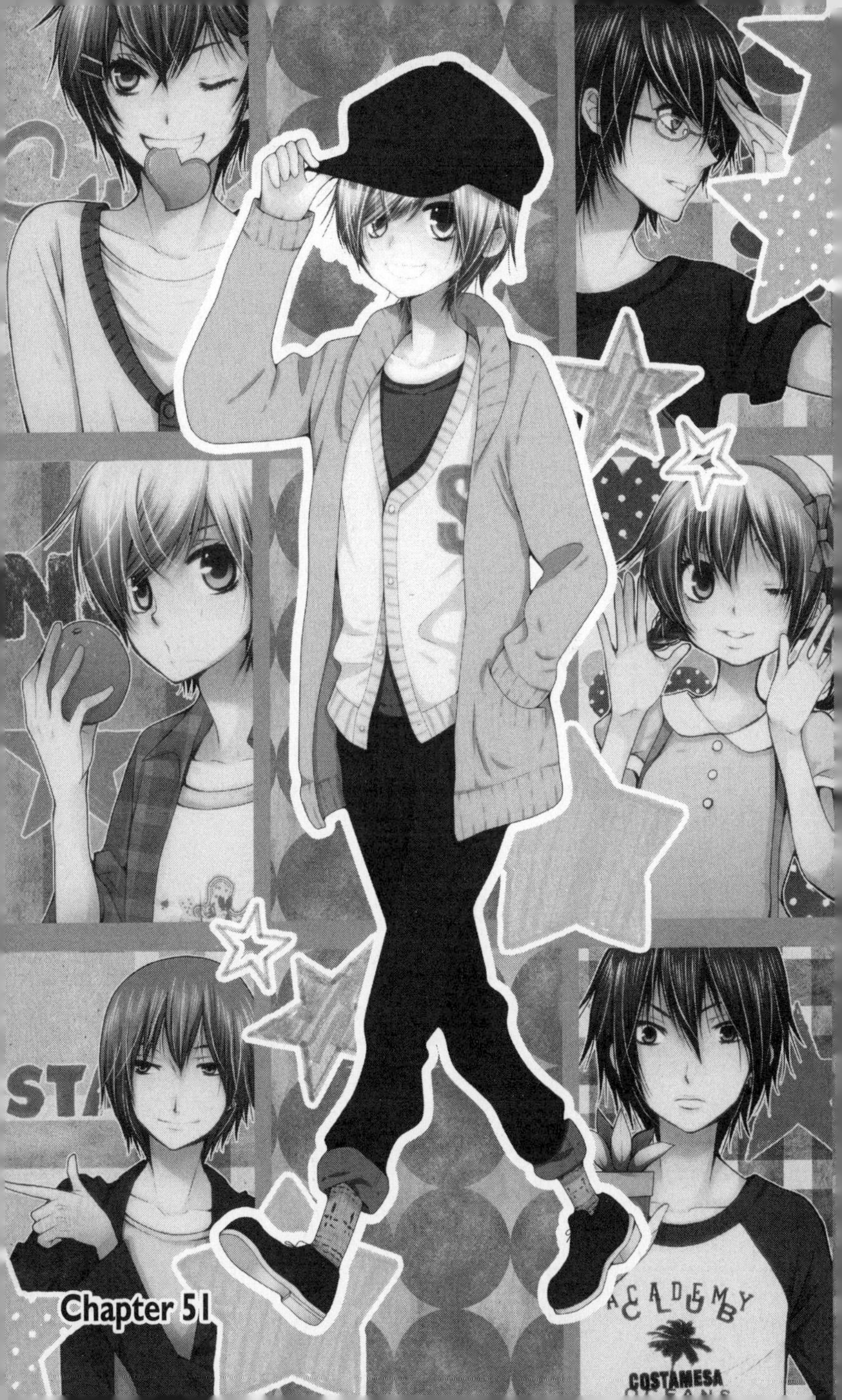
ACADEMY CLUB
COSTAMESA

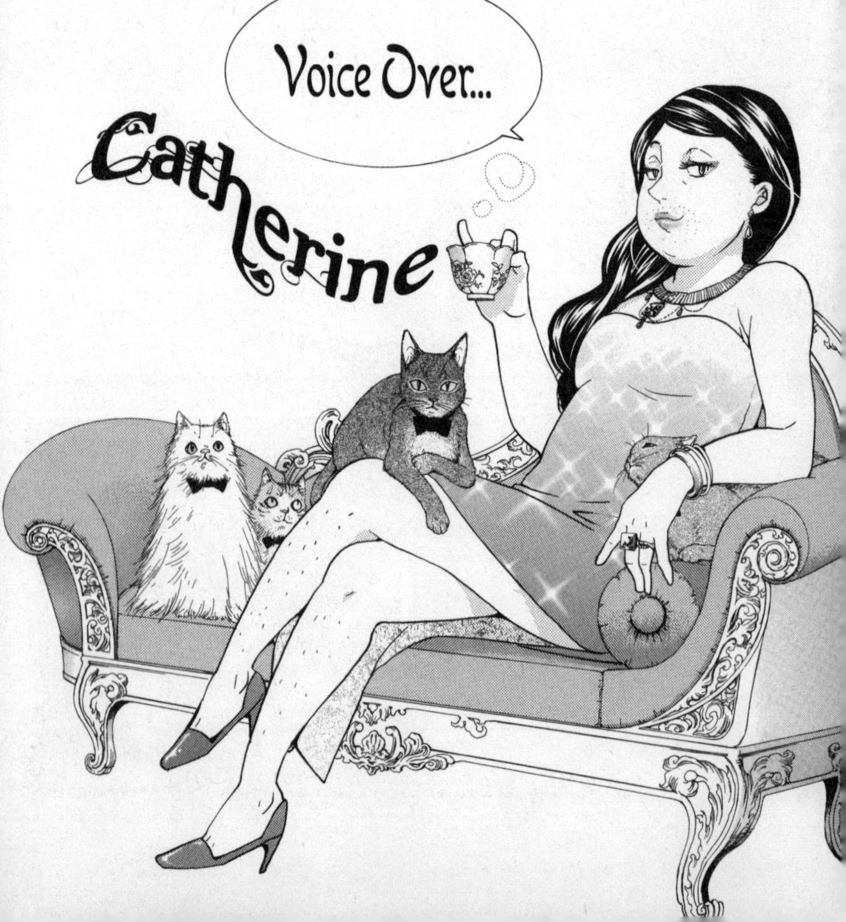
Voice Over...
Catherine

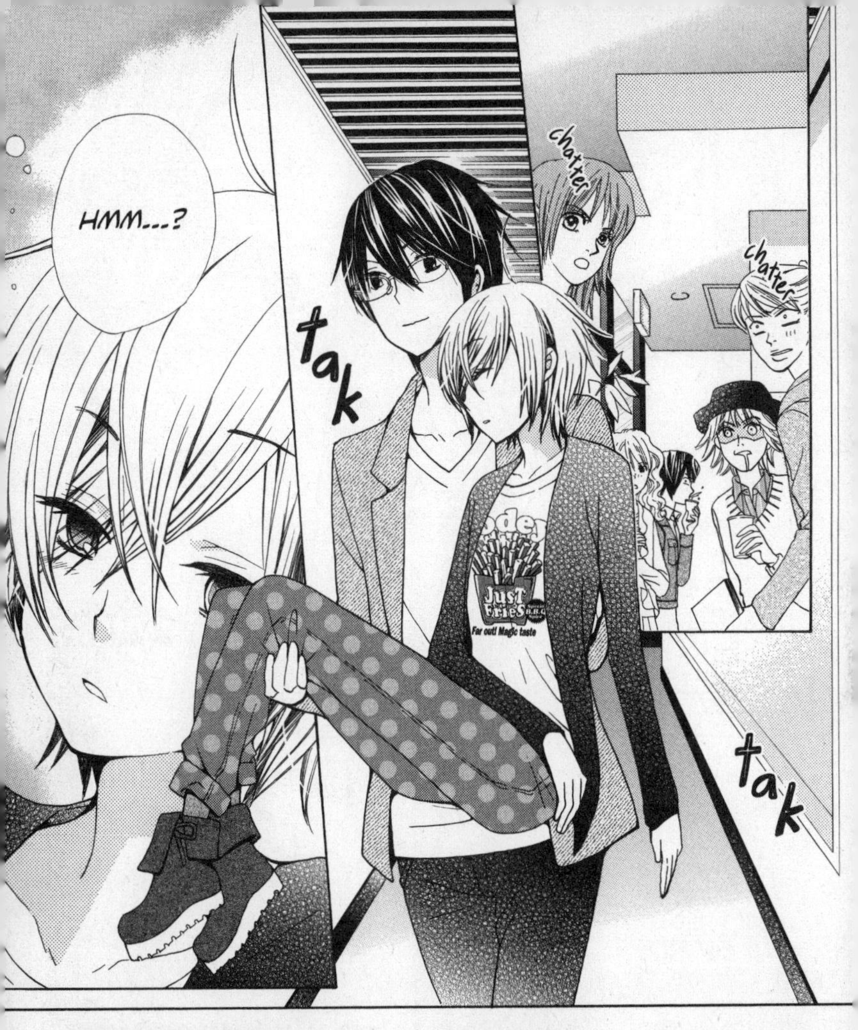
chatter
chatter
tak
tak
Just Fries
Far out! Magic taste
HMM...?

• Analog Thumbnails •

Don't people draw black-and-white thumbnails the analog way anymore? I like the old-fashioned art supplies, so if they go away, I'll be sad. If my favorite screentones get discontinued... *huff huff*

Both analog drawing and digital drawing are fun...

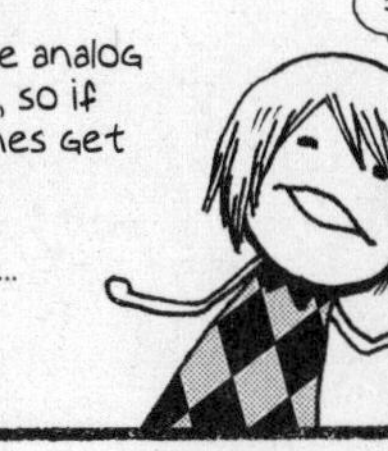
5

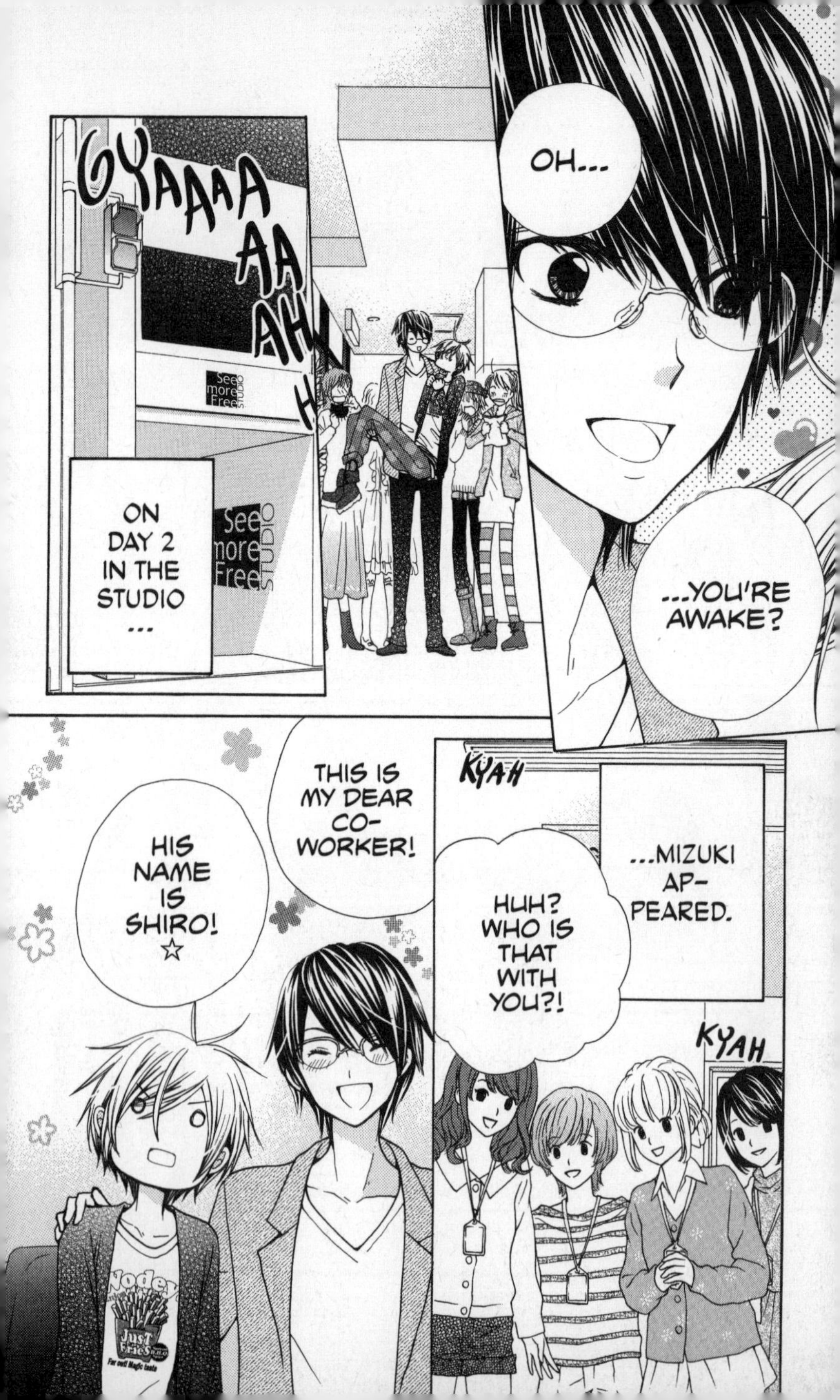
OH...
...YOU'RE AWAKE?
GYAAAAAAAAHH
ON DAY 2 IN THE STUDIO...
See more Free STUDIO
See more Free STUDIO
...MIZUKI APPEARED.
KYAH
KYAH
HUH? WHO IS THAT WITH YOU?!
THIS IS MY DEAR CO-WORKER!
HIS NAME IS SHIRO! ☆

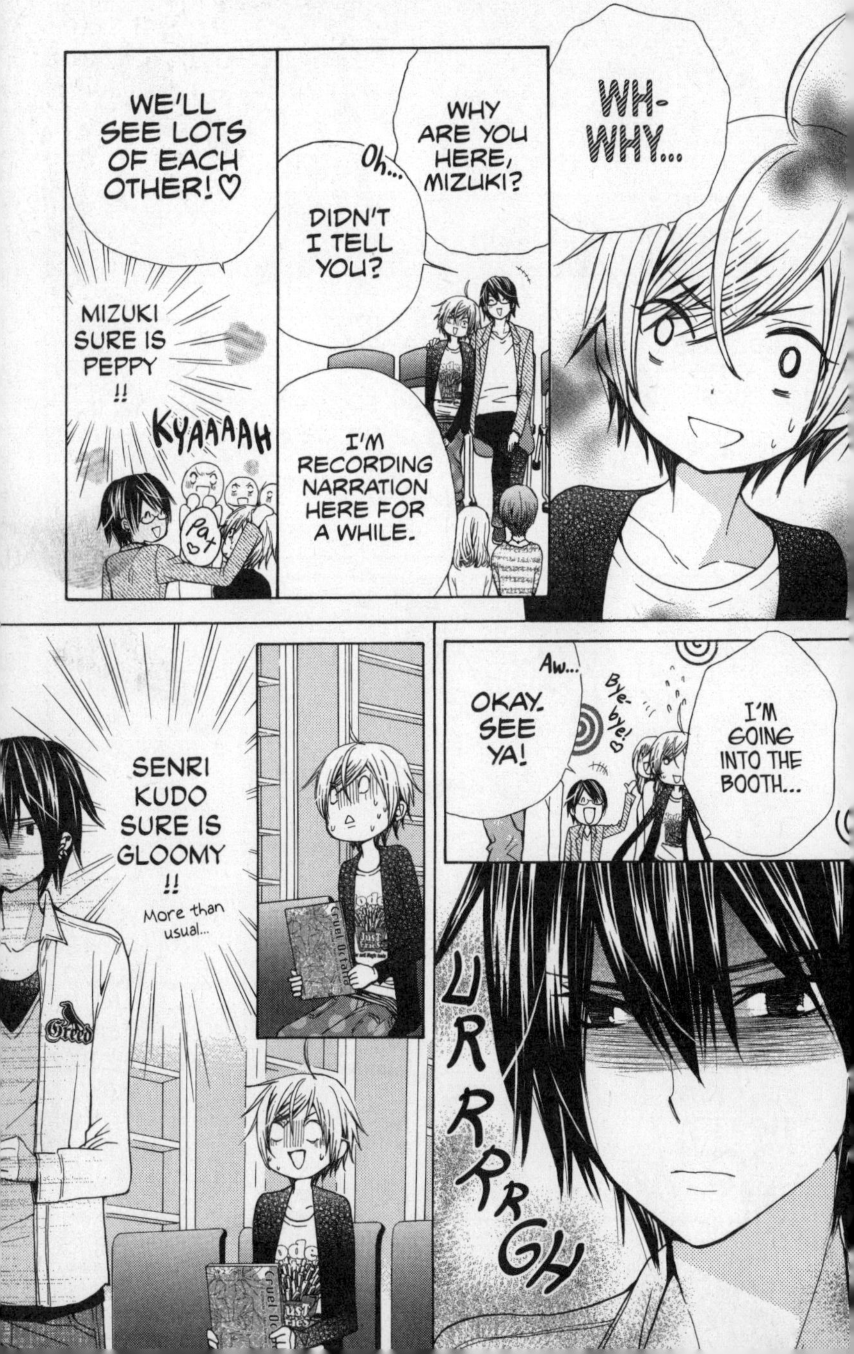
WH-WHY...
WHY ARE YOU HERE, MIZUKI?
Oh...
DIDN'T I TELL YOU?
I'M RECORDING NARRATION HERE FOR A WHILE.
WE'LL SEE LOTS OF EACH OTHER! ♡
MIZUKI SURE IS PEPPY !!
KYAAAAH
Pat ♡
I'M GOING INTO THE BOOTH...
Bye-bye! ♡
Aw...
OKAY. SEE YA!
URRRRGH
SENRI KUDO SURE IS GLOOMY !!
More than usual...

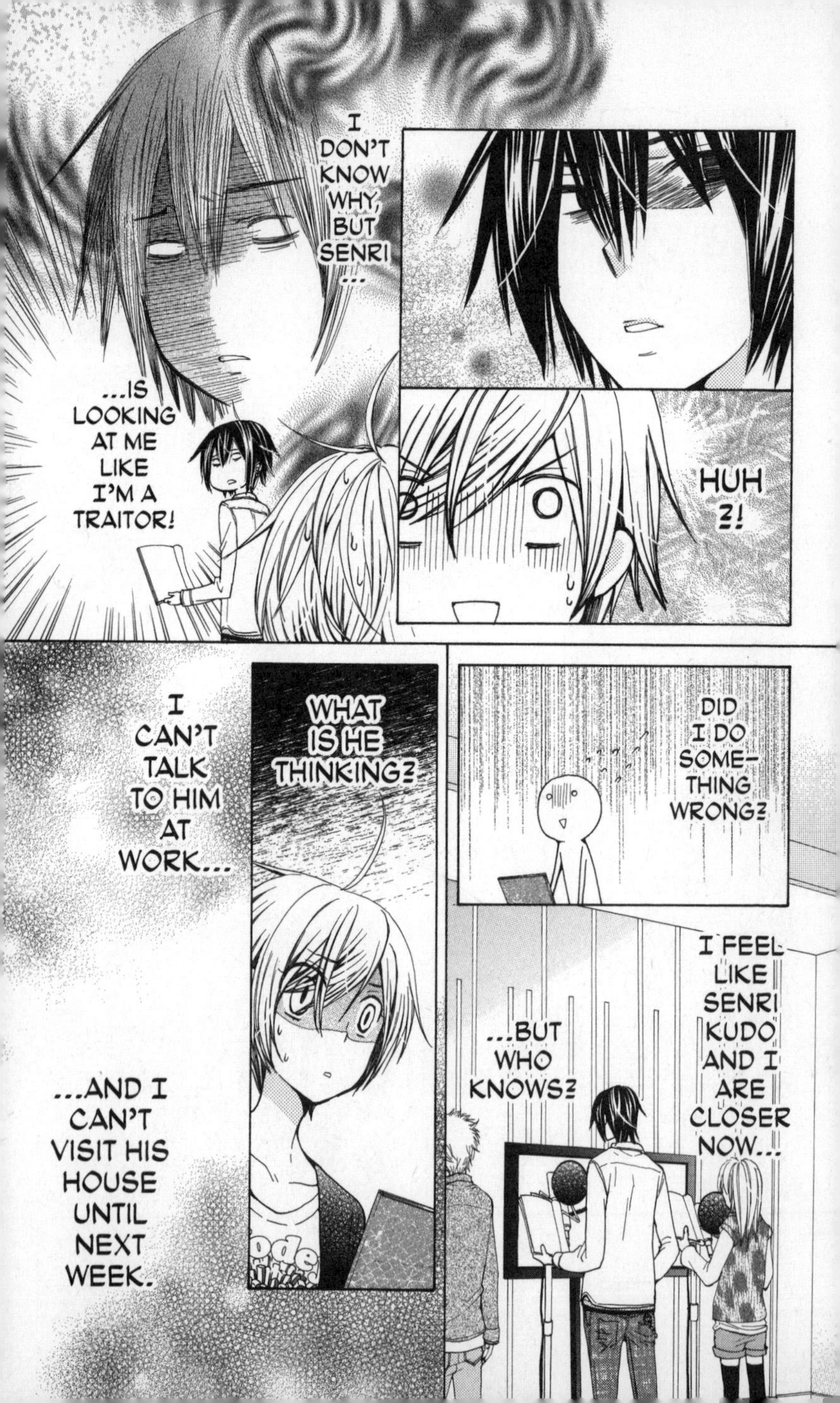
HUH?!
I DON'T KNOW WHY, BUT SENRI...
...IS LOOKING AT ME LIKE I'M A TRAITOR!
DID I DO SOMETHING WRONG?
I FEEL LIKE SENRI KUDO AND I ARE CLOSER NOW...
...BUT WHO KNOWS?
WHAT IS HE THINKING?
I CAN'T TALK TO HIM AT WORK...
...AND I CAN'T VISIT HIS HOUSE UNTIL NEXT WEEK.

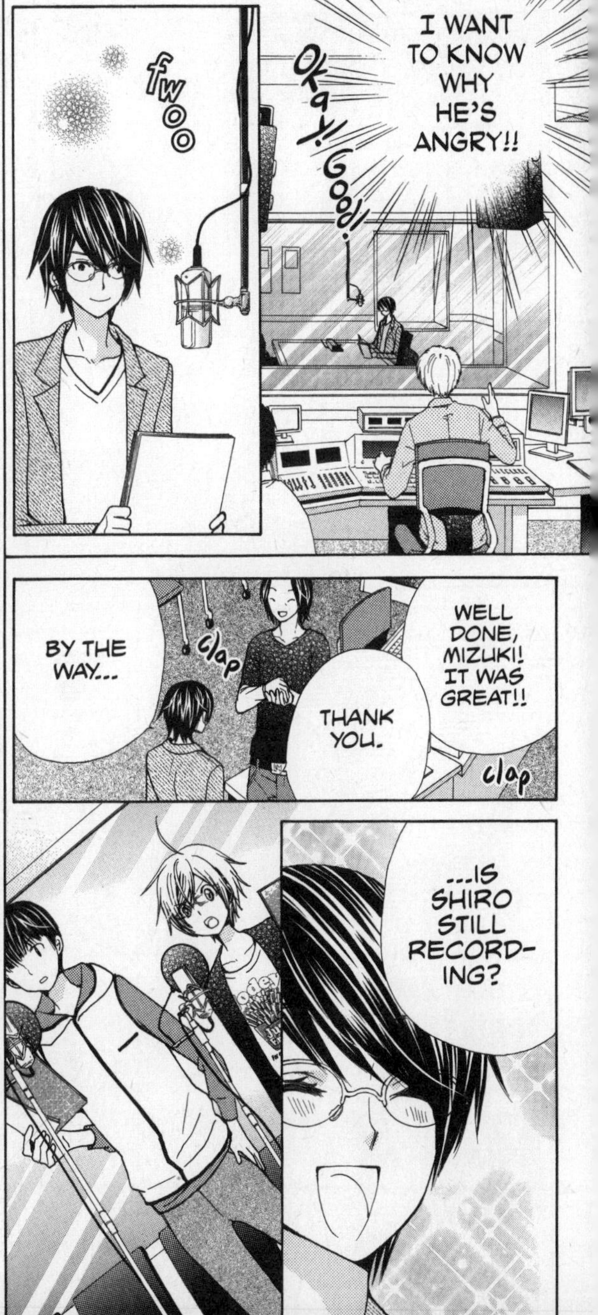
I WANT TO KNOW WHY HE'S ANGRY!!
Okay! Good!
fwooo
WELL DONE, MIZUKI! IT WAS GREAT!!
clap
THANK YOU.
clap
BY THE WAY...
...IS SHIRO STILL RECORDING?

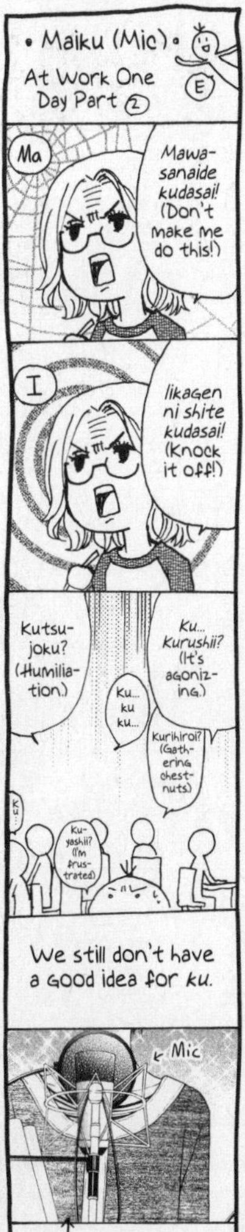
• Maiku (Mic) •
At Work One Day Part ②
E
Ma
Mawasanaide kudasai! (Don't make me do this!)
I
Iikagen ni shite kudasai! (Knock it off!)
Ku... Kurushii? (It's agonizing.)
Kutsujoku? (Humiliation.)
Ku... ku ku...
Kurihiroi? (Gathering chestnuts)
Ku...
Kuyashii? (I'm frustrated)
We still don't have a good idea for ku.
Mic
Imagine how difficult it would be to draw this mic!! Thanks for always drawing it so beautifully!!

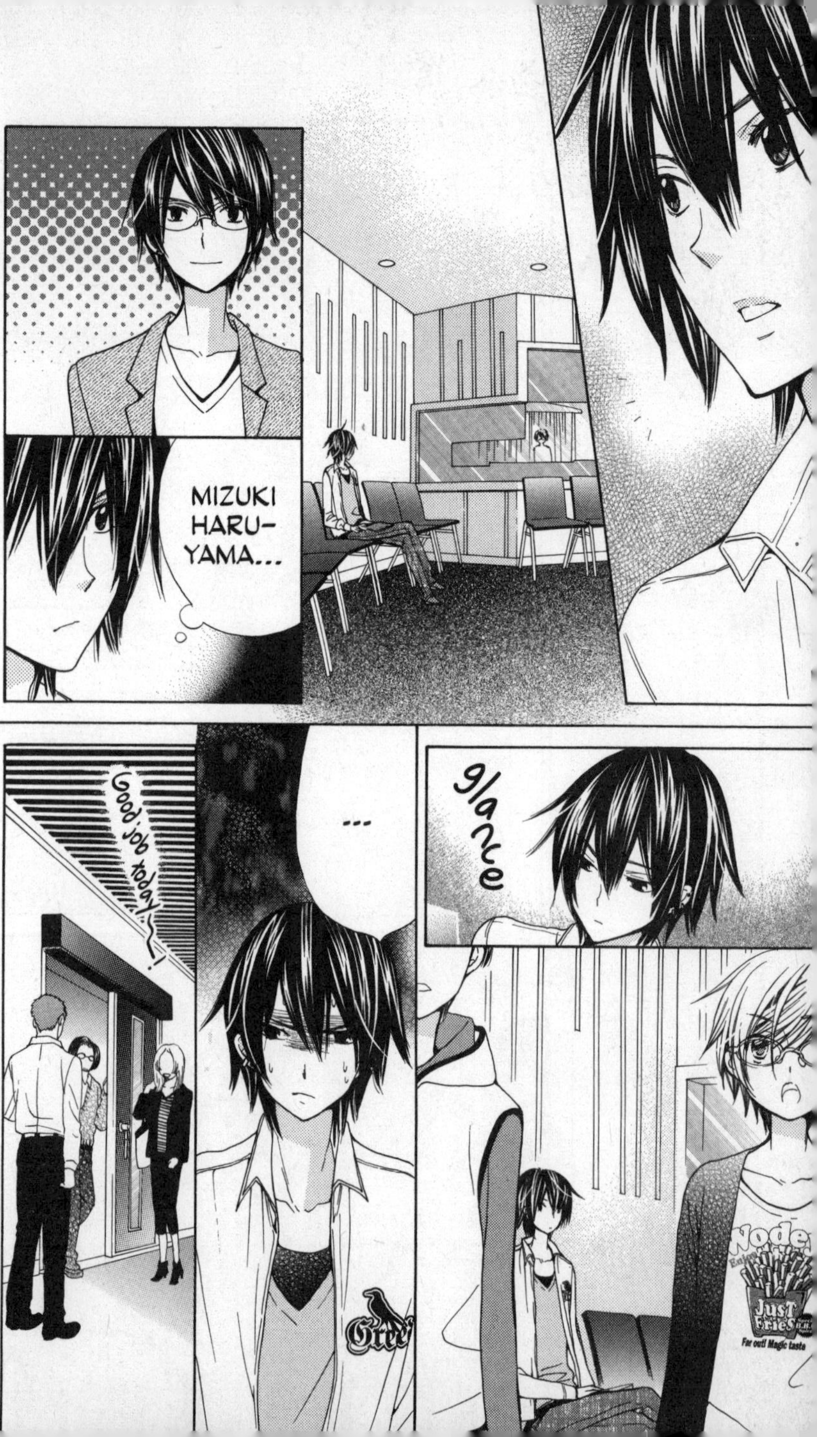
MIZUKI HARU-YAMA...
glance
Just Fries
Far out! Magic taste
...
Good job today~!

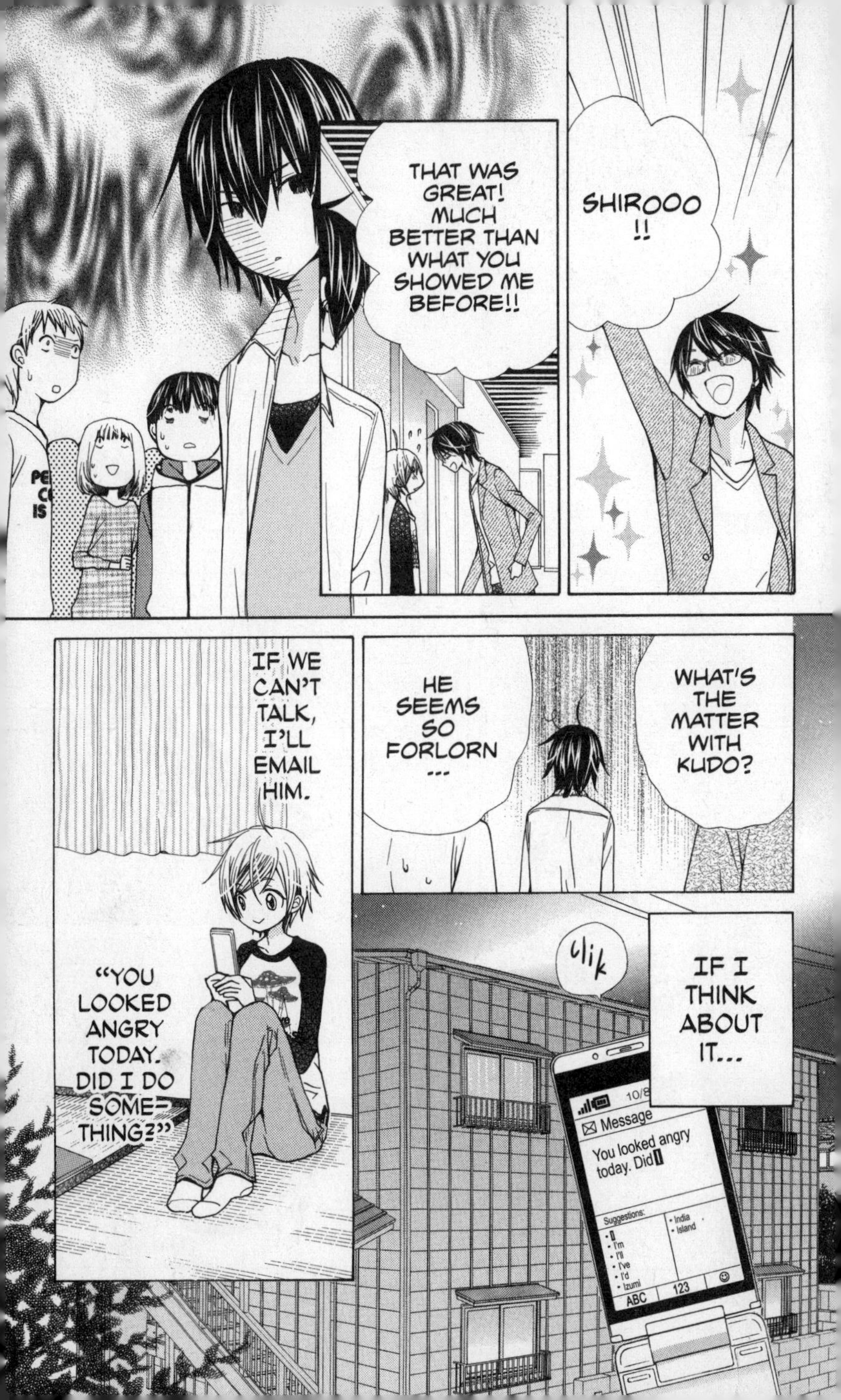
SHIROOO !!
THAT WAS GREAT! MUCH BETTER THAN WHAT YOU SHOWED ME BEFORE!!
WHAT'S THE MATTER WITH KUDO?
HE SEEMS SO FORLORN...
IF I THINK ABOUT IT...
clik
10/8
Message
You looked angry today. Did I
Suggestions:
I
I'm
I'll
I've
I'd
Izumi
India
Island
ABC
123
IF WE CAN'T TALK, I'LL EMAIL HIM.
"YOU LOOKED ANGRY TODAY. DID I DO SOME-THING?"

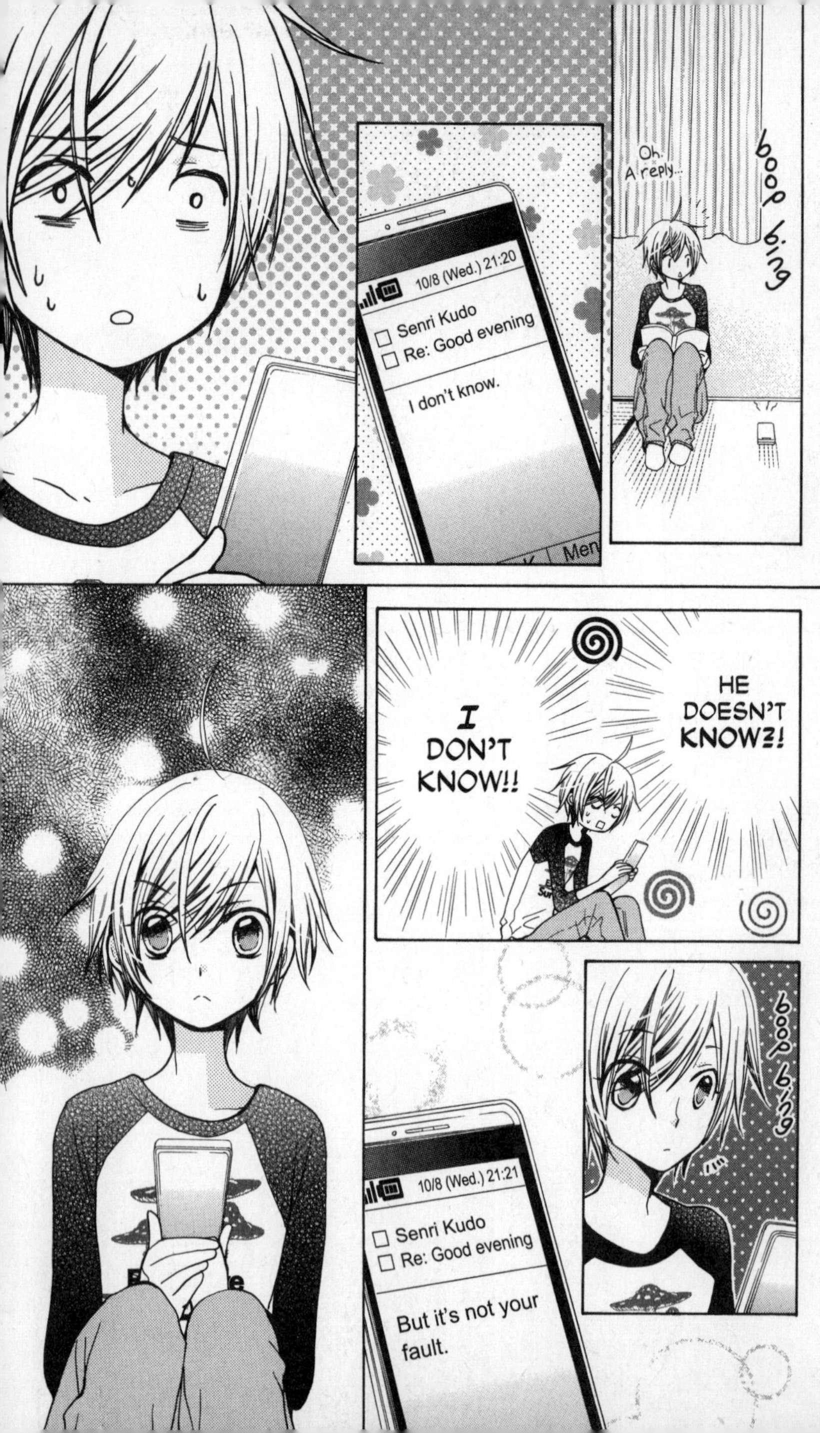
boop bing
Oh. A reply...
10/8 (Wed.) 21:20
Senri Kudo
Re: Good evening
I don't know.
HE DOESN'T KNOW?!
I DON'T KNOW!!
boop bing
10/8 (Wed.) 21:21
Senri Kudo
Re: Good evening
But it's not your fault.

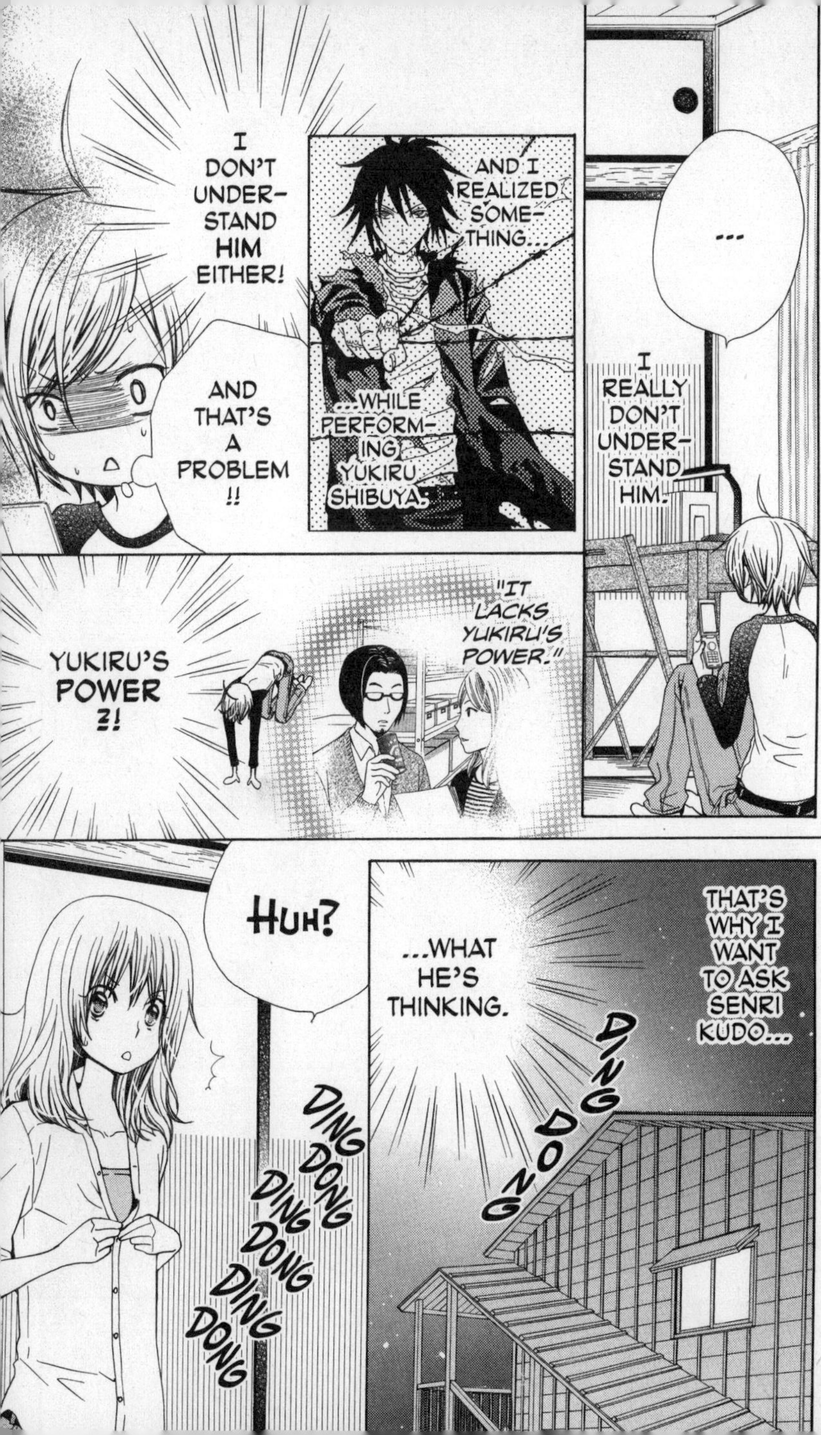
...
I REALLY DON'T UNDERSTAND HIM.
AND I REALIZED SOMETHING...
...WHILE PERFORMING YUKIRU SHIBUYA.
I DON'T UNDERSTAND HIM EITHER!
AND THAT'S A PROBLEM!!
"IT LACKS YUKIRU'S POWER."
YUKIRU'S POWER?!
THAT'S WHY I WANT TO ASK SENRI KUDO...
...WHAT HE'S THINKING.
DING DONG
HUH?
DING DONG DING DONG DING DONG

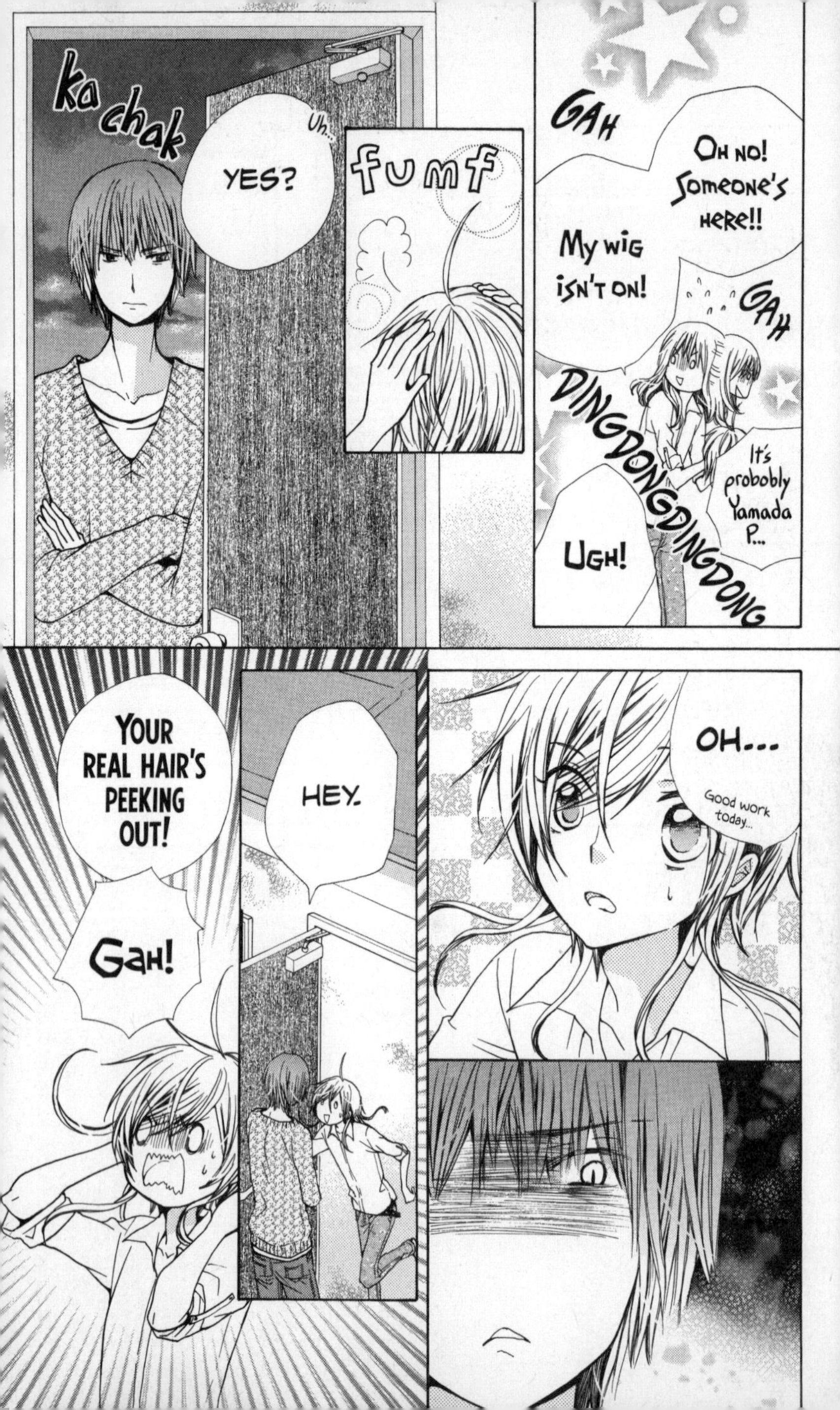
GAH
OH NO! SOMEONE'S HERE!!
MY WIG ISN'T ON!
GAH
It's probably Yamada P...
DINGDONGDINGDONG
UGH!
fumf
ka chak
Uh...
YES?
OH...
Good work today...
HEY.
YOUR REAL HAIR'S PEEKING OUT!
GAH!

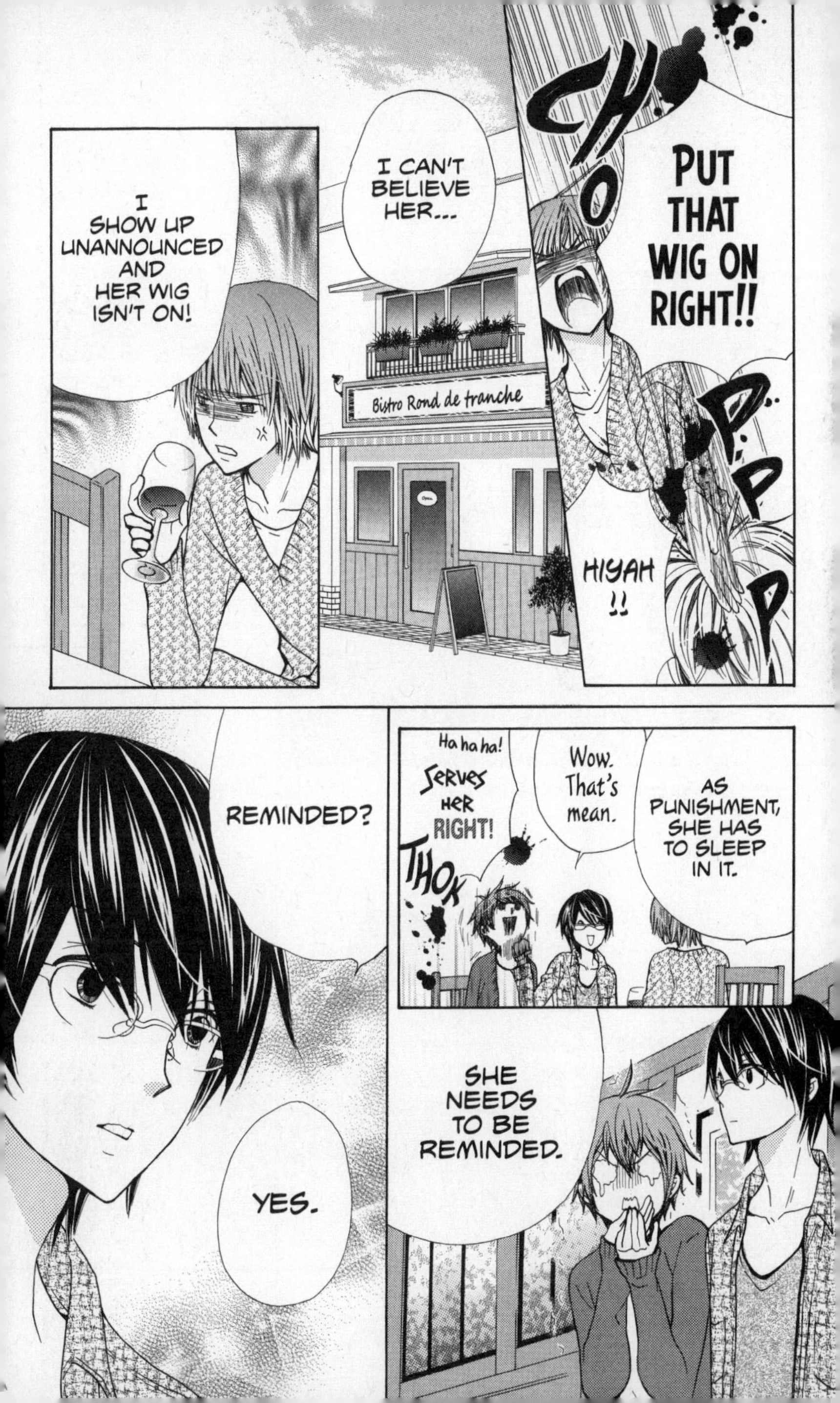
CHO
PUT THAT WIG ON RIGHT!!
P... P P
HIYAH!!
I CAN'T BELIEVE HER...
I SHOW UP UNANNOUNCED AND HER WIG ISN'T ON!
AS PUNISHMENT, SHE HAS TO SLEEP IN IT.
Wow. That's mean.
Ha ha ha! Serves her RIGHT!
THOK
SHE NEEDS TO BE REMINDED.
REMINDED?
YES.

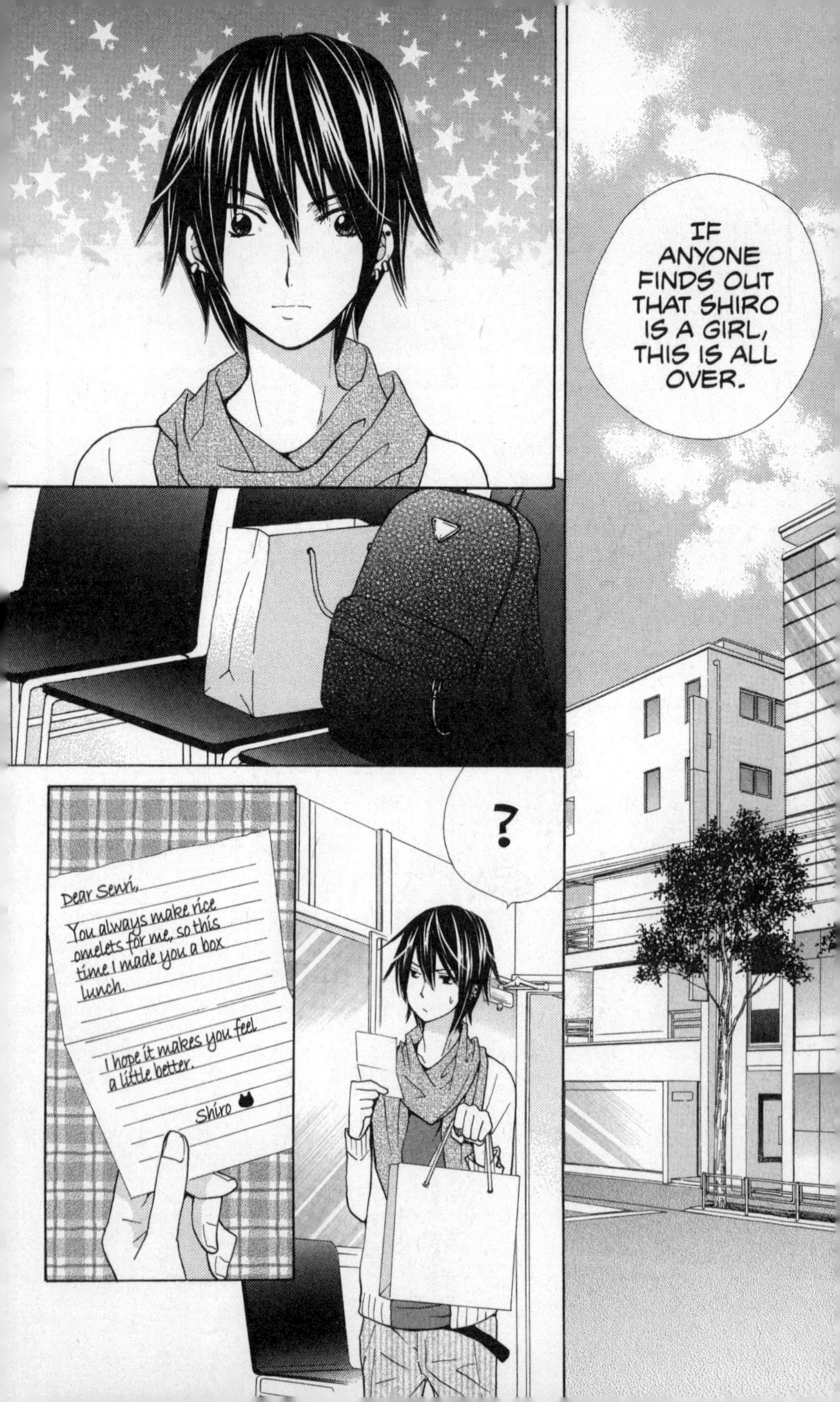
IF ANYONE FINDS OUT THAT SHIRO IS A GIRL, THIS IS ALL OVER.
?
Dear Senri,
You always make rice omelets for me, so this time I made you a box lunch.
I hope it makes you feel a little better.
Shiro

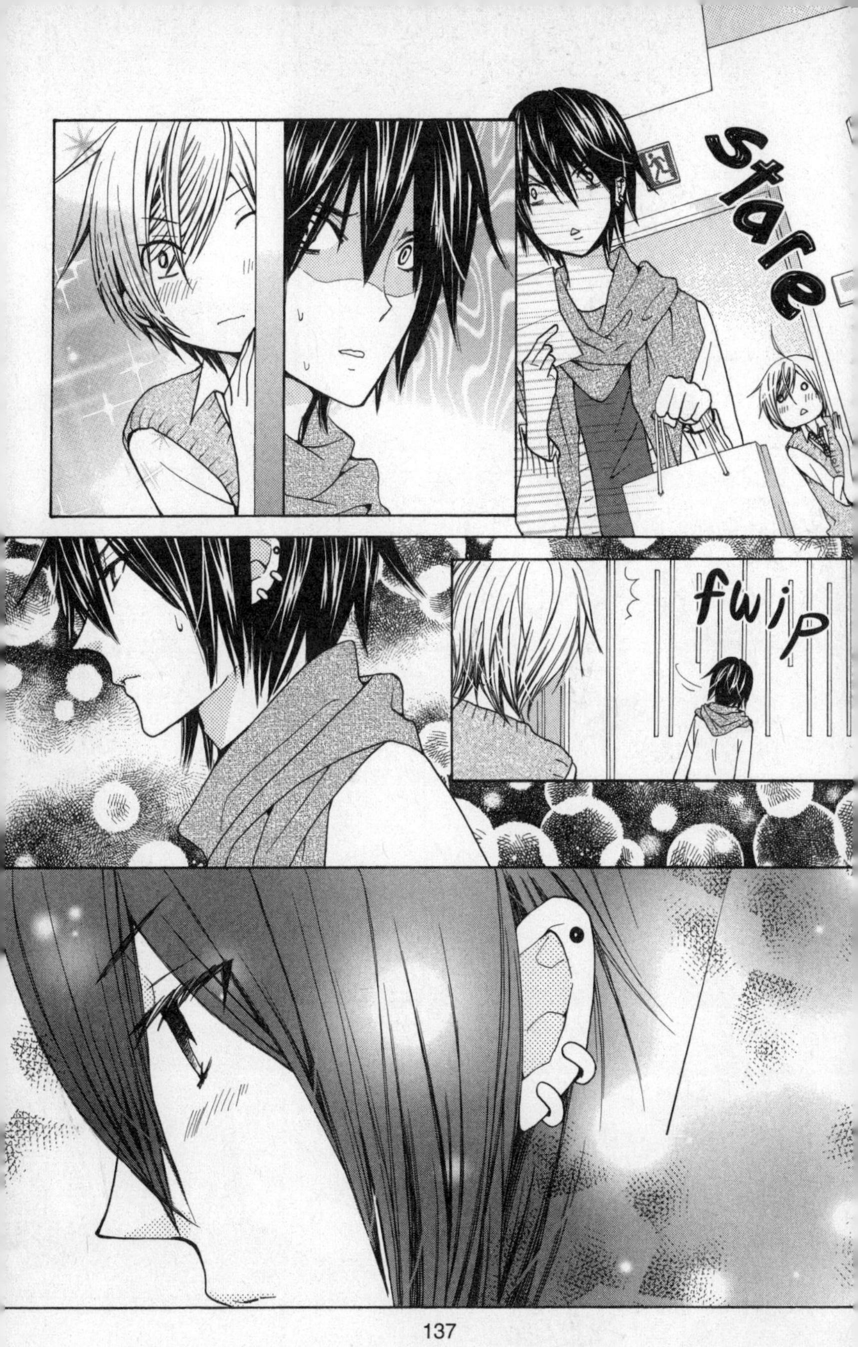
stare
fwip

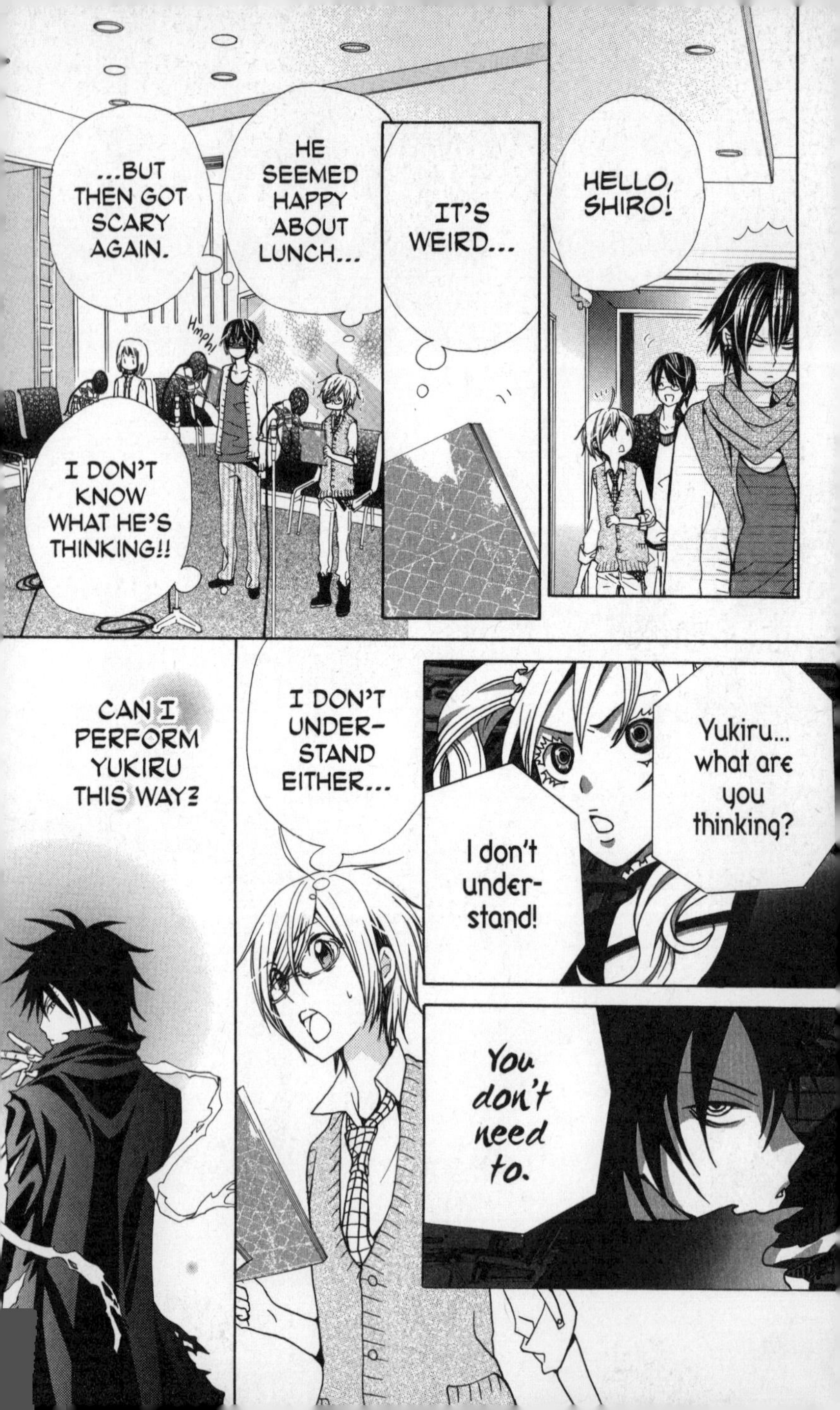
HELLO, SHIRO!
IT'S WEIRD...
HE SEEMED HAPPY ABOUT LUNCH...
...BUT THEN GOT SCARY AGAIN.
Hmph!
I DON'T KNOW WHAT HE'S THINKING!!
Yukiru... what are you thinking?
I don't under-stand!
You don't need to.
I DON'T UNDER-STAND EITHER...
CAN I PERFORM YUKIRU THIS WAY?

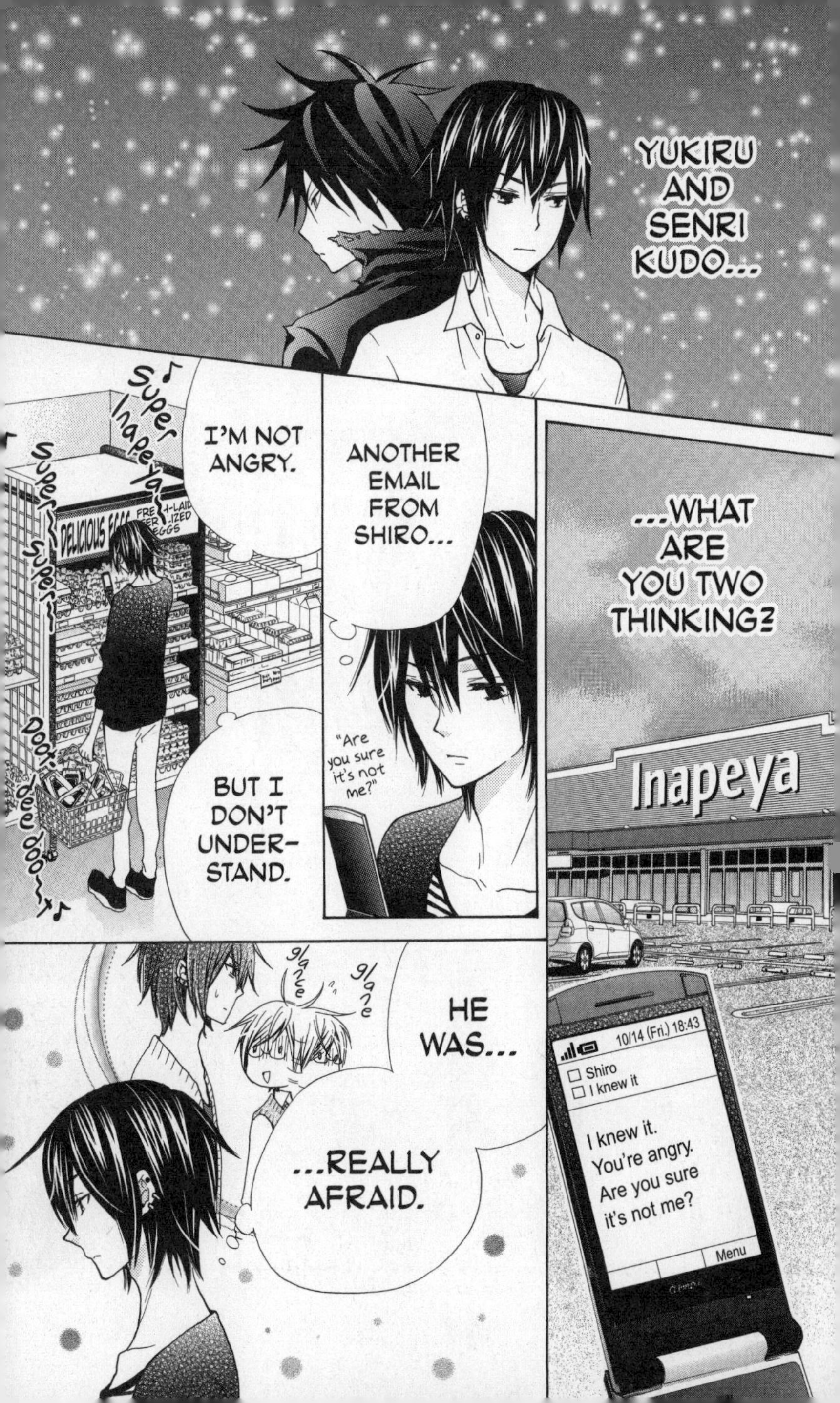
YUKIRU AND SENRI KUDO...
...WHAT ARE YOU TWO THINKING?
Inapeya
10/14 (Fri.) 18:43
Shiro
I knew it
I knew it. You're angry. Are you sure it's not me?
Menu
ANOTHER EMAIL FROM SHIRO...
"Are you sure it's not me?"
Super Inapeya~
Super~ Super~
Dooti dee doo~
DELICIOUS EGGS
I'M NOT ANGRY.
BUT I DON'T UNDER-STAND.
glance glance
HE WAS...
...REALLY AFRAID.

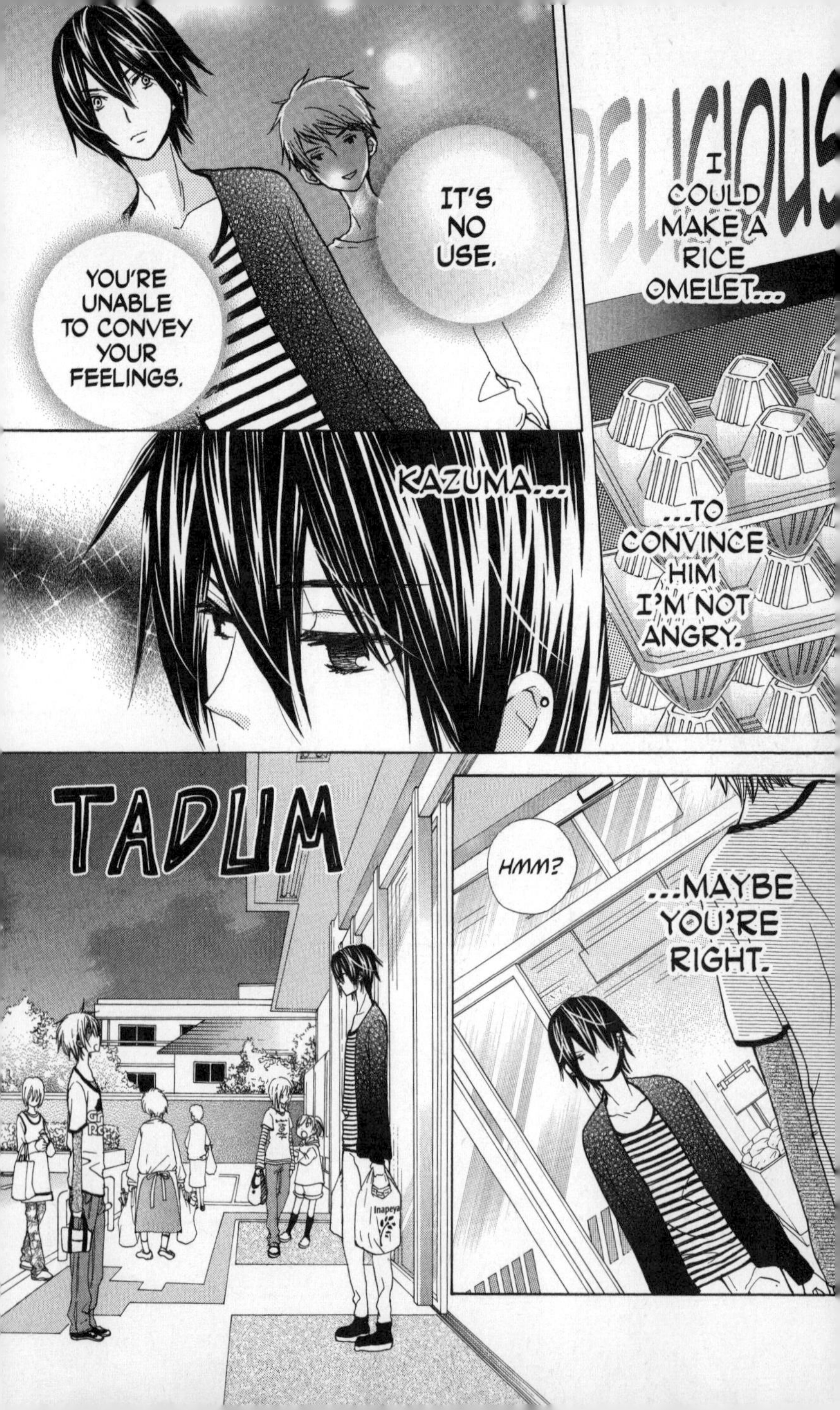
DELICIOUS
I COULD MAKE A RICE OMELET...
...TO CONVINCE HIM I'M NOT ANGRY.
IT'S NO USE.
YOU'RE UNABLE TO CONVEY YOUR FEELINGS.
KAZUMA...
...MAYBE YOU'RE RIGHT.
HMM?
TADUM
Inapeya

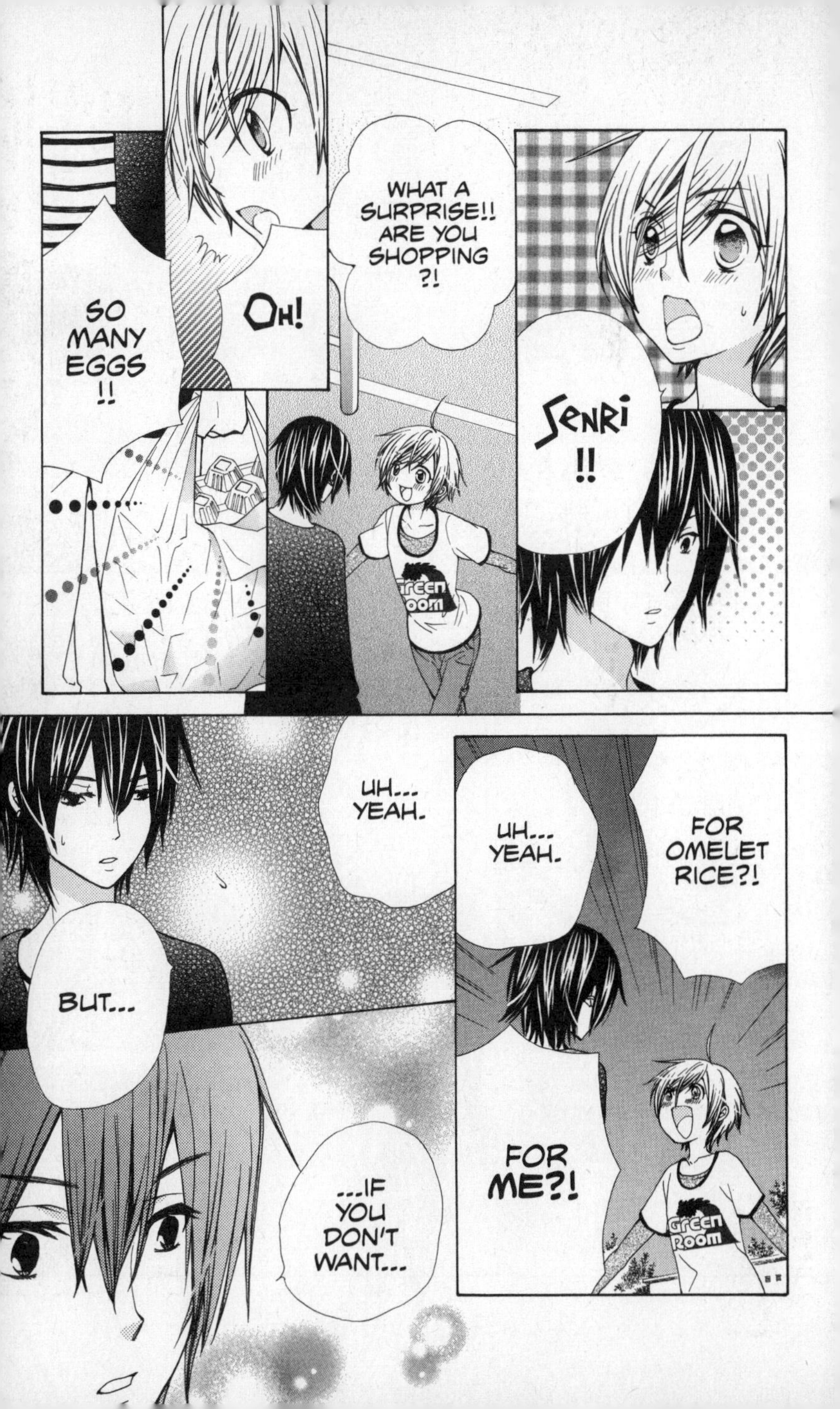
SENRI!!
WHAT A SURPRISE!! ARE YOU SHOPPING?!
OH!
SO MANY EGGS!!
......
FOR OMELET RICE?!
UH... YEAH.
FOR ME?!
UH... YEAH.
BUT...
...IF YOU DON'T WANT...

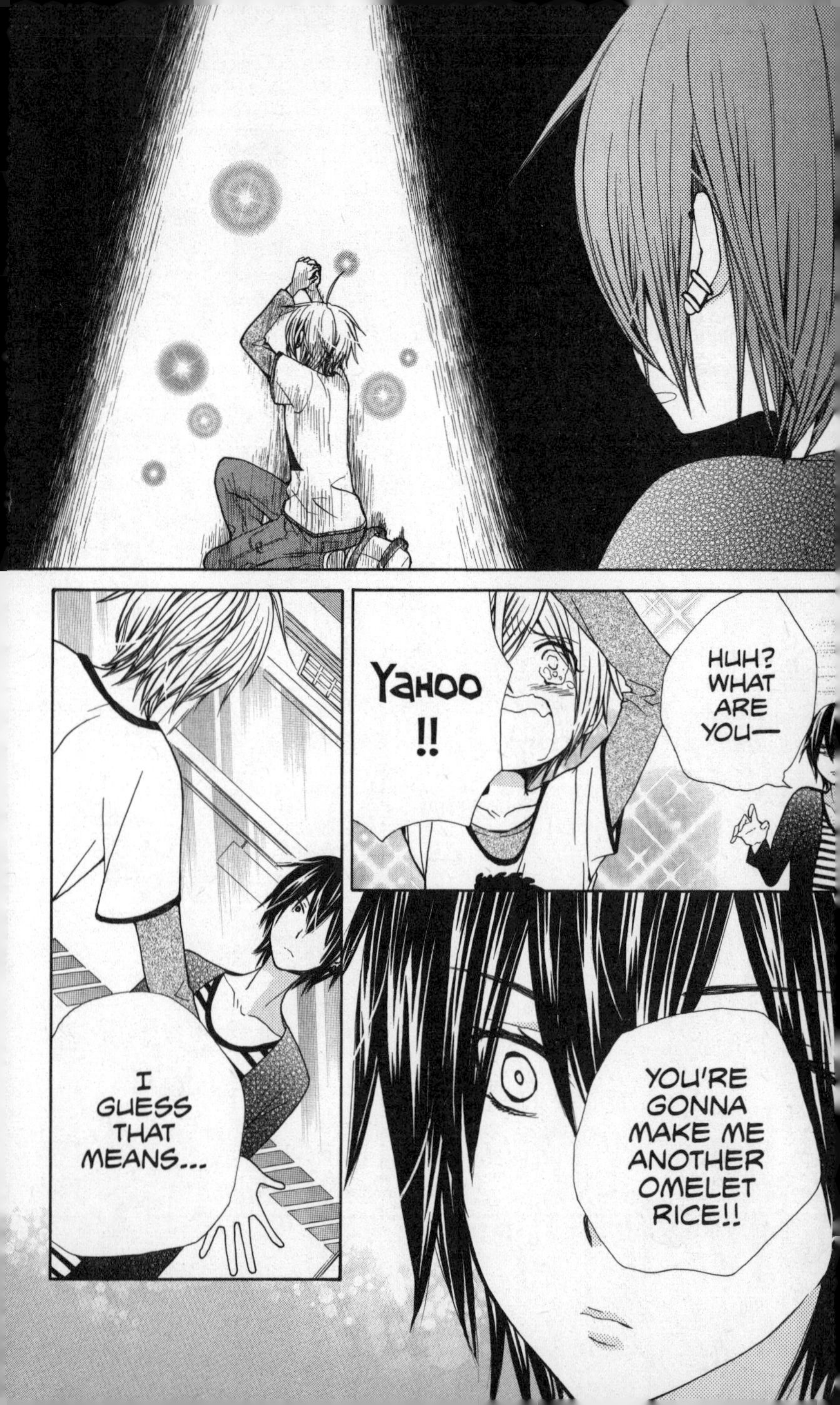
HUH? WHAT ARE YOU—
YAHOO !!
I GUESS THAT MEANS...
YOU'RE GONNA MAKE ME ANOTHER OMELET RICE!!

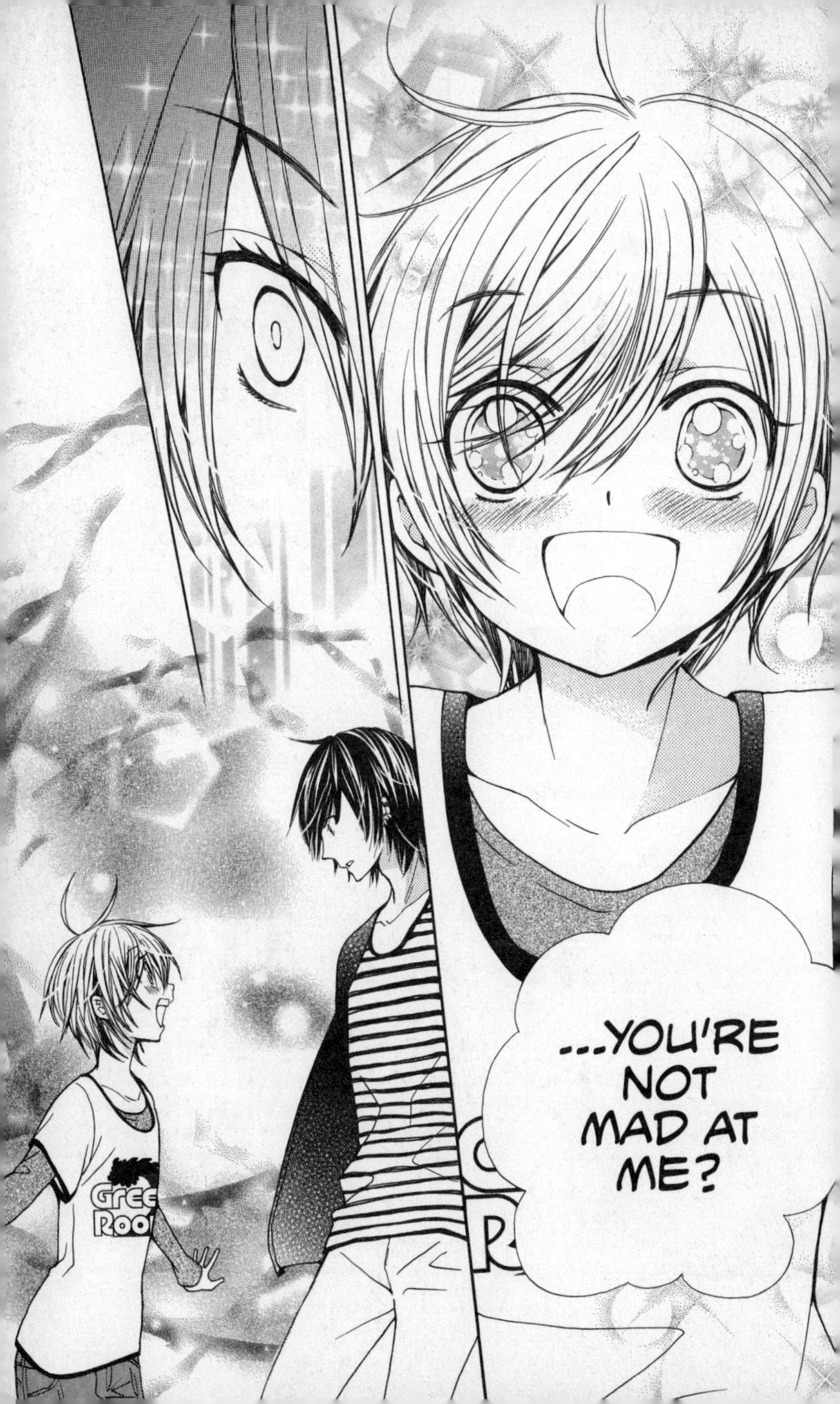
...YOU'RE NOT MAD AT ME?

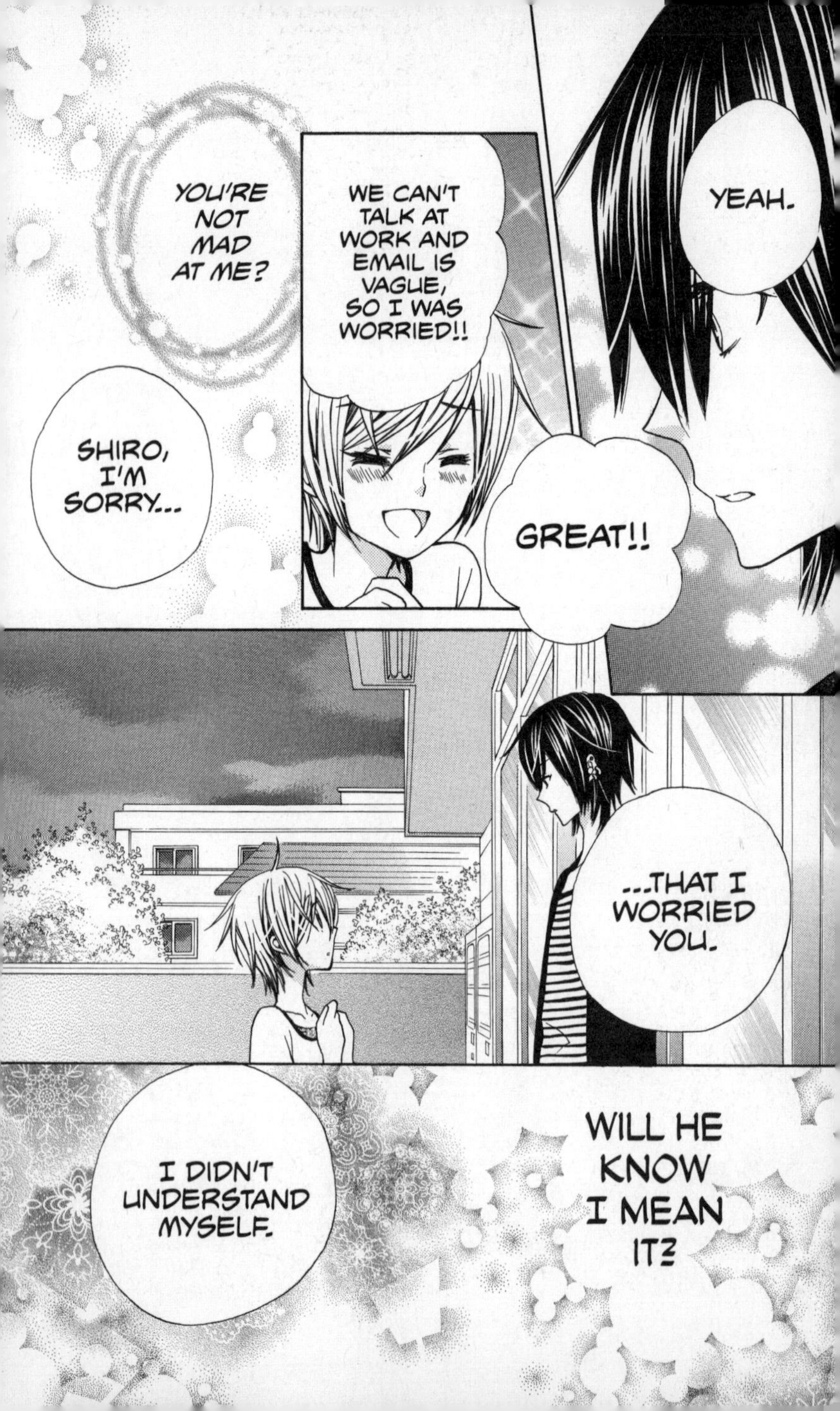
YEAH.
GREAT!!
WE CAN'T TALK AT WORK AND EMAIL IS VAGUE, SO I WAS WORRIED!!
YOU'RE NOT MAD AT ME?
SHIRO, I'M SORRY...
...THAT I WORRIED YOU.
WILL HE KNOW I MEAN IT?
I DIDN'T UNDERSTAND MYSELF.

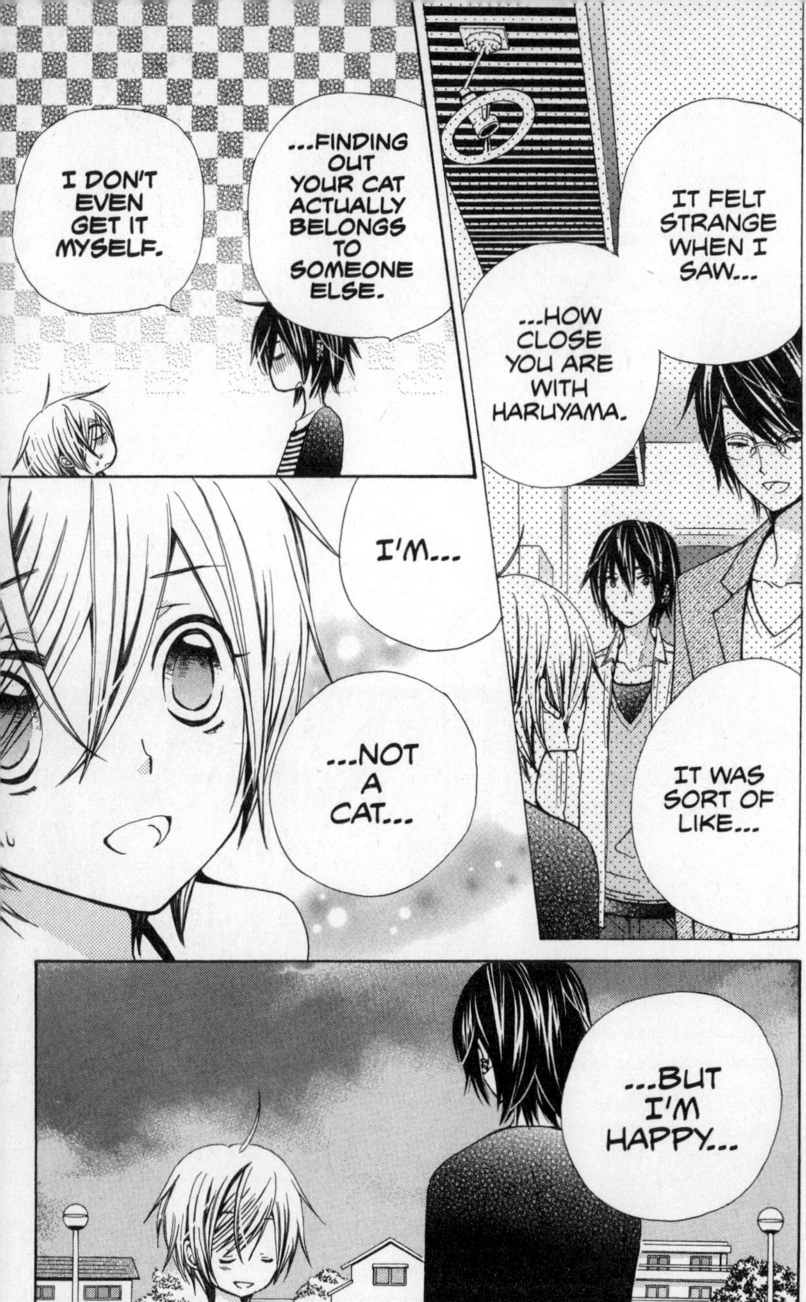
IT FELT STRANGE WHEN I SAW...
...HOW CLOSE YOU ARE WITH HARUYAMA.
IT WAS SORT OF LIKE...
...FINDING OUT YOUR CAT ACTUALLY BELONGS TO SOMEONE ELSE.
I DON'T EVEN GET IT MYSELF.
I'M...
...NOT A CAT...
...BUT I'M HAPPY...

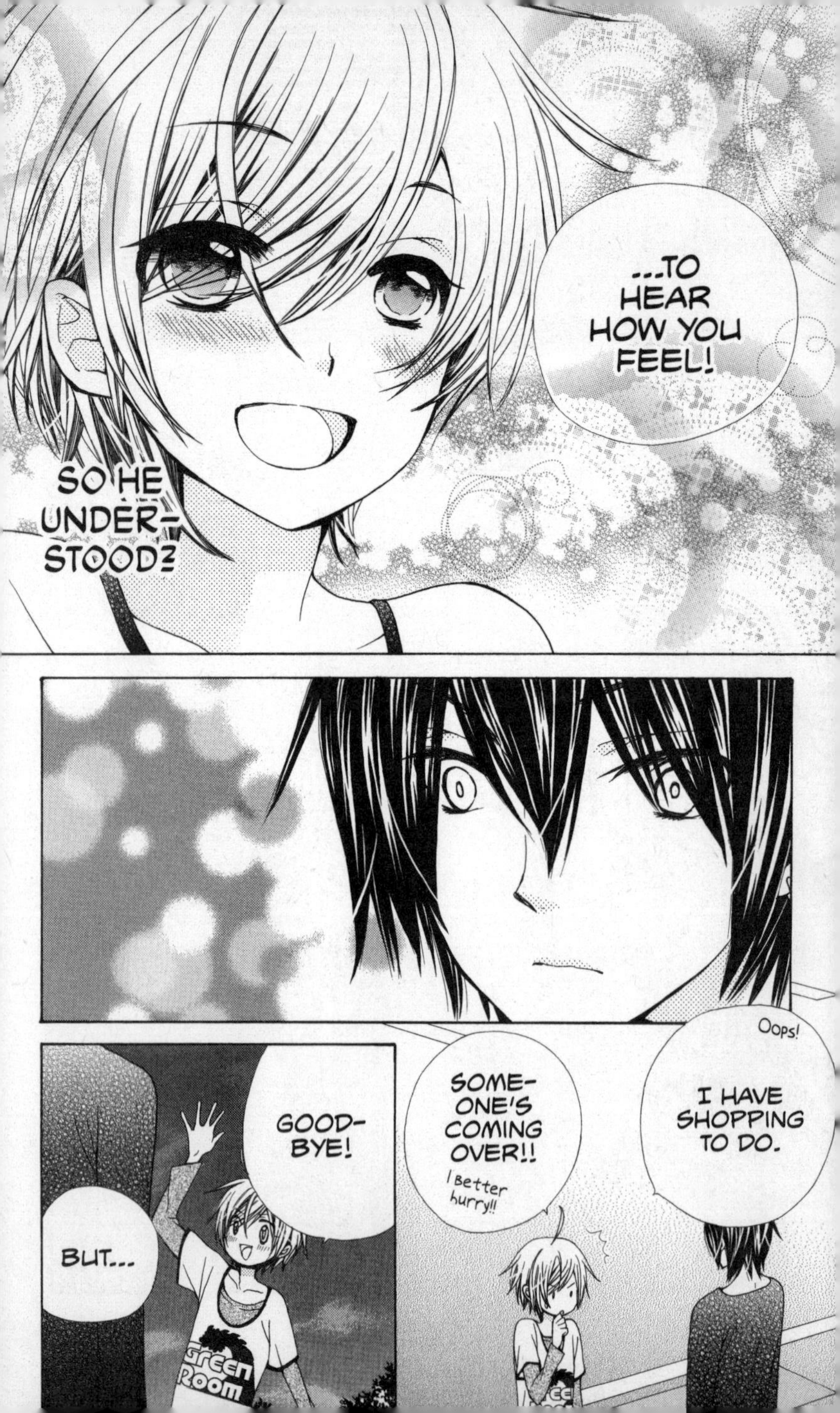
...TO HEAR HOW YOU FEEL!
SO HE UNDER-STOOD?
Oops!
I HAVE SHOPPING TO DO.
SOME-ONE'S COMING OVER!!
I Better hurry!!
GOOD-BYE!
BUT...

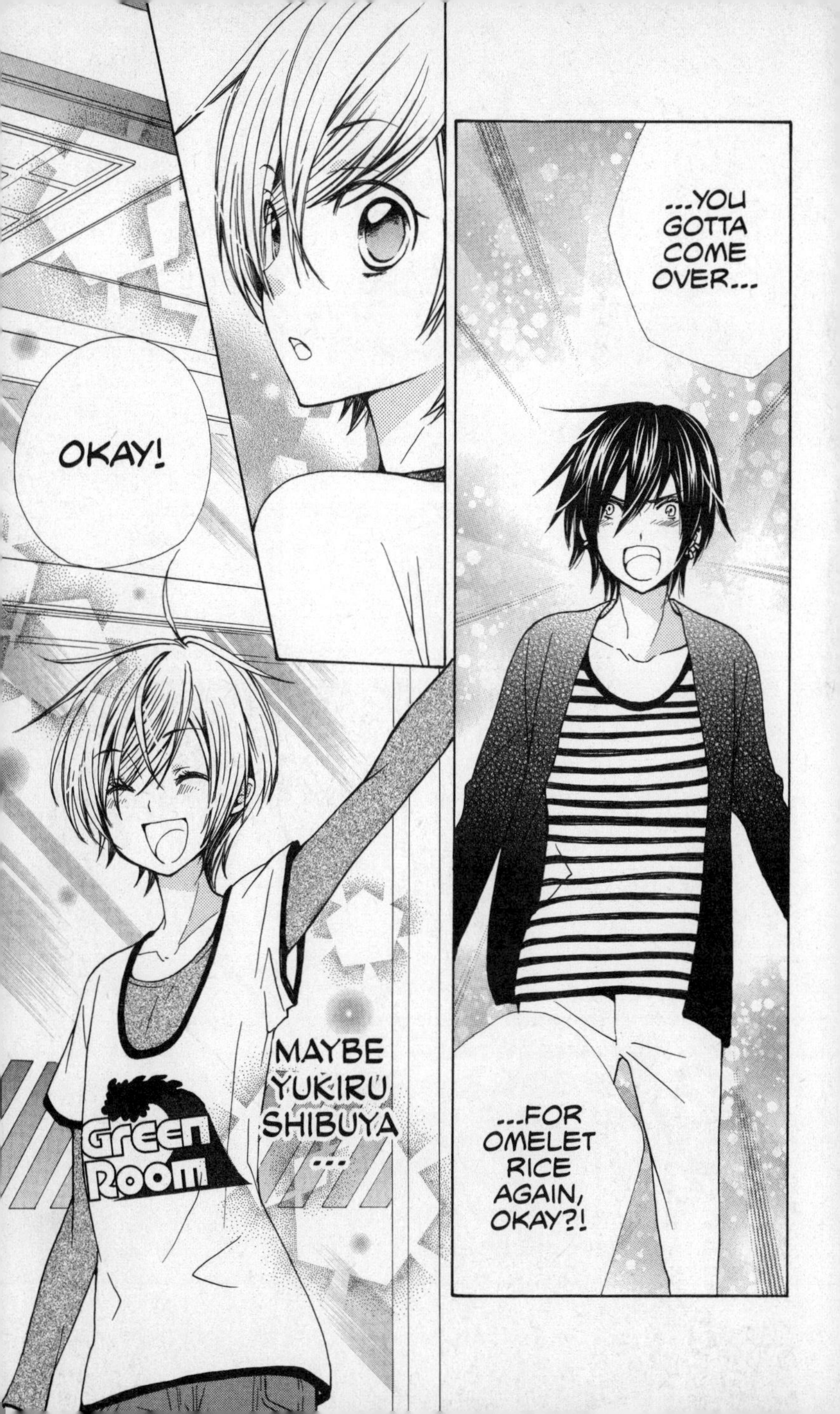
...YOU GOTTA COME OVER...
...FOR OMELET RICE AGAIN, OKAY?!
OKAY!
MAYBE YUKIRU SHIBUYA ...
Green Room

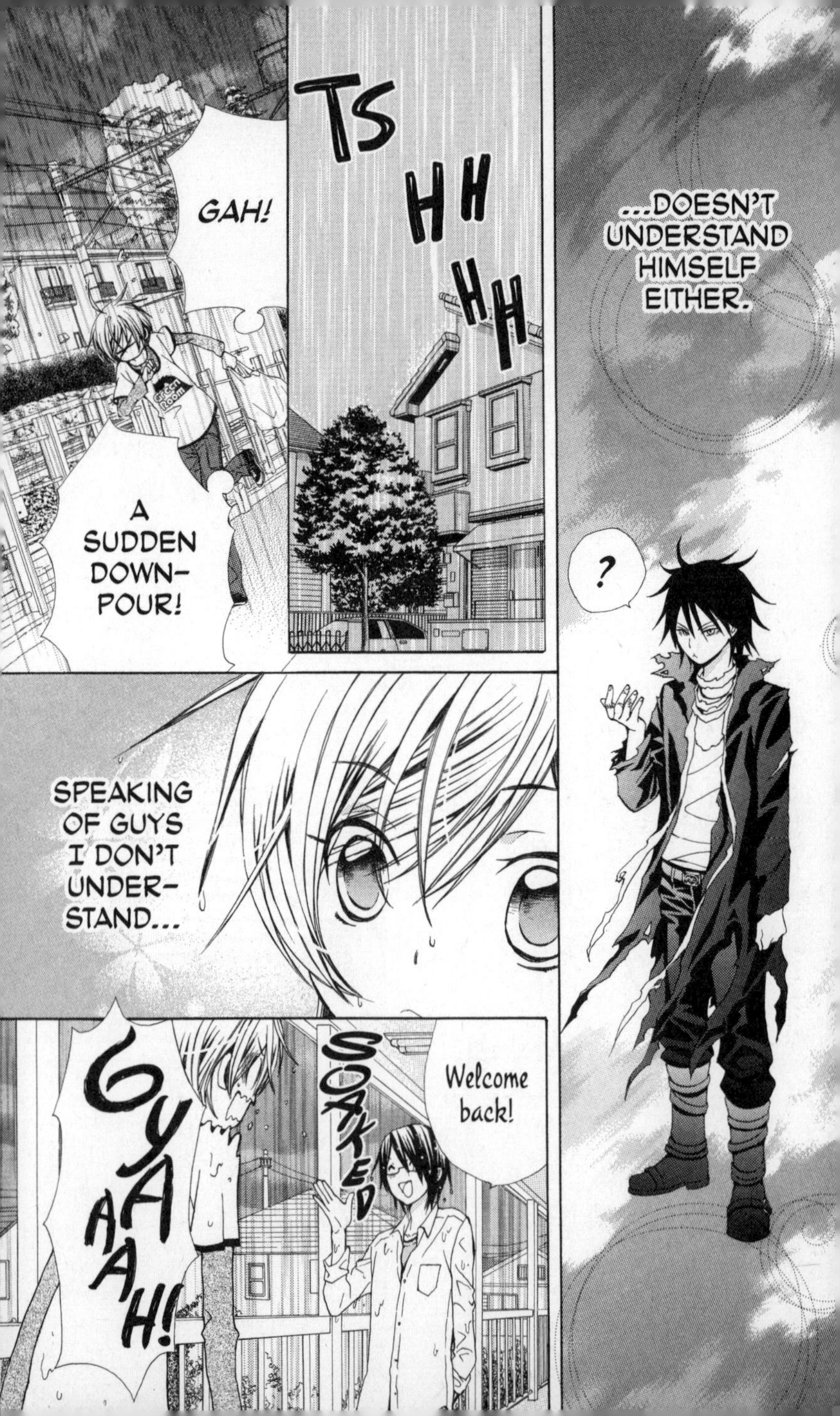
...DOESN'T UNDERSTAND HIMSELF EITHER.
?
TSHHHH
GAH!
A SUDDEN DOWN-POUR!
SPEAKING OF GUYS I DON'T UNDER-STAND...
Welcome back!
SOAKED
GYAAAH!

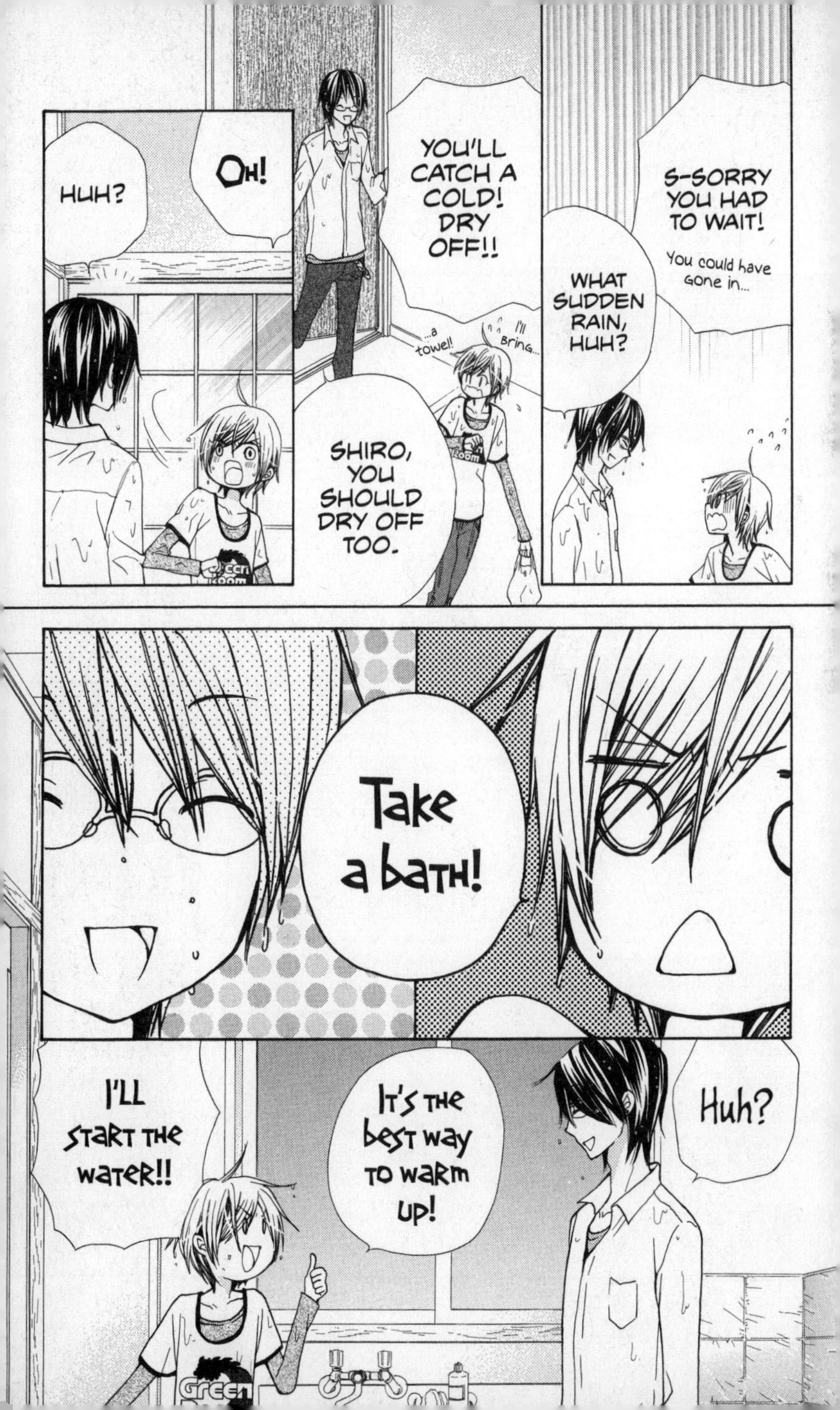

S-SORRY YOU HAD TO WAIT!
You could have gone in...
WHAT SUDDEN RAIN, HUH?
YOU'LL CATCH A COLD! DRY OFF!!
I'll bring...
...a towel!
SHIRO, YOU SHOULD DRY OFF TOO.
OH!
HUH?
Take a bath!
Huh?
It's the best way to warm up!
I'LL START THE WATER!!

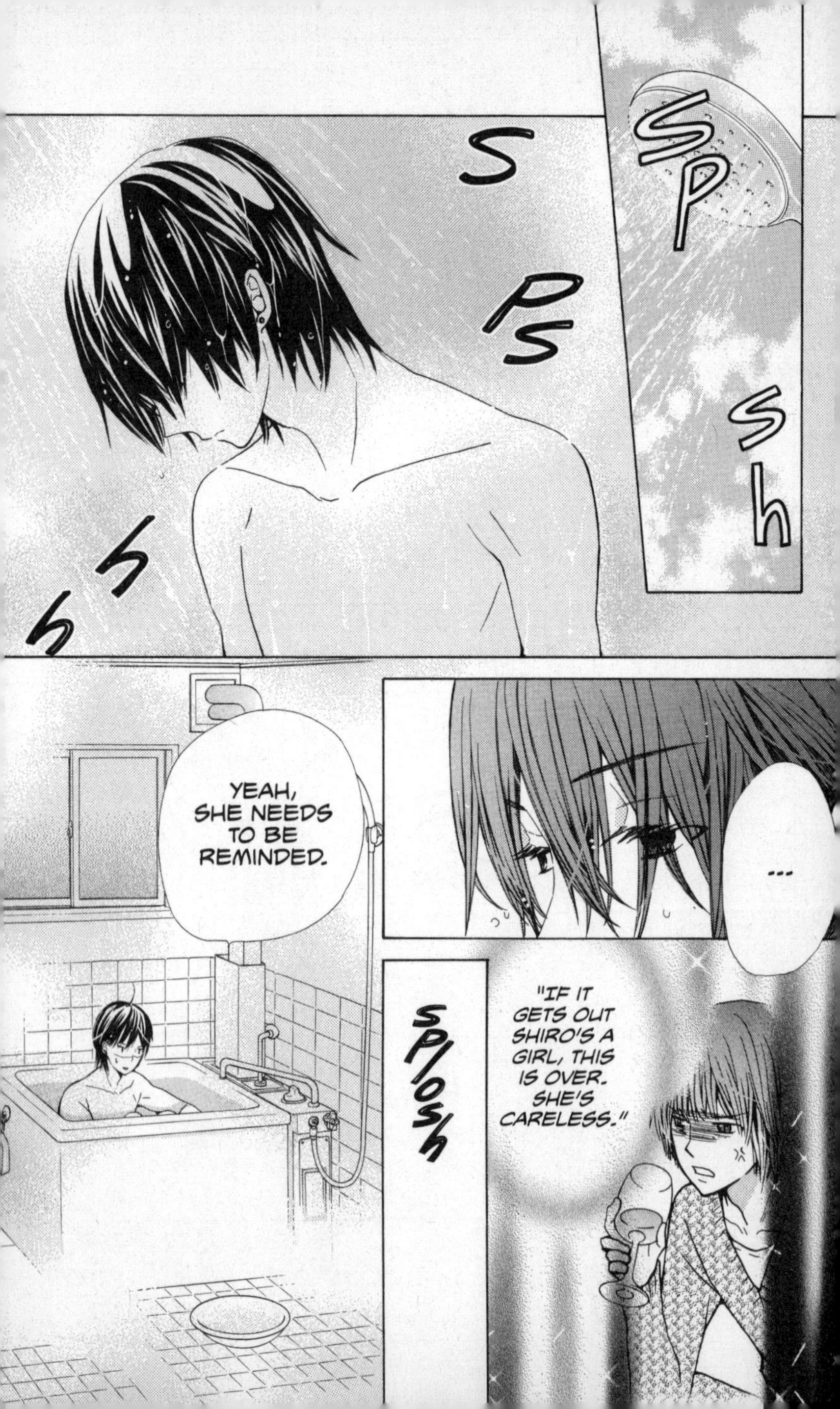
Sp
sh
S
Ps
h h
...
"IF IT GETS OUT SHIRO'S A GIRL, THIS IS OVER. SHE'S CARELESS."
Splosh
YEAH, SHE NEEDS TO BE REMINDED.

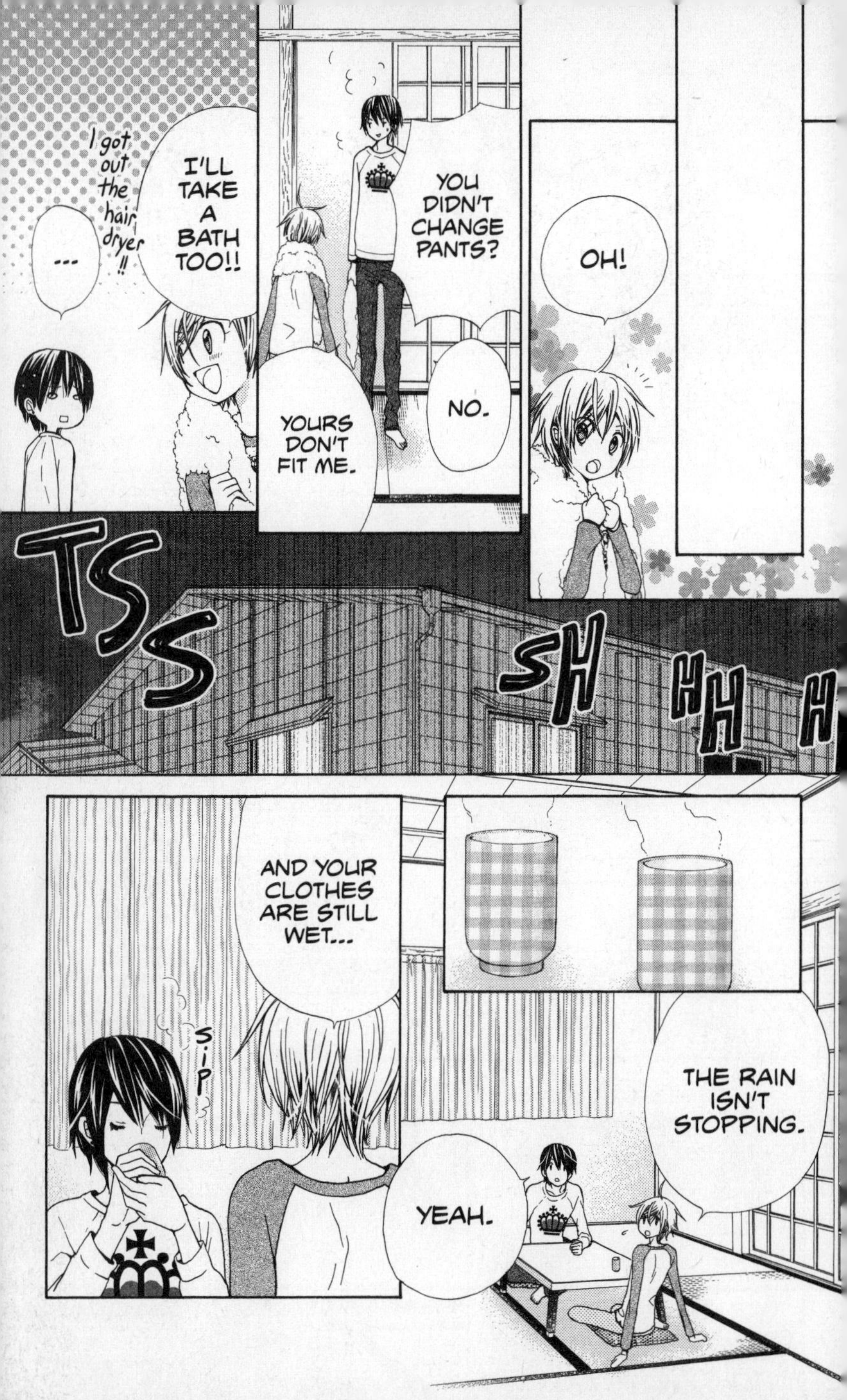
OH!
YOU DIDN'T CHANGE PANTS?
NO.
YOURS DON'T FIT ME.
I'LL TAKE A BATH TOO!!
I got out the hair dryer!!
...
TSS SHHHH
THE RAIN ISN'T STOPPING.
AND YOUR CLOTHES ARE STILL WET...
SIP
YEAH.

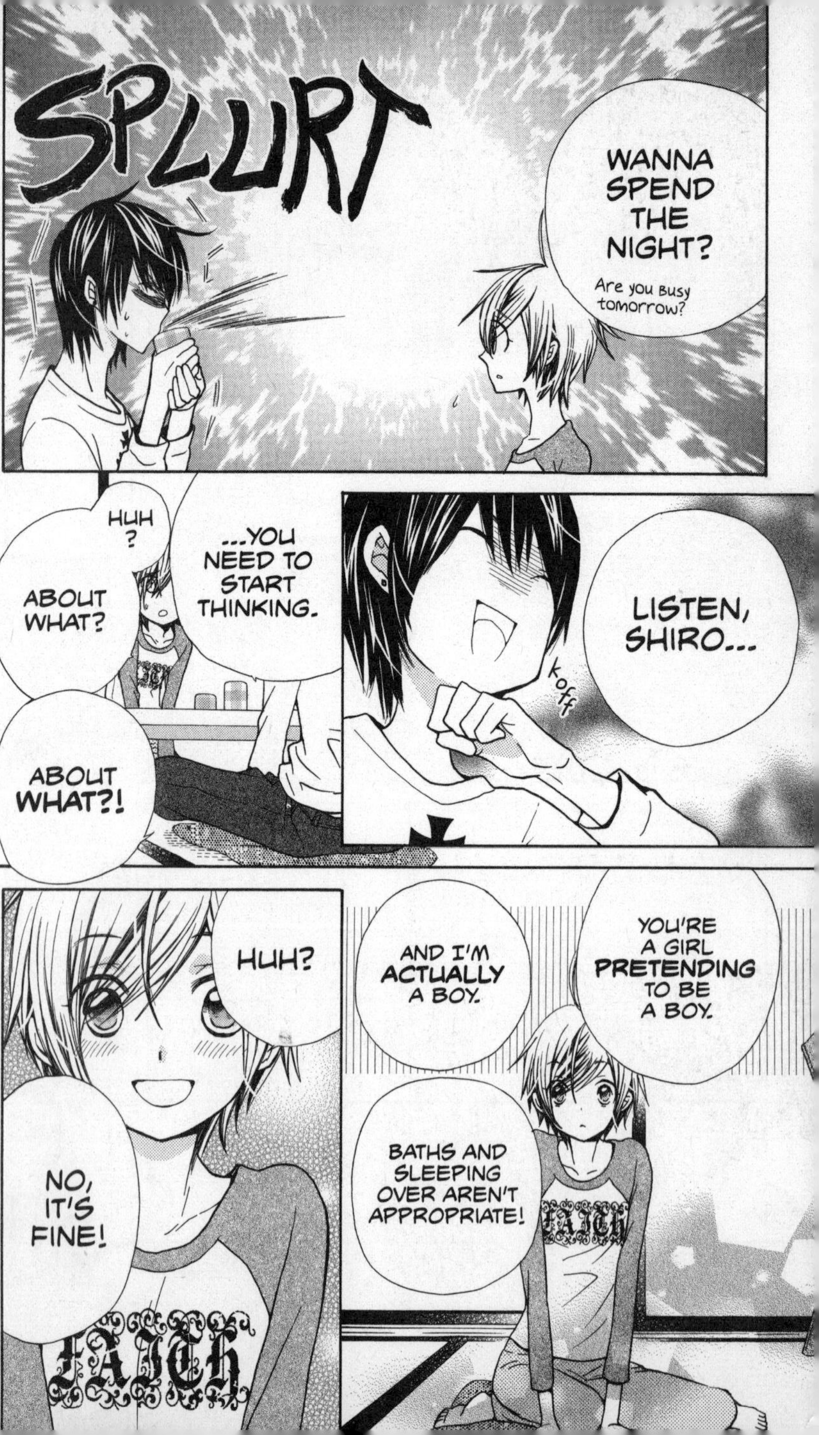
WANNA SPEND THE NIGHT?
Are you busy tomorrow?
SPLURT
LISTEN, SHIRO...
koff
...YOU NEED TO START THINKING.
HUH? ABOUT WHAT?
ABOUT WHAT?!
YOU'RE A GIRL PRETENDING TO BE A BOY.
AND I'M ACTUALLY A BOY.
BATHS AND SLEEPING OVER AREN'T APPROPRIATE!
HUH?
NO, IT'S FINE!

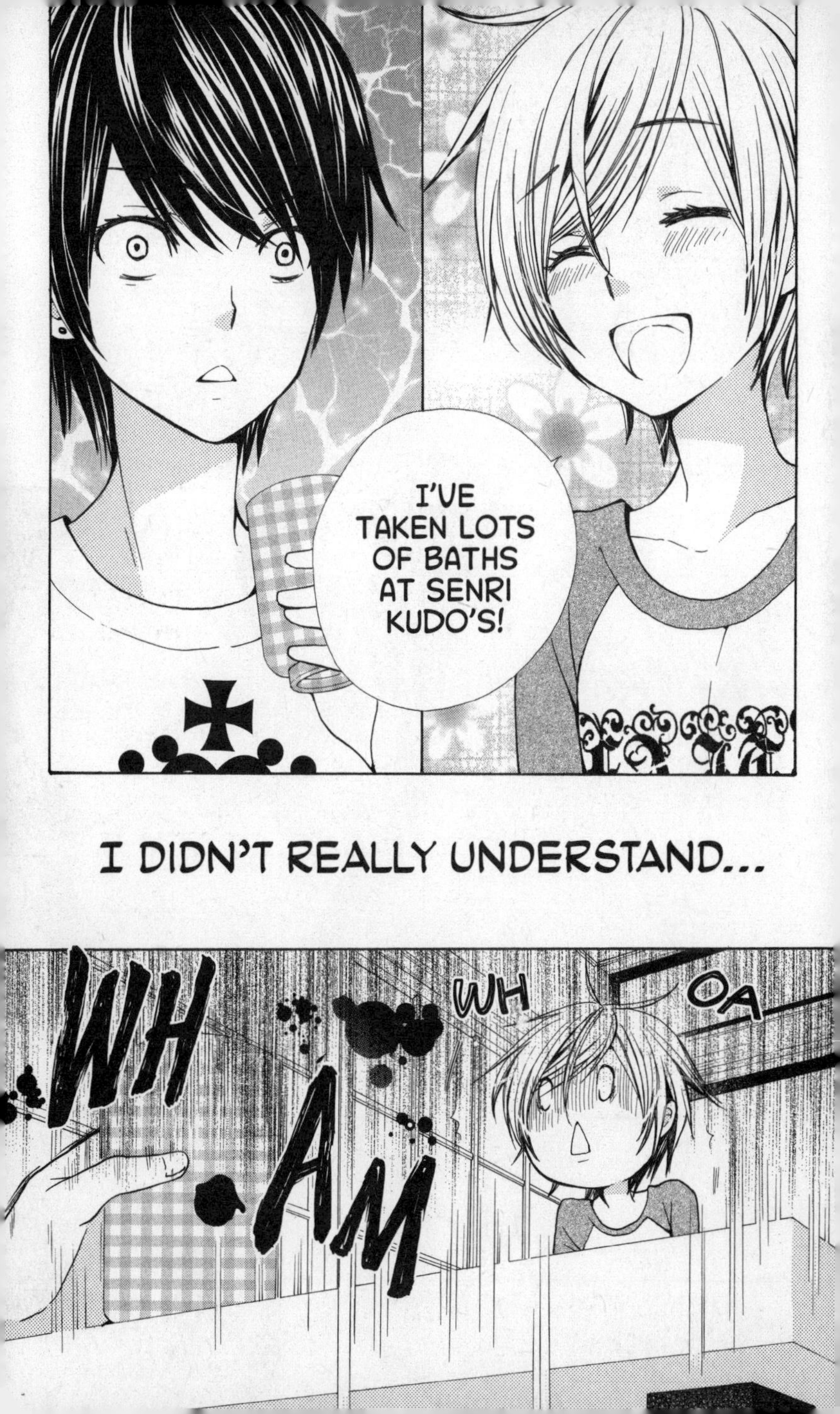
I'VE TAKEN LOTS OF BATHS AT SENRI KUDO'S!
I DIDN'T REALLY UNDERSTAND...
WH OA
WHAM

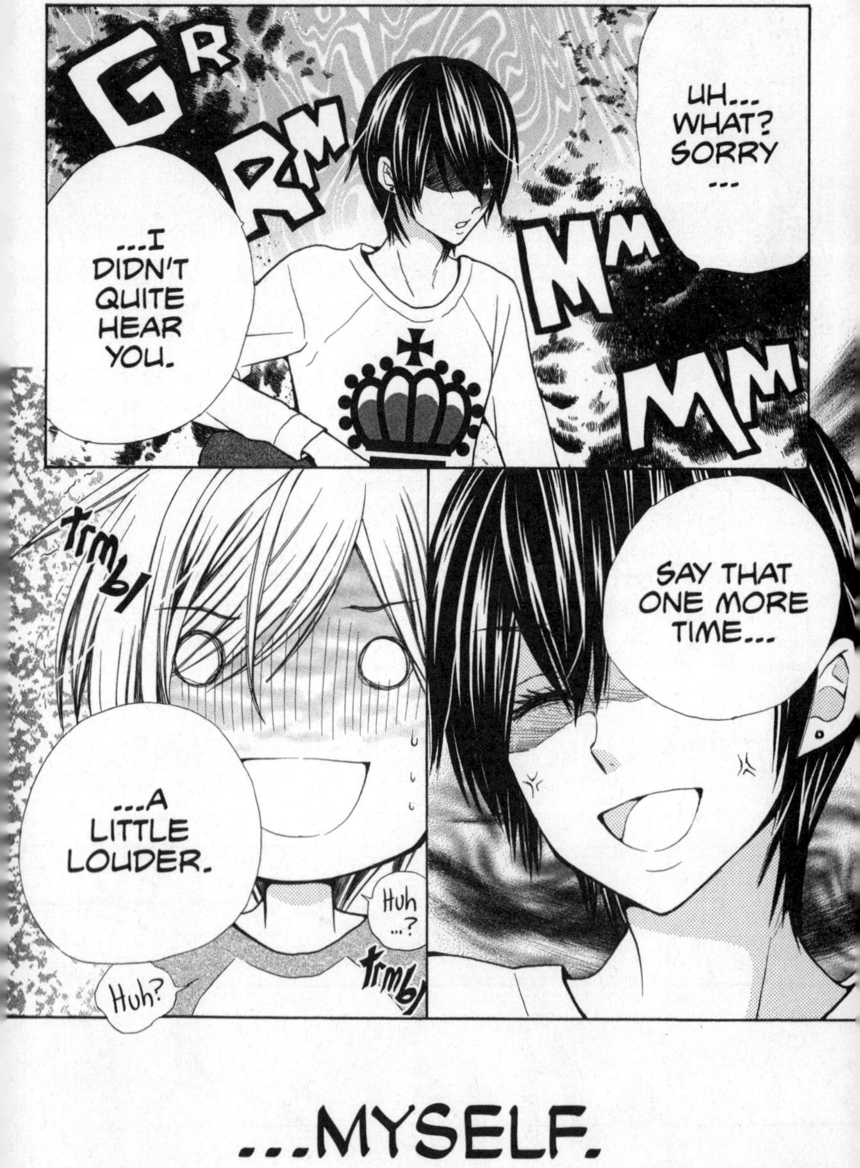
UH... WHAT? SORRY ...
GRRMMMMMM
...I DIDN'T QUITE HEAR YOU.
SAY THAT ONE MORE TIME...
trmbl
...A LITTLE LOUDER.
Huh ...?
trmbl
Huh?

...MYSELF.

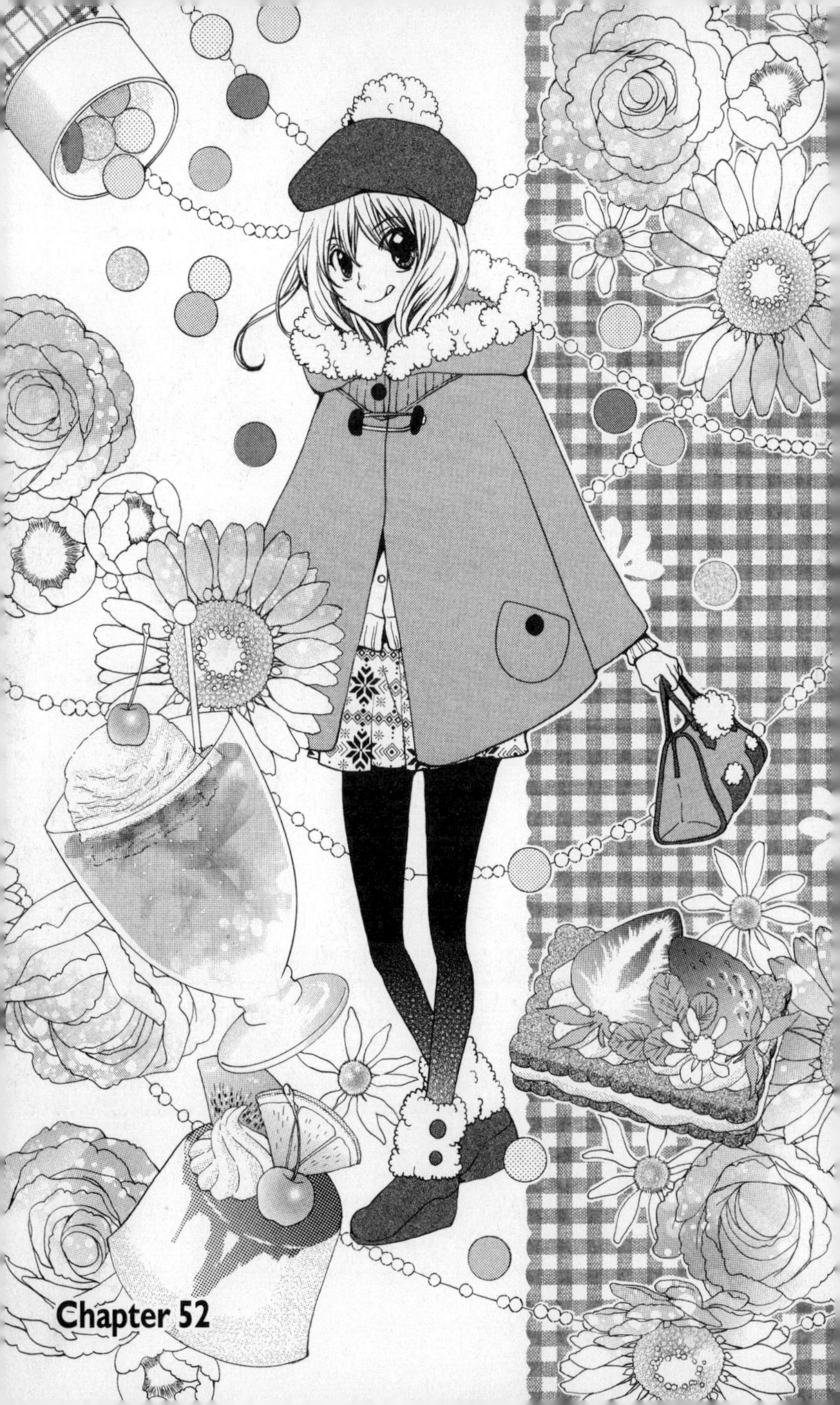

Chapter 52

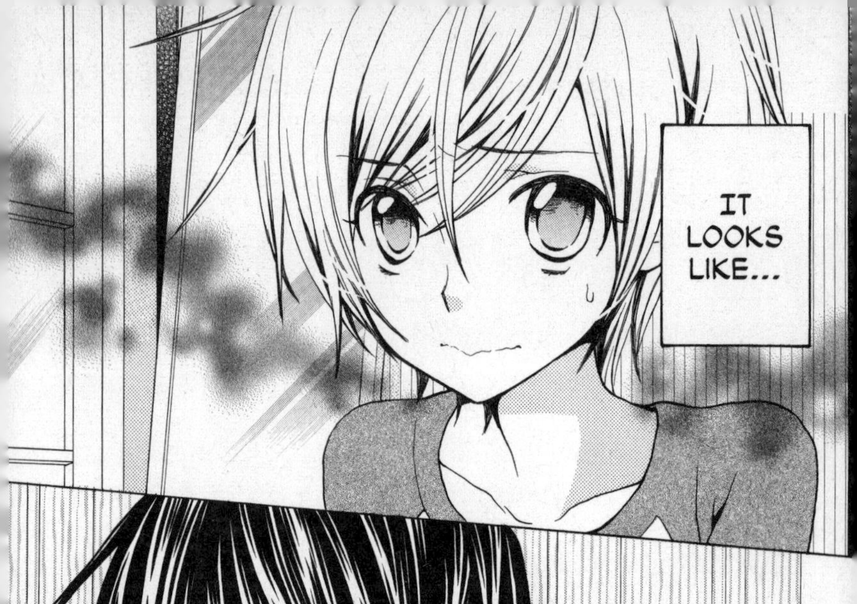
IT LOOKS LIKE...
...I'VE MADE MIZUKI MAD.
WHAT SHOULD I DO?

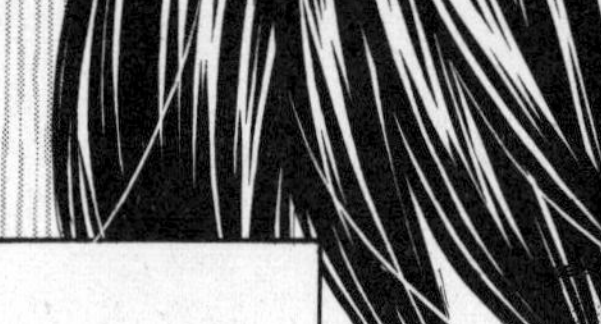

• Various Things •

• Yet again, my assistant M-san made Mitchy for the bottom notes!! They're awesome!!

• After I finish this note, I'm going to clean up this messy room!! Probably!! Yeah... Maybe...

(6)

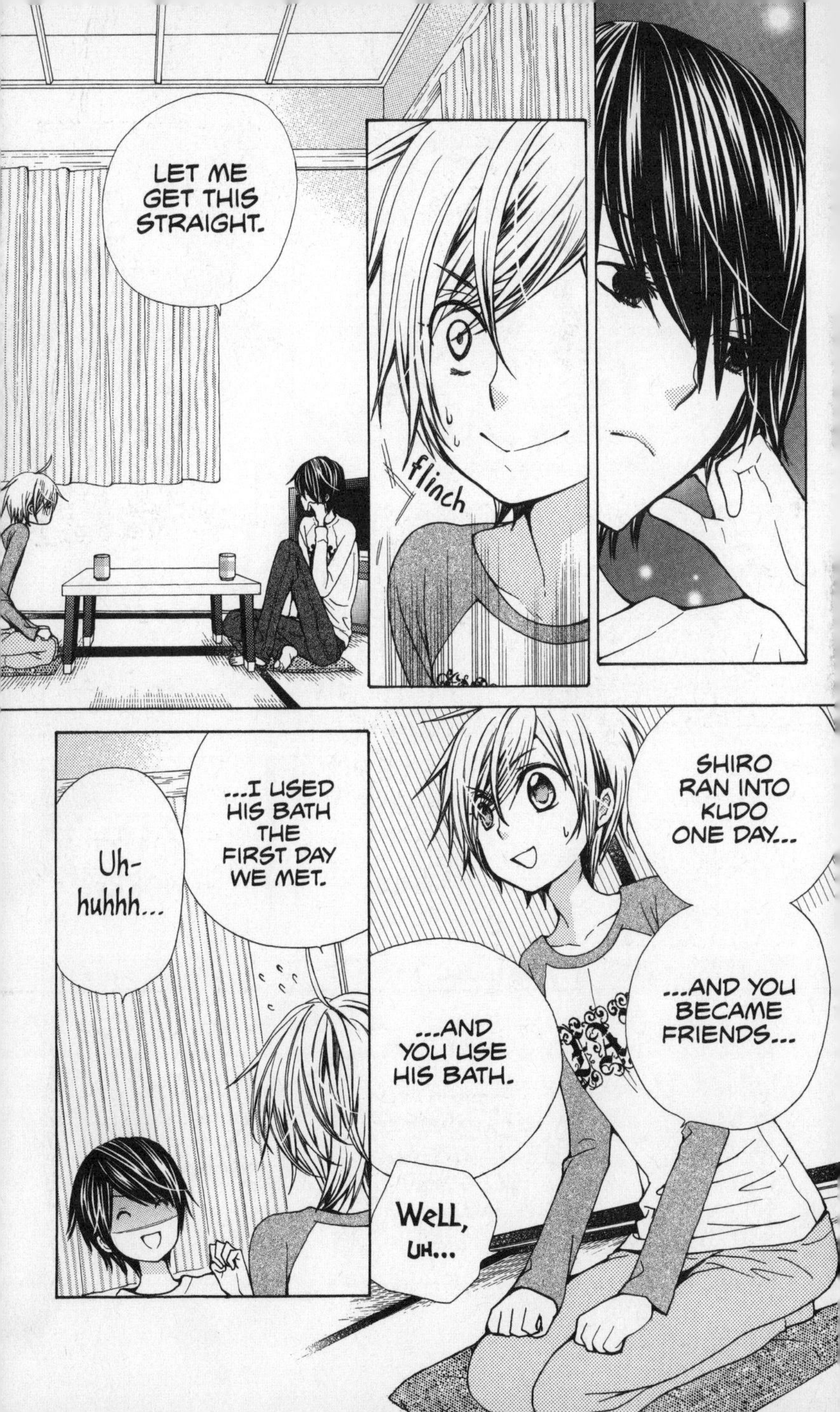
flinch
LET ME GET THIS STRAIGHT.
SHIRO RAN INTO KUDO ONE DAY...
...AND YOU BECAME FRIENDS...
...AND YOU USE HIS BATH.
Well, uh...
...I USED HIS BATH THE FIRST DAY WE MET.
Uh-huhhh...

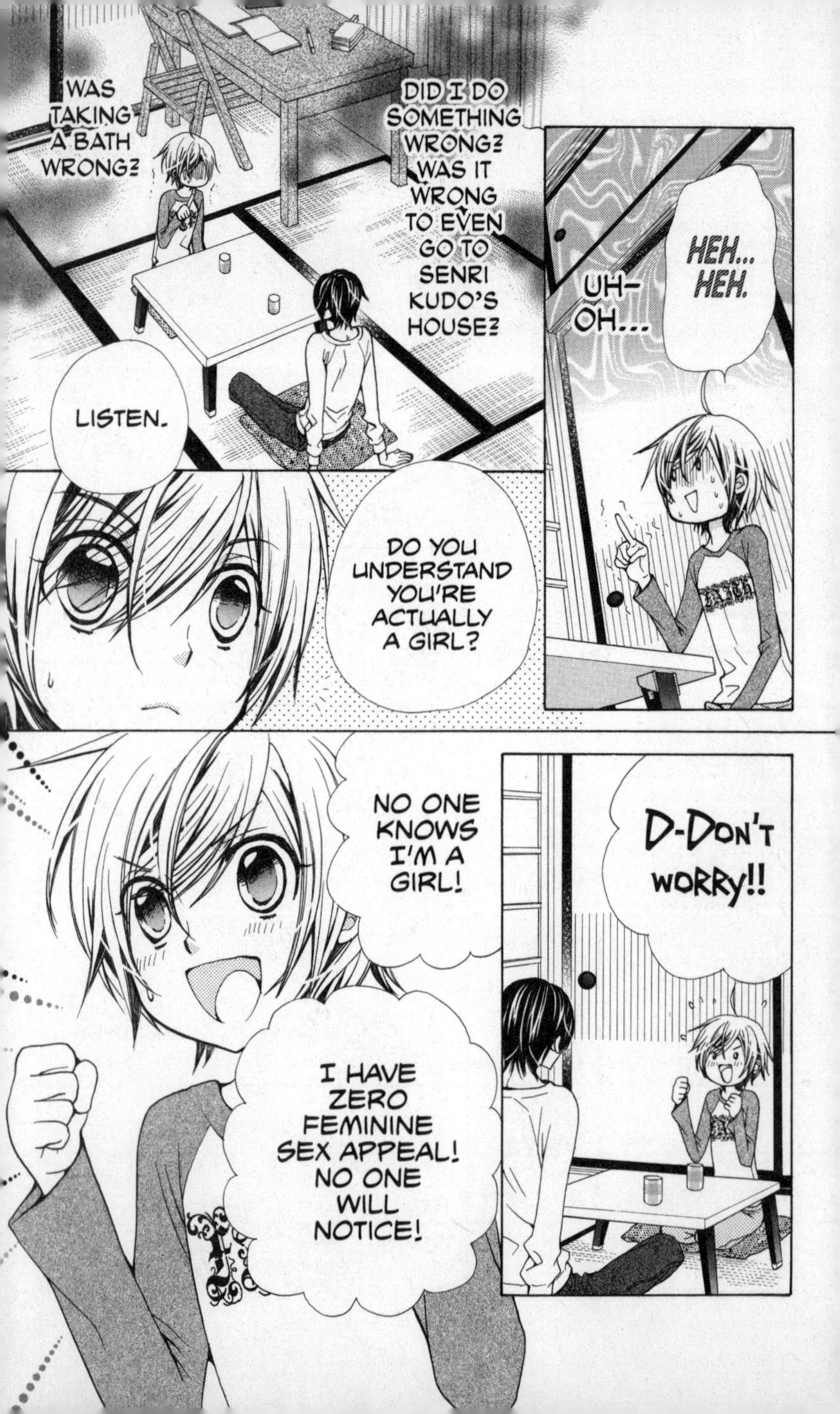
UH-OH...
HEH... HEH.
WAS TAKING A BATH WRONG?
DID I DO SOMETHING WRONG? WAS IT WRONG TO EVEN GO TO SENRI KUDO'S HOUSE?
LISTEN.
DO YOU UNDERSTAND YOU'RE ACTUALLY A GIRL?
D-DON'T WORRY!!
NO ONE KNOWS I'M A GIRL!
I HAVE ZERO FEMININE SEX APPEAL! NO ONE WILL NOTICE!

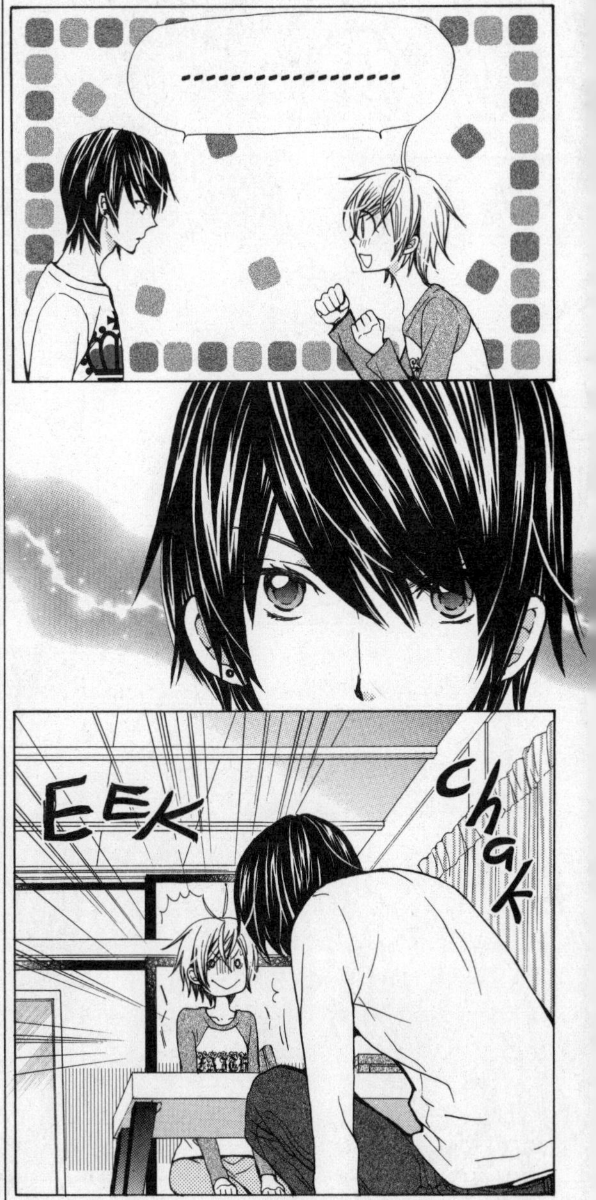

EEK
chak

• The End •

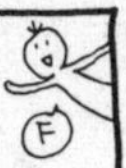

F

This is the last side-bar. Thank you for reading all this way!

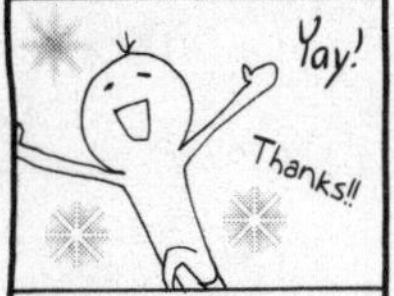

Yay!
Thanks!!

For a few years, electronic stuff hasn't worked so well here. It's so depressing...

Of the three rods in the halogen heater...

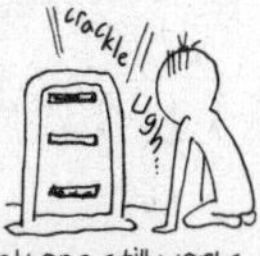

crackle
Ugh...

...only one still works.

And now...much thanks to everyone who read this far, everyone who helped with research, everyone who worked on the graphic novel, my editor, everyone who helped with composition, all my assistants, my friends and my family!!

♡ If you feel like it, lemme hear your thoughts! ♡

Maki Minami
c/o Shojo Beat
P.O. Box 77010
San Francisco, CA
94107

Maki Minami
南マキ

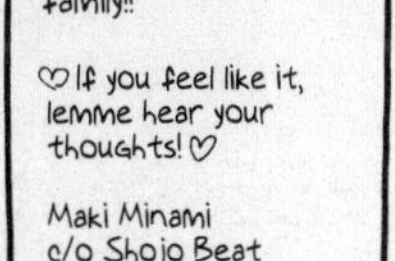

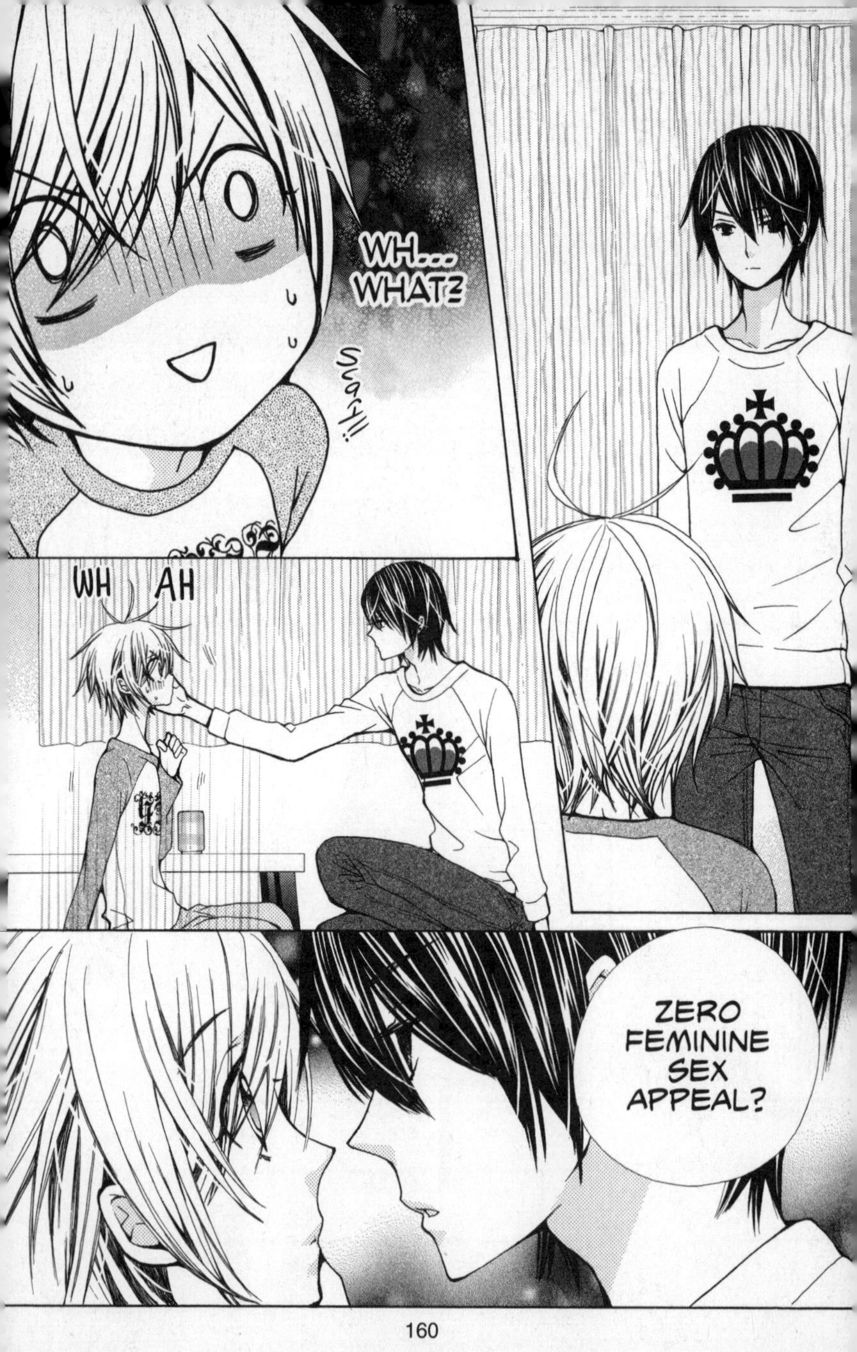
WH... WHAT?
Scary!!
AH
WH
ZERO FEMININE SEX APPEAL?

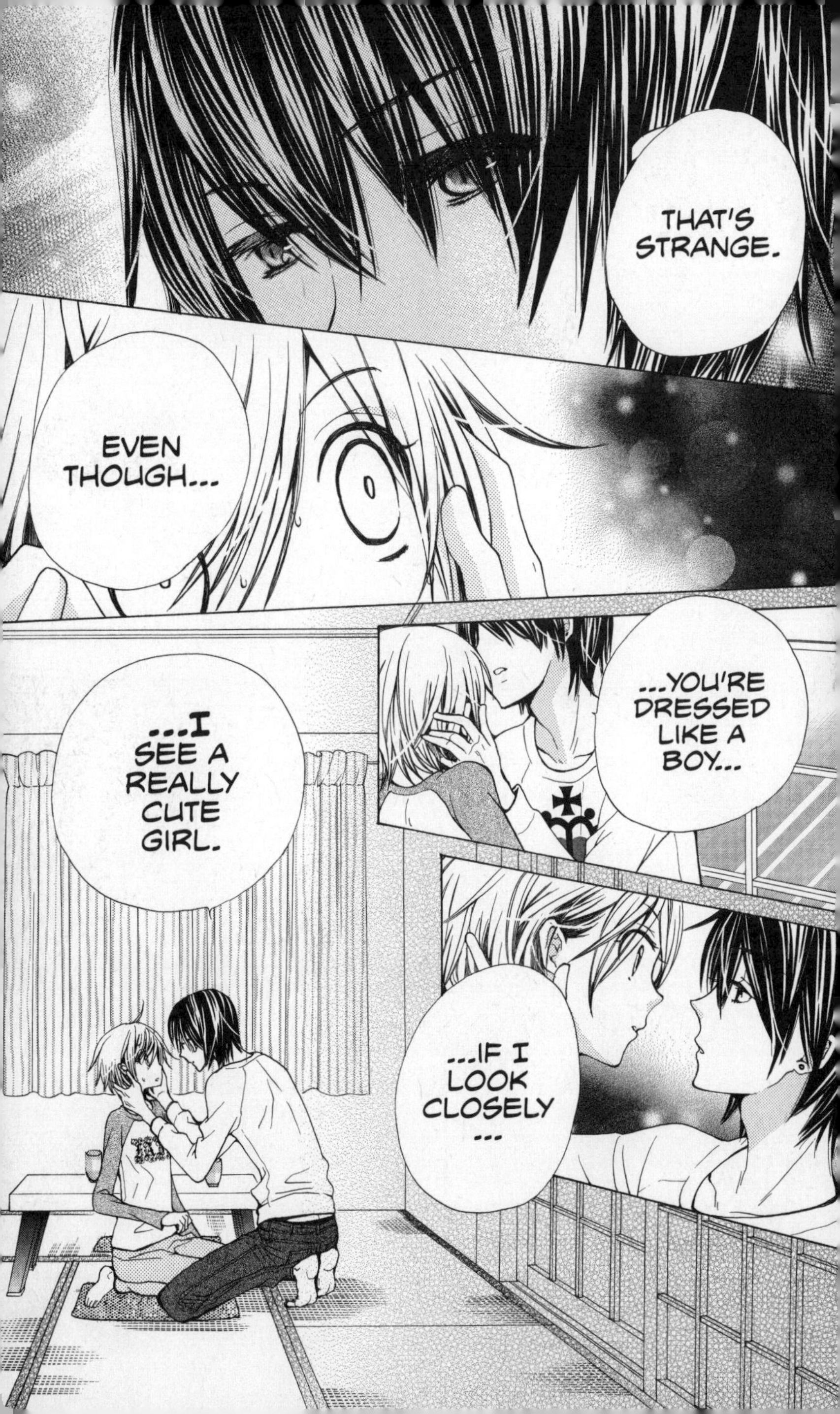
THAT'S STRANGE.
EVEN THOUGH...
...YOU'RE DRESSED LIKE A BOY...
...IF I LOOK CLOSELY ...
...I SEE A REALLY CUTE GIRL.

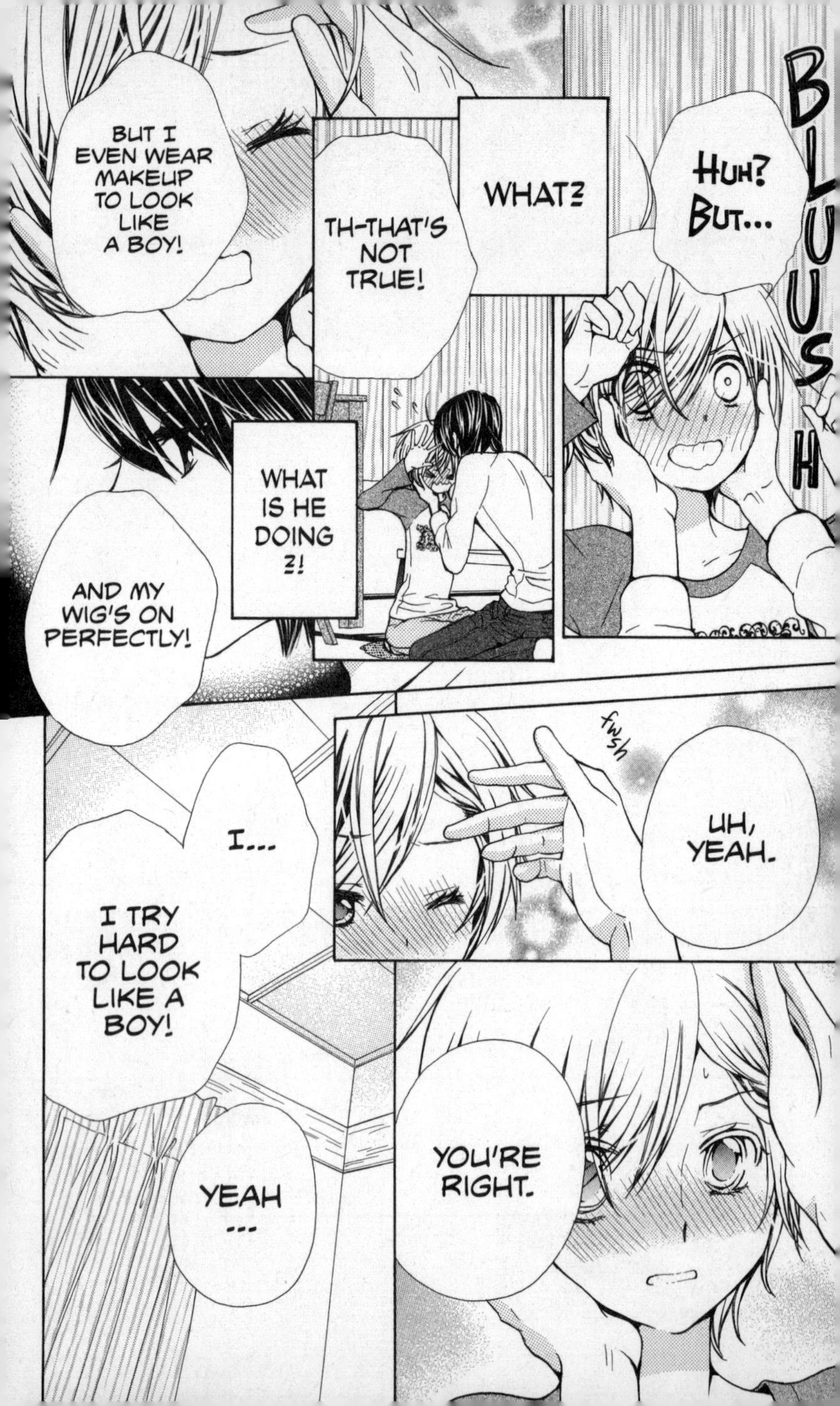
HUH? BUT...
BLUUSH
WHAT?
TH-THAT'S NOT TRUE!
BUT I EVEN WEAR MAKEUP TO LOOK LIKE A BOY!
WHAT IS HE DOING?!
AND MY WIG'S ON PERFECTLY!
I...
I TRY HARD TO LOOK LIKE A BOY!
fwsh
UH, YEAH.
YOU'RE RIGHT.
YEAH...

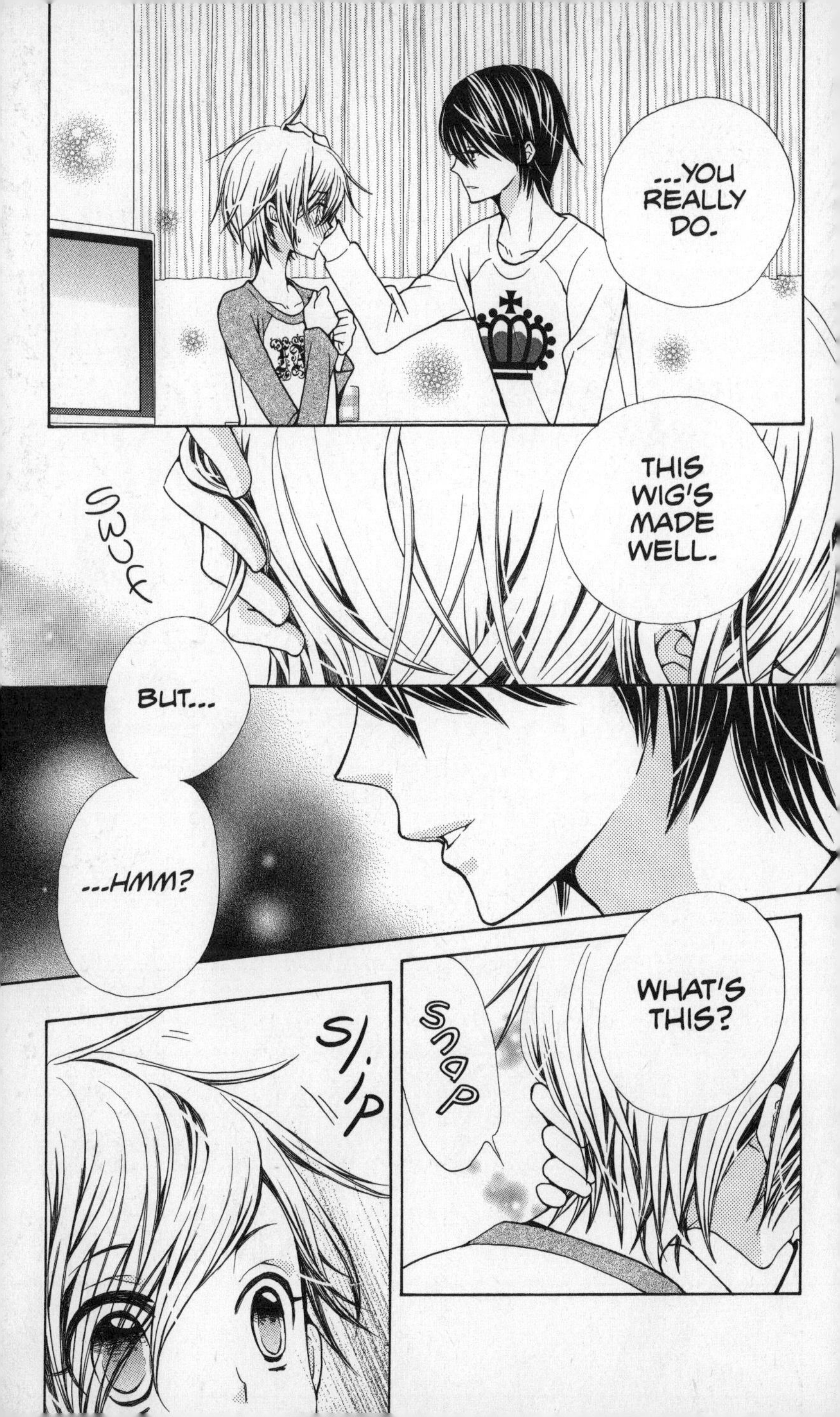
...YOU REALLY DO.
THIS WIG'S MADE WELL.
BUT...
...HMM?
WHAT'S THIS?
Snap
Slip

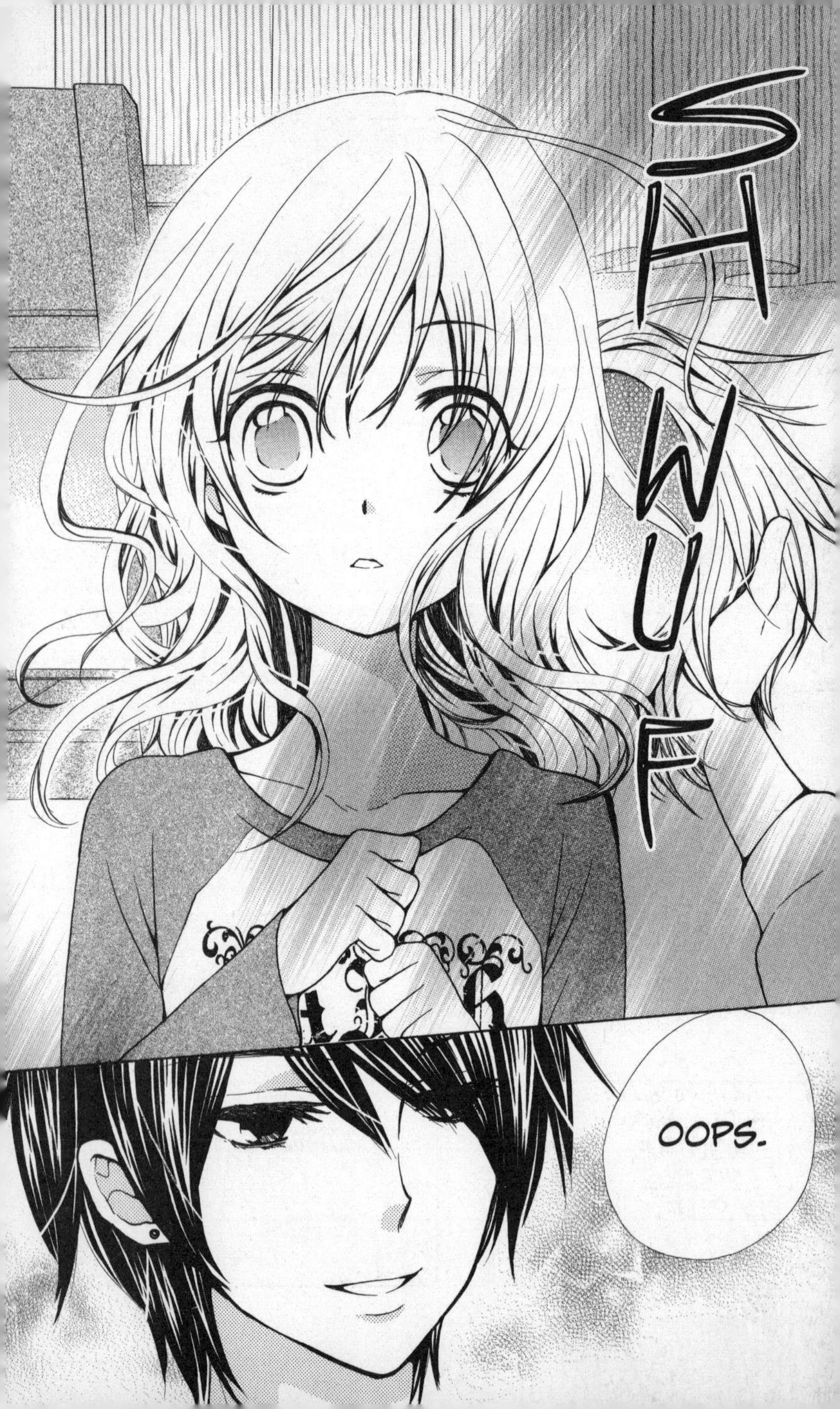
SHWUF
OOPS.

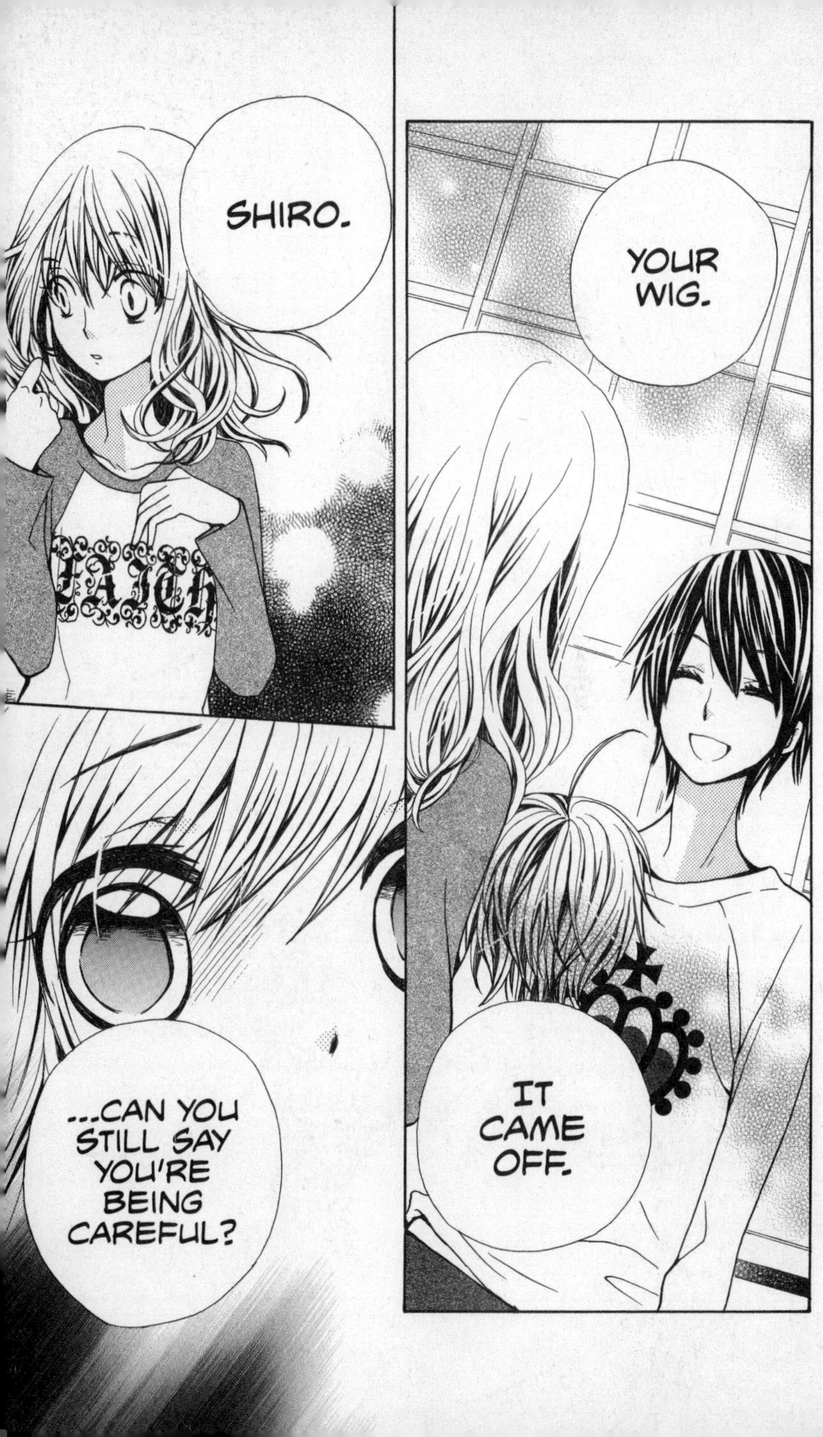
YOUR WIG.
IT CAME OFF.
SHIRO.
...CAN YOU STILL SAY YOU'RE BEING CAREFUL?

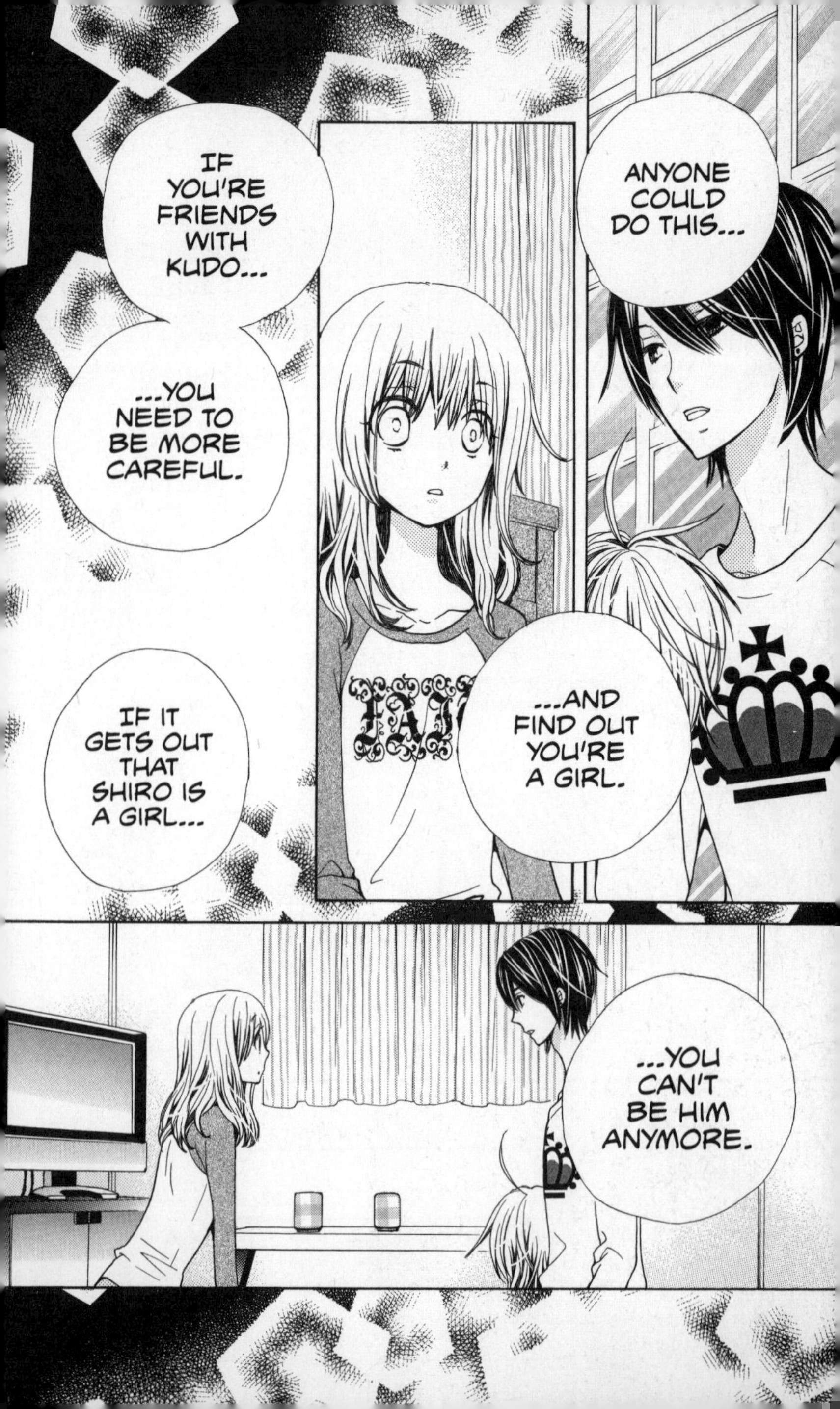
ANYONE COULD DO THIS...
...AND FIND OUT YOU'RE A GIRL.
IF YOU'RE FRIENDS WITH KUDO...
...YOU NEED TO BE MORE CAREFUL.
IF IT GETS OUT THAT SHIRO IS A GIRL...
...YOU CAN'T BE HIM ANYMORE.

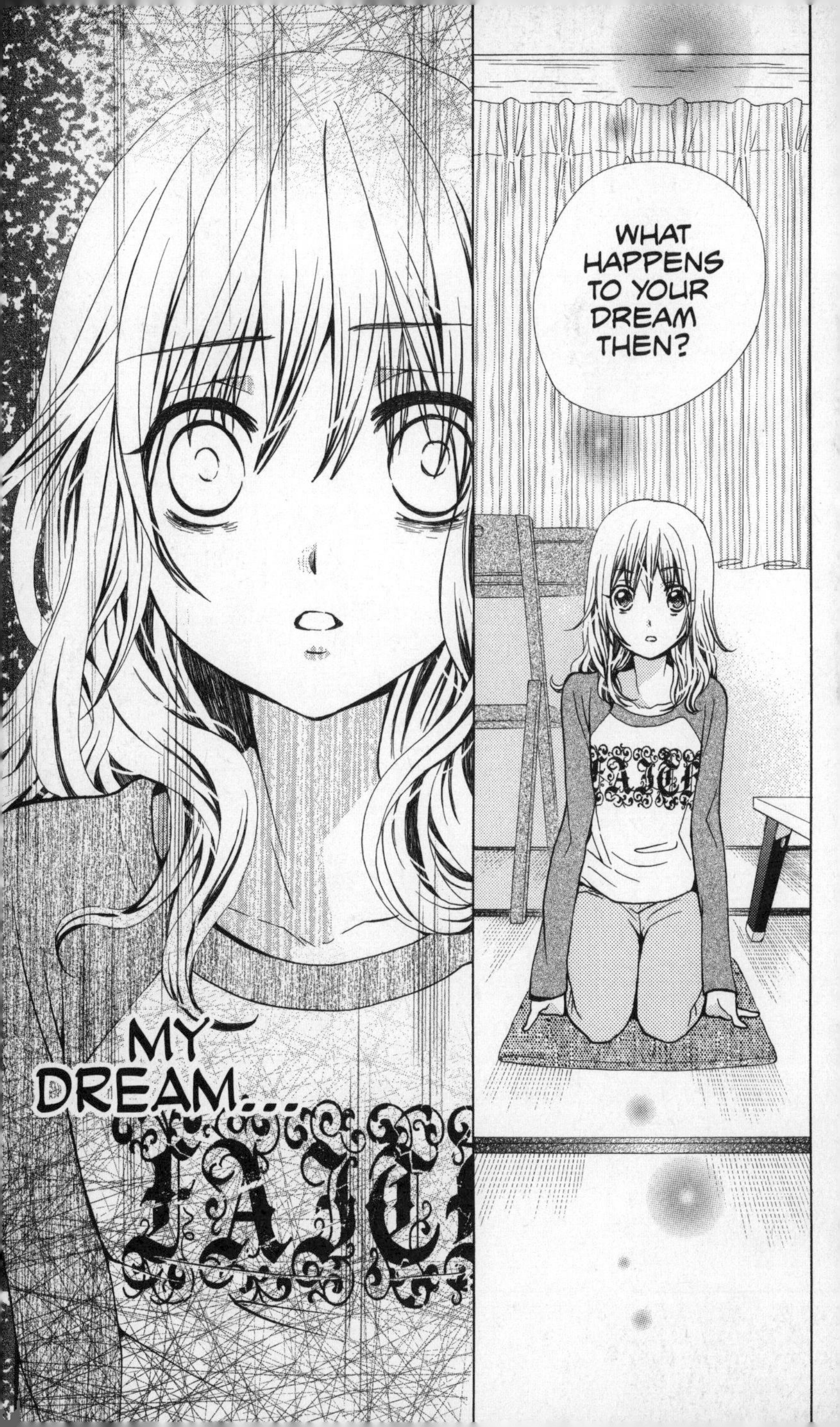
WHAT HAPPENS TO YOUR DREAM THEN?
MY DREAM...

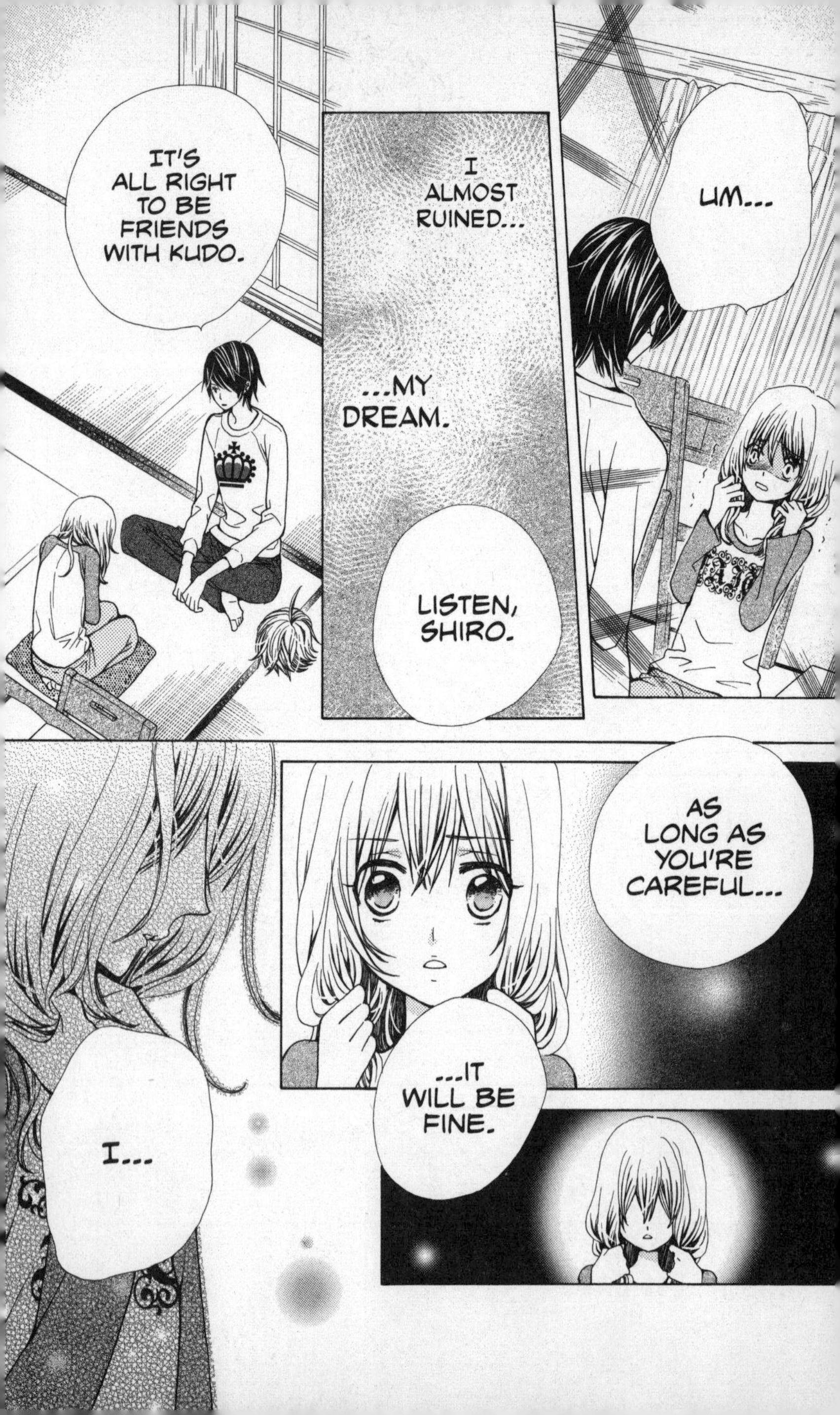
UM...
I ALMOST RUINED...
...MY DREAM.
LISTEN, SHIRO.
IT'S ALL RIGHT TO BE FRIENDS WITH KUDO.
AS LONG AS YOU'RE CAREFUL...
...IT WILL BE FINE.
I...

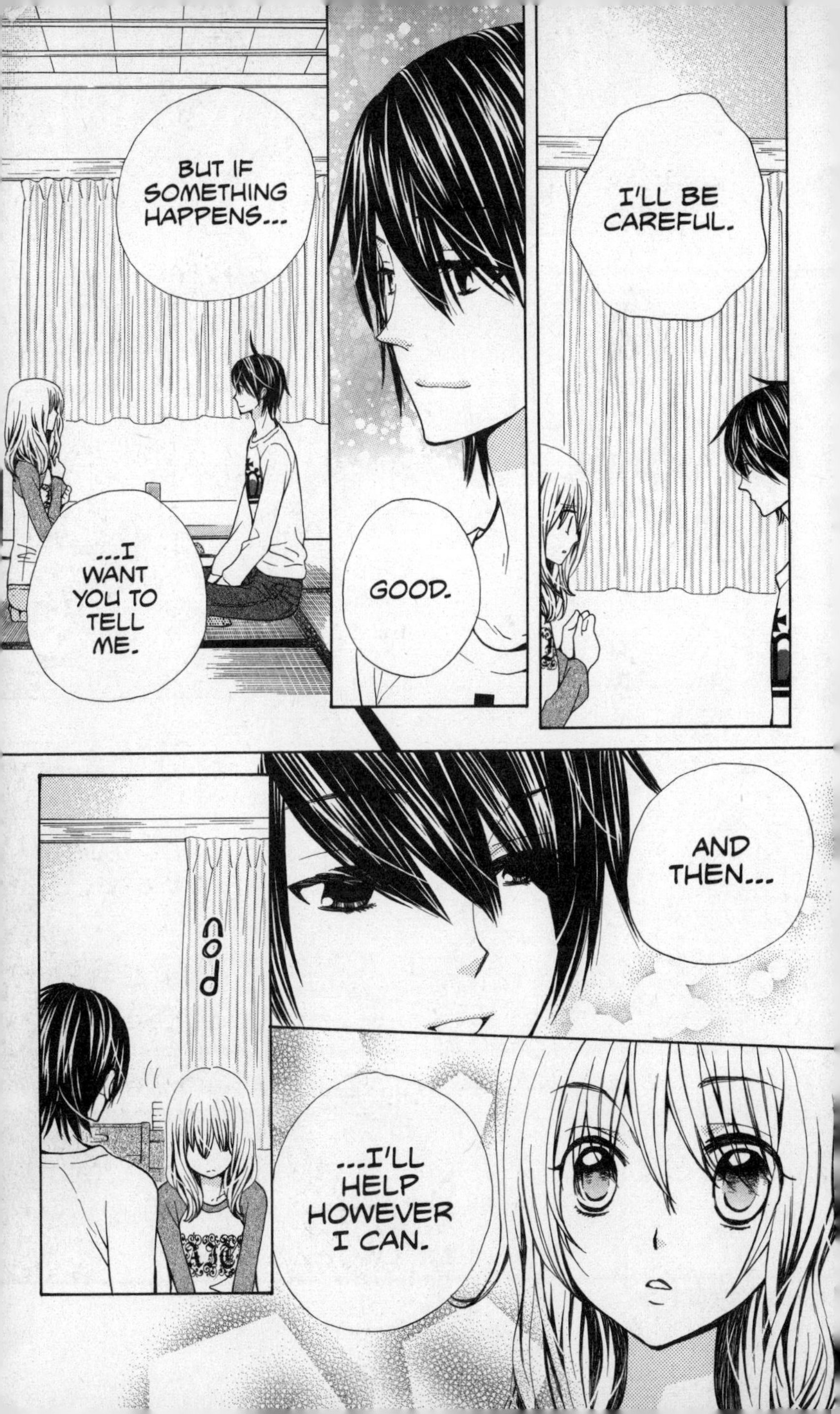
I'LL BE CAREFUL.
GOOD.
BUT IF SOMETHING HAPPENS...
...I WANT YOU TO TELL ME.
AND THEN...
...I'LL HELP HOWEVER I CAN.

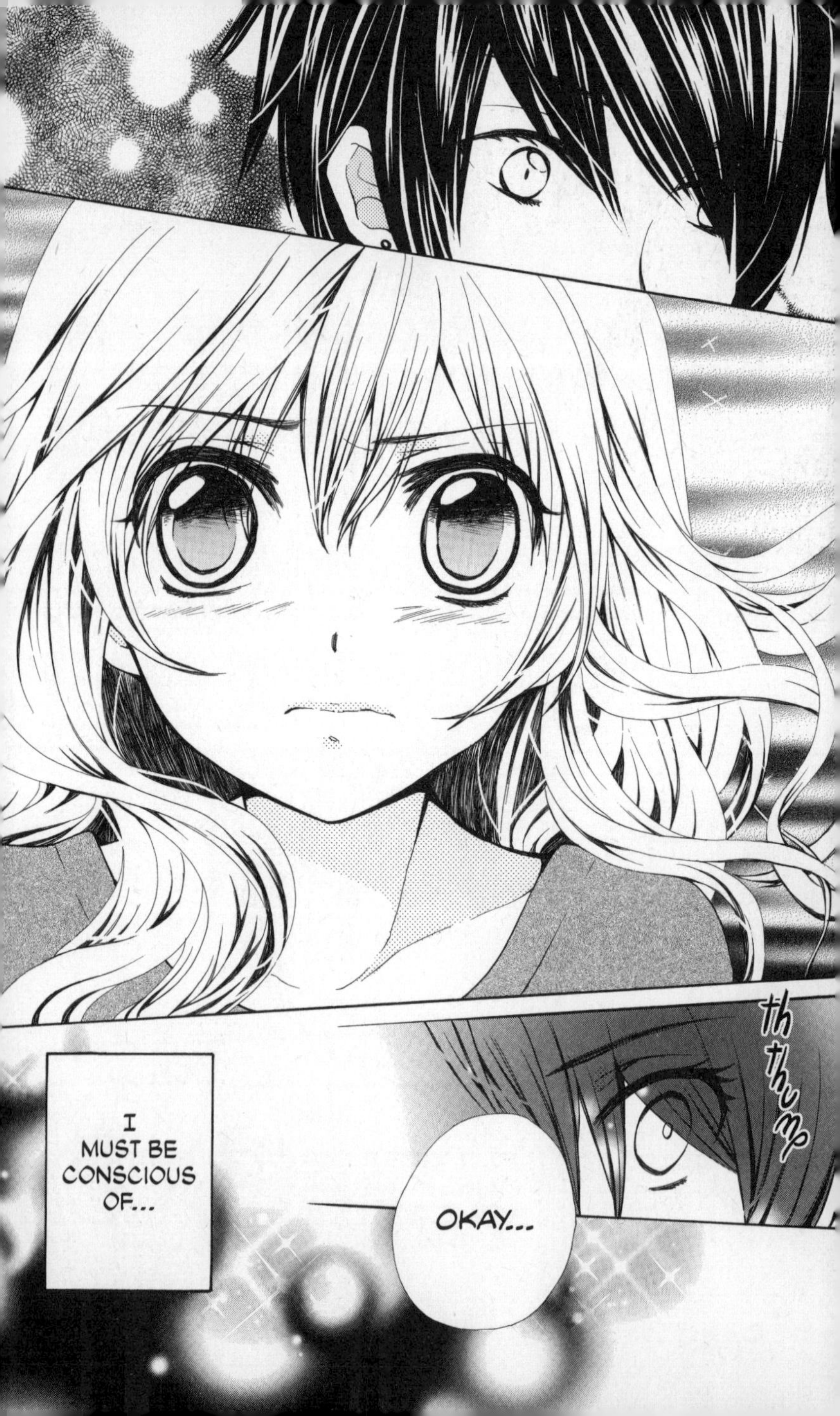
th thump
OKAY...
I MUST BE CONSCIOUS OF...

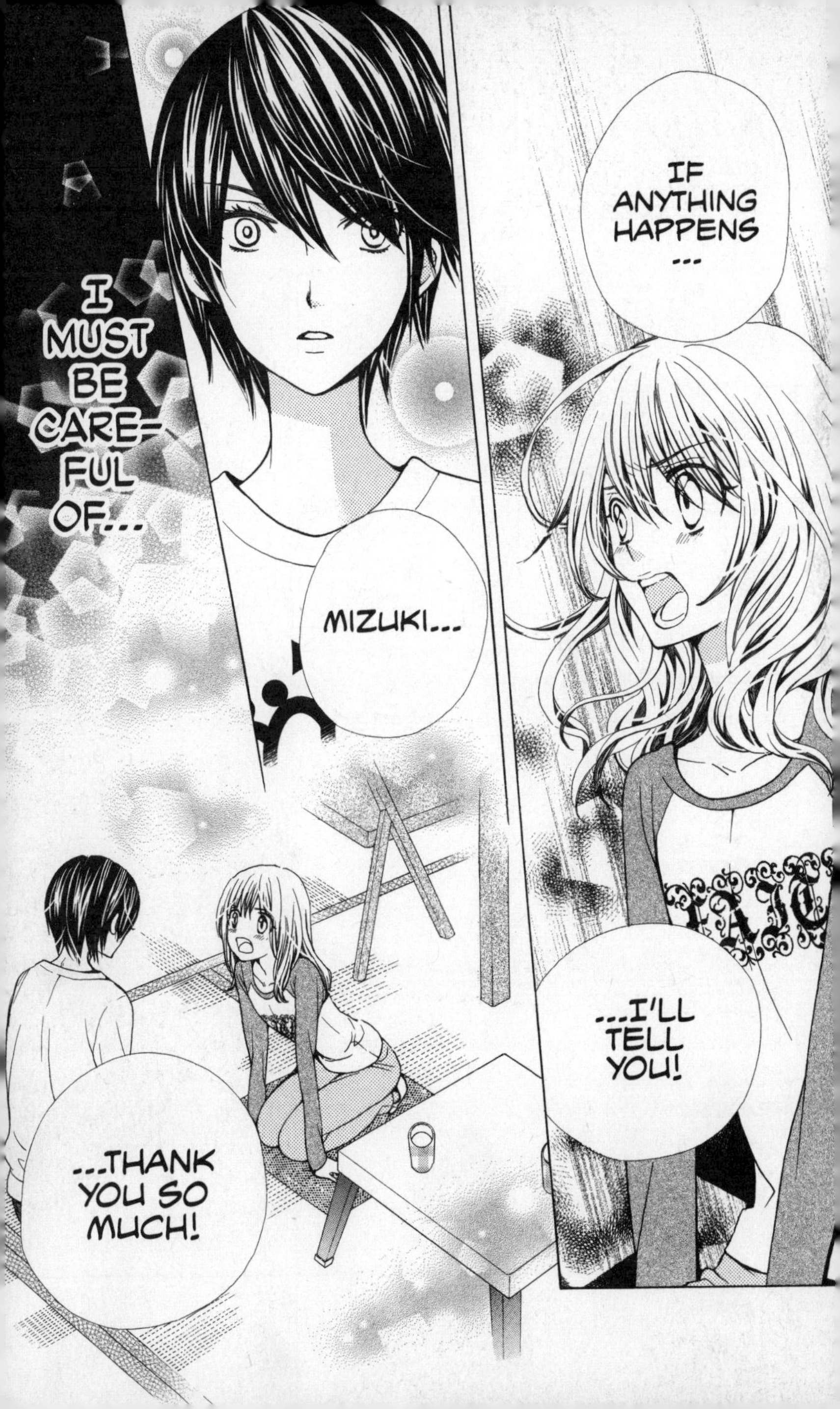
IF ANYTHING HAPPENS...
...I'LL TELL YOU!
MIZUKI...
I MUST BE CARE-FUL OF...
...THANK YOU SO MUCH!

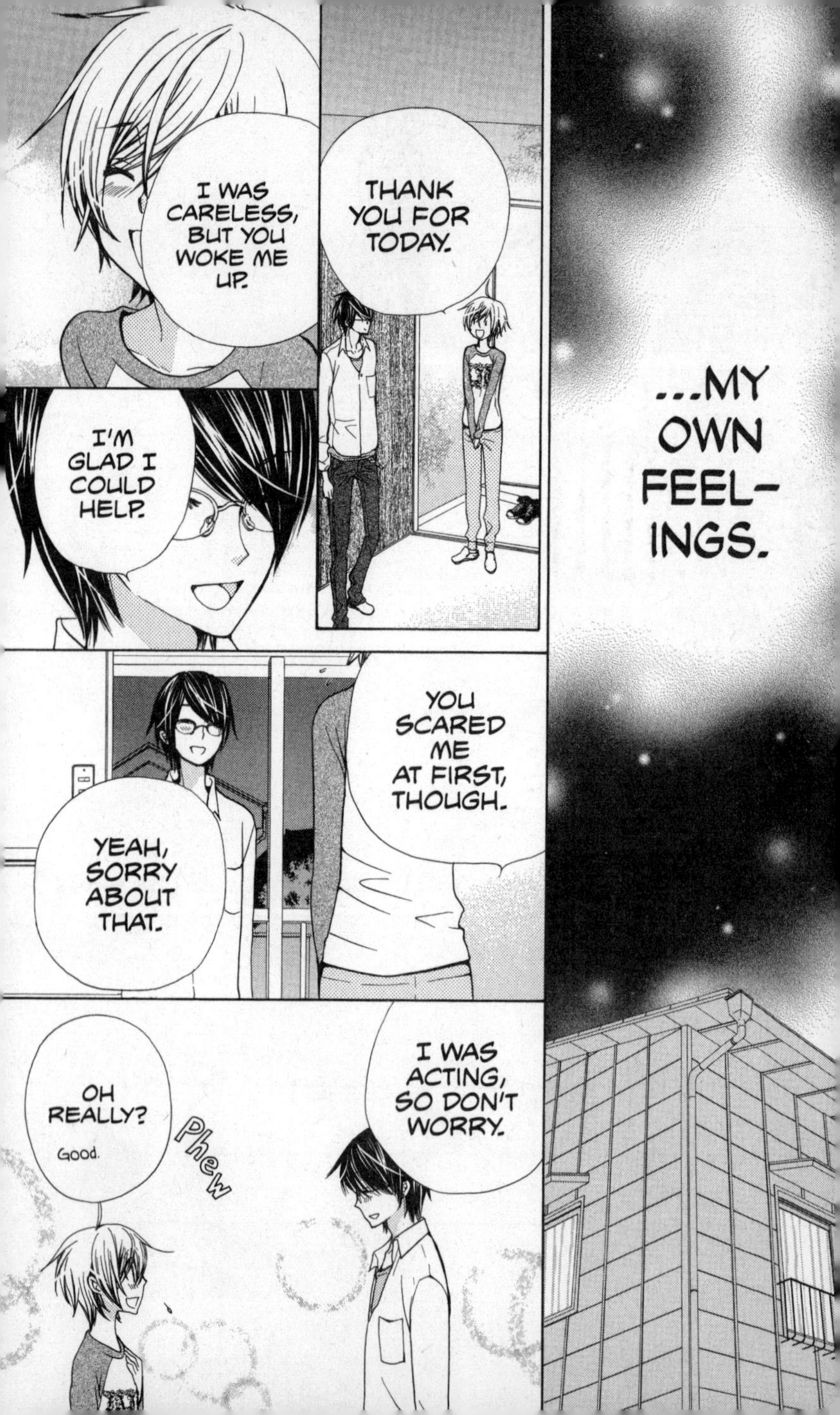
...MY OWN FEEL-INGS.
THANK YOU FOR TODAY.
I WAS CARELESS, BUT YOU WOKE ME UP.
I'M GLAD I COULD HELP.
YOU SCARED ME AT FIRST, THOUGH.
YEAH, SORRY ABOUT THAT.
I WAS ACTING, SO DON'T WORRY.
Phew
OH REALLY?
Good.

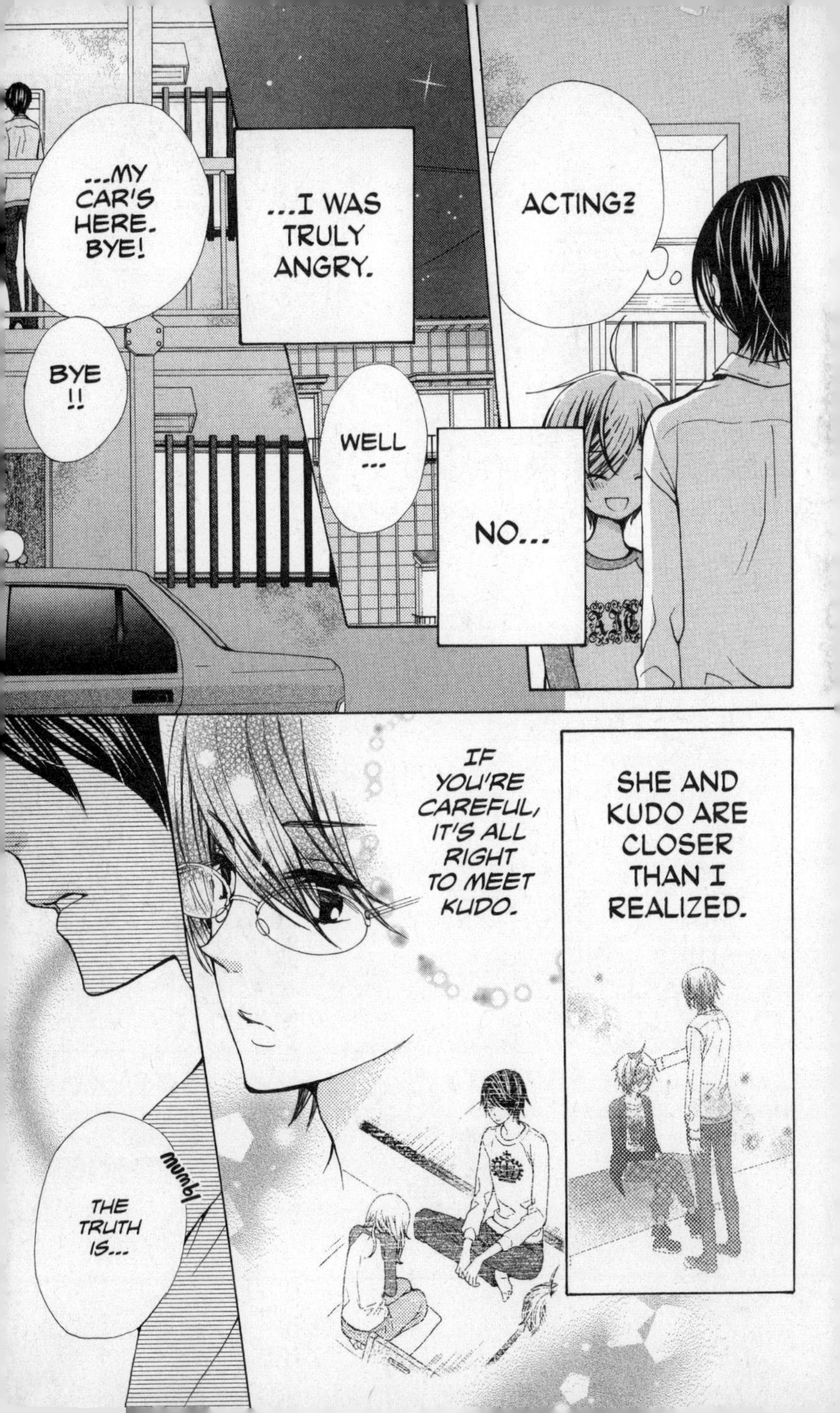
ACTING?
WELL...
NO...
...I WAS TRULY ANGRY.
...MY CAR'S HERE. BYE!
BYE!!
SHE AND KUDO ARE CLOSER THAN I REALIZED.
IF YOU'RE CAREFUL, IT'S ALL RIGHT TO MEET KUDO.
mumbl
THE TRUTH IS...

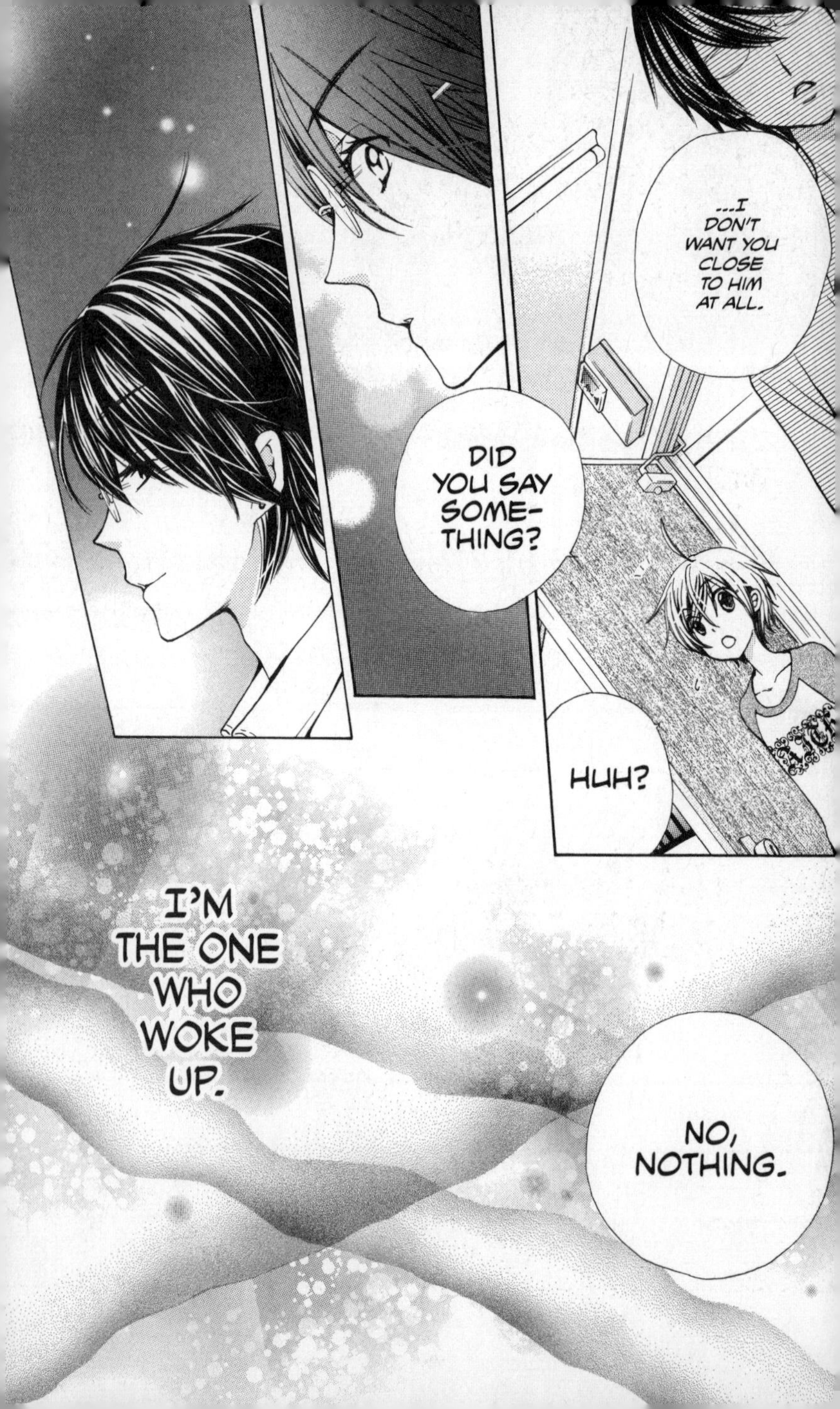
...I DON'T WANT YOU CLOSE TO HIM AT ALL.
HUH?
DID YOU SAY SOMETHING?
NO, NOTHING.
I'M THE ONE WHO WOKE UP.

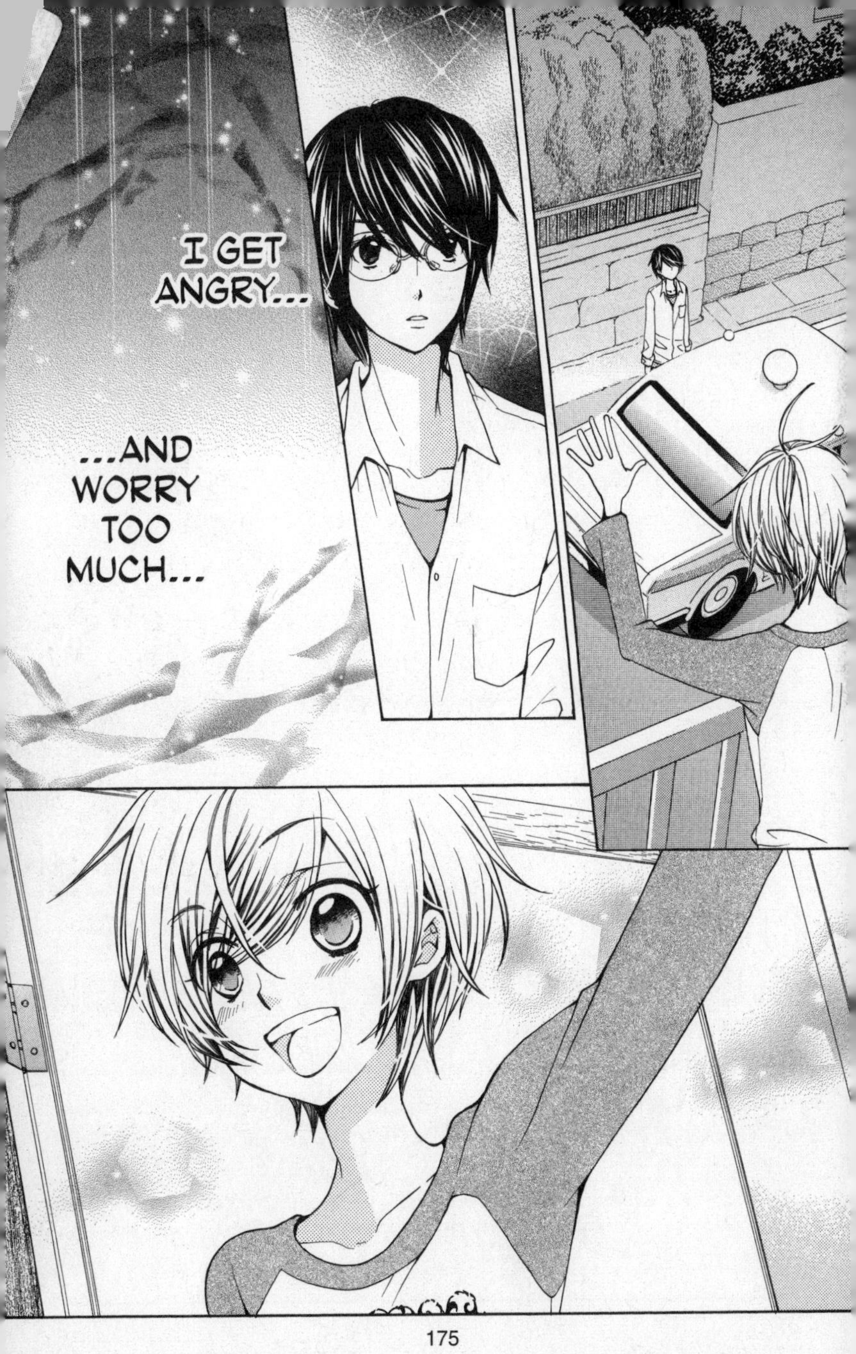
I GET ANGRY...
...AND WORRY TOO MUCH...

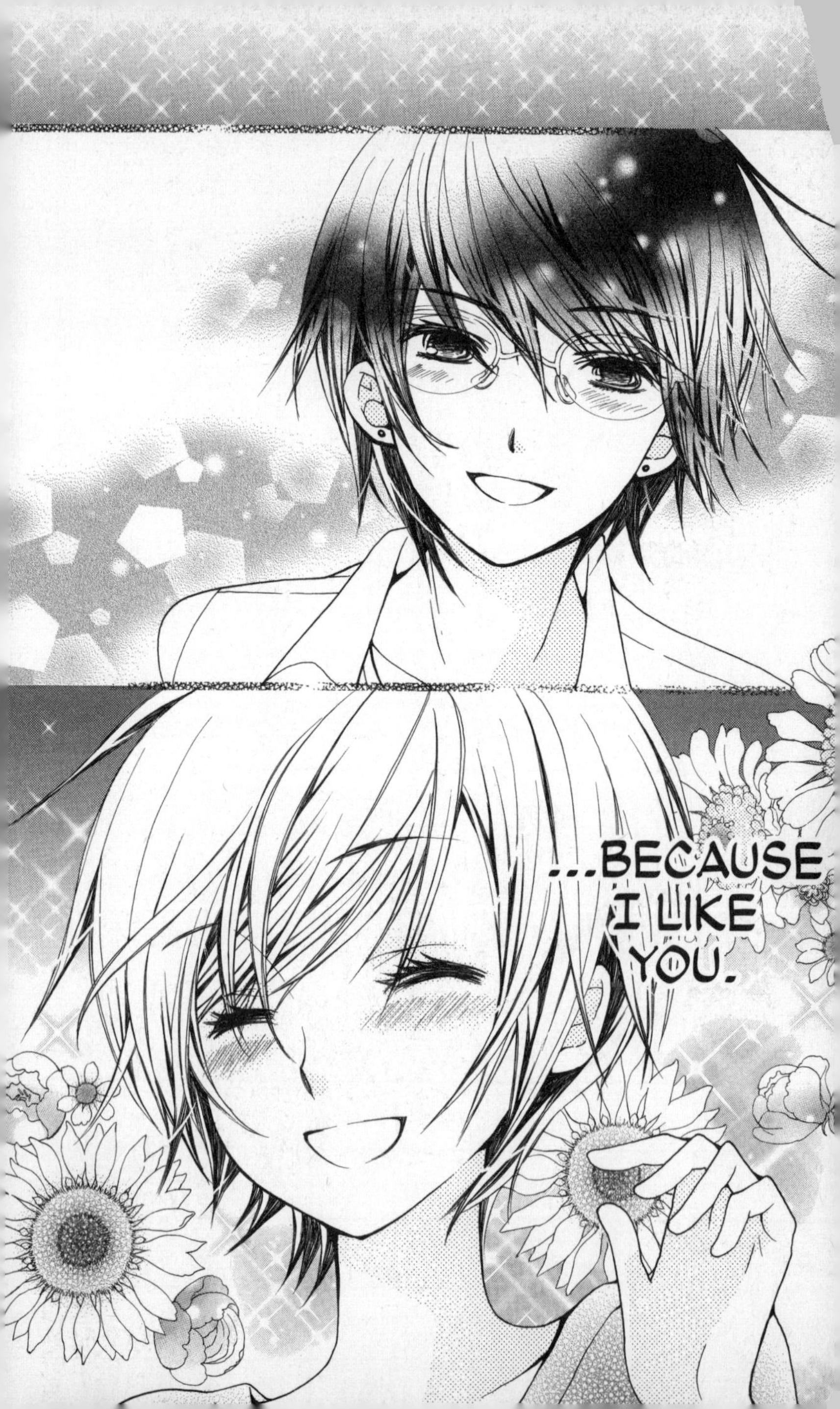
...BECAUSE I LIKE YOU.

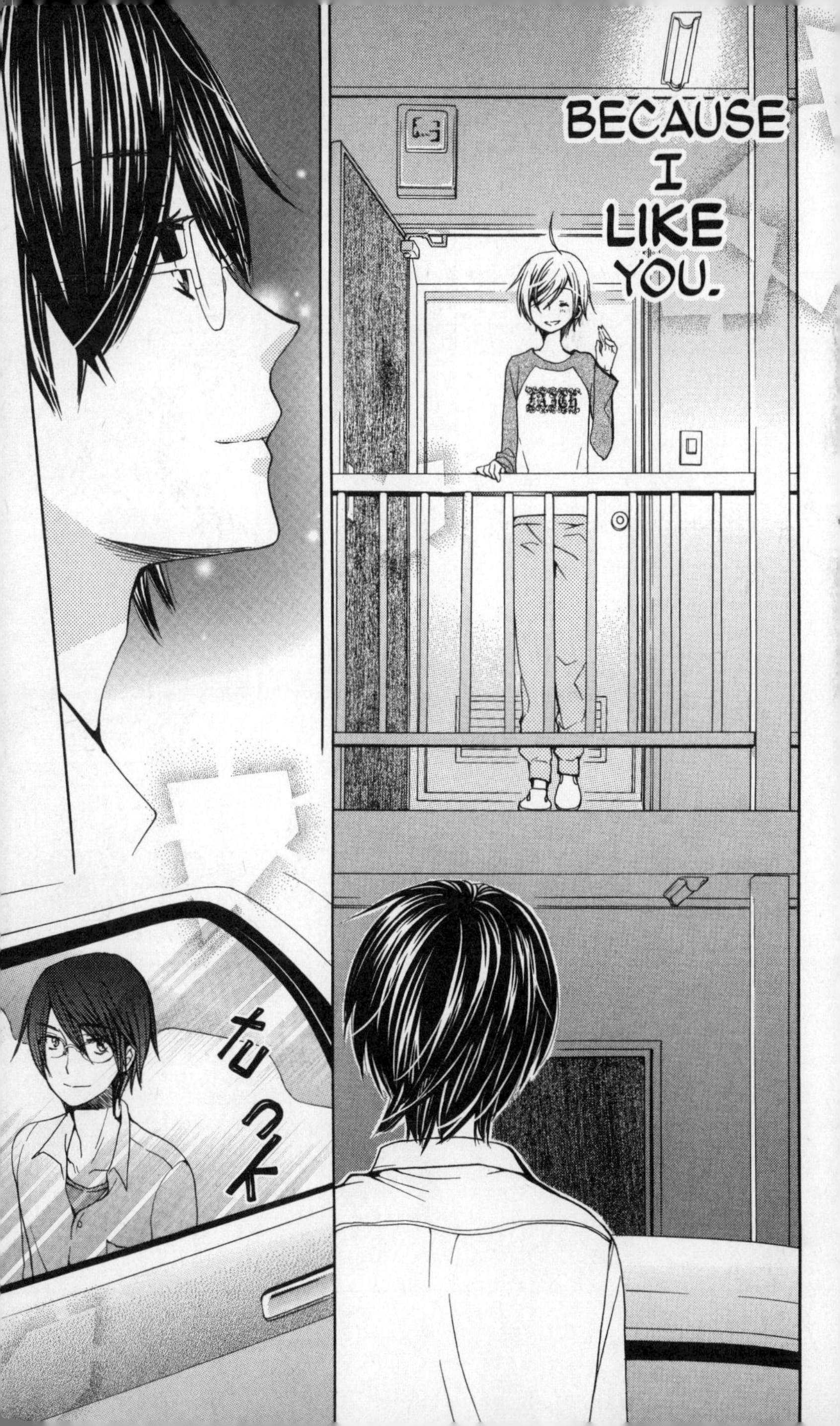
BECAUSE I LIKE YOU.

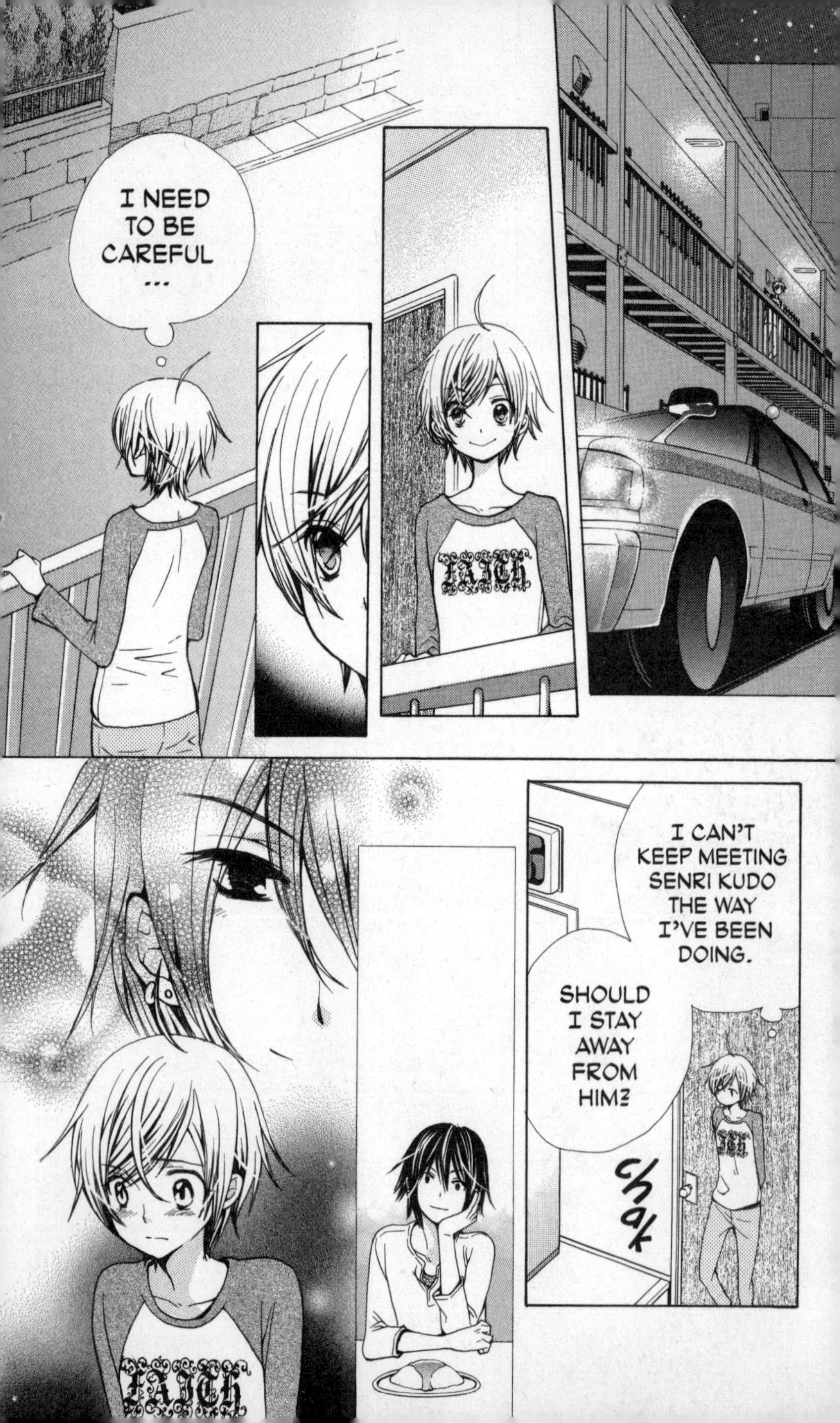
I NEED TO BE CAREFUL...
I CAN'T KEEP MEETING SENRI KUDO THE WAY I'VE BEEN DOING.
SHOULD I STAY AWAY FROM HIM?
chak

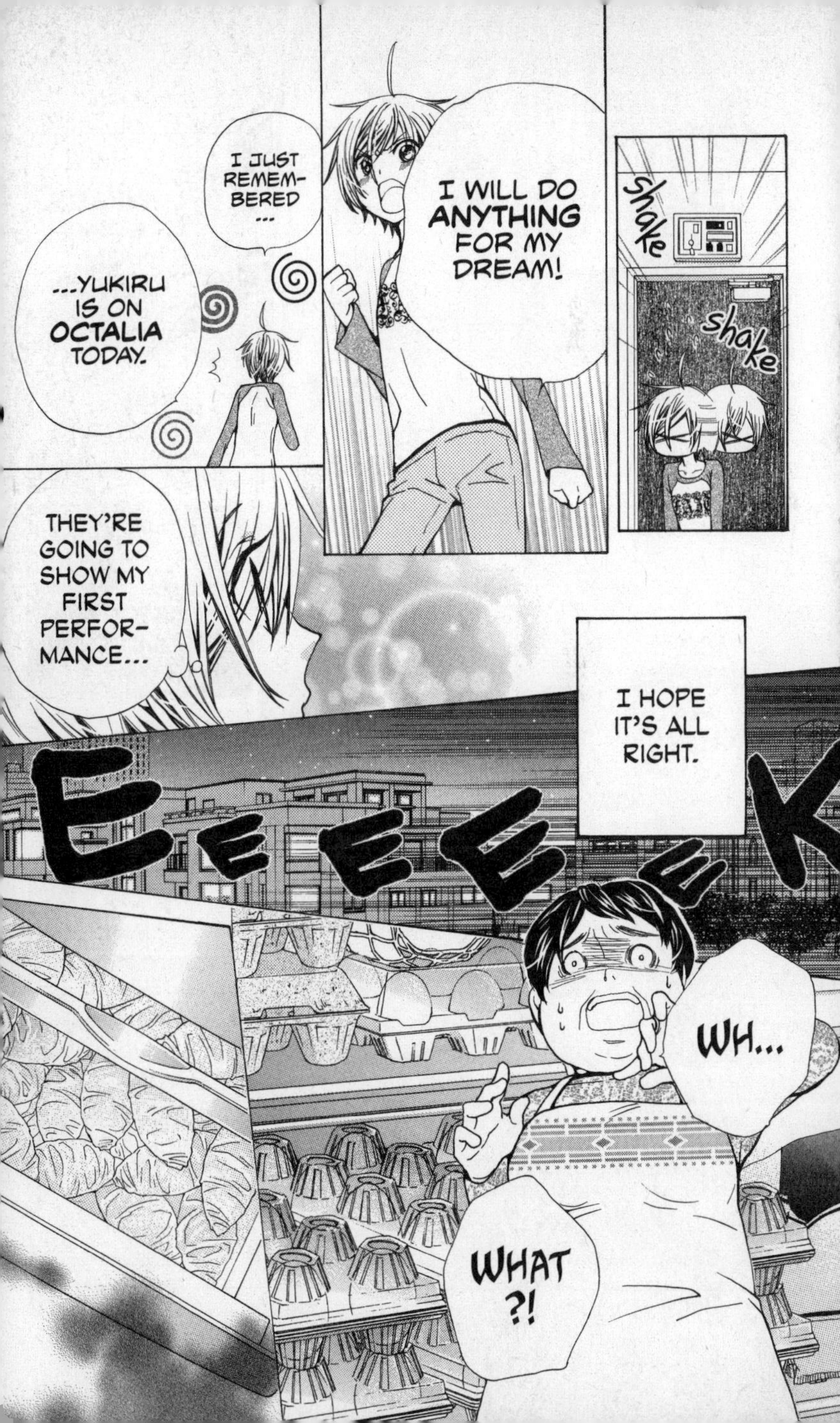
shake
shake
I WILL DO ANYTHING FOR MY DREAM!
I JUST REMEMBERED ...
...YUKIRU IS ON OCTALIA TODAY.
THEY'RE GOING TO SHOW MY FIRST PERFORMANCE...
I HOPE IT'S ALL RIGHT.
EEEEEK
WH...
WHAT ?!

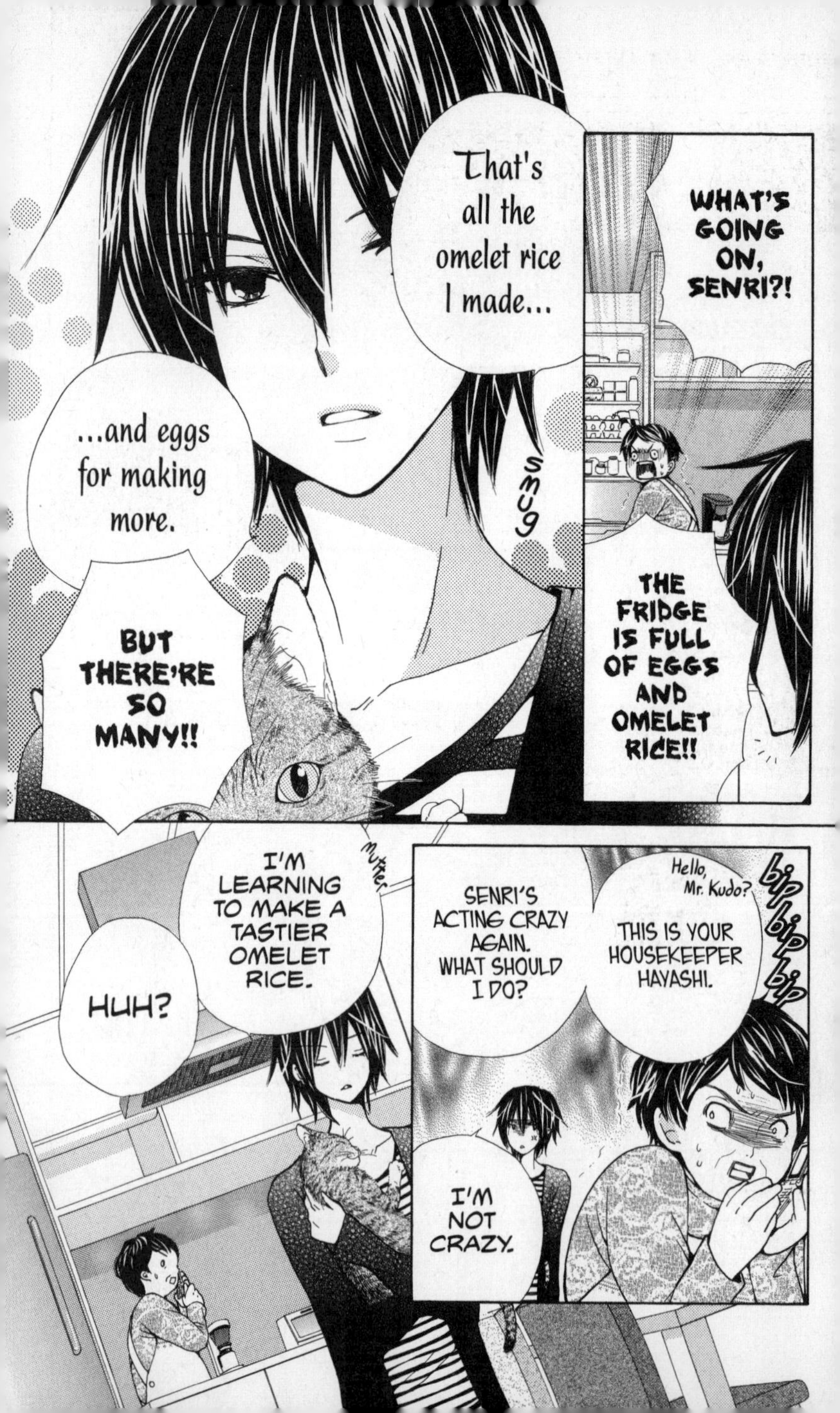
WHAT'S GOING ON, SENRI?!
THE FRIDGE IS FULL OF EGGS AND OMELET RICE!!
That's all the omelet rice I made...
SMUG
...and eggs for making more.
BUT THERE'RE SO MANY!!
bip bip bip
Hello, Mr. Kudo?
THIS IS YOUR HOUSEKEEPER HAYASHI.
SENRI'S ACTING CRAZY AGAIN. WHAT SHOULD I DO?
I'M NOT CRAZY.
mutter
I'M LEARNING TO MAKE A TASTIER OMELET RICE.
HUH?

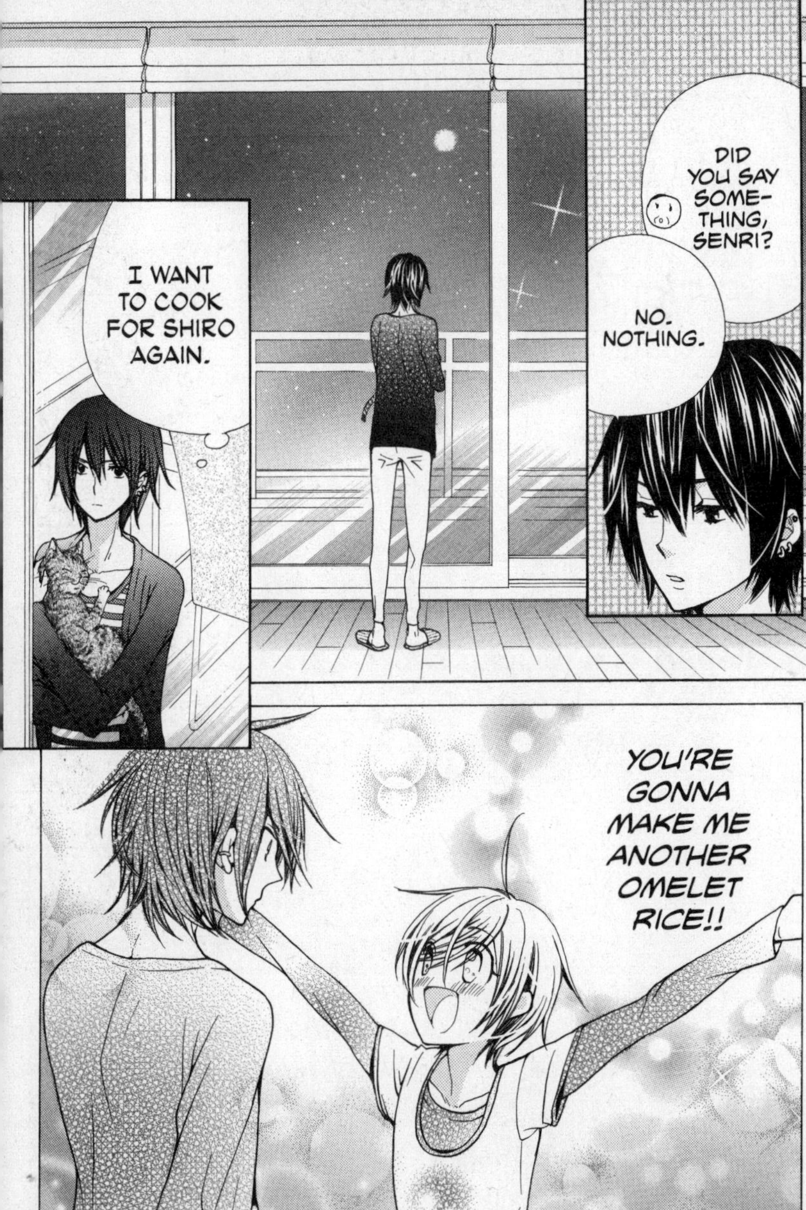
DID YOU SAY SOME-THING, SENRI?
NO. NOTHING.
I WANT TO COOK FOR SHIRO AGAIN.
YOU'RE GONNA MAKE ME ANOTHER OMELET RICE!!

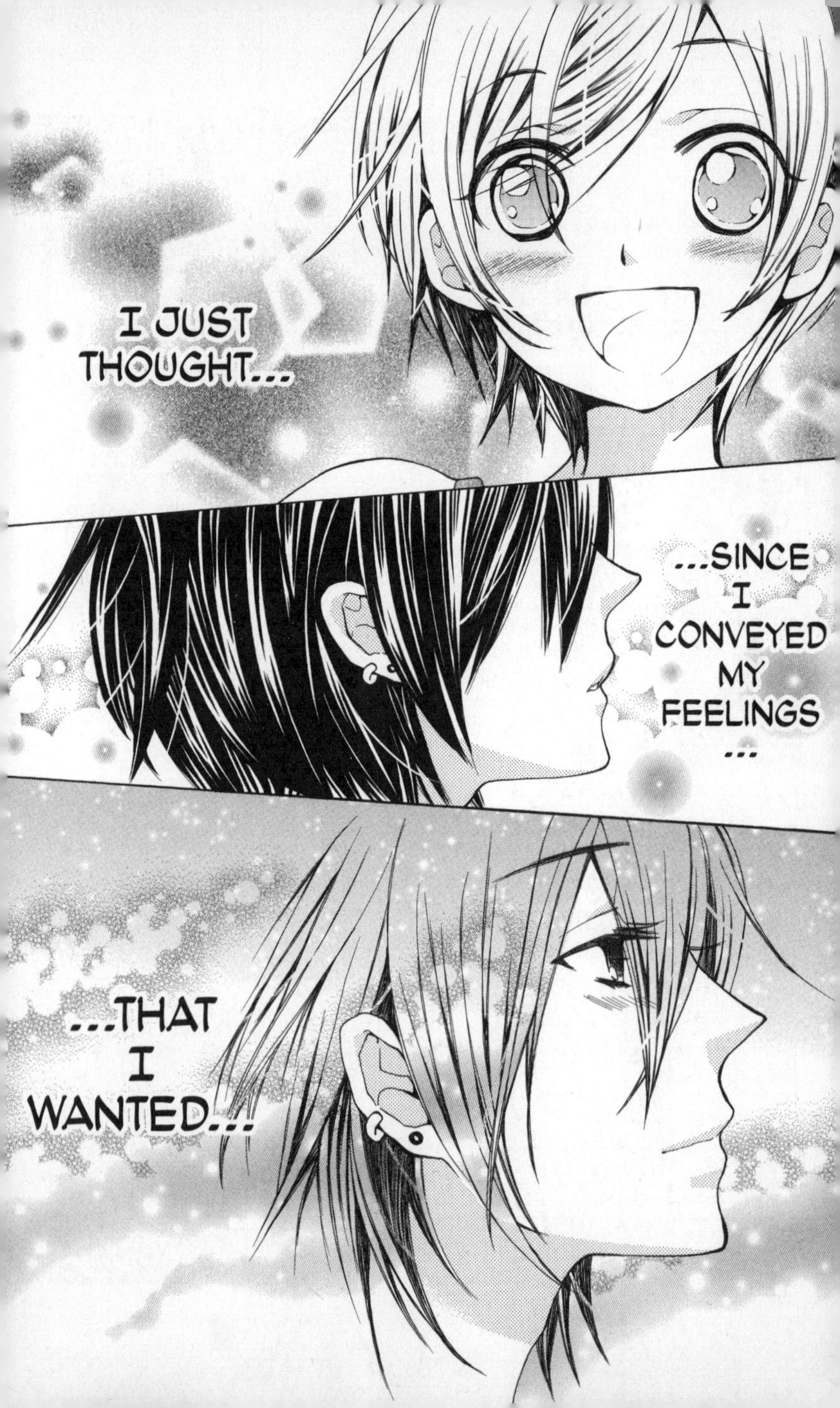
I JUST THOUGHT...
...SINCE I CONVEYED MY FEELINGS...
...THAT I WANTED...

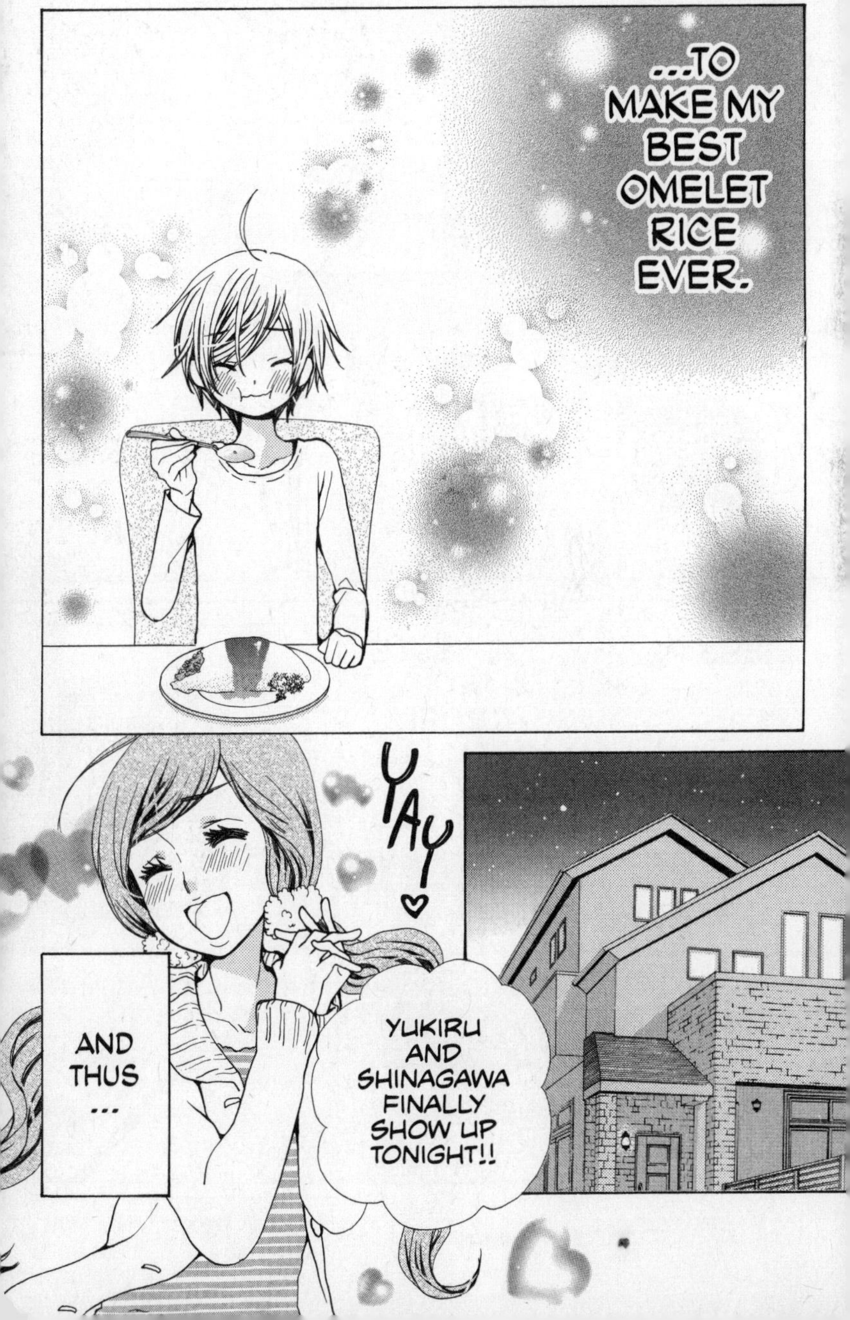
...TO MAKE MY BEST OMELET RICE EVER.
YAY! ♡
YUKIRU AND SHINAGAWA FINALLY SHOW UP TONIGHT!!
AND THUS...

I'VE SET IT TO RECORD IN SUPER HIGH-DEF!
I'll take notes for a review in my blog!
KYAH
KYAH
gasp
WHAH! IT'S START-ING!!
Kyaaah!
...WITH MUCH INVESTED EMOTION ...
...EPISODE 15 OF CRUEL OCTALIA...
...BEGAN.

Voice Over!: Seiyu Academy Volume 9/ End

▂▃▄	10/15 (Sat.) 21:33

| Return | Select | Menu |

Sudden Bonus Content Corner!!
Cell phone lock screen

★ This time it's Senri's lock screen. It's a picture of Gonzales. Catherine is slightly jealous.

He takes lots of cat videos with his cell phone.

M-yama-san did the screen! S-san did the cat!!

Team work!!!

The poster below is for the movie that Senri's mother Sakura starred in. It's a horror flick. I-san provided the poster. The illustration was my own...

Team work!!

KiMOGURENSU
I love you...and your blood...and flesh.

★Starring: Sakura Aoyama
Kyoko Mori Byou Kato Tai Koizumi Mikata Tanaka.

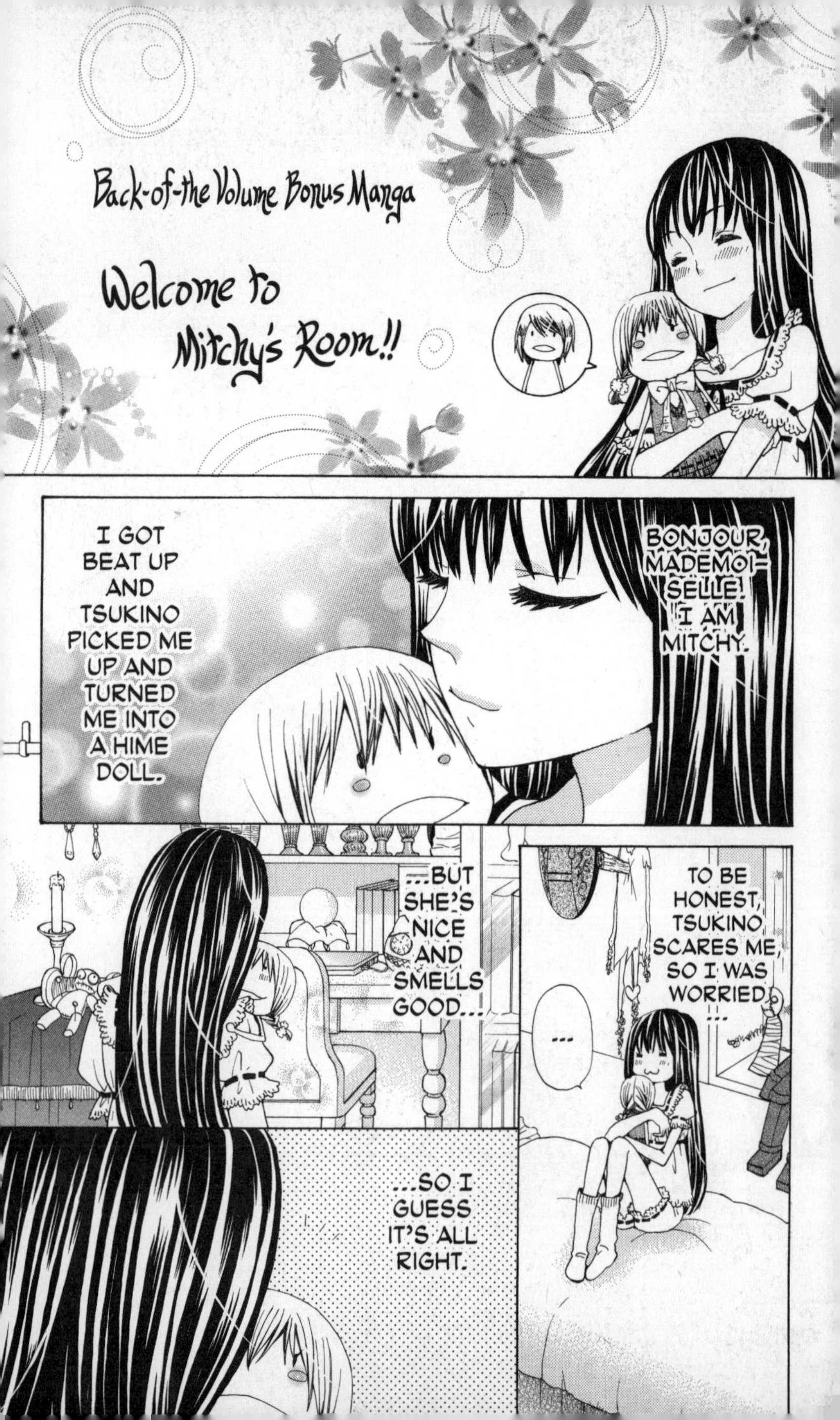
Back-of-the Volume Bonus Manga
Welcome to Mitchy's Room!!
BONJOUR, MADEMOI-SELLE. I AM MITCHY.
I GOT BEAT UP AND TSUKINO PICKED ME UP AND TURNED ME INTO A HIME DOLL.
TO BE HONEST, TSUKINO SCARES ME, SO I WAS WORRIED...
...
...BUT SHE'S NICE AND SMELLS GOOD...
...SO I GUESS IT'S ALL RIGHT.

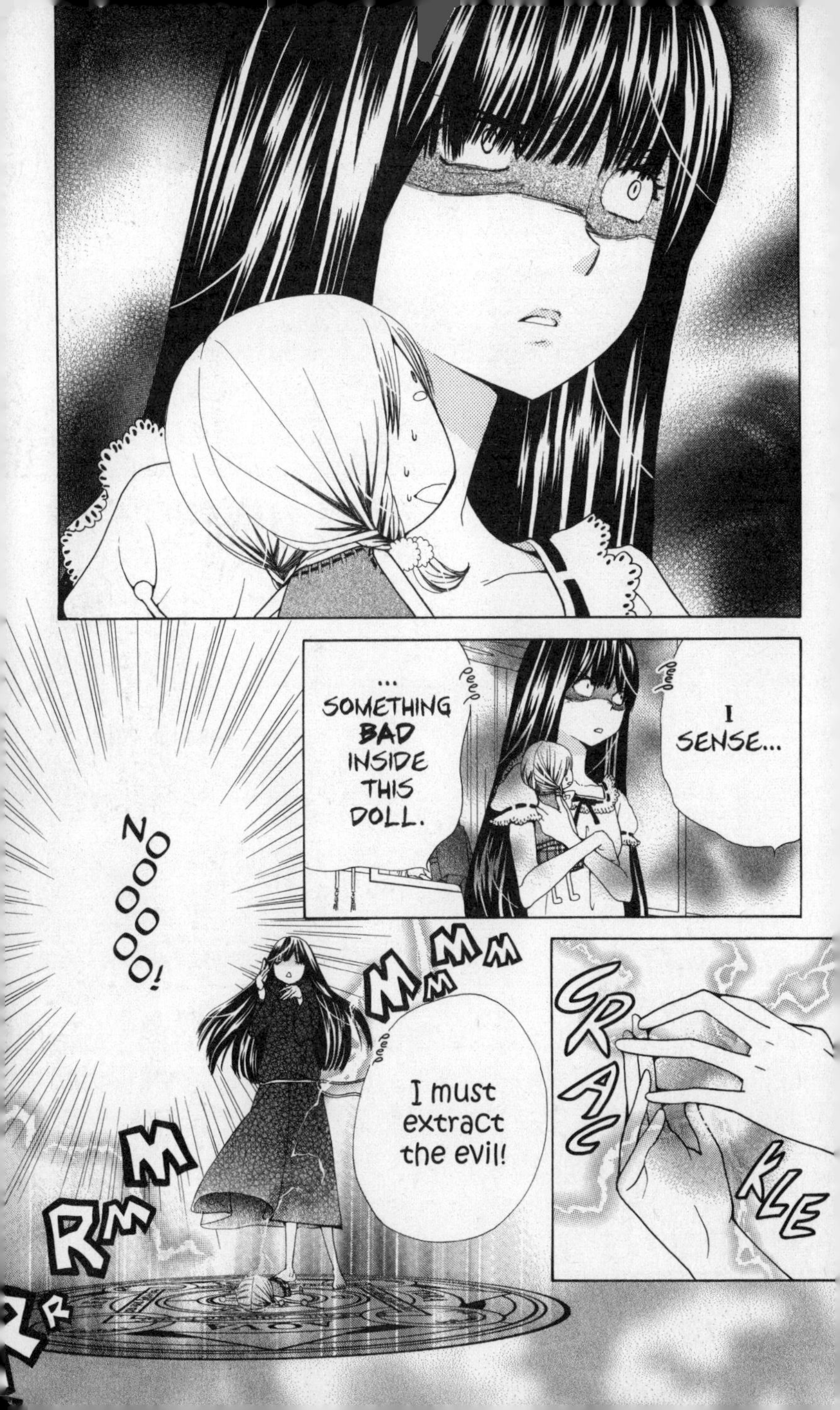
I SENSE...
...SOMETHING BAD INSIDE THIS DOLL.
NOOOOOO!
CRACKLE
MMMMM
I must extract the evil!
RMM
RR

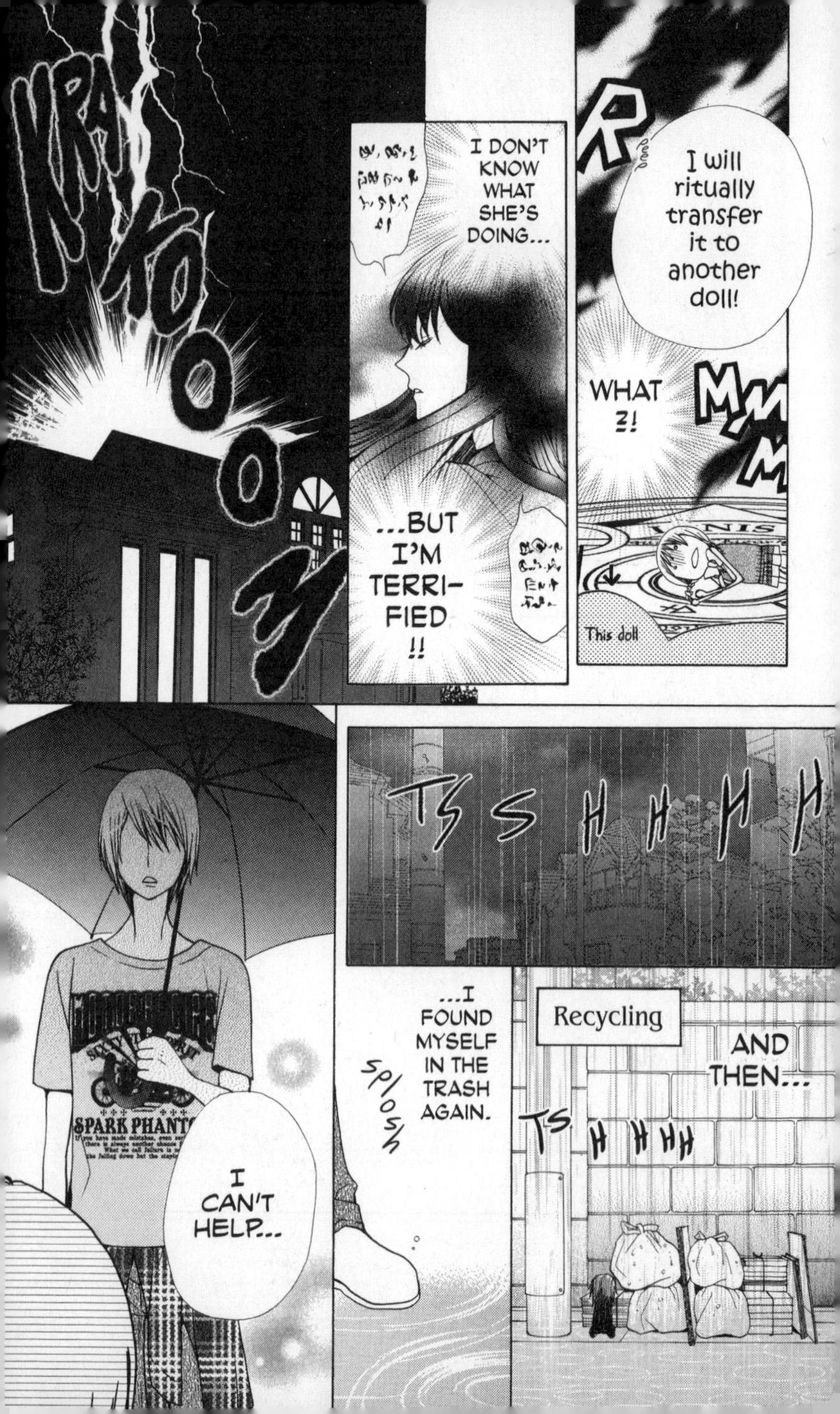
I will ritually transfer it to another doll!
WHAT ?!
This doll
I DON'T KNOW WHAT SHE'S DOING...
...BUT I'M TERRI-FIED !!
KRAKOOOOM
TSSHHHHH
Recycling
AND THEN...
TSHHHH
...I FOUND MYSELF IN THE TRASH AGAIN.
splosh
I CAN'T HELP...

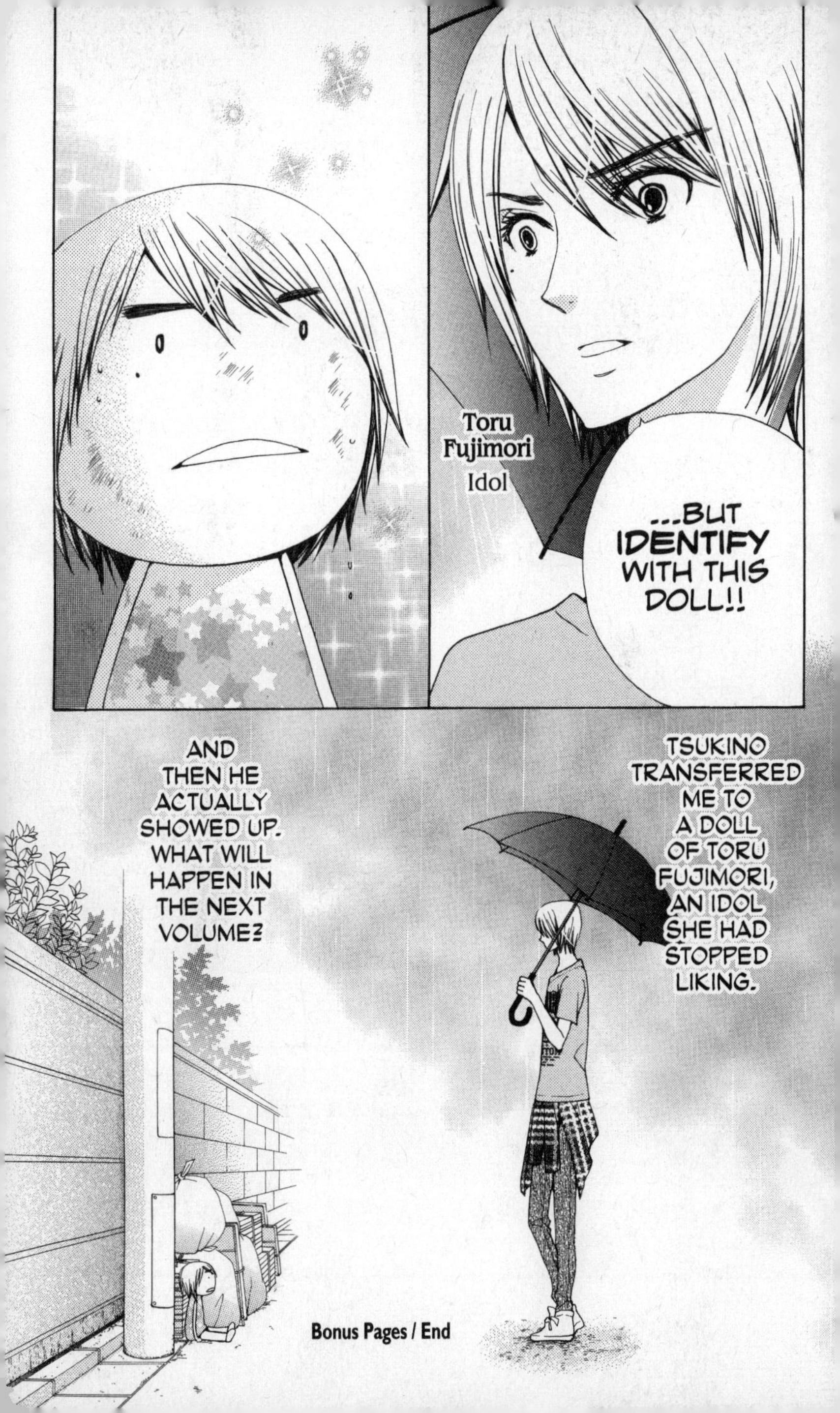
Toru Fujimori
Idol
...BUT IDENTIFY WITH THIS DOLL!!
TSUKINO TRANSFERRED ME TO A DOLL OF TORU FUJIMORI, AN IDOL SHE HAD STOPPED LIKING.
AND THEN HE ACTUALLY SHOWED UP. WHAT WILL HAPPEN IN THE NEXT VOLUME?
Bonus Pages / End

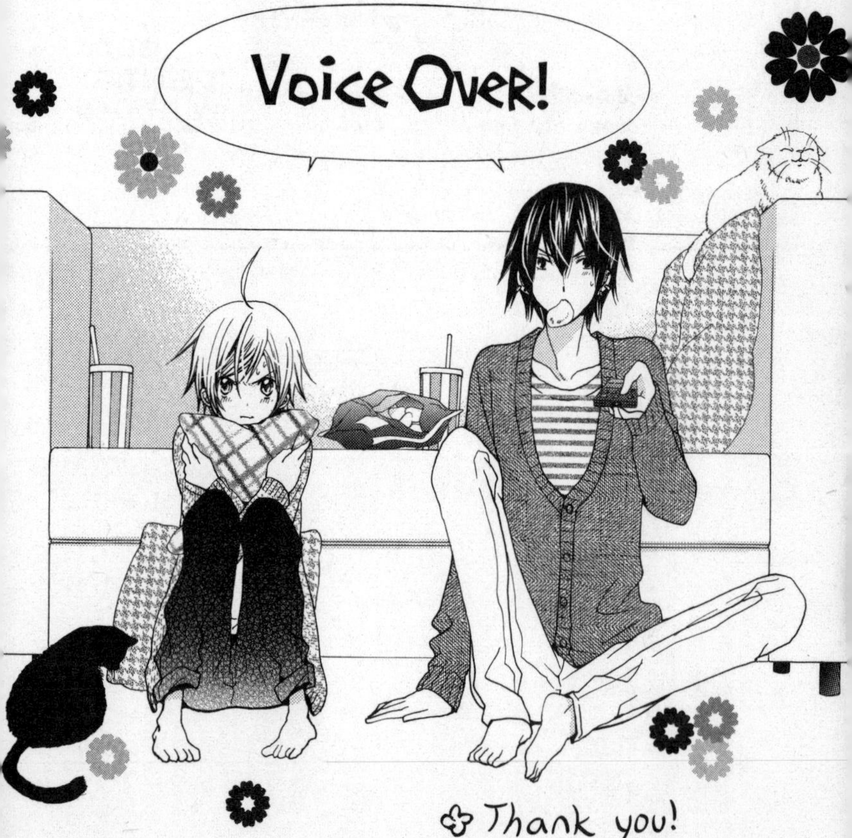
Voice Over!
Thank you!